Lockdown 1:
March -Augus

The Lockdown Diaries of two Harmless Criminals

Sally Featherstone

Although this work is intended to be a true account no responsibility is taken by the author or publisher for the accuracy or otherwise of any of the information presented, or for any action taken by any party arising from this.

ISBN 9781739745509

First published by Opitus Books, United Kingdom, 2022.

Opitus Books

www.opitus.net

Foreword

One day in early Spring 2020, my partner Phill found a card I sent him some time ago, never thinking how relevant it might become in this pandemic year.

Inside the card it said:

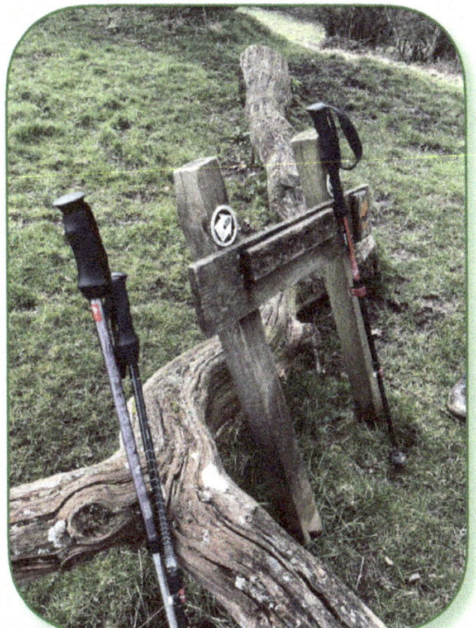

Can we, shall we?
One day very soon
Let us go away
Together, just you and me,
Call in sick and go to the sea
And hold hands all day,
Eat our sandwiches on the train,
Get drunk on fresh air
And come home tired
And never tell anyone...ever.

Rob Ryan

I include the verse here, not as an excuse for what we begin to do, but in an attempt to explain what I am revealing in these pages from my Lockdown Diaries, and the photographs and drawings that accompany them, as we become a pair of 'harmless criminals' in the Coronavirus stricken countryside.

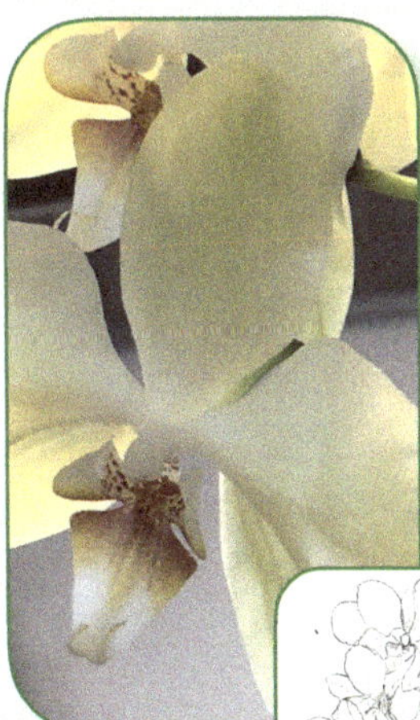

On 11th March 2020, the World Health Organisation (WHO) declares COVID-19 to be a pandemic.

On 15th March 2020, in a house in central Sheffield, I open a new sketch book and make a drawing of an orchid on the table in front of me. As usual, I am half listening to Radio 4, murmuring in the background, and warning us that people over 70 should prepare for 'a long period of shielding' to avoid the growing risk of catching the new 'Coronavirus' sweeping across the country.

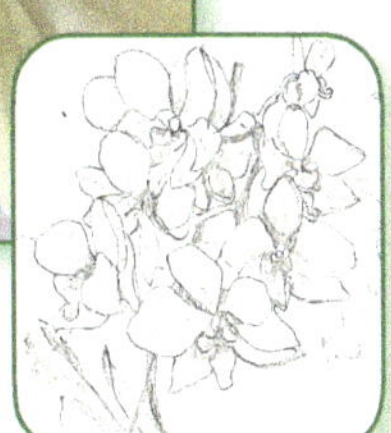

In the same bulletin, the Old Vic Theatre announces its closure, and the total number of deaths from the virus in the UK exceeds 108. The Lockdown Diaries are born.

11 days later, on 23rd March, the Government declares a lockdown across all four countries of the UK, ordering everyone to 'Stay at home'.

From that day, I begin to photograph, draw and write about the experiences of two people attempting to manage the combined pressures of living through a locked down pandemic; renovating a deserted, neglected, decidedly quirky, round-ended, ex-children's home; and responding to the government's seeming inability to get ahead of this deadly microscopic enemy or give clear advice on how we should behave.

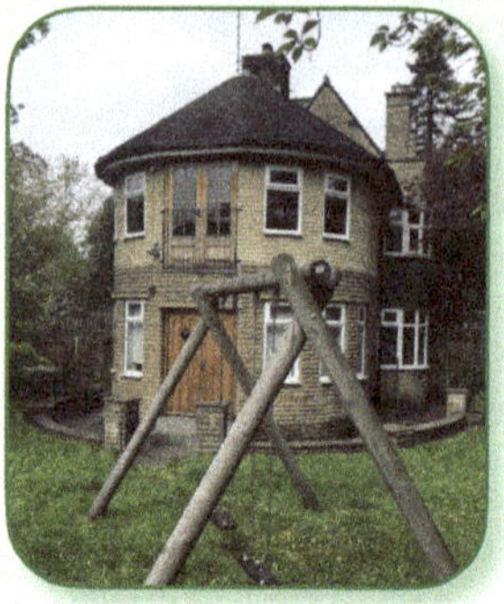

In the beginning, I record the natural beauty of a dormant hawthorn tree, emerging bulbs in garden pots, or a sprig of forget-me-nots in a jam jar. Later my entries include the 'harmless criminality' of our expeditions into the Derbyshire countryside.

Daily drawing, often using photographs taken during that day, proves to be a therapeutic discipline, helping me to manage the stress of being locked away from family and friends, and the abrupt end to experiences of the arts, previously essential to both Phill and me.

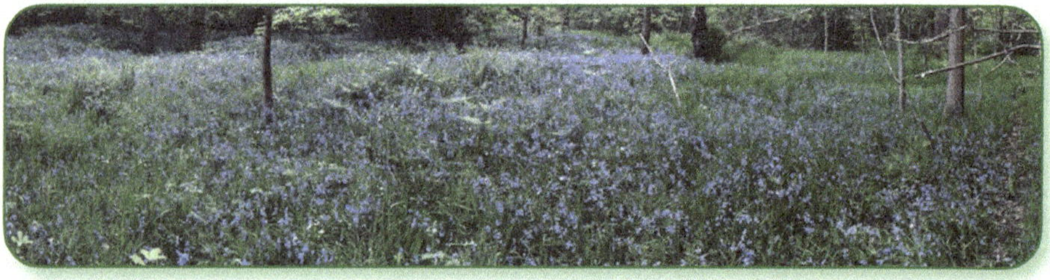

As Lockdown looms, we have only recently moved from the top of an isolated Pennine hillside to a rental property in the middle of Sheffield, while we find a house to buy and settle in for the rest of what we hope will be a long retirement. We have recently found just the unusual property we need - previously a children's home, much in need of renovation, with a garden neglected for many years; a challenging project at any time, but particularly now, as Lockdown looms.

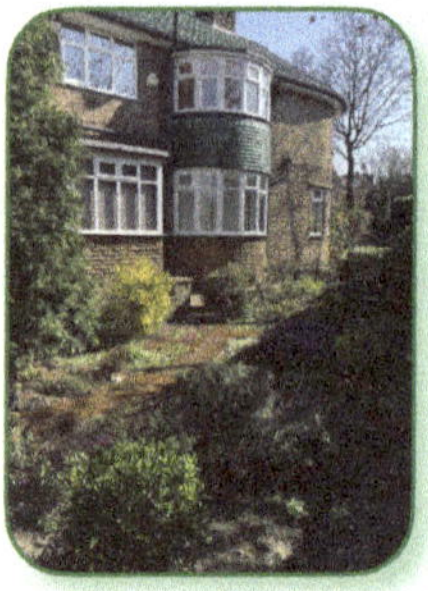

Our daughter Sarah, her husband Jeff and their two sons, Bruce and Lenny live locally, and our USA-based family, John, Kathy and daughters Hailey and Ella , are in regular contact.

We are beginning to rediscover activities we enjoyed in our early married life in London - theatres, museums and galleries, shops, restaurants and coffee bars, the noise and bustle of living in a city. We take up neglected interests, join local groups and classes, make new friends and contact old ones.

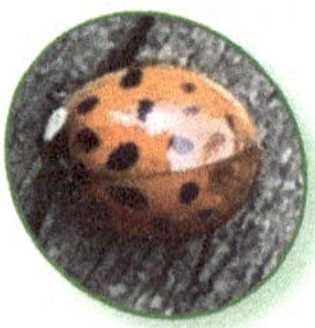

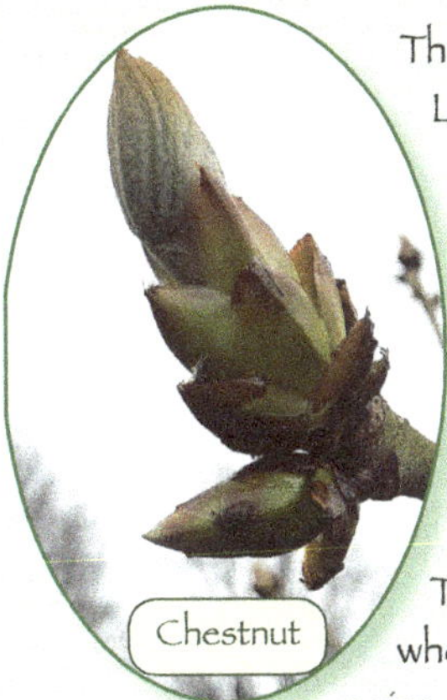

Chestnut

Then the Pandemic is declared, and during the periods of imposed Lockdown, three major traits of my personality begin to take over. They have circulated around each other since my childhood, but become particularly obvious during this extraordinary year in imposed isolation.

The first is a visceral need to be outside, rooted in a country childhood, roaming free in field, shore and woodland; steeped in the natural surroundings of the 'green and the blue' of trees, flowers, birds and insects.

The second is a tendency to depression, tolerated in a big family when, as the middle child of five, I retreated into myself from their noise and bustle, but never named until I diagnosed myself in adulthood.

The final aspect of my personality relevant to this locked-down situation is a resistance to authority, probably inherited from my mother, a strong and independent woman, widowed young with five young children.

My rebellious nature proves to be particularly troublesome during lockdown, and is destined to feed our joint decisions to step round government guidance and directives and continue our commitment to 'the green and the blue' of the English countryside. The Government's Covid restrictions have been met by many with dread, and I know they will be very hard for us too. Like most other people, we never dream that lockdown will become a way of life for us all, extending for many months.

Sheffield City contains more than 4.5 million trees, over 250 public parks and 52 square miles of national park, so we are lucky to live in one of the greenest cities in Europe, but untamed natural countryside is very different, and finding access to this has been a priority for us since we moved here.

As the spring buds of greening begin to arrive we are reminded of the open views and abundant wildlife just outside the door of our former home, high on a hill in West Yorkshire, and realise that the threatened lockdown will leave us bouncing against the walls of our rented house, and the city boundaries of Sheffield.

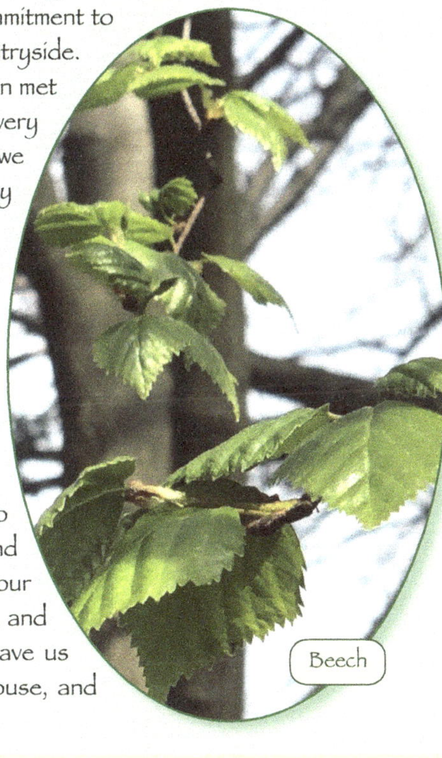

Beech

In the green and the blue with my mother and my brothers.

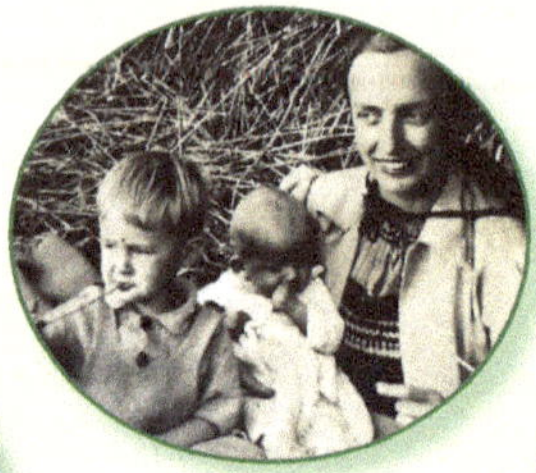

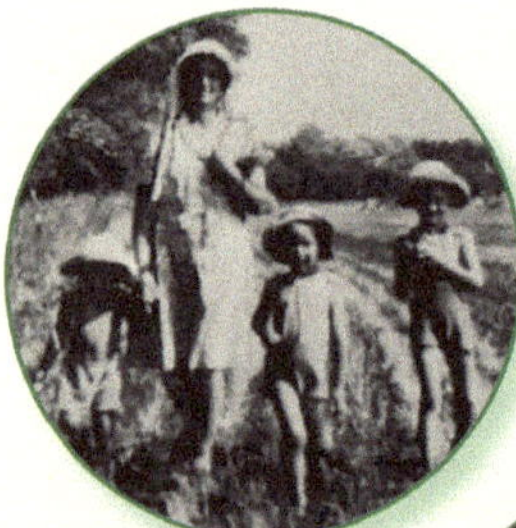

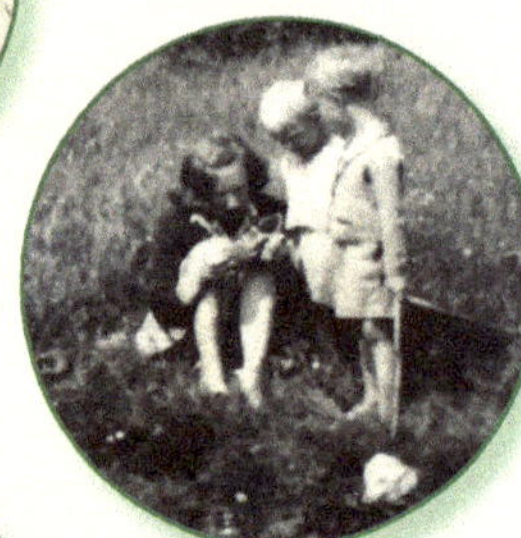

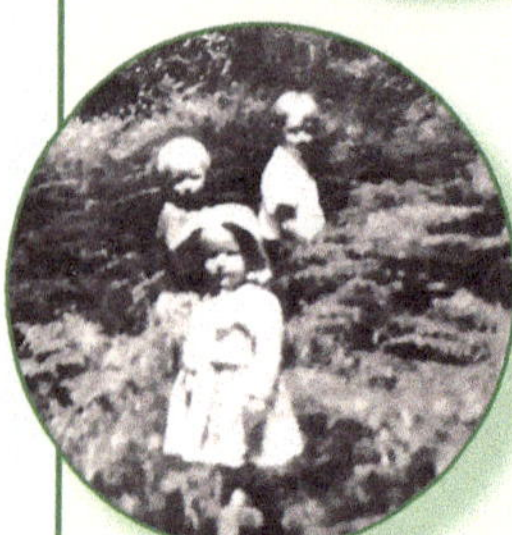

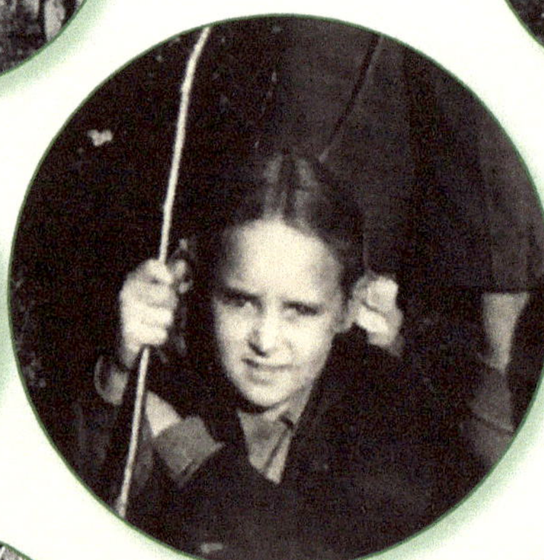

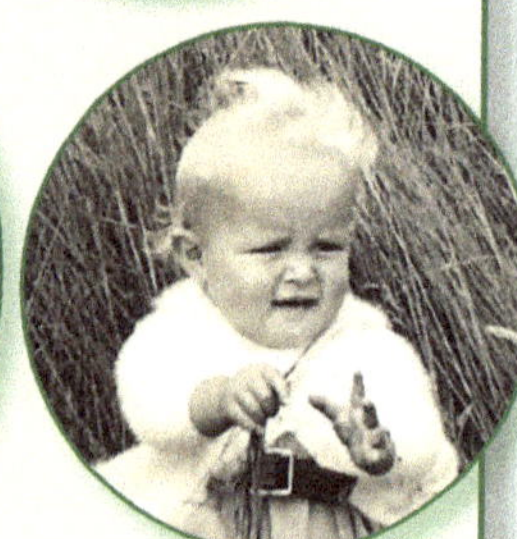

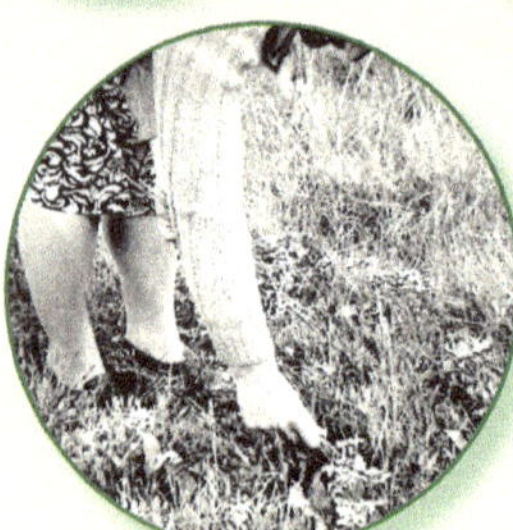

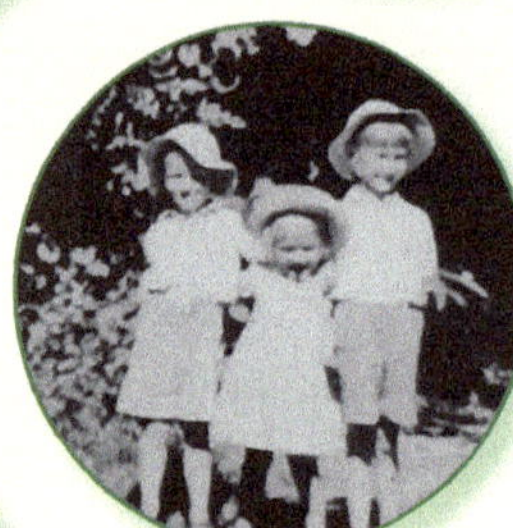

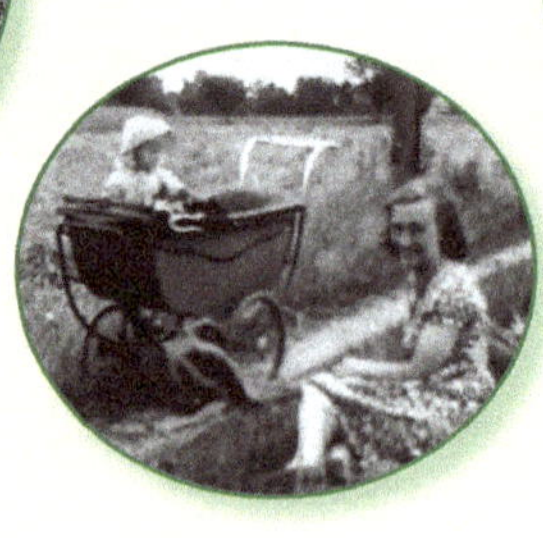

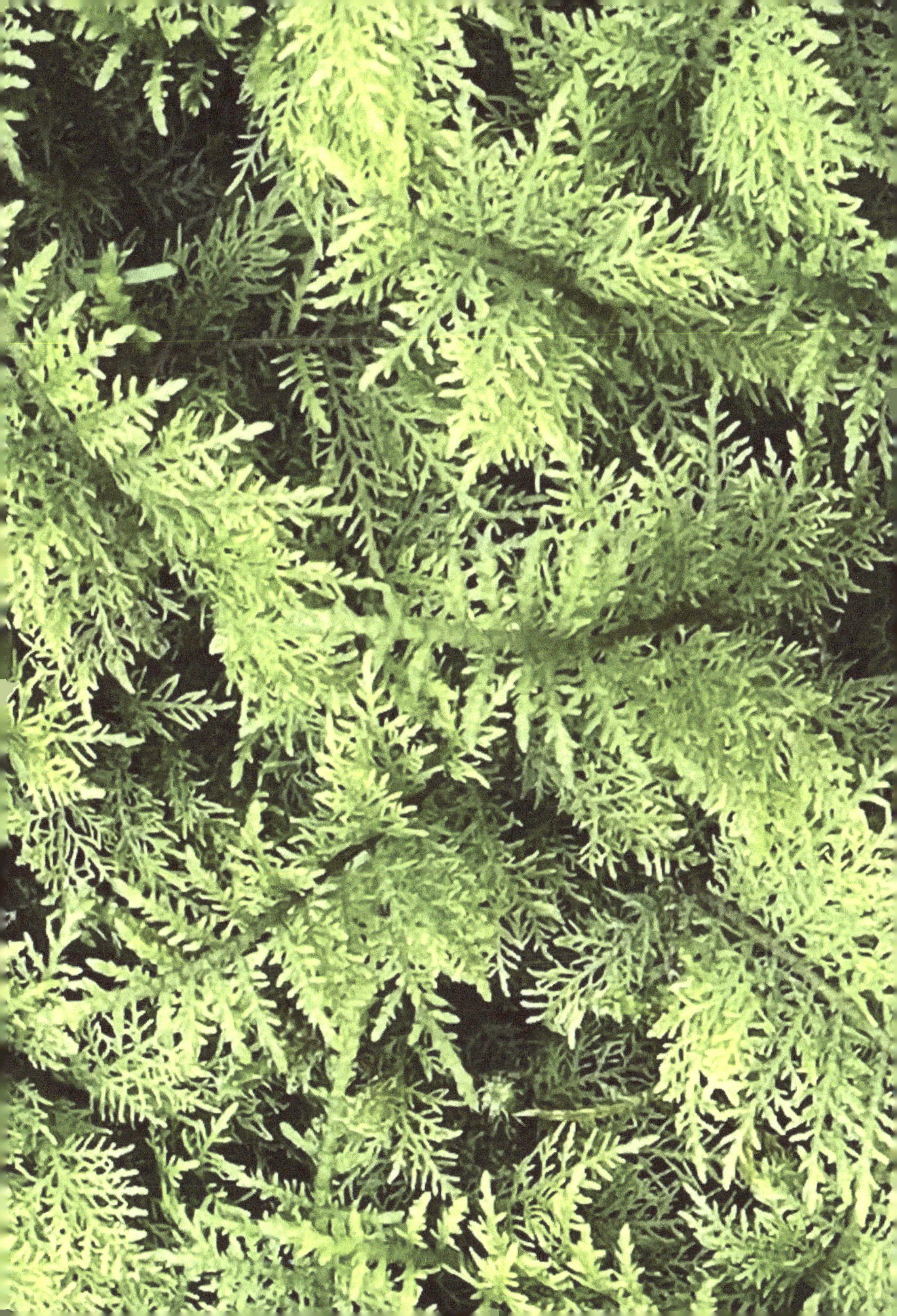

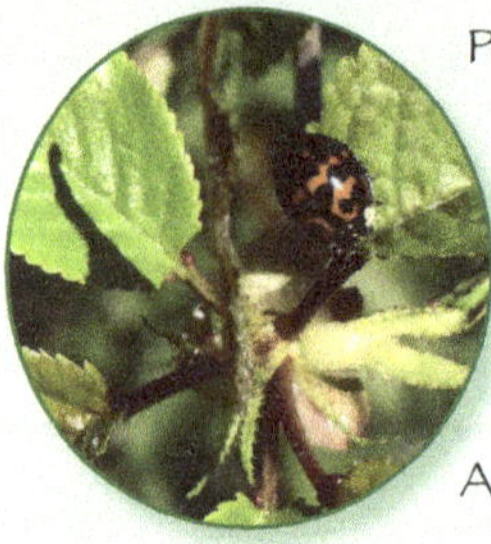

Permission to go out for exercise is one thing, freely exploring the countryside, walking footpaths, stopping to look at single flowers, gazing at great vistas, and hearing the sounds of birds and animals may prove to be near impossible during lockdown, without bending or re-interpreting the National Lockdown regulations.

And this is when my resistance to authority begins to surface.

My mental health, although it can be temporarily controlled by the familiar medication of alcohol, is really only lifted by regular exposure to being out of doors, in 'the green and the blue' of sky, sea, trees and plants, so I already know that lockdown will be very hard for me.

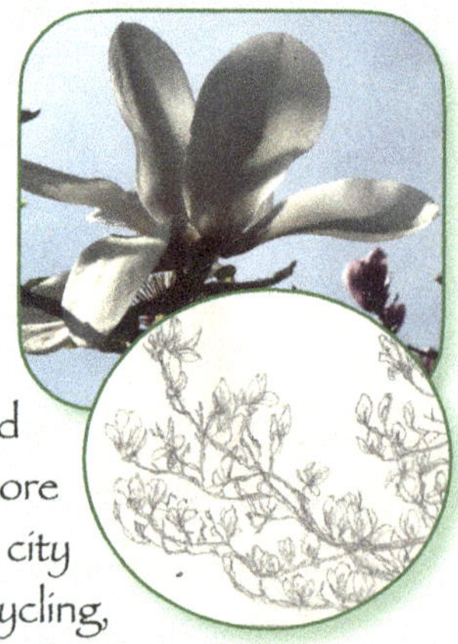

Fortunately, my partner, Phill, understands my need for and shares my love of the outdoors, so from 19th March, as well as drawings, I begin to enhance my diary with notes of our local walks and permitted 'daily outdoor exercise' in the immediate area, including the wonderful resource that is the Sheffield Botanical Gardens. However, this permitted and limited 'physical activity' quickly becomes more and more constraining as we take our daily walk in crowded city parks with hundreds of other locked-down people, cycling, running, walking, and exercising children and dogs.

The pressure results in an almost unconscious 'boundary pushing escapism', as we quickly realise we will have to walk further and further from home to get outside this tight ring of activity, gradually extending our range as everyone struggles to get away from each other - partly from fear of infection, partly to find some privacy for their exercise.

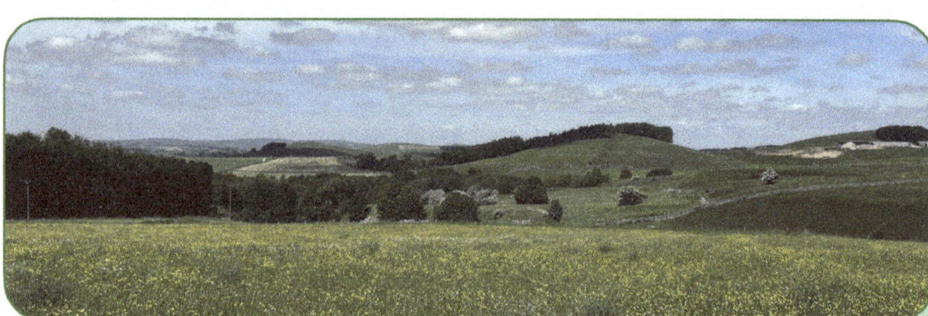

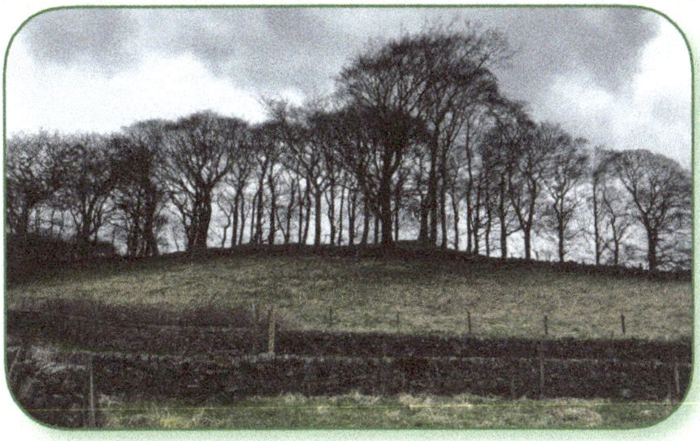

As lockdown becomes established as a way of life, we begin to feel like storybook characters, locked in our turrets, so the only way to maintain my equilibrium is for us to get in the car and follow the advice at the time, which is to; 'walk for longer than you drive'.

At this point we begin to become the 'harmless criminals' of this book's title, which involves us in going outside the local area to places where few if any other people are walking. Such expeditions are not strictly legal, but begin to be our escape from the claustrophobia of the city.

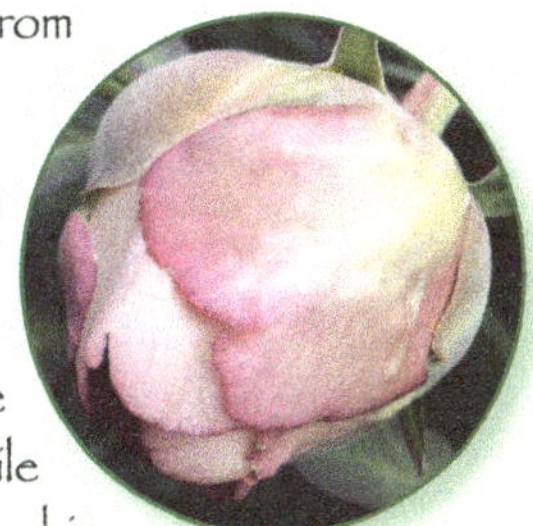

The first Lockdown continues, and although I write something about lockdown life almost every day, I begin to concentrate on these walks in the 'green and the blue', making longer accounts of these illicit outings. Slowly I become aware that I have inadvertently discovered a way to manage Covid Lockdown, while preserving my mental health and the equilibrium of my partnership with Phill, without whom I would not have survived this terrible time.

A life remembered today: Kevin Priestley; 56, Tool setter; Goldthorpe, UK.

To bring me down to earth, and to remind me of the developing situation, every evening I add to my entries the names of individuals who have died from Covid in the UK or in countries across the world, and news items, government edicts, and some of the many statistics on cases and the subsequent deaths.

As I make continuing entries in my Lockdown Diaries into 2021, and extend these into a record of the Second and Third Lockdowns, and the periods of anxiety filled calm between them, I think back to March 2020, when we felt sure that Lockdown would be something short and relatively pain-free.

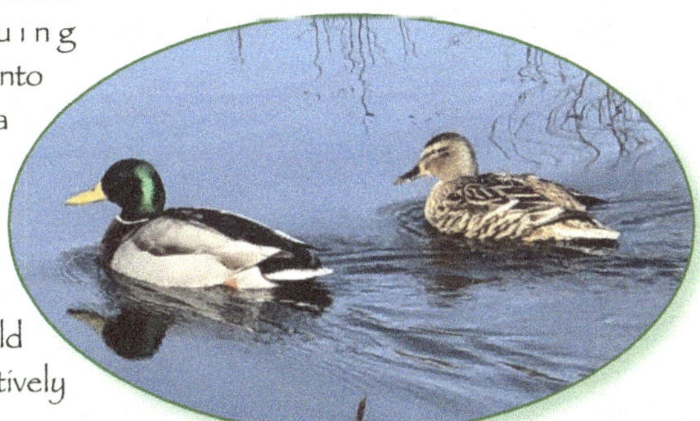

How innocent we were!

MARCH 2020

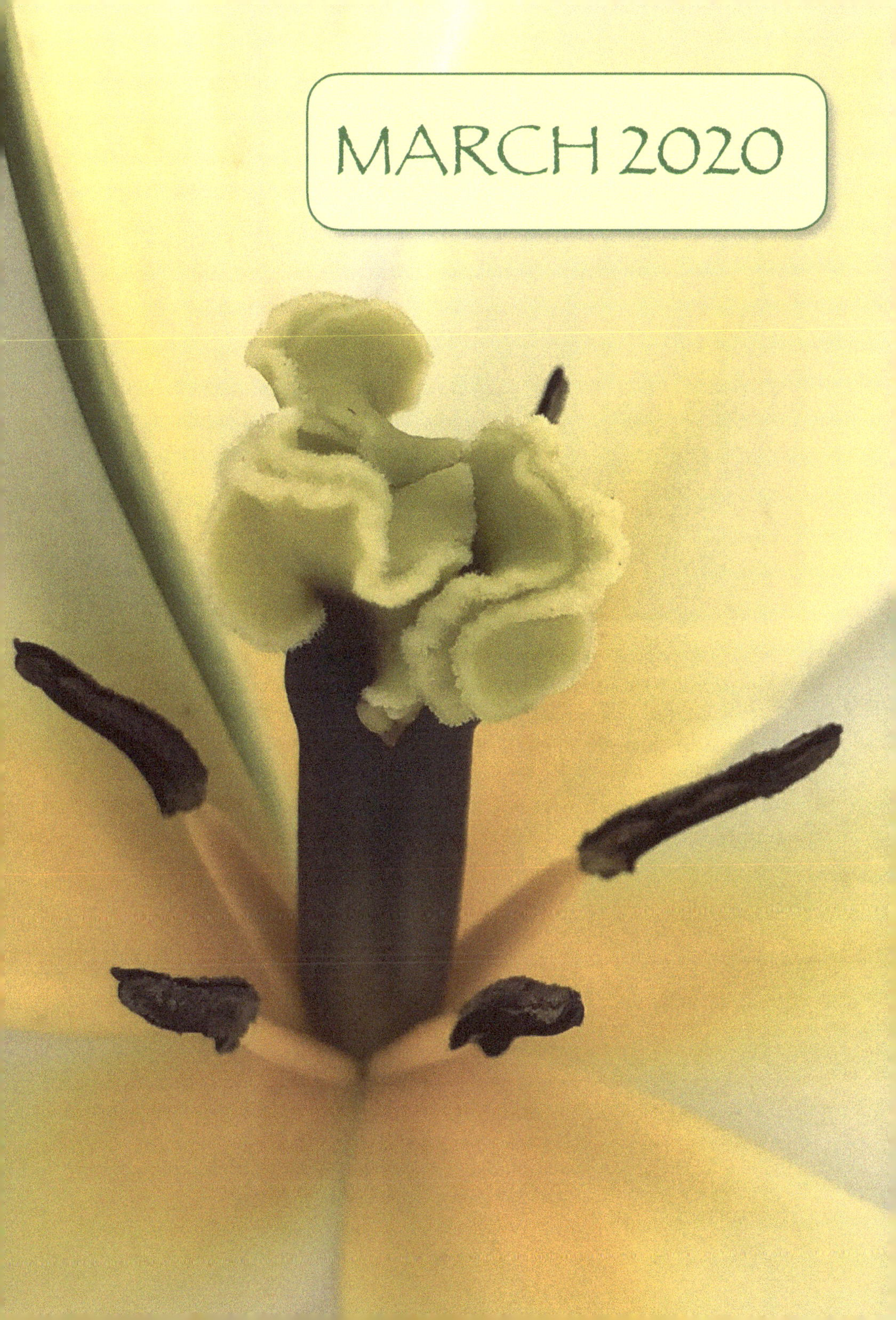

16th March 2020 Confirmed Cases: 1,500 Total deaths: 155

THE DEPARTMENT FOR DIGITAL, CULTURE, MEDIA & SPORT STATES 'IT IS ADVISED THAT LARGE GATHERINGS SHOULD NOT TAKE PLACE'.

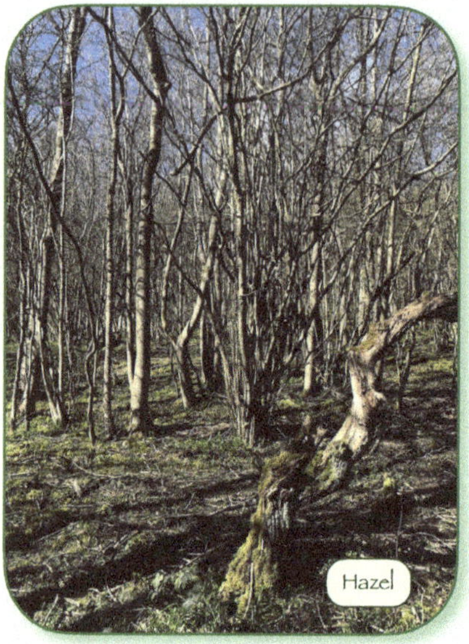
Hazel

We really should have thought more carefully about the route, the recent heavy rain, and the season, but having lived on the well-drained Pennine hills for ten years, we forget what low level paths can be like. We innocently set out, not in our walking boots, but in shiny, pavement, town boots, completely unsuitable for the terrain we meet - a land full of water, brought down over the limestone valley sides by recent torrential rain, forming lakes of mud in the riverside meadows.

We walk down from the car park, negotiating a wet field and a wonky wooden bridge over a lively bubbling stream, to enter hazel woodlands where primrose leaves and wood anemones are emerging among the coppiced hazels. The challenges of this popular footpath through Monsal Dale soon become clear as we teeter on tufts of grass, hop and jump over puddles and squidgy moss, skirt seas of mud and small streams, and push our way through brambles and thickets of hawthorn, their sharp winter thorns grabbing our clothing and hair.

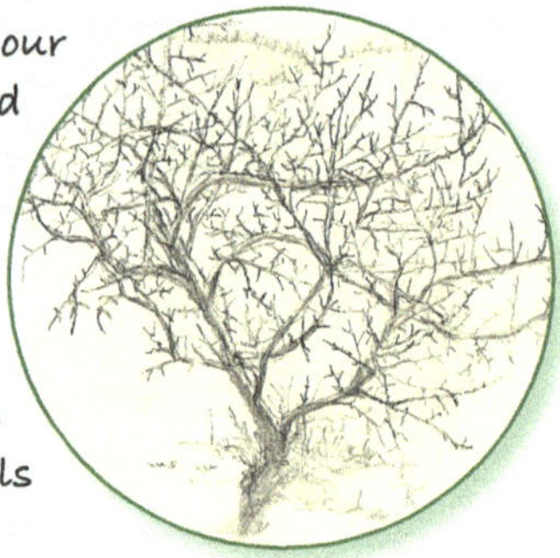

We scramble and slide along, embarrassed by our unsuitable footwear, now covered in sticky mud, and losing grip on the slick surfaces, we are overtaken by groups in sensible walking boots or wellingtons.

Other walkers' looks are alternately sympathetic or scornful as we doggedly press on until we reach the wide grassy fields by the wonderful water-fuelled falls of the River Wye.

A life remembered today: Rod Moore;. 63, Ambulance paramedic; Falkirk.

Here, seated on a blanket on the wet grass, an Indian family in bright saris brave the cold, picnicking as their children paddle, shrieking joyously in the freezing water, clothing pulled high like Victorians in petticoats, to avoid the chilling splashes of the river.

After a much needed rest, leaning on the fence to watch rainbows and sunlight caught in the spray from the falls, we decide it would be sensible to cut our walk short at this point, and retrace our steps along the muddy banks.

The return path seems even longer, even more slippery, and muddier, but we are cheered by bright faces of celandines, and catkins wave from hazel thickets.

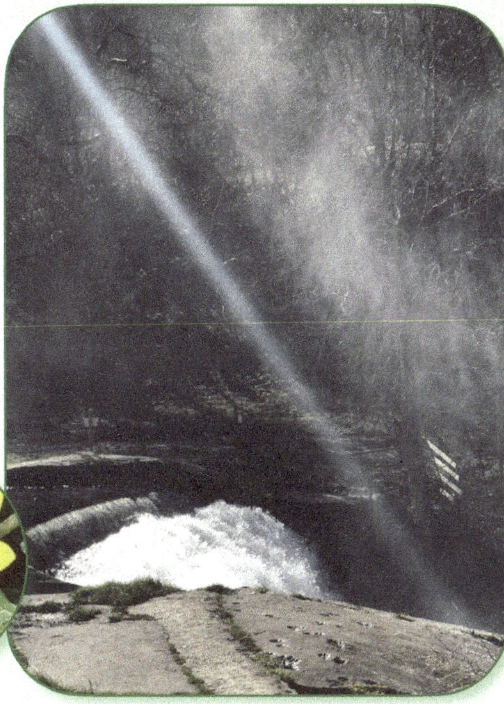

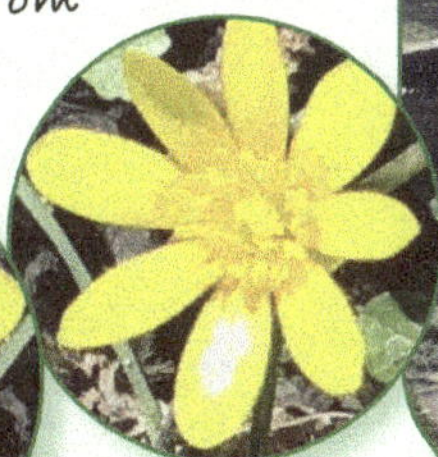

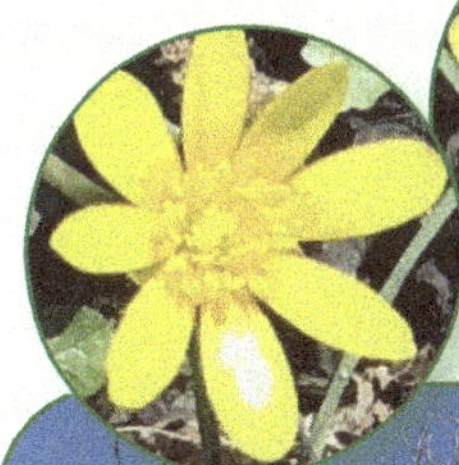

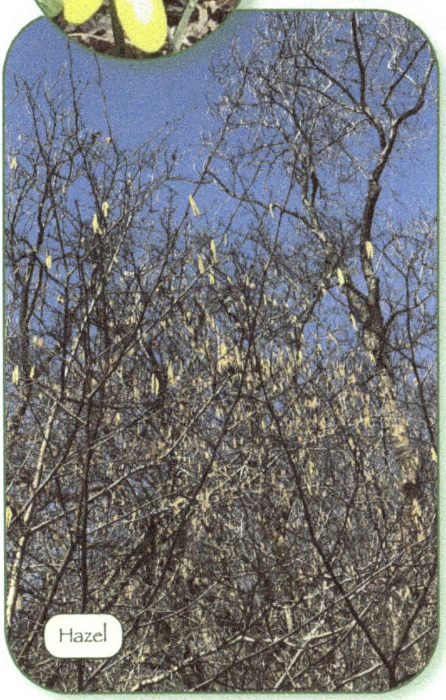

Hazel

Finally, crossing the bridge and climbing the waterlogged grass of the sloping fields to the car park, we remove our mud encrusted boots for the drive home, vowing that our walking boots will always be with us for future walks in this new wet landscape, so different from the gritty, well-drained Pennine hilltop paths where we have walked over the past decade.

and meanwhile, as we were looking for signs of Spring: *The UK death toll reaches 47, with the number of cases passing 1,500. The Prime Minister advises everyone in the UK against 'non-essential' travel and contact with others, to work from home if possible and avoid pubs or theatres.*

Pandemic Day: 1 Legal Lockdown 1: minus 10

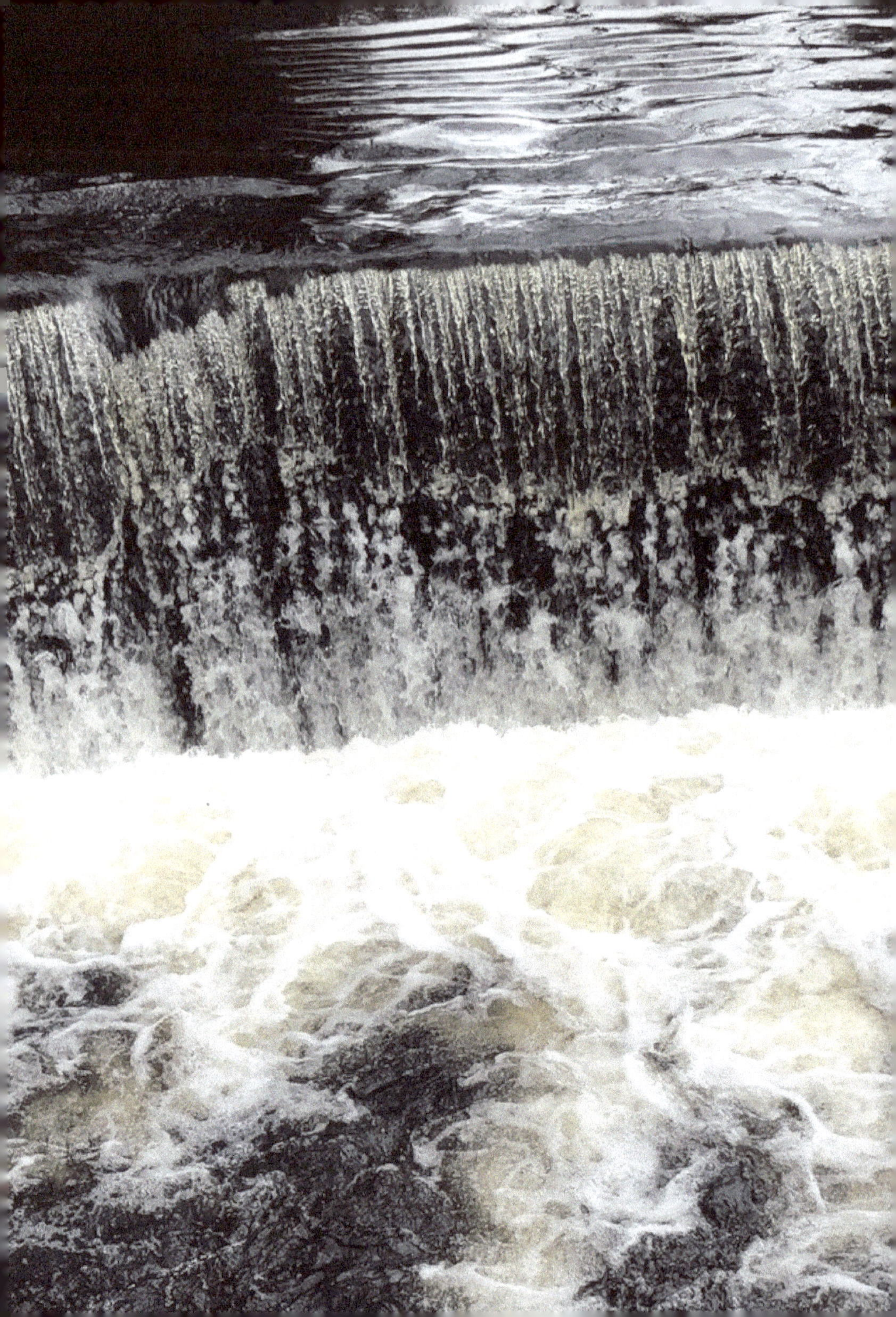

17/18th March 2020 Confirmed Cases: 2,182 Total deaths: 348

17th - THE UK GOVERNMENT PROVIDES A £3.2MILLION EMERGENCY SUPPORT PACKAGE TO HELP ROUGH SLEEPERS INTO ACCOMMODATION.

In the days that follow, we listen to the radio and watch TV news, but are still no clearer about what will happen if Covid cases continue to rise. It is a time for endless speculation, discussion and disbelief about the coming 'lock down', which everyone expects, but knows little about.

I am terrified at the thought of being locked in this house, with no view, no freedom, and such a tiny garden, with its fake grass lawn. It is the only house in a small cul-de-sac, so we have no neighbours, no facing houses, and not even any passers-by to create movement or interest My compromised immune system means I will be more vulnerable, and the regulations are likely to be even more strict than for others. Not knowing is the worst thing, and the PM seems reluctant to take the decision already made in many other European countries.

Lives remembered: Roger Lemin; 79; Care home resident; Cornwall, & Suzanne Loverseed; 63; Care home nurse; London.

18th - THE PRIME MINISTER ANNOUNCES, 'NOW IS THE TIME FOR EVERYONE TO STOP NON-ESSENTIAL TRAVEL OR CONTACT'.

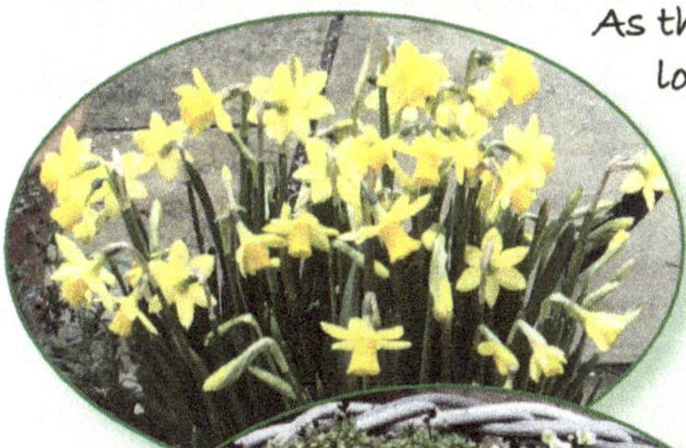

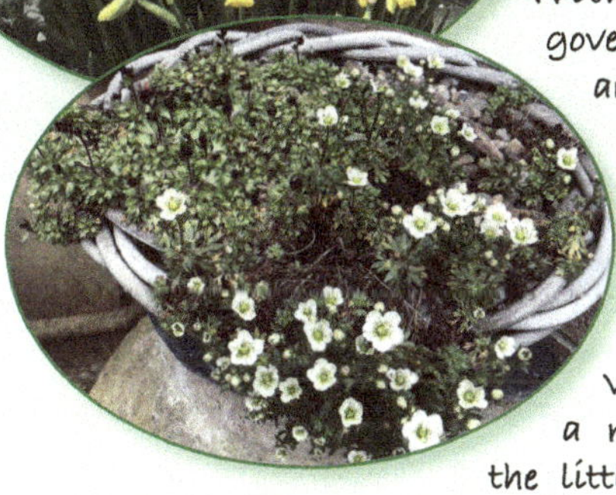

As the spring begins to move forward, regardless of lockdown, we watch the plants in the garden of our rental house in the city. Rockery plants begin to flower, and daffodils push their leaves and greeny-yellow buds through the soil, opening with a gold flourish.

With no other information from the government, we decide that we will go for another day of discovery in the White Peaks. And so begins our series of walks which could now be described as 'benign or harmless criminality'.

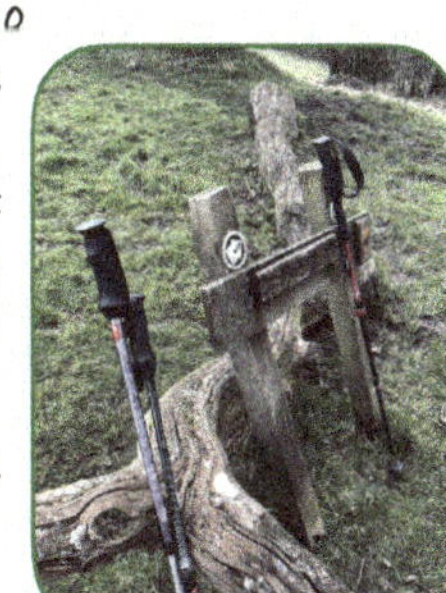

We choose to go along the Dane Valley from Wincle, a riverside walk past the little brewery and the trout farm, along a secluded valley, through water meadows where we are unlikely to meet anyone.

Pubs are now closed, so we must rely on our own resources and what we can carry in our coat pockets and daypacks.

Pandemic Day: 6/7 Legal Lockdown 1: minus 8/9

19th March 2020 Confirmed Cases: 3,269 Total deaths: 275

THE GOVERNMENT GUIDANCE IS STILL UNCLEAR ABOUT WHAT WE SHOULD OR SHOULDN'T DO, AND THERE APPEARS TO BE NO LIMIT ON WHERE WE CAN GO.

With walking boots, poles and a picnic, we set out from Wincle, a tiny village nestled in a valley by a bridge over the river Dane, and featuring a micro-brewery and a trout farm. Although the path is obviously well used, the valley is deserted, as people begin to stay at home to avoid the virus. The first part of the walk is through the puddling green water meadows beside the river, showing evidence of the wettest winter on record with pools of grassy water and streams flowing across every meadow from the woods above.

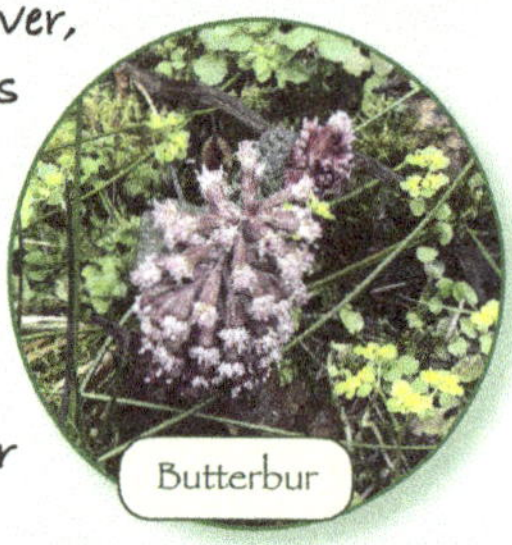
Butterbur

We cross the river by a waterfall, to follow an old canal, full of the big leaves and pink flower-buds of butterbur, and the tall green spears of iris, as yet without their signature yellow or blue 'flags'.

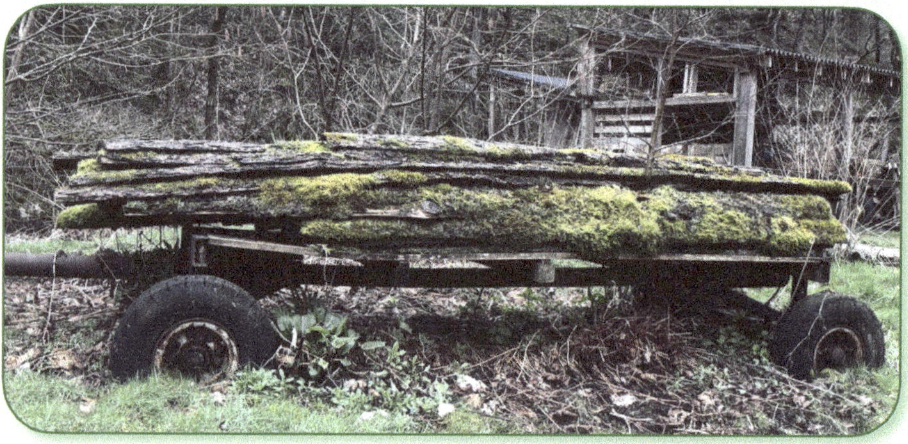

Beside the canal, among the emerging grasses and tall weeds, old buildings and farm vehicles gently decompose as moss, weeds and tall tree saplings reclaim this previously man-managed land.

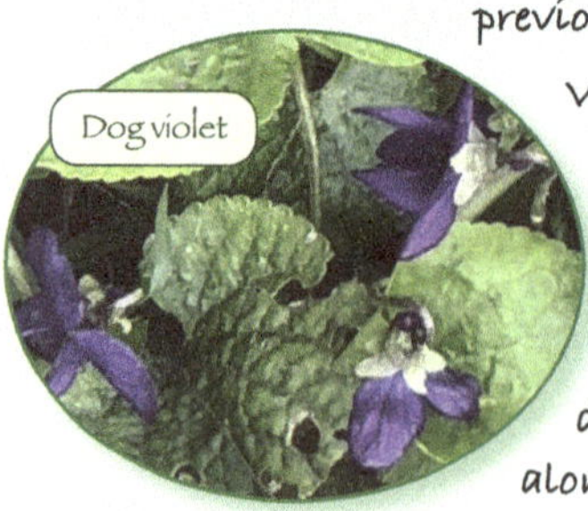
Dog violet

Violets nestle in the verges, and feathery green tendrils of moss reach out with an obvious intention of decorating every surface.

In this almost forgotten valley, where some people evidently still live, even going to school must be a daily adventure, with animal and plant life left alone to grow and thrive at will.

A well maintained black-cindered track then leads us along between river and canal to the relative civilisation of a concrete field path, and we leave the valley sleeping in voluntary lockdown, to climb to the Gritstone Trail, gaining the summits of a row of hills, with sloping fields dripping and running with water, dotted with ruined buildings and gradually being re-wilded with natural tree planting and fenced nature reserves to deter grazing deer.

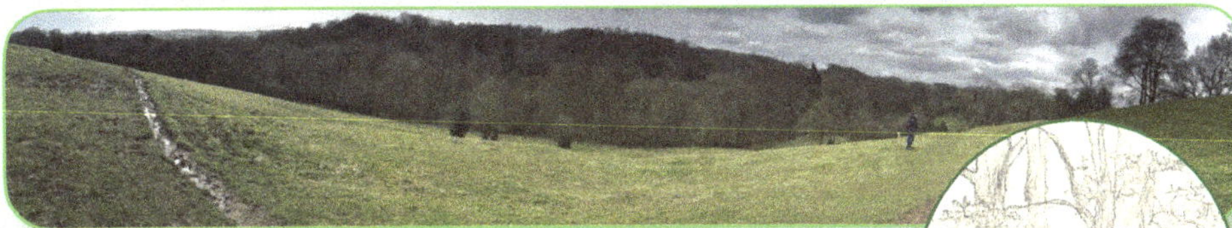

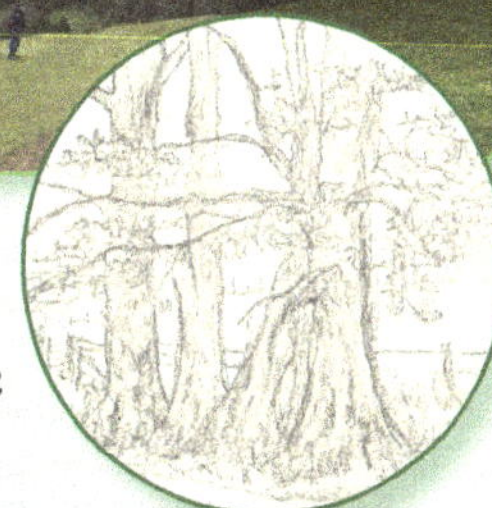

We pause under the great beech trees here, perching on a footpath sign to avoid the wet grass, and look down on deserted meadows and woods, devoid of any sound but the birds and the constant running of water.

A life remembered today: <u>Bill Jackson</u>; 89; Retired; Hertfordshire.

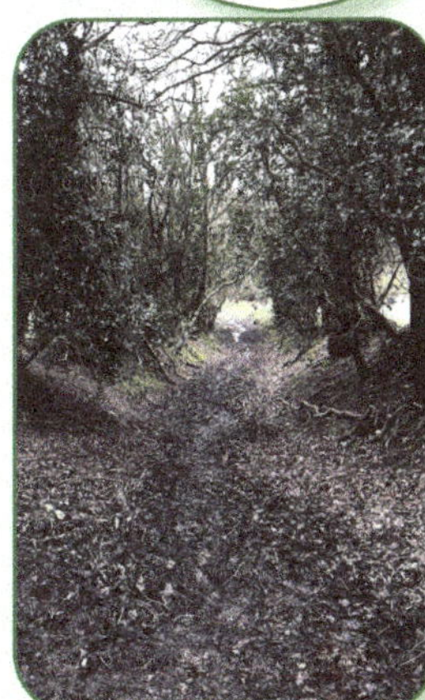

Ancient sunken footpaths carve deep, shady, leaf-littered ways along this hilltop ridge, conjuring up ghosts of farmers' wives travelling to market with chickens and pigs, eggs and butter, sheltered by ancient oaks, dark hollies and twisted hawthorns, with children trudging behind, often barefoot, cold, and hungry.

As we reach the top of the hills, the view opens onto park-like sheepy fields with great lines of giant oaks marching towards Wincle Grange, a late 15th Century farmhouse, with pale decorative stonework among the old timbers.

and as we walk those rain-soaked hills: *The government announces that all schools in England will shut on Friday 20 March, except for vulnerable and key worker children. No exams will take place this academic year.*

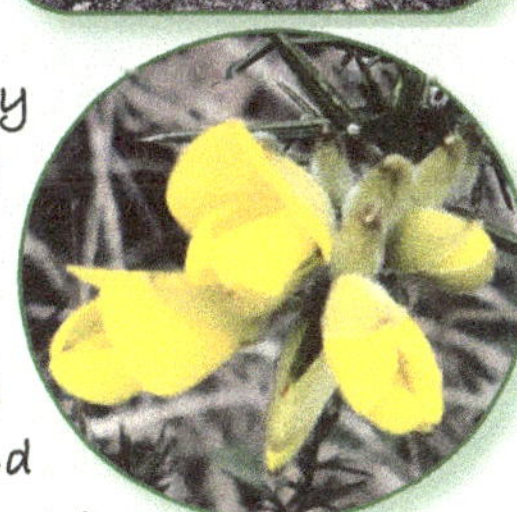

In the field margins gorse flowers shine yellow and prickly, and the path leads past the house and down the narrow lane, back to Wincle village, for a risky but welcome pint at the local brewery, with hand sanitiser available, but no masks.

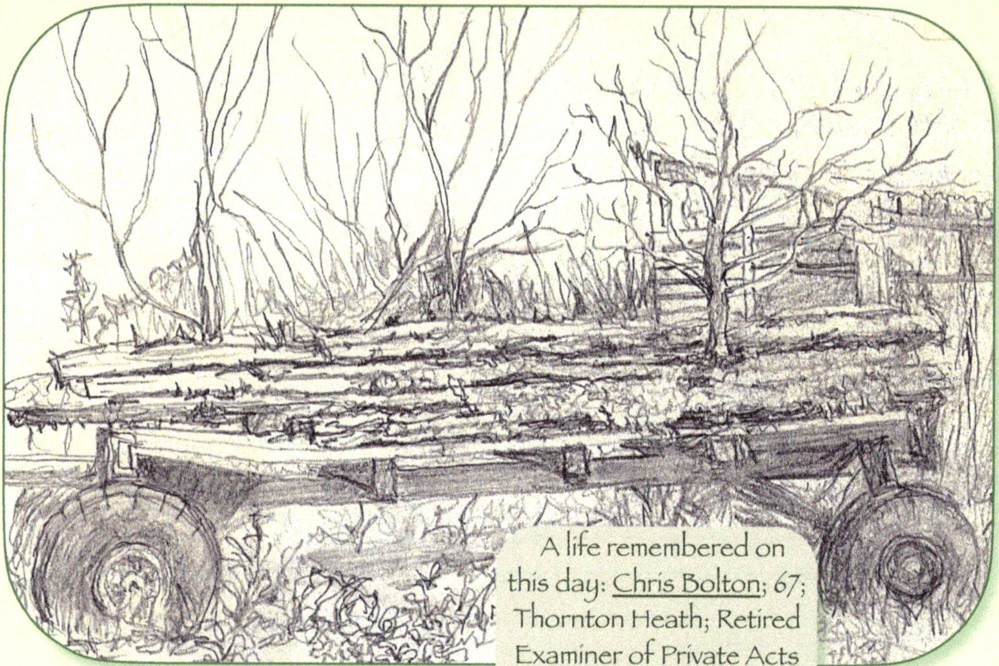

A life remembered on this day: Chris Bolton; 67; Thornton Heath; Retired Examiner of Private Acts - House of Lords.

It is far too cold and wet to draw in the open air today, so I must wait till we get home to do any drawing, using photos taken on our walk. This cart, rotting quietly beside the disused and weed-filled canal, will become a favourite for drawings over this locked down time. During the year, it slowly disappears into the Spring weed growth of dandelions, tall docks and the seedlings of nearby trees, the Summer scramble of blackberry and bindweed, and the magenta flowers of Autumn willow herb, before emerging even more ramshackle, skeletal and mossy as the next winter returns.

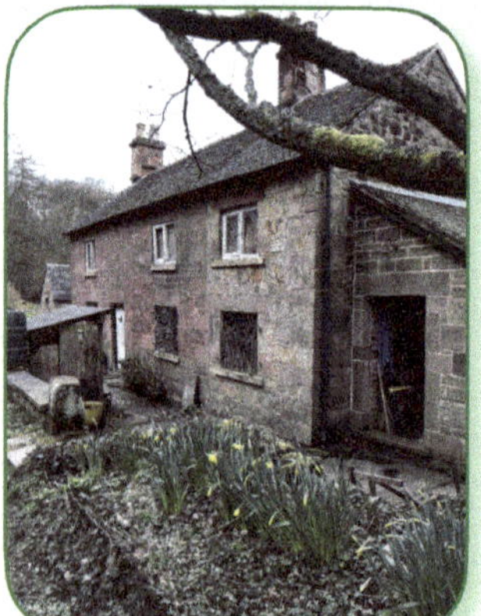

This little collection of buildings must once have been a busy place, as lock-keepers and other canal workers dredged and cleared this little feeder canal, running parallel with the winding rocky, fast flowing Dane River, on its way to the Mersey. Water wheels once provided power for flour, cloth and paper mills, but these buildings are now mostly disused, although there is still some evidence of current inhabitants.

Pandemic Day: 8 Legal Lockdown 1: - minus 7

22nd March 2020 Confirmed Cases: 4,792 Total deaths: 587

THE PRIME MINISTER FINALLY GIVES US DUE WARNING THAT LOCKDOWN WILL START IMMEDIATELY, AND WE REALISE THAT THE HORIZONS ARE REALLY CLOSING IN ON THE CITY.

A life remembered on this day: Emily Perugia; 29; health care worker; London.

For me, writing and drawing in my Lockdown diary now becomes a way of shutting out this terrible time, where the COVID quiet of the city threatens, like a living grey entity, just out of sight, but caught in the corner of your eye, a reflection in a window or a ghost in the rear-view mirror. Things are normal, yet frighteningly abnormal, and as we all wait for the certainty of lockdown, things get even stranger. Silence rules the night, where, apart from the sounds of foxes and owls emerging from the local park, the streets get quieter and quieter, as people voluntarily lock themselves away in their own houses, waiting for an official announcement.

At this time, while wrestling with the new realities of Lockdown, I sometimes slip into a state of unbelief, becoming convinced that, 'It's all a dream, and soon we'll wake up to normality,' or I lie awake in the dark silence of Lockdown night, and for just a second my brain tricks me into thinking, 'There must be a place where we can hide and just sit out this horrible virus.' But of course I soon come to my senses and realise that the declaration of a pandemic does really mean that the virus can and will spread everywhere. We are all in this together!

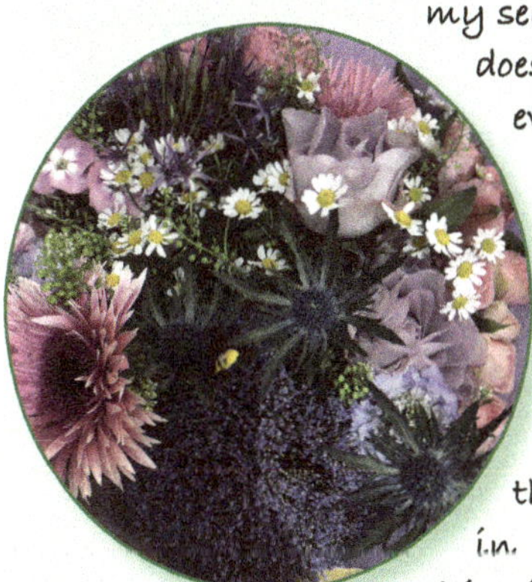

I marvel that people in countries all over the world immediately and mostly obediently lock themselves in, stop going to work, driving their cars, eating in restaurants and drinking in pubs, and take on the challenging task of educating their own children at home.

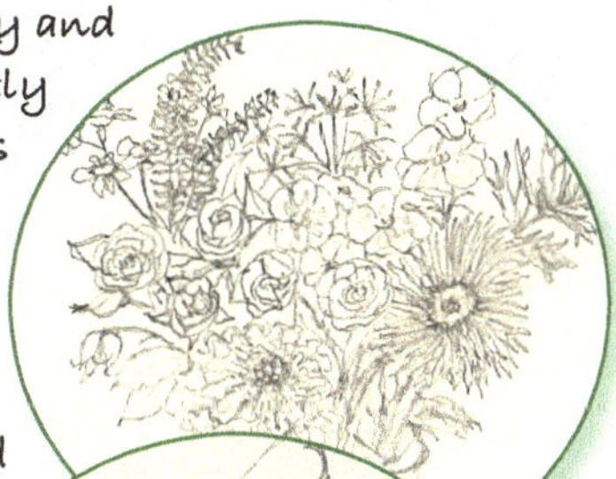

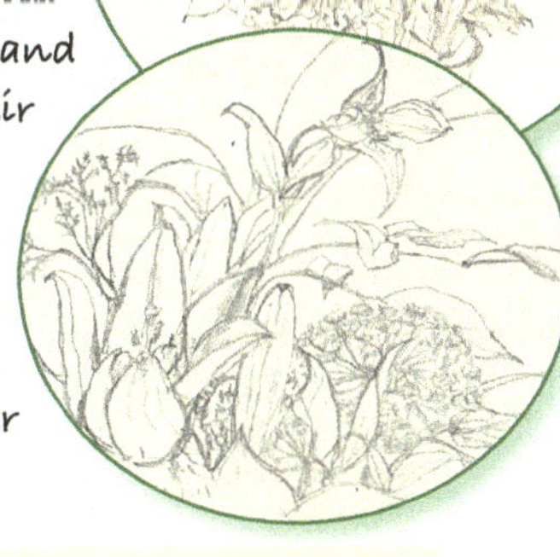

But no-one has yet said we CAN'T drive out for a walk. The weather has improved, so, leaving behind two beautiful Mothers' Day bouquets, we drive to Monk's Dale for another walk.

Pandemic Day: 11 Legal Lockdown 1: minus 4

23rd March 2020 Confirmed Cases: 6,650 Total deaths: 937

THE BRITISH PUBLIC ARE INSTRUCTED THAT THEY MUST STAY AT HOME, EXCEPT FOR SHOPPING FOR BASIC NECESSITIES; ONE FORM OF EXERCISE A DAY; ANY MEDICAL NEED; AND TRAVEL TO AND FROM WORK WHEN 'ABSOLUTELY NECESSARY'. WHEN THESE RESTRICTIONS COME INTO FORCE ON 26 MARCH, THE STATUTORY INSTRUMENT FOR ENGLAND OMITTED TO DEFINE ANY LIMIT ON THE NUMBER OF EXERCISE SESSIONS.

Remembered today: Stuart Hayes; 72; Security guard; Hornchurch; UK.

A sunny drive through deserted lanes takes us to the empty station car park at Miller's Dale. The route lies over the dizzying Headstone Viaduct spanning road and river, then past looming grey walls of abandoned lime kilns, and down a watery, slippery, celandine lined path to a wooden bridge across the river we saw from the viaduct high above.

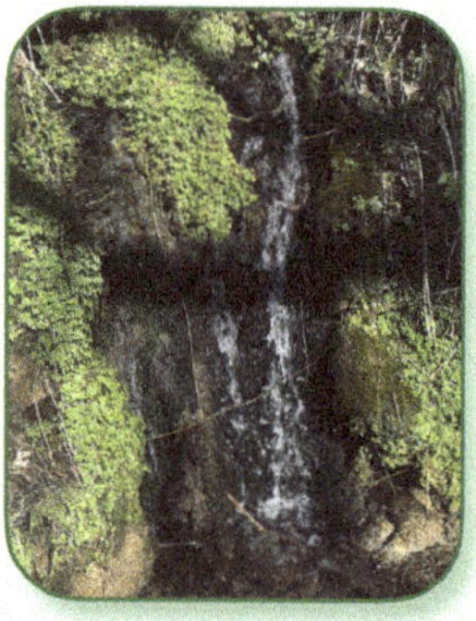

We choose the road to the right along the river bank where emerging leaves of forget-me-nots and budding brambles tangle on the wet banks, and water runs from every slope and bank. Little flowery islands in the river, like floating plates at a Spring wedding, offer refuge among their trees and grasses for birds and small mammals. Green, heart-shaped leaves show that there will soon be even more starry golden celandines among the dark green, rushing into flower before tree canopies shut out the light.

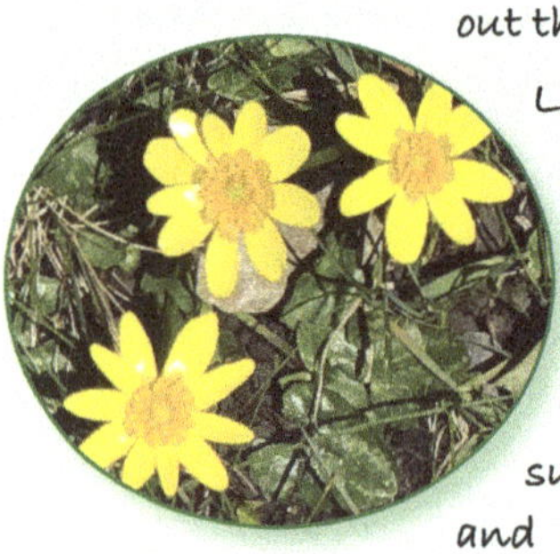

Looping back after a map-reading error, we now climb the hill from the Angler's Rest to reach the tidy, stony yards of Monks Dale Farm, protected by KEEP OUT signs that reflect the anxiety felt by country dwellers at this challenging time. Avoiding the farm, we enter a double walled track across sunny fields, where daisies and more celandines lift their faces against pale stone walls and ash trees clench their black buds tight despite the sun.

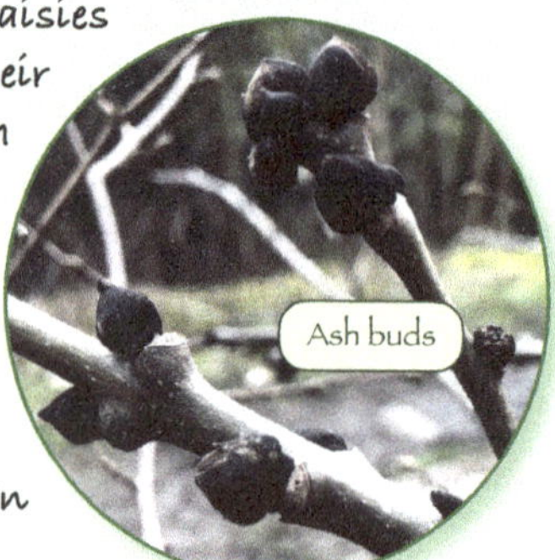

Ash buds

We stop to rest under one of the ash trees, pruned short to stop them undermining the walls. Here, sitting in the Spring sunshine, it is hard to believe that we are in such a dreadful position, with strangers avoided and the protection of our own family's safety a priority for us all.

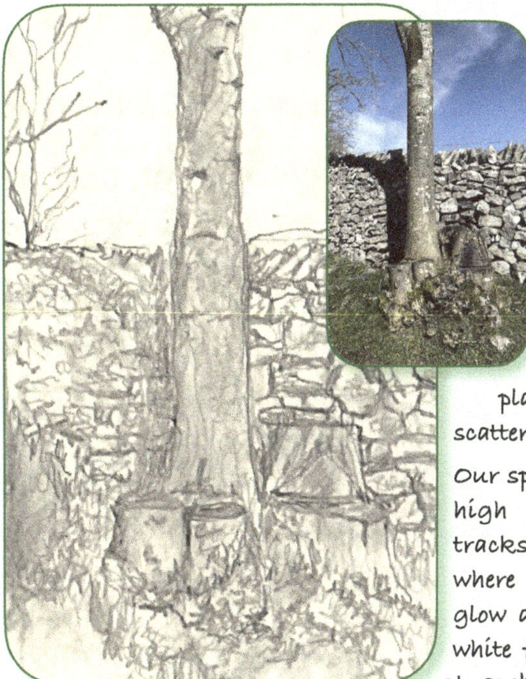

The track continues up the hill, through fields of sheep, all corralled by the limestone walls that march across the landscape, white-lining fields and farmsteads, and opening out onto muddy hilltop fields. As we climb higher, the views expand to the South and West where white rock faces and gorges split the green fields, and sheep hide in plain sight, white as the boulders scattered among them.

Our spirits lift as we meet no-one in this high quarantined landscape. Rutted tracks lead past viewpoint gateways where first dandelions glow among the tiny white flowers of wild strawberries, and circular rosettes of lichens slowly and stealthily decorate the walls, sometimes mingling white and yellow to make fried egg shapes, crisping in the bright Spring sunshine.

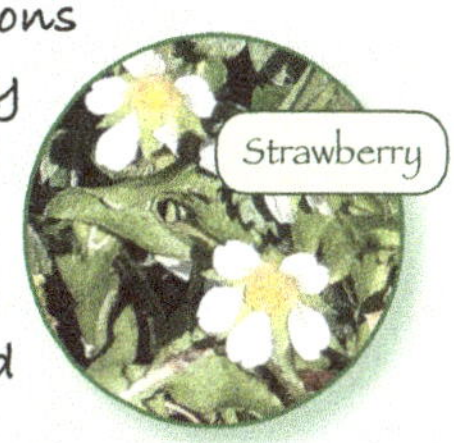

Strawberry

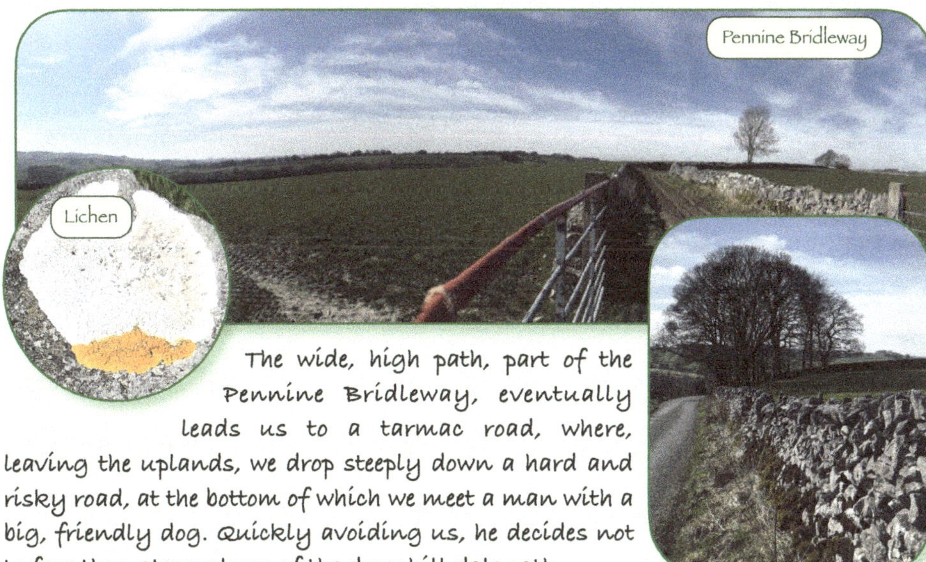

Pennine Bridleway

Lichen

The wide, high path, part of the Pennine Bridleway, eventually leads us to a tarmac road, where, leaving the uplands, we drop steeply down a hard and risky road, at the bottom of which we meet a man with a big, friendly dog. Quickly avoiding us, he decides not to face the watery gloom of the downhill dale path.

In this deep, dark greenness, trees lie as they fall from the white walls of the gorge above, to rest tumbled in the shady gloom. Long, feathery blankets of moss cover every rock, tree and bank, and even hang from trunks, branches and twigs. Rocks tumble unheard, fences and old walls crumble into the moss-covered ground, swallowed up in the dim greenness. Among the moss and ivy, dog's mercury and a tiny yellow spurge struggle to flower. Herb Robert with hairy red stems spider-legs itself over the rocks, and everywhere is the sound of water, as we struggle to keep our footing on sharp, white, loose, moss-covered rocks, clamber under and over fallen trees, and navigate huge boulders. What seem like miles of wobbly walking are punctuated only twice, as we keep the regulation 'ironing board' distance from young and agile walking couples on this unusually deserted walk.

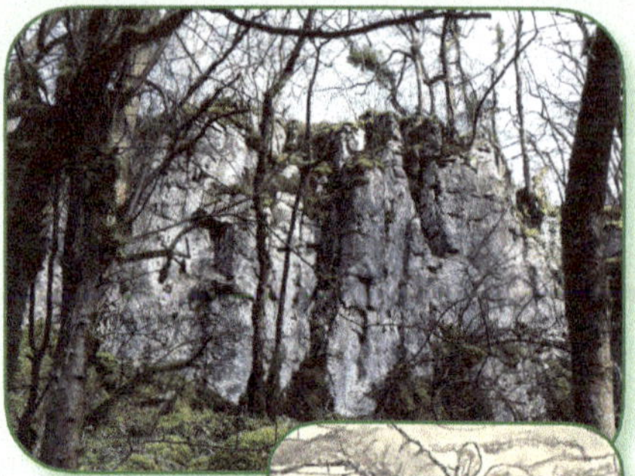

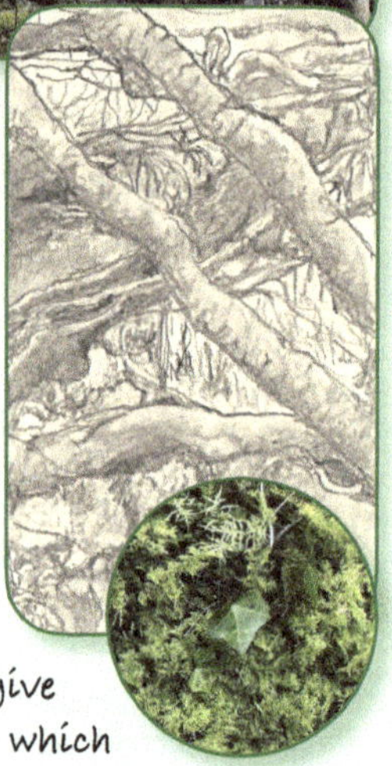

We leave the reserve at a sign warning us of 'ROAMING LIVESTOCK', and gradually the path widens, becomes less stony, and rises up the steep, grassy side of the gorge to give stunning views over the length of our woodland journey, which proved a longer and much more difficult walk than we had planned.

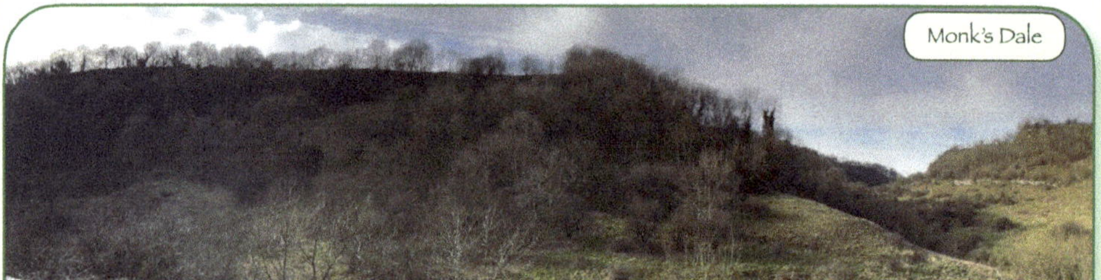

Monk's Dale

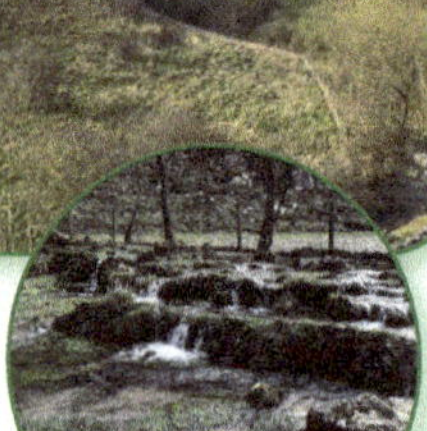

Negotiating the narrow sloping path, we wind down again to the river where water meadows lie, with natural rapids and pools of weed-filled water surely full of fish and frogs.

Two lives remembered on this day: Husband & wife; Eileen and John Carroll; 76 & 75, Retired; Motor trade; Paisley.

Now, among coppiced hazels, sheltered by white cliffs, we meet the 'roaming livestock' warned on the sign. Gentle brown highland cattle paddling up to their knees in the weedy river, or standing on the path, moving aside only very reluctantly for us to pass. These gentle giants are some of the few signs of life we have met today, on the first of our 'harmlessly criminal' outings.

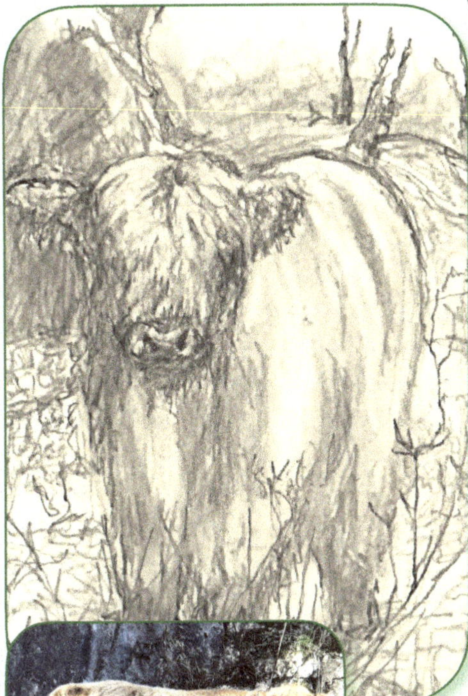

We reluctantly leave these characterful and unusual inhabitants and, crossing a rather rickety timber bridge, climb steep wooden steps from the valley, wondering what can possibly come next, and if this walk will ever reach its end.

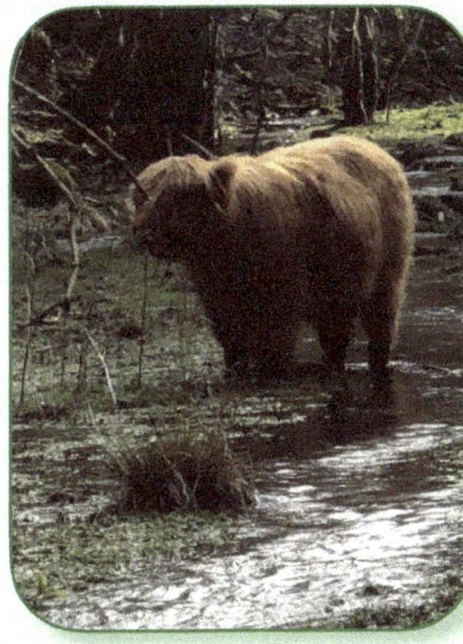

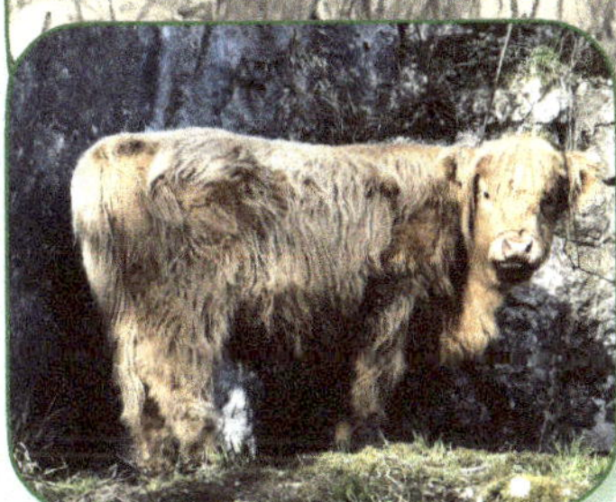

We emerge from the watery green valley into grassy, daisy filled meadows and the welcome sight of the huge viaduct that we left this morning, which seems a lifetime ago. it's almost a surprise to see that the station car park is just a daisy-studded field and a final stile away.

Back to the car and the drive home - to hear on the car radio that, as we take another country walk, the Prime Minister has at last announced the start of the expected national lockdown.

***and meanwhile**: With all schools closed, home learning starts in earnest, except for the children of key workers and those seen as 'vulnerable'.*

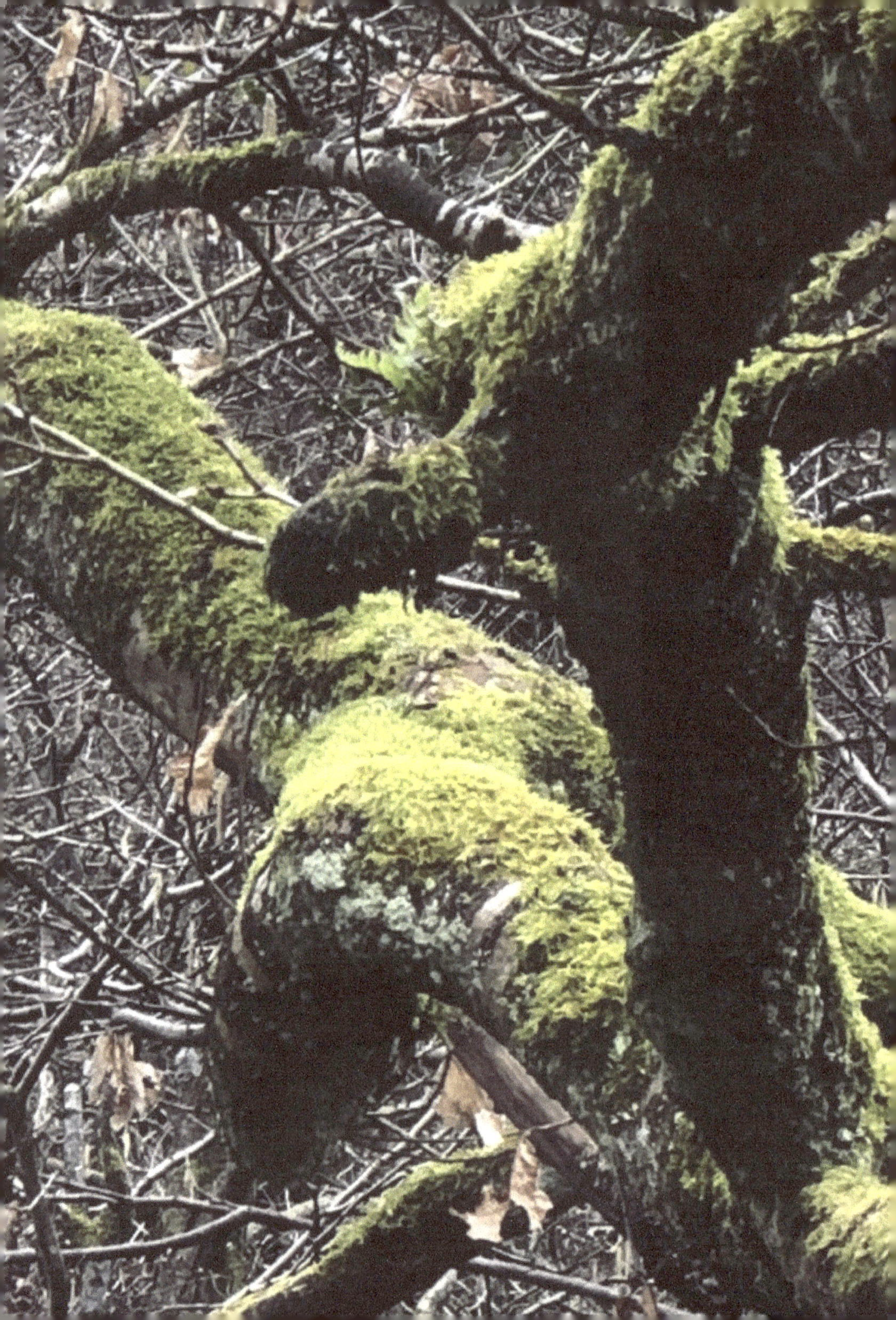

25th March 2020 Confirmed Cases: 7,973 Total deaths: 1,477

THE POLICE WILL BE GIVEN THE POWER TO USE 'REASONABLE FORCE' TO ENFORCE LOCKDOWN REGULATIONS.

Lockdown is really here now, and we practice being alone in our house, where it feels quiet, but strangely normal. Facing the reality of lockdown, there is even a sort of adrenaline rush about the newness of it all, and it's difficult to understand how I feel about it. I still don't know how I will react to being kept indoors, and I already miss contact with human groups and individuals and, almost more importantly, with the wild natural world.

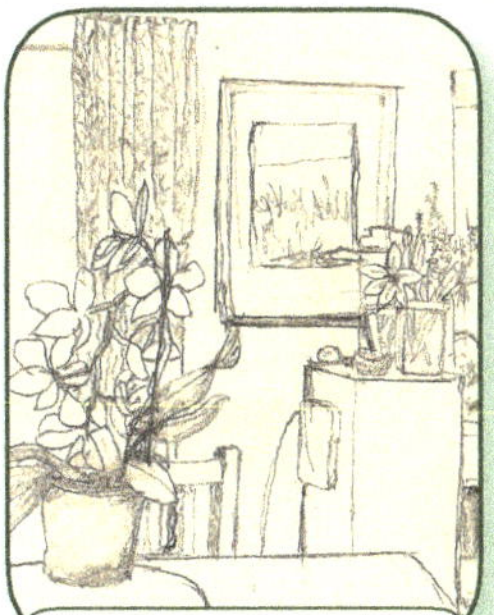

Our lockdown house

A life remembered on this day: Jean Gibbons; 89, Retired; Christchurch.

I must be careful to find plenty of things to do, download some more books for my Kindle, and fight the feeling of sliding uncontrollably downwards, which often heralds an impending depression. I feel homesick for the wide hilltop views and airy freedom of our old house on the Pennines, where everything had space to grow and we could walk unhindered into our own fields instead of having to look at the artificial lawn and red brick walls.

But I must keep positive! We have planted pots of bulbs in this garden, and they are blooming. We have a home, our health is good, we have family nearby, and we are living in one of the greenest cities in Europe.

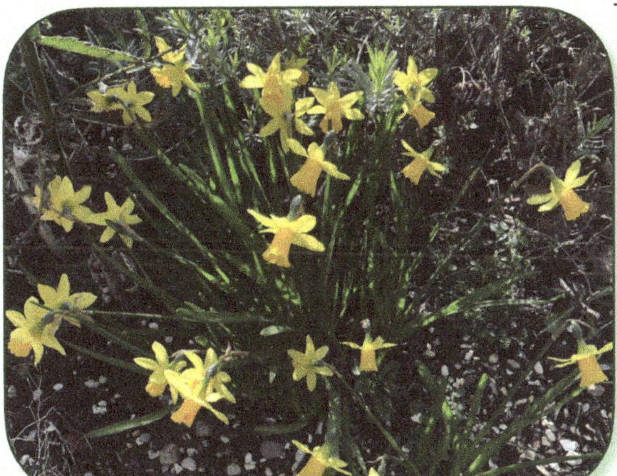

Tomorrow is the first day of legal lockdown, and we intend to escape again, this time with some anxiety that we may now really be 'harmless criminals', doing no harm but still officially breaking the law.

and meanwhile: The first two working doctors working for the NHS die from COVID-19 on the same day. One was a GP, the other was a hospital surgeon.

Pandemic Day: 14 Legal Lockdown 1: minus 1

26th March 2020   Confirmed Cases: 11,658   Total deaths: 1.839

THE LOCKDOWN REGULATIONS COME INTO EFFECT, AND INCLUDE SIGNIFICANT RESTRICTIONS ON FREEDOM OF MOVEMENT: 'NO PERSON MAY LEAVE THE PLACE WHERE THEY ARE LIVING WITHOUT REASONABLE EXCUSE'.

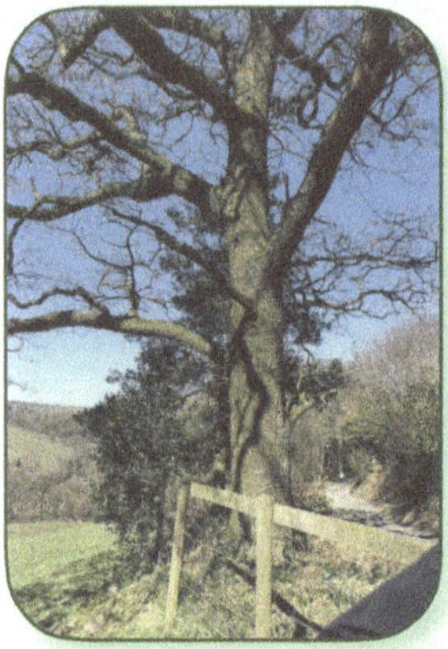

On the first day of legal lockdown, we drive to Shuttingsloe, for what we think may be be our last walk until Lockdown ends, and comfort ourselves with the government assurances that lockdown is just a very temporary measure.

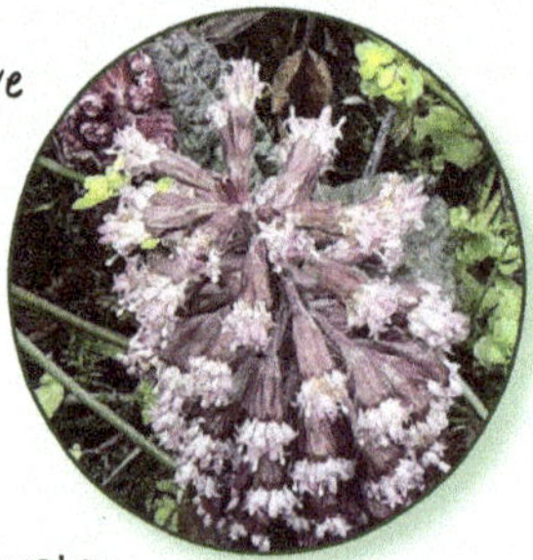

Starting out in a positive mood, we miss a turning, end up on a completely different footpath from the one we intended, and follow a less interesting, less isolated route, where we often see other people.

The weather is sunny and warm as we walk through water meadows, watching peacock butterflies on the strange dirty pink flowers of butterbur growing by the stream. The Spring wildflowers are not out yet - just an occasional dandelion or celandine, but banks of planted daffodils shine out in golden splendour from farm gateways and farmhouse gardens, tempting bumblebees into their trumpets, where they buzz loudly before reversing out again, yellow with pollen.

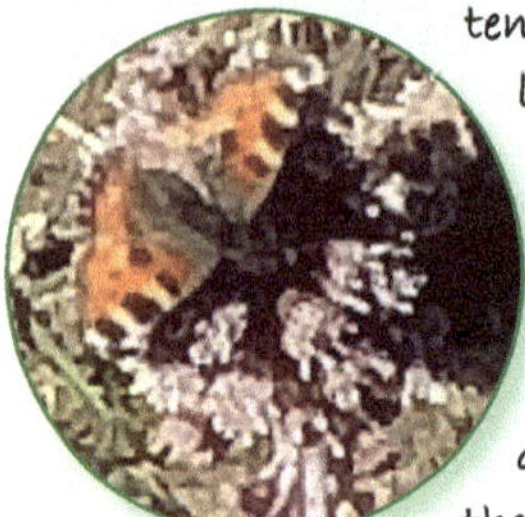

Our walk is mainly on farm tracks through fields, and on country roads, quiet apart from thundering lorries driving from the limestone quarries to the continuing road building. There is little other traffic, and even fewer people, those we do meet giving us a wary wide berth as they walk their dogs or tend their gardens. Pubs and cafes are shut, car parks cordoned off, windows closely curtained - how long before they will be allowed to open their doors to weekend walkers again?

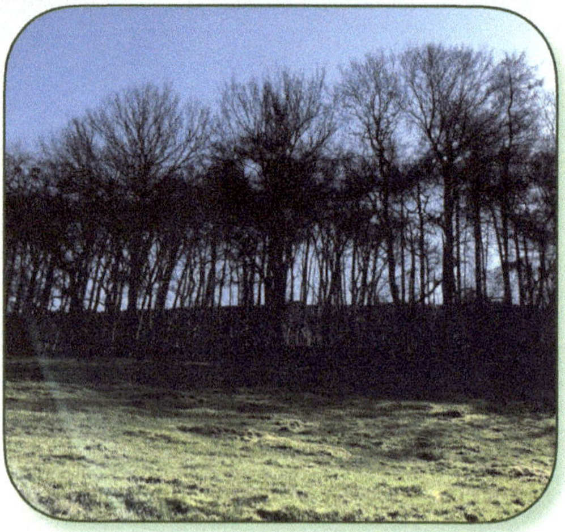

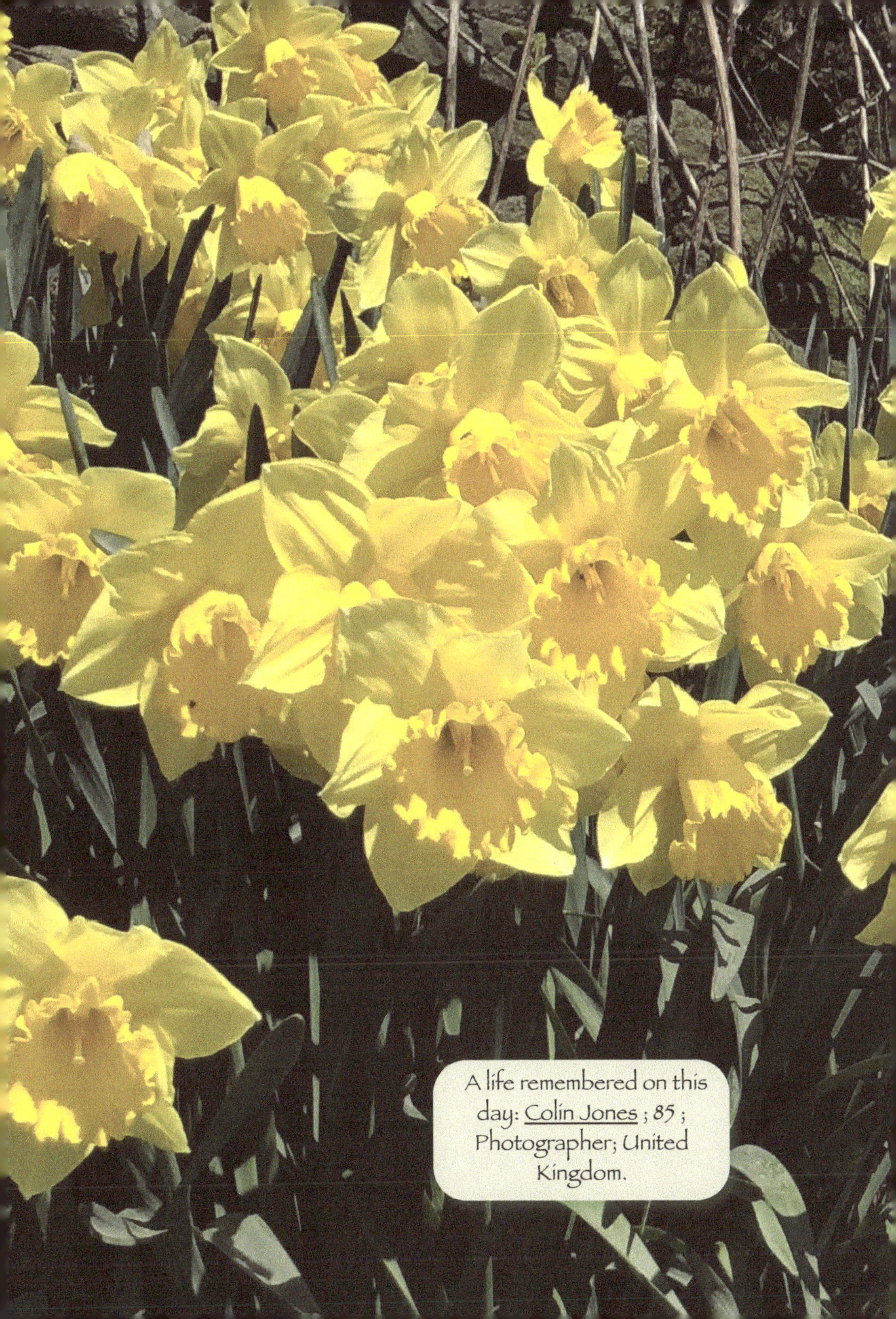

A life remembered on this day: Colin Jones ; 85 ; Photographer; United Kingdom.

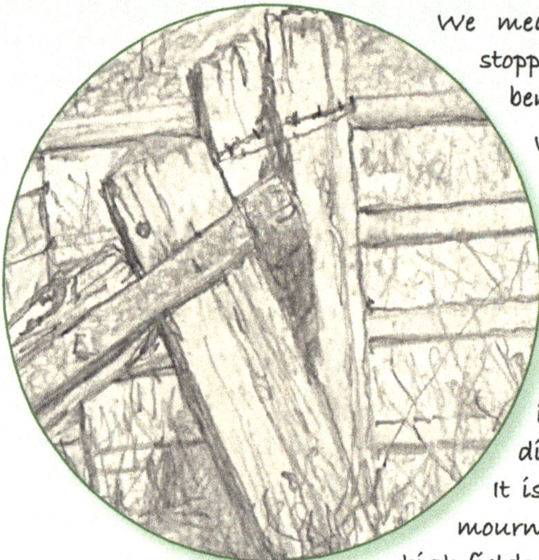

We meander among fields and farms, stopping for lunch at a grassy gateway beneath steep, bracken covered hills.

We are passed by more local dog walkers who give us suspicious looks before moving swiftly on. Either they are too polite or too scared to ask who we are!

Returning to the river, we sit listening to water and birds, including the mournful cry of a distant curlew from across the valley. It is two years since we last heard that mournful, but unforgettable sound on the high fields of West Yorkshire.

Buds on hawthorn, larch and bramble are swelling under a bright blue sky and warm sun, but there are no leaves yet on the big hedgerow trees, although the silver birch look freshly painted against the blue of the cloudless sky. A wet winter and a sunny spring raised our hopes of an early greening of these trees, but the white-barked birches, great elms, ashes and sycamores by the river are still bare, with just the tint of olive green lichen on their trunks and branches.

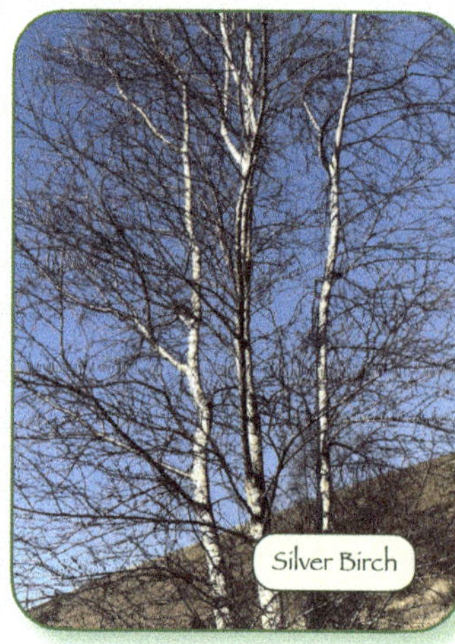

Silver Birch

and as birds ignore the exercise limits: *The 'Lockdown Regulations' come into effect, significantly extending the range of businesses that are required to close with immediate effect including retail businesses not on an approved list.*

We drive home by a different route, along deserted lanes, past car parks cordoned off with official black and yellow tape, and unofficial barriers across farm gateways. The local people give very clear messages of their feelings for city dwellers invading the countryside they see as their own.

At 8 o'clock we go out in the road with neighbours to bang saucepans and clap, joining the first 'Clap for Carers' in support of everyone working in the NHS.

Pandemic Day: 15 Lockdown 1: day 1

Acorns grow into little oaks

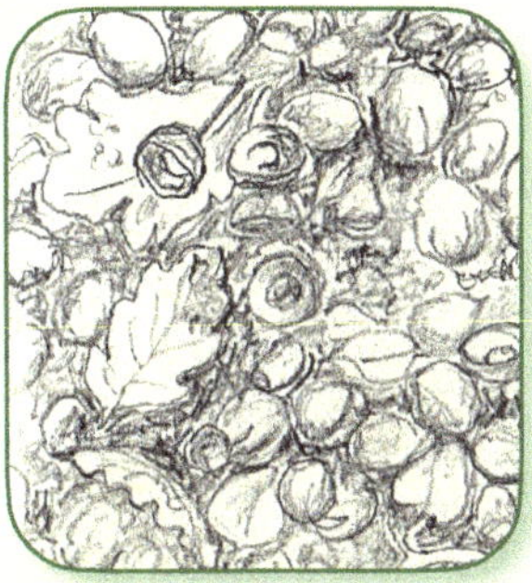

12th October 2019

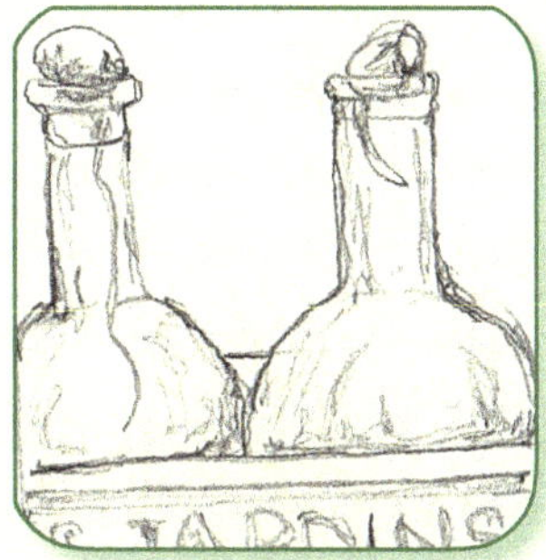

27th October 2019

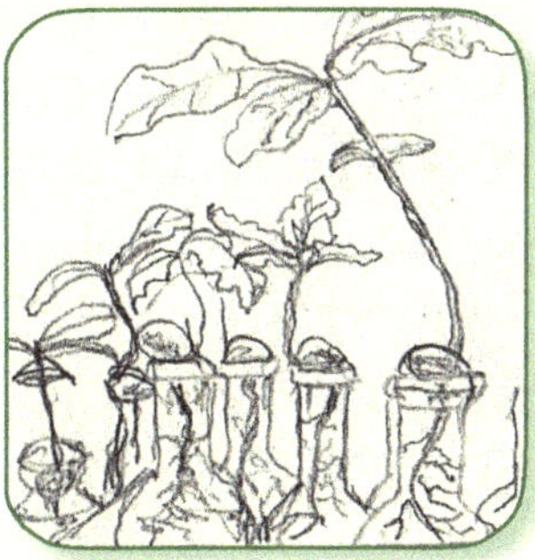

13th December 2019

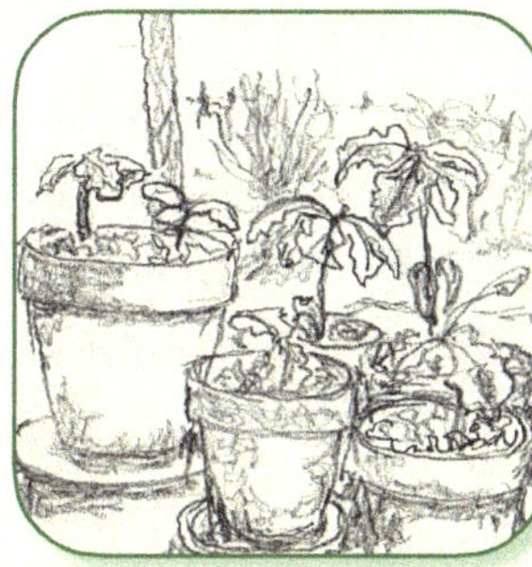

14th February 2020

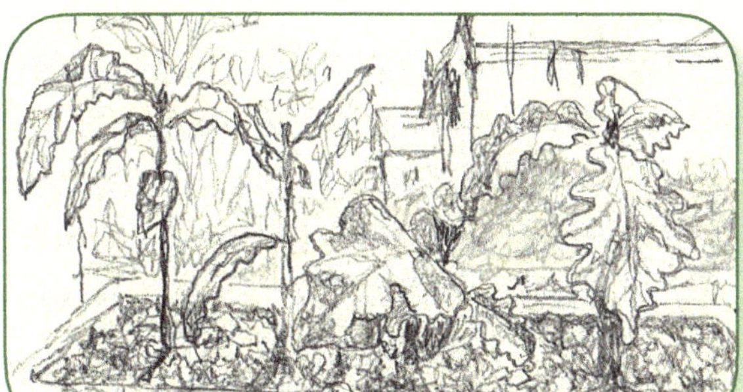

29th March 2020

Remembered on this day: Barbara West; 64; patient with Downs Syndrome; London.

27th March 2020 Confirmed Cases: 12,288 Total deaths: 2673

A GOVERNMENT CLARIFICATION CONFIRMS THAT WE ARE NOT TO DRIVE OUT TO WALK AND TAKE EXERCISE. WE MUST STAY IN 'THE IMMEDIATE LOCALITY'.

And then we hear of Dominic Cummings' drive north. Unlike Mr Cummings, our 'New Normal' life must now be the four walls of our living room, and this makes us feel even more disobedient!

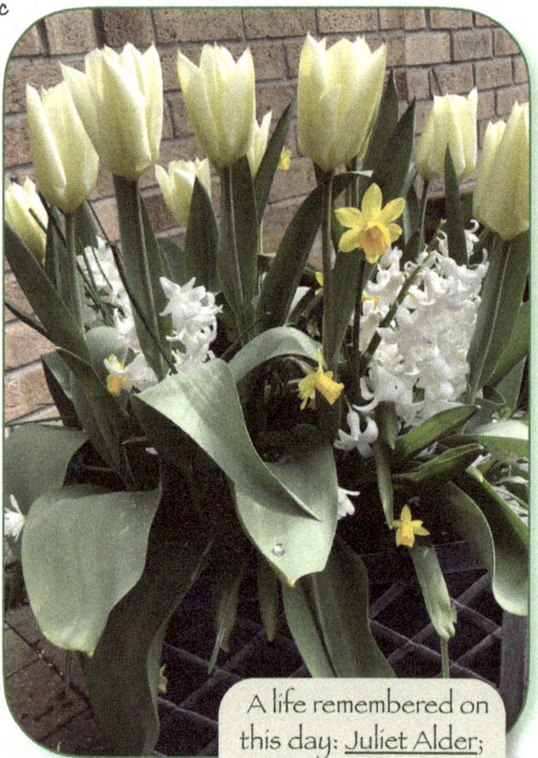

A life remembered on this day: Juliet Alder; 58; Healthcare assistant; London.

Two days at home, and I already feel really 'locked in'. Our horizons shrink as Spring advances. Buds begin to break on hawthorn and sycamore in the warmer city, and spring flowers are at their best, but many will never be seen, with parks and public gardens locked down. Our tubs of yellow tulips, perfumed white hyacinths and little daffodils flower by the front door, but we are the only people who see them.

In the last days of March, we obediently walk round local parks, where horse chestnuts are unfurling their green hands and magnolias opening furry buds.

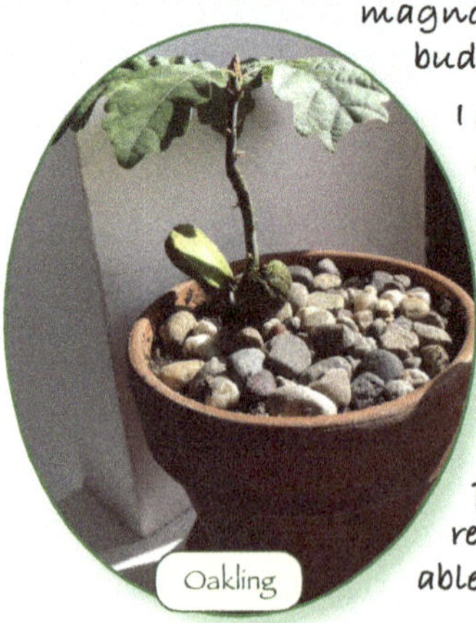

Oakling

I spend time drawing from photos the development of some acorns that we have been growing into little oak trees on our windowsill. We collected them in the local park last autumn, where they lay deep in the mud at the edge of the football field, and balanced them on little glass bottles, where they all rooted.

I have read that of all the thousands of acorns produced by a single oak tree, only one will ever reach maturity. I wonder when and where we will be able to find a place to plant our little trees.

Pandemic Day: 16 Lockdown 1: day 2

March 2020 ends

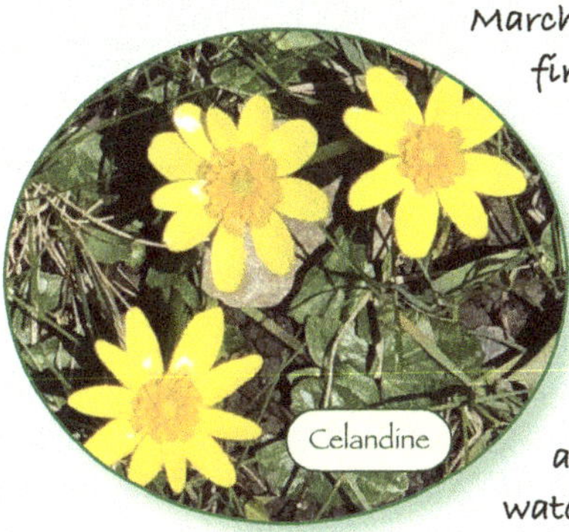

March is over, and we reach the end of Day 2 of the first National Lockdown.

I swing from confidence that the measures will work to reduce our risk, to doom and gloom that the lockdown will go on for much longer than the few weeks promised by an impossibly unrealistic and 'gung-ho' government.

Airports, schools and pubs close, and children and their parents get used to learning at home, watching PE lessons on line, completing computer worksheets printed at home, welcoming work sent from schools, and engaging (or not) with quickly assembled 'learning; programmes on TV. Parents and programmers suddenly realise that school is not just maths and English, and cannot all be delivered through pencil and paper exercises. They hurriedly begin to address the issues connected with teaching PE, drama, art, music and science remotely, without gyms, labs or studios. The youngest children, used to hands-on learning with specially chosen educational resources and skilled teachers, find worksheets quickly become boring, as parents wrestle with 'phonics' and try to master the mysteries of learning to read.

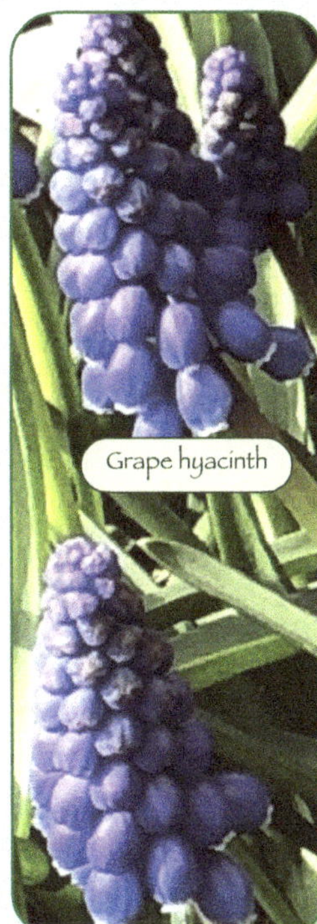

Our own horizons are reduced and we begin to get used to the silence - no noise from pedestrians and road users, no chat when deliveries are left on the doorstep, no conversations with people we meet on walks, no shopping, no theatre, exhibitions, cinema or pubs, and most strangely no traffic noise at night. At this point physical links with our families are broken, but a government adviser is able to drive hundreds of miles to see his parents, apparently feeling he is outside the law.

The restrictions on our movement immediately begin to chafe. We race the regulations to get in walks before the deadline, and then as the details of regulation are clarified, we become 'harmless criminals', interpreting the letter of the law in a way that suits our need to be in the blue and the green.

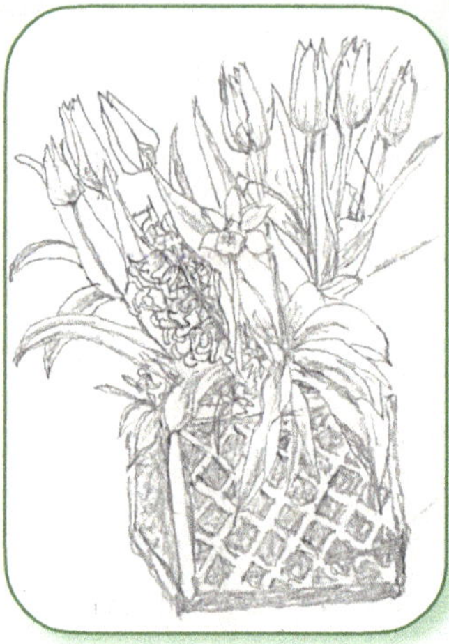

As human life becomes more restricted, natural life continues its unstoppable progress into Spring. Planters and beds of bulbs bloom, and trees begin to open their leafy hands, as the parks and public gardens provide a welcome space for our restricted exercise. Foxes, badgers, owls and other wildlife, normally hidden from city dwellers roam freely and fearlessly down city streets, even in daylight.

The garden at the Children's House begins to surprise us with shoots and buds of hidden plants. We manage to extend our outings by the 'two plus one' of three long walks in the deserted local countryside of the White Peaks. Two of these walks are completed before the regulations become law, and we must stay within the City limits, our final 'legal' walk is on the very first day of National Lockdown

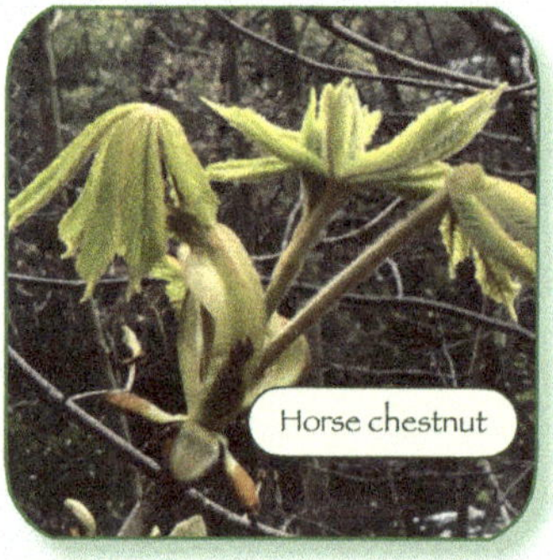
Horse chestnut

In the UK, there have been over 38 thousand reported cases, and more than four thousand people have already lost their battle with this virus. How many more lives will be lost before its deadly stalking progress across the world finally loses its grip and it returns to its secret lair to prepare for another strike?

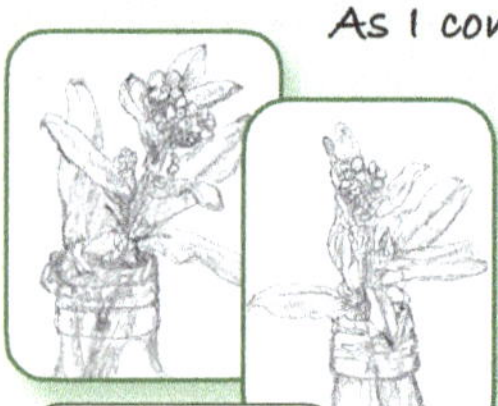
Forget-me-not

As I continue to wonder how long this lockdown will last, I think about the many families destined to mourn those who have died in hospitals and care homes without the support of family or friends, while a government adviser seems free to go wherever he likes!

We are lucky that no-one we know has been infected, but we are evidently only at the beginning of this process, and no-one can assume they are safe.

UK CASES AND DEATHS: 31st March 2020

Confirmed Cases - 38,025

Deaths to date - 4,430

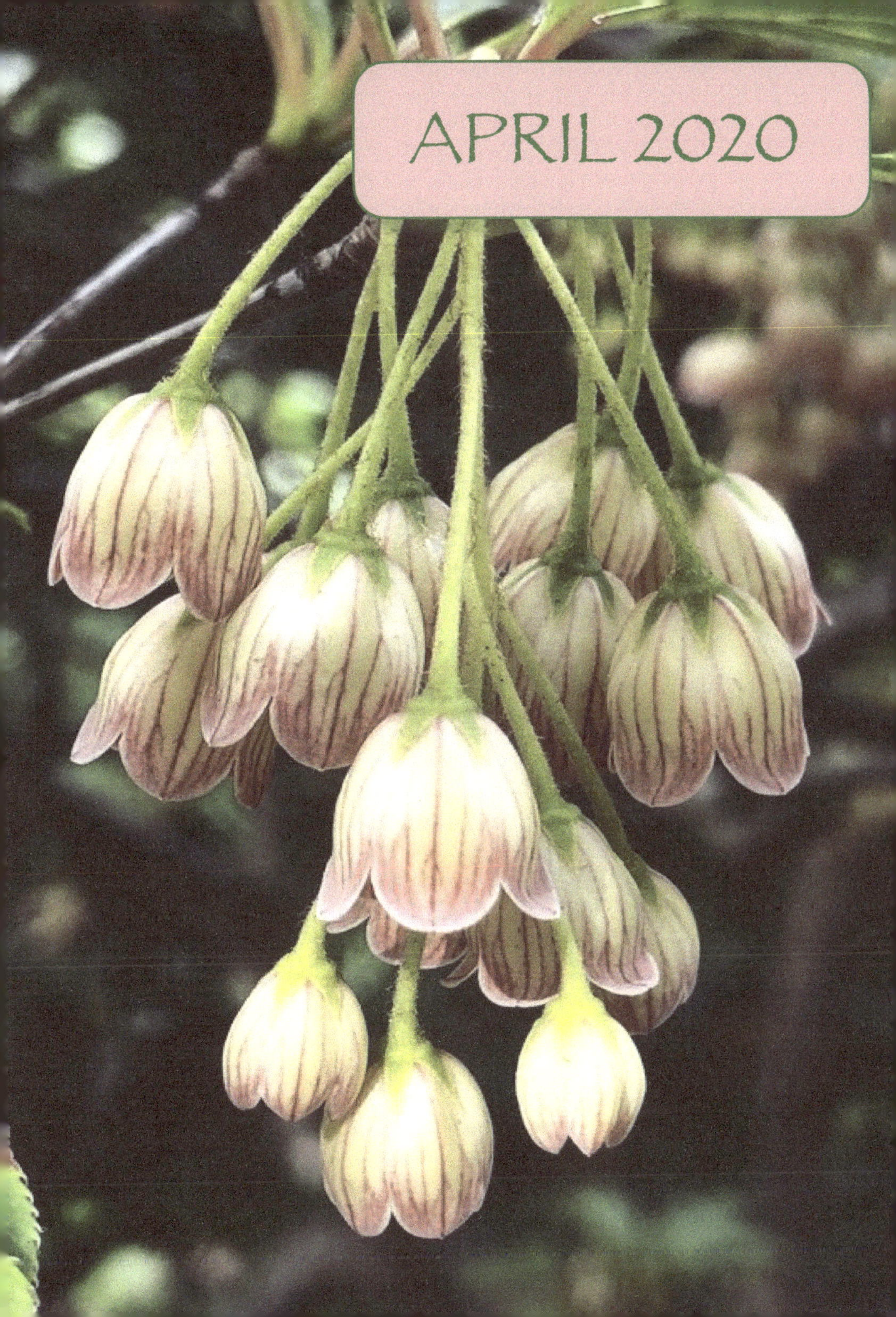
APRIL 2020

1st April 2020 Confirmed Cases: 24,638 Total deaths: 5,199

SHORTAGES OF PPE CAUSE FRICTION BETWEEN GOVERNMENT AND NHS, AS HOSPITALS AND CARE HOMES FAIL TO GET SUPPLIES.

Terry Waite, who spent 1,763 days as a hostage, and four years in solitary confinement, advises:

> 'Keep your own dignity, form a structure for the day, be grateful for what you have, read and be creative.
>
> You are not stuck at home, you are safe at home.'

A life remembered on this day: George Georgiou; 62; Chip shop owner; Muswell Hill. London.

Such sensible and thought-provoking advice from a man who was confined for so long, but after just ten days of lockdown, I find it difficult to heed his words. I am grateful for what I have, but I still feel locked in like some storybook Rapunzel in her tower, waiting for the prince with the cure to come riding in.

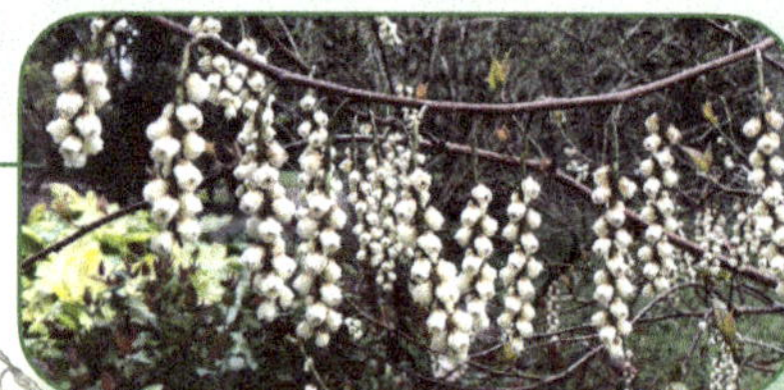

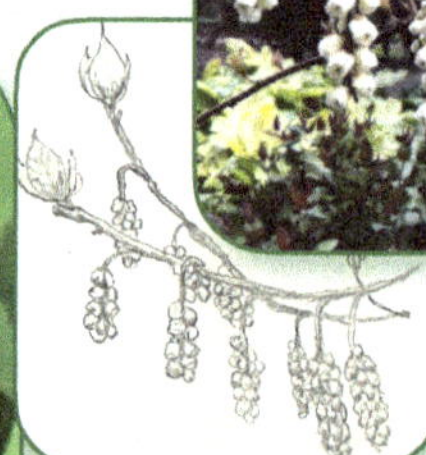

Spiketail; Stachyrus praecox

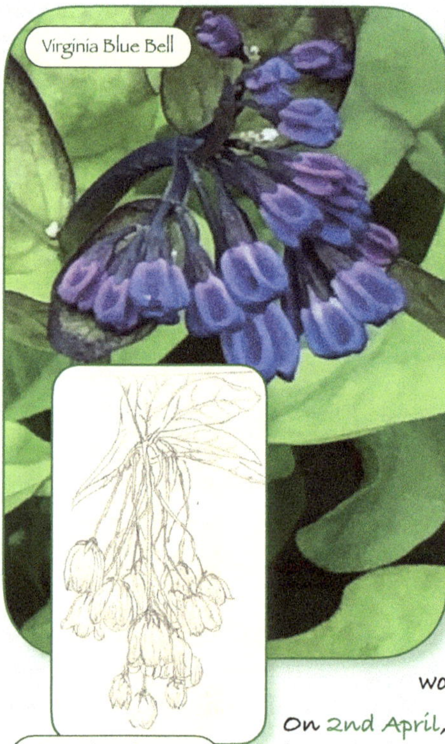

Virginia Blue Bell

Enkianthus Campanulatus; Red Bells

We are forced to restrict our daily outings, and the nearby Sheffield Botanical Gardens become our refuge for experiencing nature as we watch the Spring unfold. Spectacular blooms, perfect in the still air, call to bees, flies or beetles. Rare shrubs hang their strange flowers like crafted decorations or long strings of perfect pearls. The park attendants are locked down too, so there is no-one to ask about the names of these strange plants, so I must resort to the wonderful resource of Google.

On 2nd April, we make a longer circuit of Norfolk Park, down the nature reserve where birds sing Spring songs, and leaves of new growth thrust through the soft earth.

Pandemic Day: 21 Lockdown 1: day 7

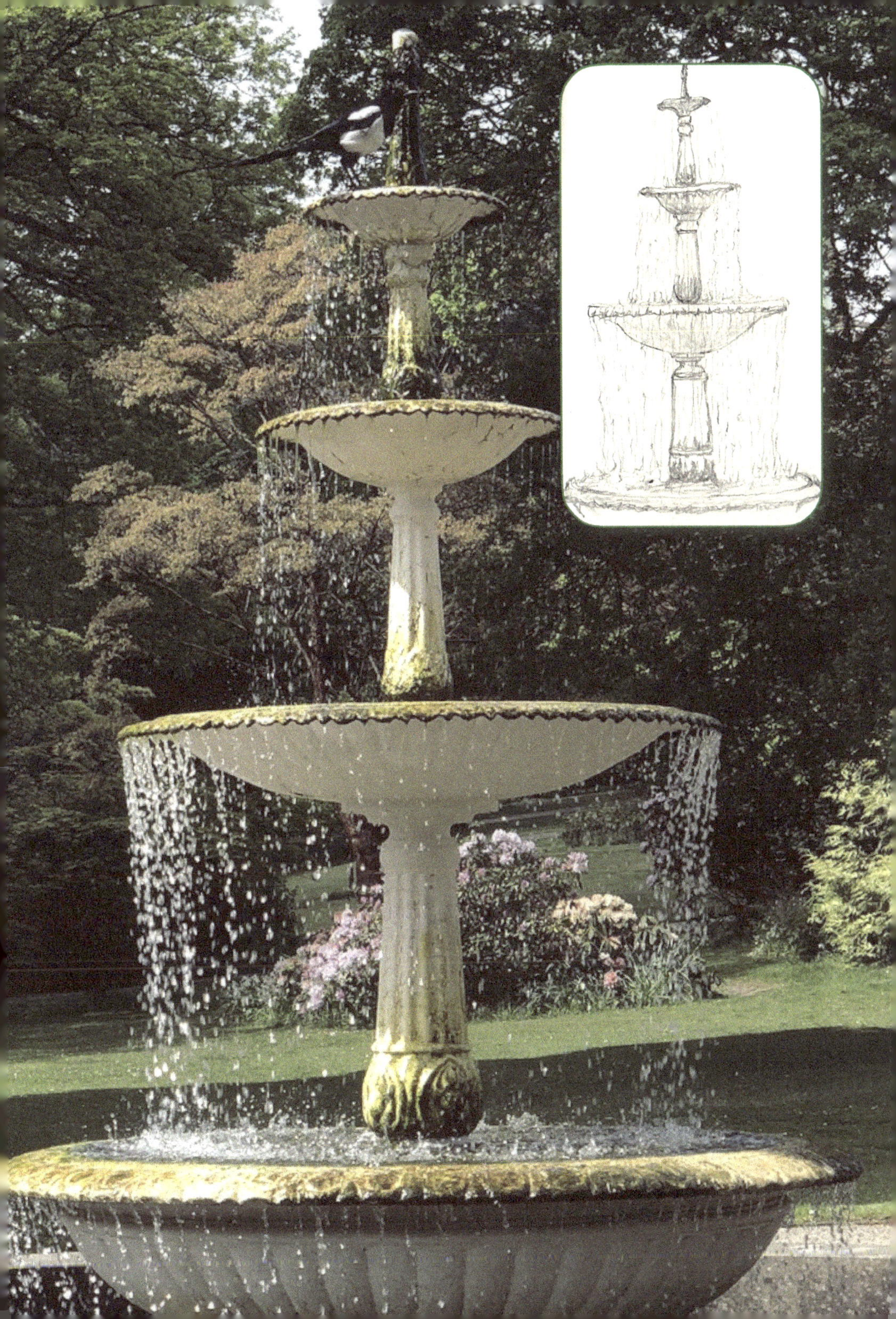

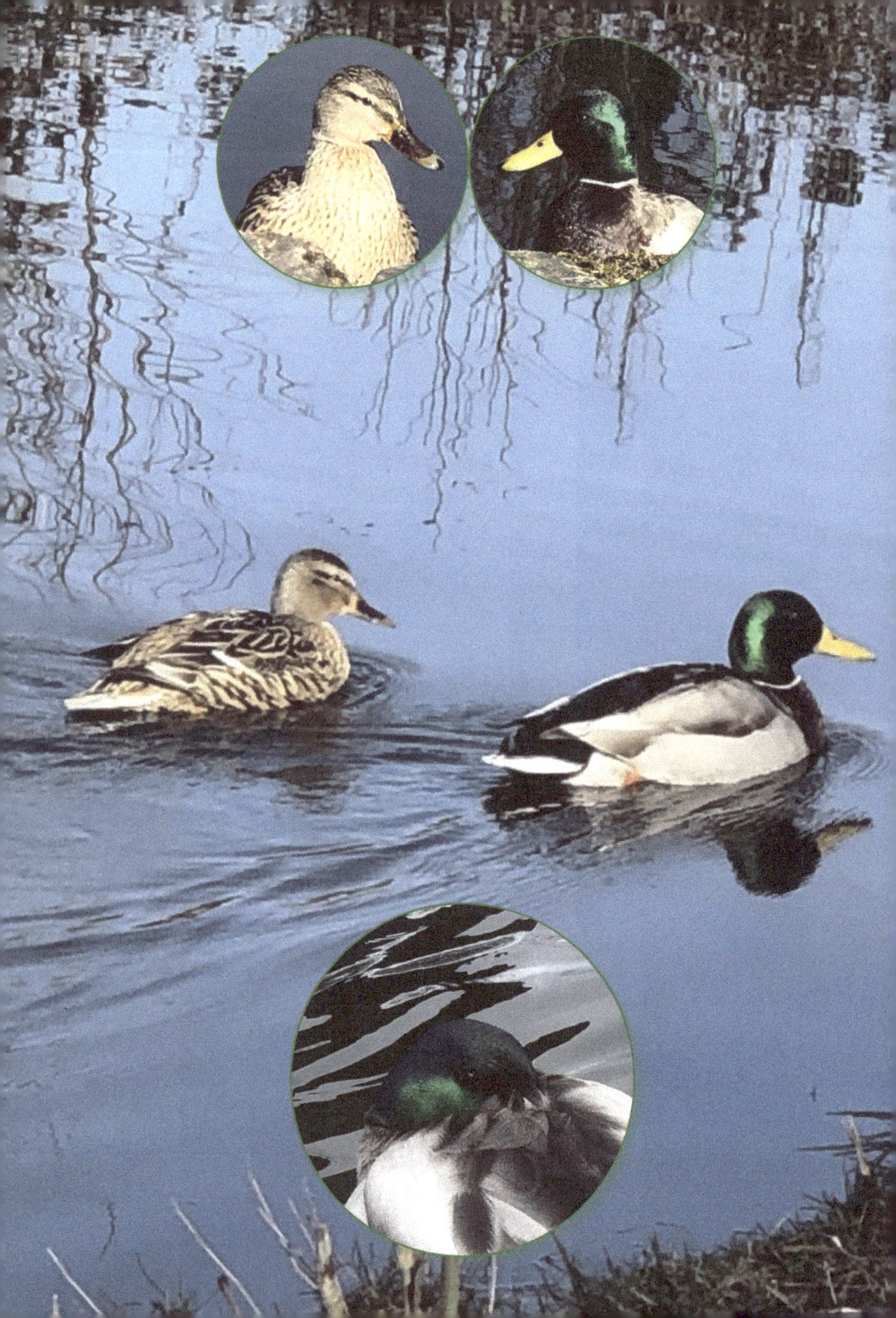

3rd April 2020 Confirmed Cases: 39,282 Total deaths:7,751

NHS NIGHTINGALE, THE FIRST TEMPORARY HOSPITAL TO TREAT CORONAVIRUS PATIENTS, OPENS AT THE EXCEL CENTRE IN EAST LONDON.

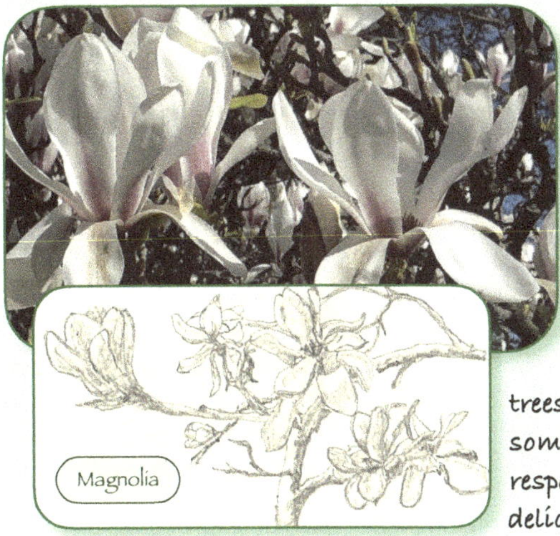

Magnolia

On a sunny Spring afternoon, we enjoy a walk along quiet residential roads lined with desirable, spacious, Victorian and Edwardian houses with established, well maintained gardens full of shrubs bursting into Spring bloom. More and more magnolias hold furry buds and pale, pink suffused cups of petals. Chestnut trees open from their 'sticky buds', and some early blossom trees begin to respond to the sunshine by unfolding delicate shoots and pink petals.

In one front garden a teddy is carefully balanced in a tree, signalling a family's support for the NHS, and children's paintings of rainbows decorate windows.

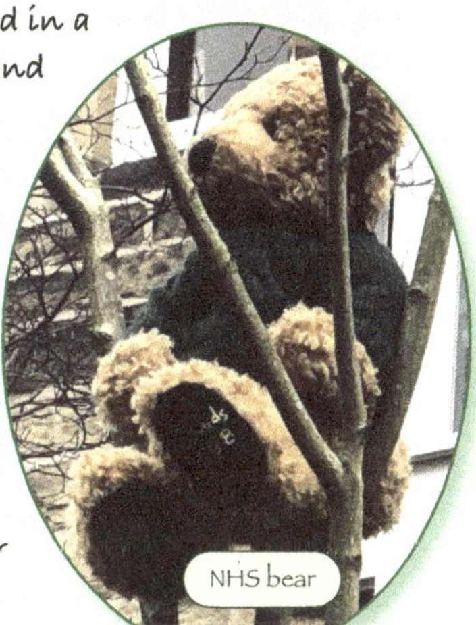

NHS bear

The sunlit paths in Endcliffe Park are busy with walkers trying politely to keep their 'social distance', but as runners and cyclists also abound here, with earbuds firmly fixed, and clouds of heavy breathing escaping into the air, proper separation is difficult. They ride or run in the middle of the path, pushing pedestrians to the verges - I wish we could agree to make some paths just for cyclists and runners, and leave others for those of us who only want to walk!

Our 'daily exercise' continues beyond the playgrounds and sports fields, past the park, where the ducks are puzzled by the lack of crusts, and up through the top part of Endcliffe Park, which is less managed, and where the paths are wider and quieter. Here we can linger in the places where the rush of bikes and panting of energetic runners are less intrusive.

Lives remembered today:
Bassodeo Rambojun; 85; Royal Mail; London, and Areema Nasreen; 36; NHS nurse; Walsall; West Midlands.

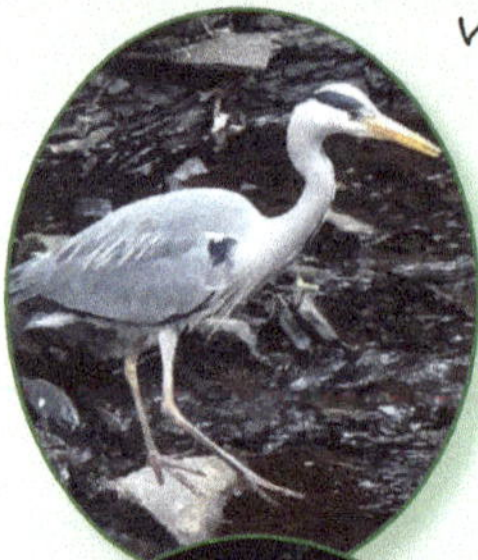

We spend some time watching a big grey heron stalking in the cold water of Porter Brook, ignoring us as it walks slowly upstream, enjoying the unusual quiet, with no enthusiastic dogs or noisy children to disturb its fishing. It walks, freezes motionless, then daggers its beak into banks and between rocks in the water, before stepping carefully on until it reaches the deep pond and shallow rapids under the bridge over the Porter Brook.

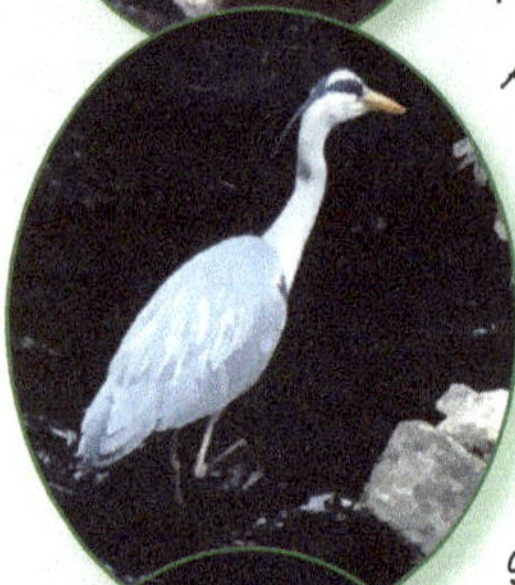

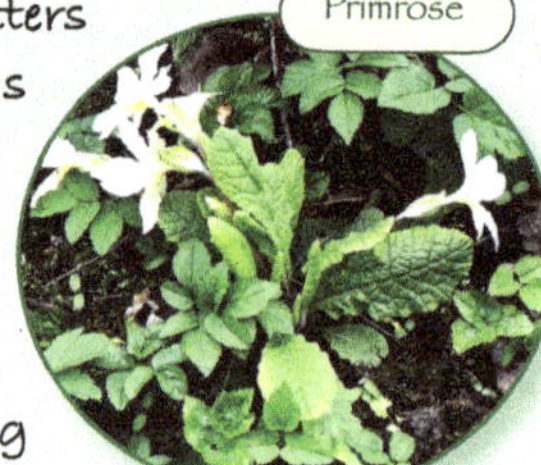

Primrose

A wagtail hops, dips and flutters around the heron, perhaps waiting for food disturbed by the bigger bird, but the heron suddenly spreads its great grey umbrella wings and lifts over the bridge and the road, long grey legs dangling, just managing to avoid a collision with an astonished cyclist.

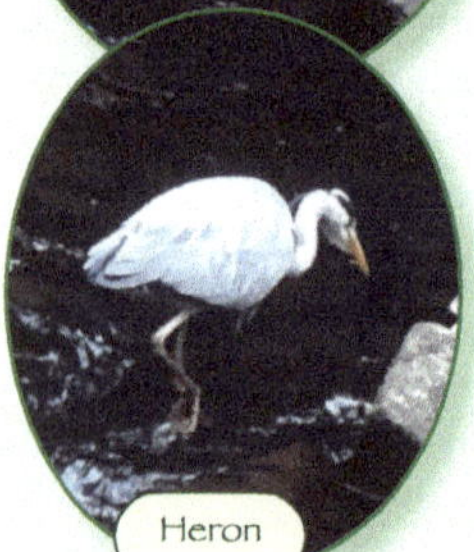

Heron

At Shepherd's Wheel the restored knife grinders' workshop is closed and bolted, with only the ghosts of the workers among the dusty spider webs. Beyond the workshop and water wheel, we find mallards on the bright blue water of the reflected sky, and early primroses, palest yellow among the greenery, and as we continue our walk round the edge of the allotments, brambles lean over the path with fresh bunches of leaves, and new sharp thorns ready to snag our coat sleeves.

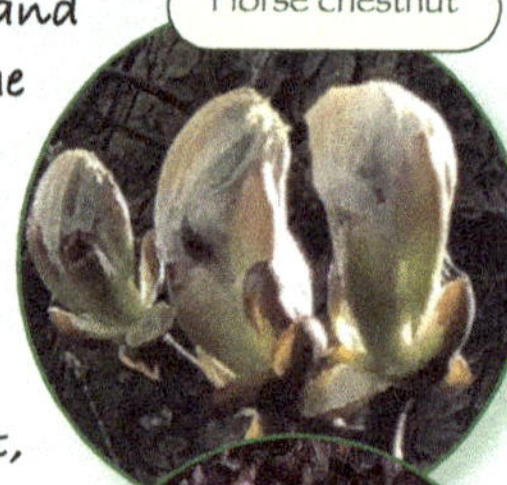

Horse chestnut

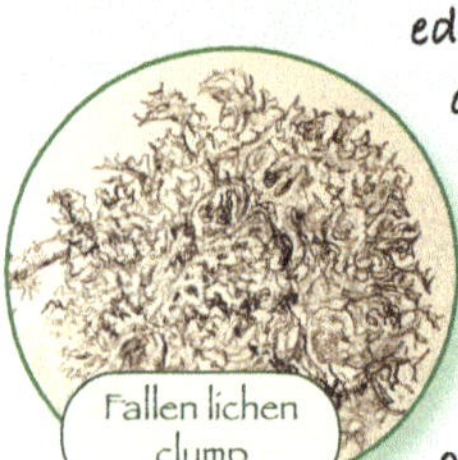

Fallen lichen clump

This is a pavemented circuit, unlike our usual muddy, grassy outings, but being outside in 'the green and the blue' anywhere helps to dispel the insistent locked in frustrated feeling. We discuss the possibility of going further to walk, and decide that for now, we will abide by the rules, but make no promises for the future!

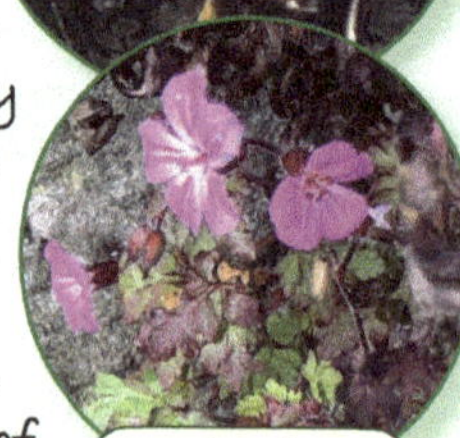

Herb Robert

and meanwhile: *Health Minister, Matt Hancock sets a target of carrying out 100,000 tests a day by the end of the month.*

Pandemic Day: 23 Lockdown 1: day 9

KIER STARMER IS ELECTED AS LEADER OF THE LABOUR PARTY, SUCCEEDING JEREMY CORBIN.

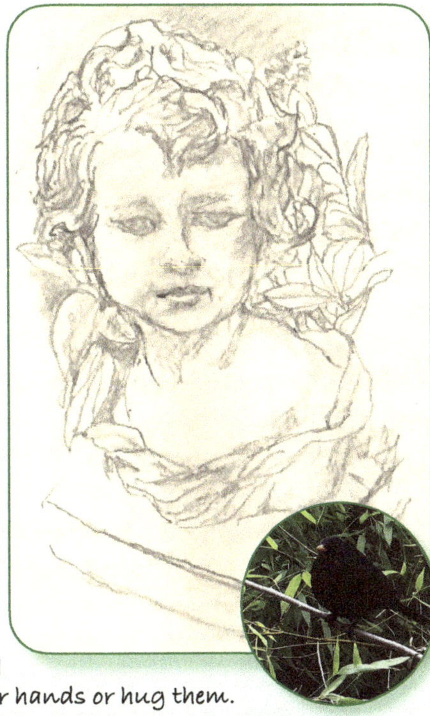

As the days pass, the virus continues to take its toll, and there is no sign of a let up. We take some of our exercise in Norfolk Park, often stealing into the unlocked garden of the house we hope to buy. Estate agents are closed, so progress on the sale is still achingly slow, and we see no early way forward.

I spend some time drawing a little sculpture from the garden, which I have had for many years.

5th - It's no surprise that, in such lovely weather, families without gardens congregate in parks, where both adults and children, who really need their friends, can at least see them, talk to them and play with them, even if they can't hold their hands or hug them.

In a change to the rules, we are now told that we can drive for five minutes to a place of exercise!

Five lives remembered today: London bus drivers - Kenneth Yeboah, 55; Nadir Nur, 48; Emeka Nyack Ihenacho, 36; Ranjith Chandrapala, 64; Rodolfo Silva.

6th - THE QUEEN SPEAKS TO THE NATION, TO RAISE NATIONAL MORALE AS THE PRIME MINISTER IS HIMSELF HOSPITALISED WITH THE COVID VIRUS.

Male London bus drivers aged 20-65 are found to be more than three times more likely to die from Covid than men in other jobs.

Assistant Head Zane Powles of Western Primary School, Grimsby, walks more than five miles every day to deliver free school meals, and check on children in need from his school. Lockdown has truly brought out the very best in some people!

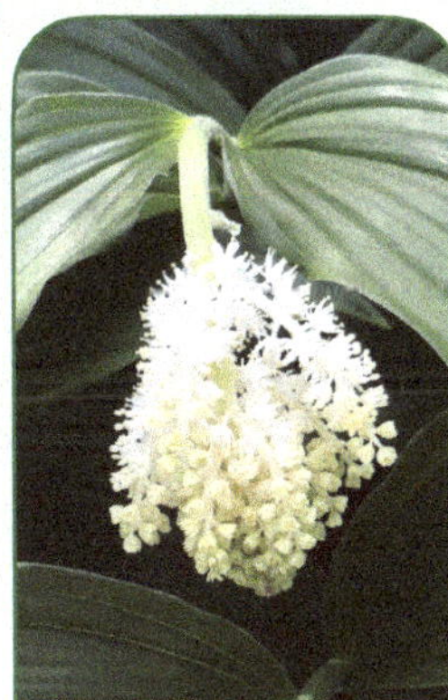

Maianthemum raceemosum; false Solomon's Seal

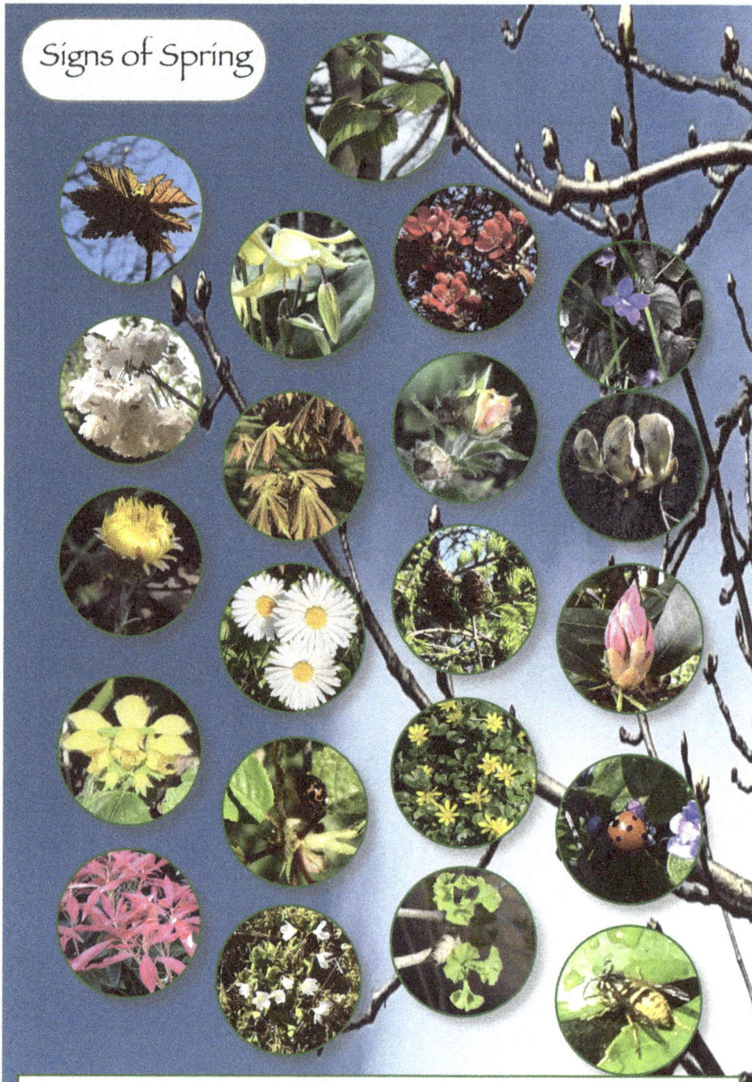

Sycamore, cherry, coltsfoot, pieris, beech, chestnut, daisy, ladybird, wood anemone, crab apple, gum, larch, celandine, ginkgo, dog violet, horse chestnut, rhododendron, another ladybird, wasp.

13th/20th April 2020 Confirmed Cases:93,030 Total deaths: 16,393

13th - Our daughter Sarah is making PPE for local hospitals. Just like story book elves, people drop off bags of clean fabric on her drive, and volunteer stitchers come later to pick up instructions and bring finished work.

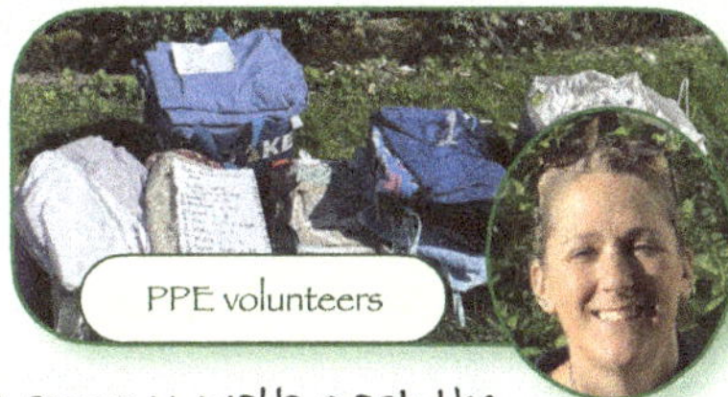

PPE volunteers

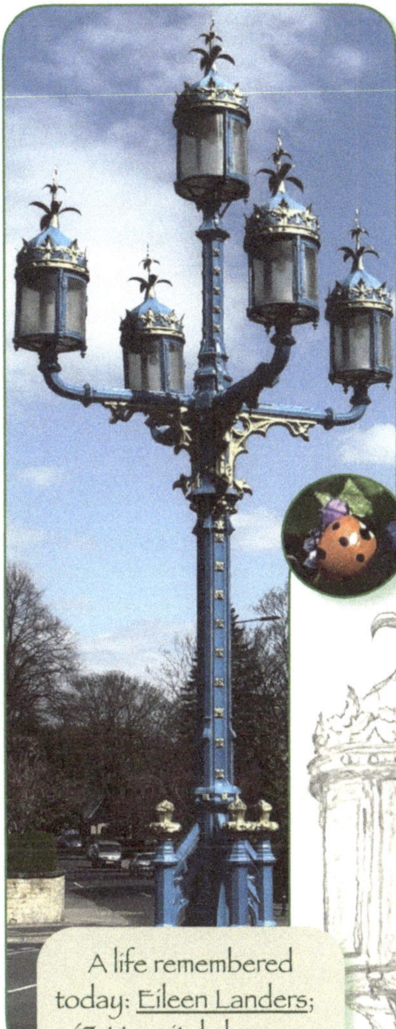

16th - The sunny walk past the blue lamp-post, through the gates and up the Turkey Oak Drive in Norfolk Park is less crowded, and the birds still visit in remembered hope of picnics and playgroups, while a woodpecker drums in the trees.

At 99, Captain Tom Moore begins walking round his garden for NHS charities.

20th* - *THE PM LEAVES HOSPITAL.

A walk in the Botanical Gardens where the bluebells are now out, and the beeches, ashes, oaks and horse chestnuts are greening. The daffodils are over, and the grass is carpeted with pale petal confetti from magnolia and cherry trees. Ladybirds emerge from hibernation, ducks sleep by the pond, and a robin with a worm comes close, in the hope of crumbs. We intend to escape to Ladybower Reservoir tomorrow!

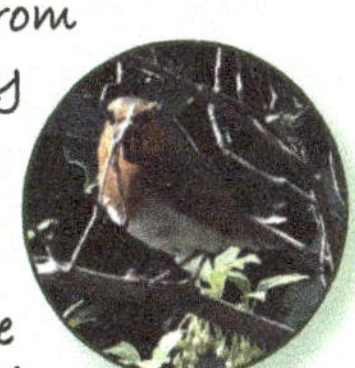

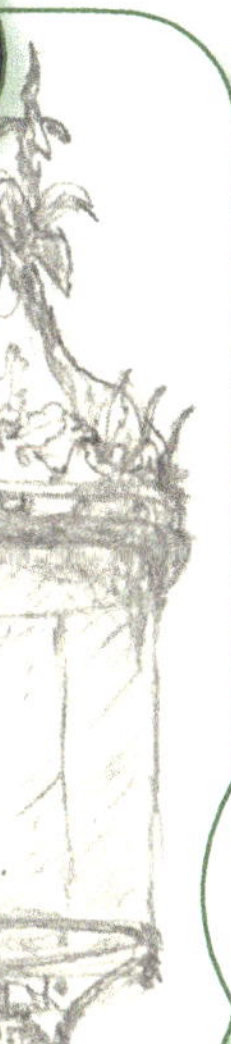

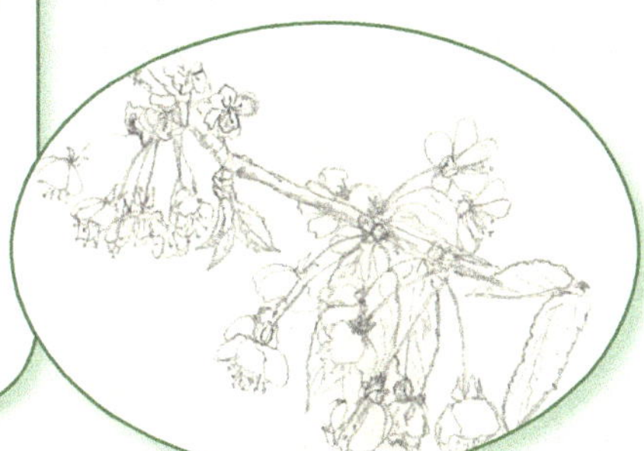

A life remembered today: Eileen Landers; 67; Hospital cleaner; Burton on Trent; UK.

Pandemic Day: 33/40 Lockdown 1: day 19/26

Today Dorothy Duffy dedicated this poem to her sister:

Rose (Billy) Duffy; 81; died in London.

This is an extract from the poem, which you can find at:

https://www.irishtimes.com/news/health/my-sister-is-not-a-statistic-poem-honours-death-of-irish-woman-in-london-1.4229377

From 'My sister is not a statistic'

Tomorrow, when the latest Deathometer of Covid is announced in sonorous tones,
Whilst all the bodies still mount and curl towards the middle of the curve
Heaped one atop and alongside the other
My sister will be among those numbers, among the throwaway lines
Among the platitudes and lowered eyes, an older person with underlying health conditions,
A pitiful way to lay rest the bare bones of a life.
My sister is not a statistic
Her underlying conditions were
Love
Kindness
Belief in the essential goodness of mankind
Uproarious laughter
Forgiveness
Compassion
A storyteller
A survivor
A comforter
A force of nature
And so much more....

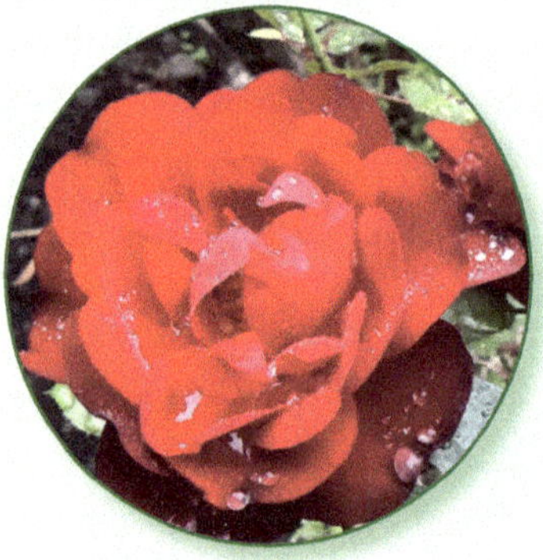

Dorothy Duffy 2020

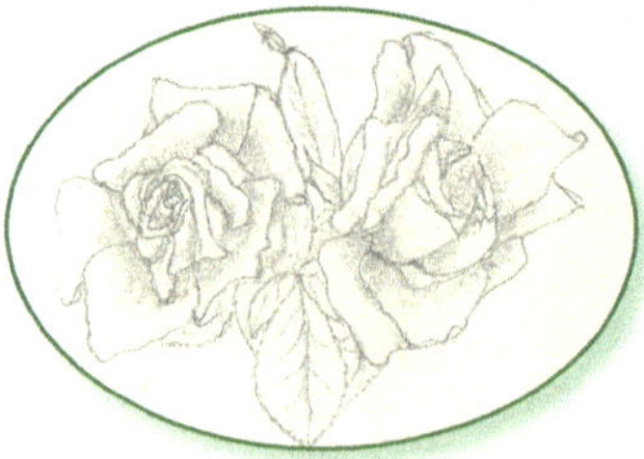

***and meanwhile:** Matt Hancock tells the daily briefing that a 'Herculean effort' is being made to ensure daily deliveries of PPE to frontline workers, including the establishment of a domestic manufacturing industry to produce the equipment.*

21st April 2020 Confirmed Cases: 129.004 Total deaths: 22,886

DAME ANGELA MACLEAN, DEPUTY CHIEF SCIENTIFIC ADVISER, SAYS THE NUMBER OF CONFIRMED CASES IS 'FLATTENING OUT'. THE NUMBER OF PEOPLE IN HOSPITAL HAS BEGUN TO FALL IN SCOTLAND, WALES AND EVERY REGION OF ENGLAND.

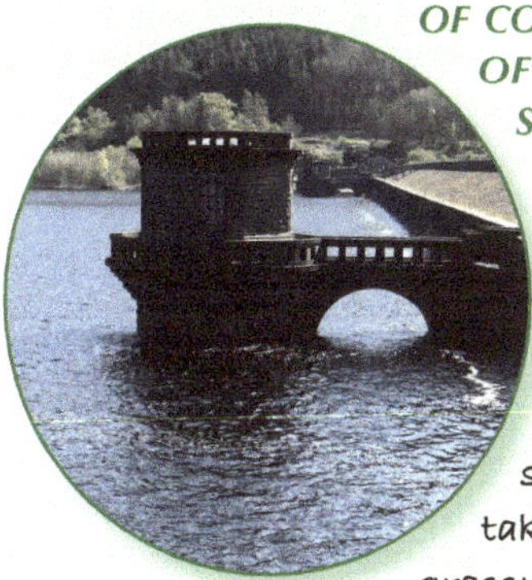

We are not flagged down or monitored on our way out of the city, which we confidently expected, and after a traffic-free drive, we find an isolated parking space on the far side of the Ladybower Reservoir, helpfully shielded by trees. Our first secret walk begins with a steep flight of wooden steps, taking us breathlessly up through the woods to a grassy ride where we turn to walk near the edge of the dam. The vast concrete water management structures, sunk deep into the water have an air of mystery, like a computer game abandoned by a teenager deep in a midnight mystery challenge.

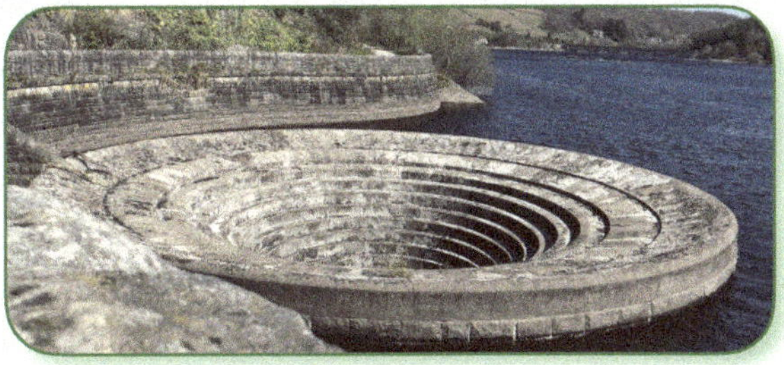

The ground is concrete hard after such a long dry spell, but it is obvious from the stone-strewn paths and stream beds that water has recently rushed freely and frequently down these slopes in gullies and streams, even flooding over footpath stones and across the waterside country road that encircles the reservoir, and is usually full of visitors.

This morning it is deserted.

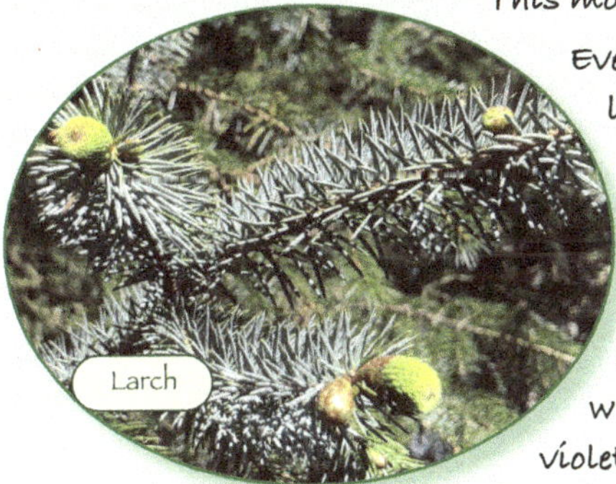

Larch

Everywhere the trees are exploding into leafy life. Larches are spiking green buds, and firs have new blue-ish needles at the end of every branch.

Everywhere the banks are sprinkled with purple violets, pale wood sorrel, sparky dandelions and shiny yellow celandines.

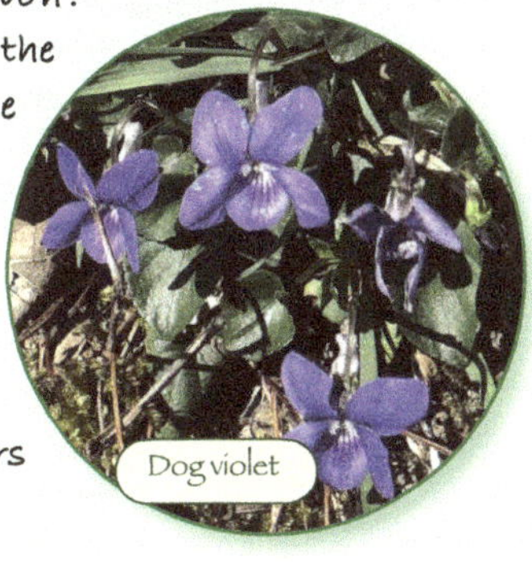

Dog violet

How is it possible that that no-one but risk-takers can come here to enjoy it all in its Spring beauty.

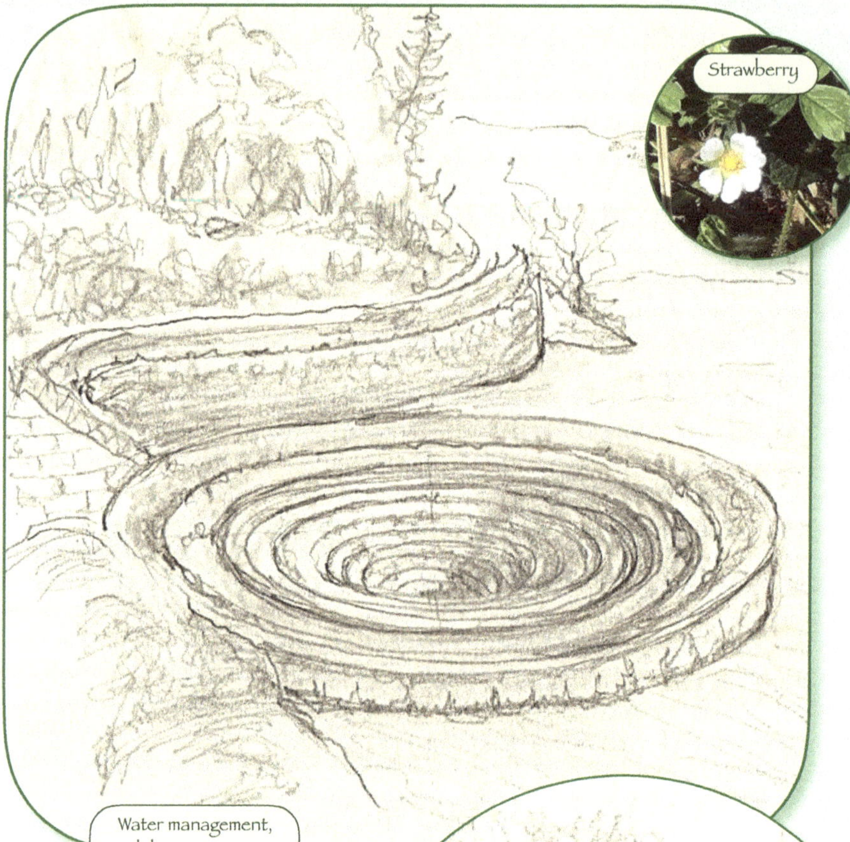

Strawberry

Water management,
Ladybower Reservoir

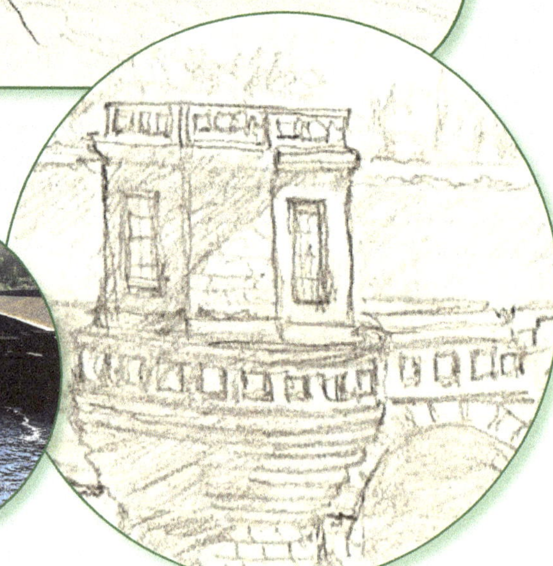

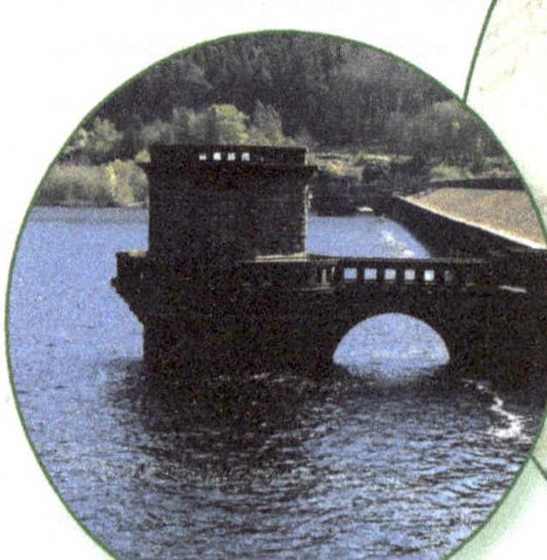

We continue uphill through deserted dark woods of conifer, and along shady green rides where sheep lift their heads from the emerald Spring grasses to gaze at our passing, startled by visitors in this time of lockdown.

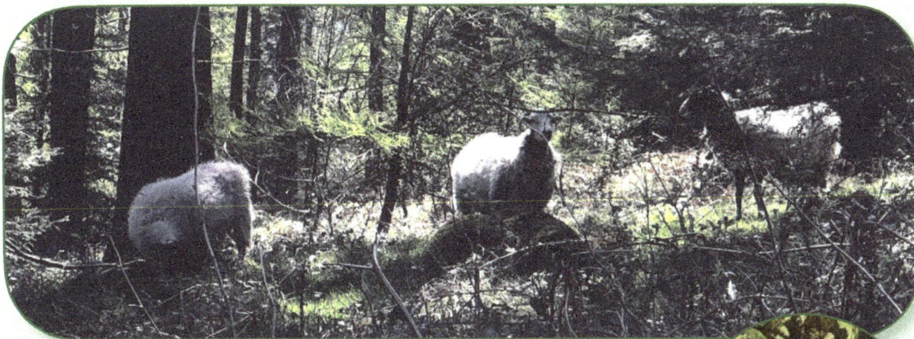

Looking down between the green sprouting larch trees we can see the deep blue of the water reflecting the featureless azure skies. It is so quiet in these locked down woods, we can almost believe that a national Lockdown and Covid are just dreadful nightmares, and we have just woken to a normal world.

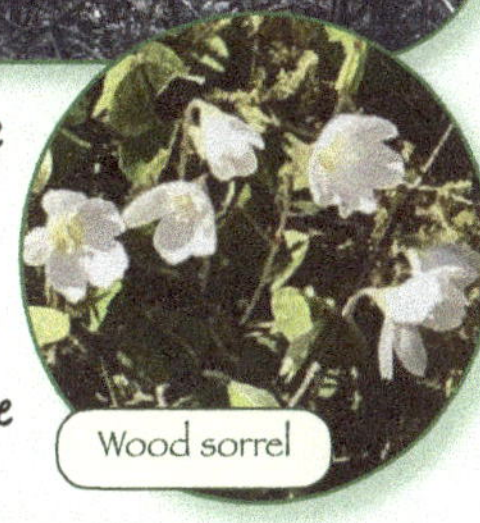

Wood sorrel

Two young lives remembered: Ismail Mohamed Abdulwahab; 13; schoolboy; London; and a 7-week old baby in Connecticut, youngest person so far to die of the virus.

On our steady walk uphill we randomly take likely-looking turns, referring occasionally to our guide book and map. The path takes us through native woodland with beech, sycamore, oak and alder, white wood sorrel flowers lighling up the shady leaf litter and fragile spring grasses growing beneath the lowest branches.

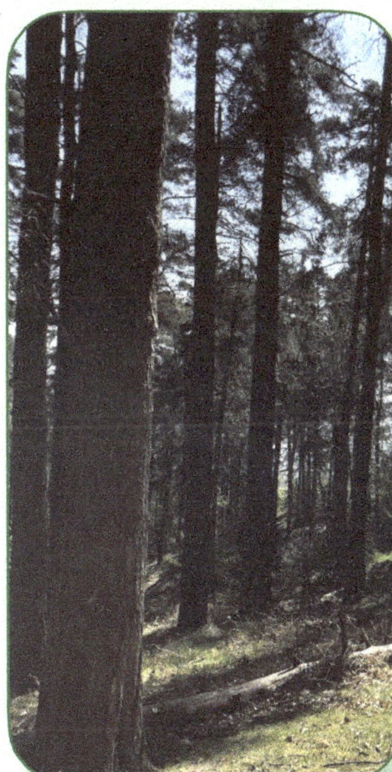

In the 1930's the native woodland trees here were over-planted with tall sitka spruces, but the conifers are now gradually being replanted with native species to return the woods to their original beauty. In the sunlit glades of these quiet and empty woodlands, the trees are full of song from small but invisible birds.

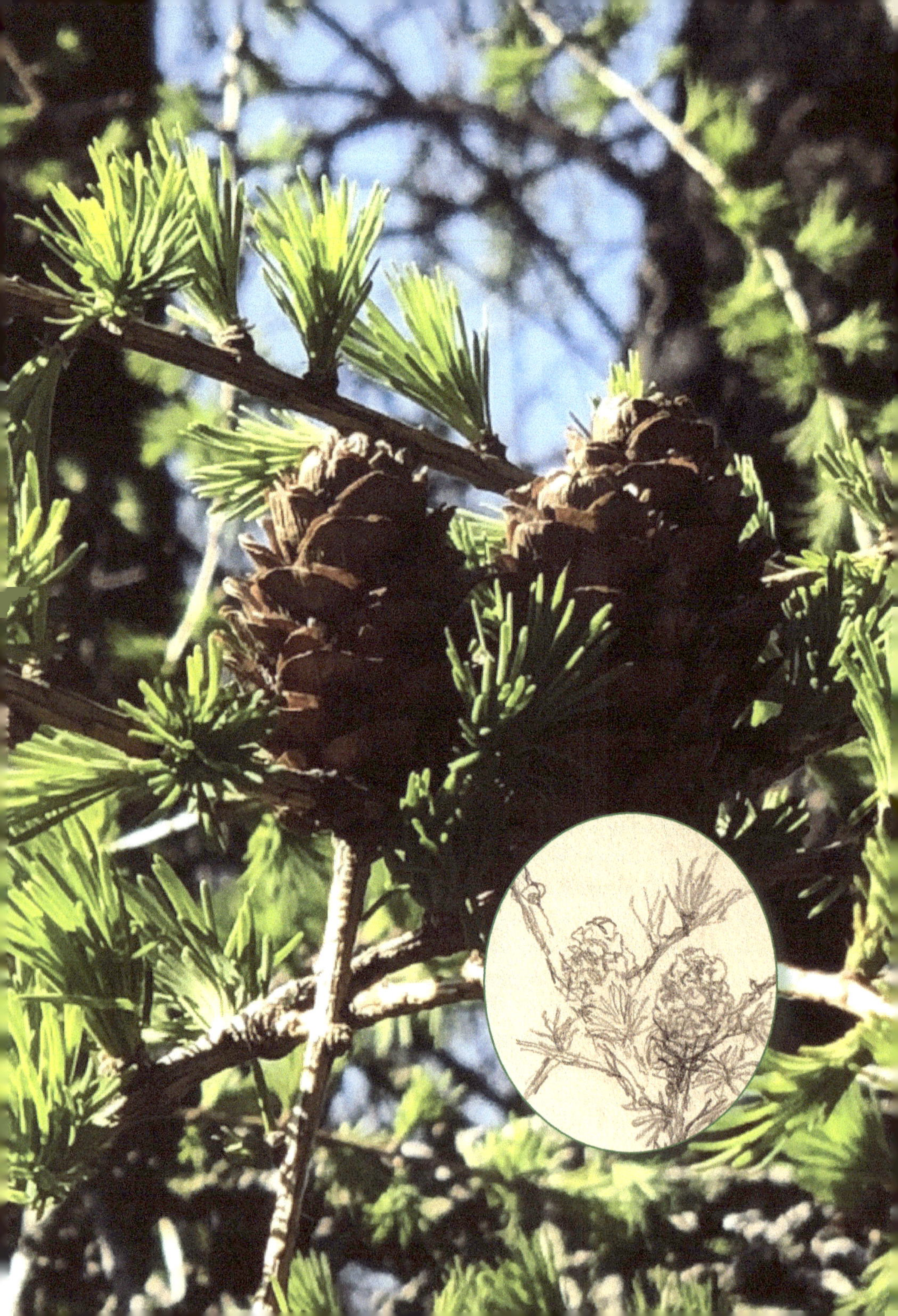

It is so good to be out in the open air, under a blue sky and with only the small sounds of birds and wind in the trees to keep us company. Just being here is such a pleasure, and a breathtaking release from the oppression of lockdown in the frightened, frightening city, where everything is familiar and new at the same time, and we are all free citizens in a prison of our own making.

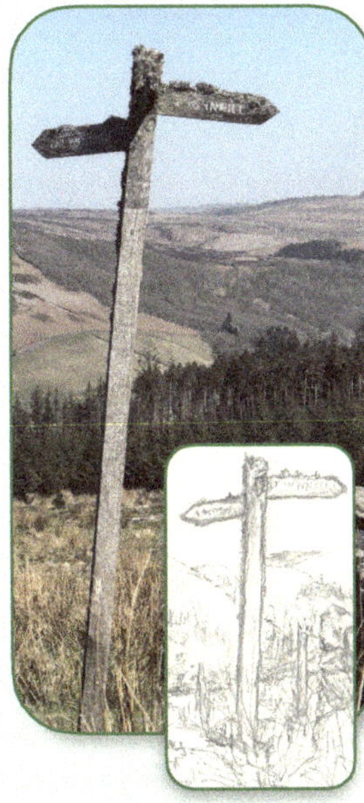

Climbing up to the tree line we meet the east wind, blowing hard across the heather moorland above the woods, and finding a sheltering wall by a mossy signpost, we sit on moss and heather cushions for a picnic.

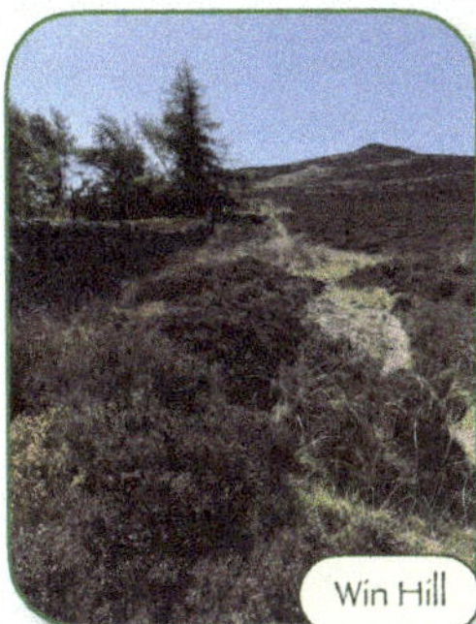

Win Hill

We turn to look up behind us at the last bit of the walk to the top of Win Hill, still a challenging height above us.

This last part of the climb is a sometimes wobbly scramble up the steep, slippery, windswept, heather lined, dry and scratchy slope to the top of the hill.

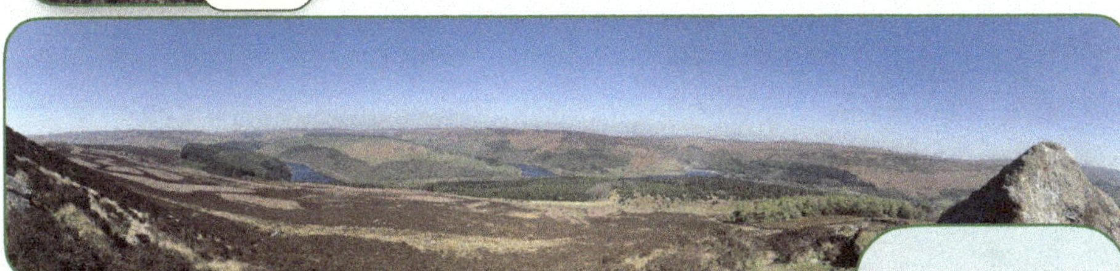

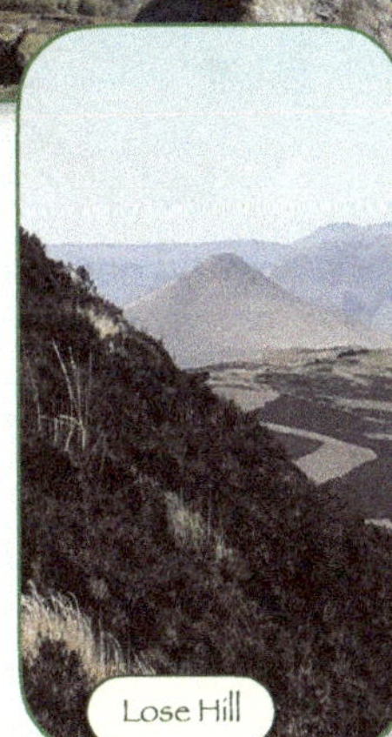

Lose Hill

Here we are met with panoramic views across the reservoir, down to Stanage Edge, and away up to the North to the far edges of the Peaks and the misty blue Pennines beyond. We recall clear days when we looked South from the same range of Pennine Hills to the misty Peaks of Derbyshire.

Below us, to the West, the pyramid-shaped top of Lose Hill is obvious, and to the South and East we see the footpath down towards the Hope Valley and Castleton, and the sight of the wide and gentle footpath that we could have chosen to get to the top, if only we had taken the right path before lunch!

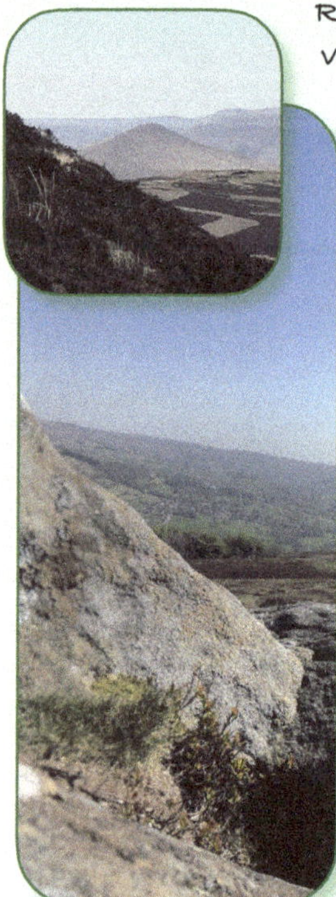

Reluctantly tearing ourselves away from the panoramic views, we sensibly take the easier way back down the hill.

This path, although very well trodden has its own challenges, as among the heather, huge white boulders, worn smooth by weather and walkers, lie in wait to twist an ankle or grab a foot when we are distracted by the views, and the old gnarled woodland that fills every sheltered corner and mossy stream valley.

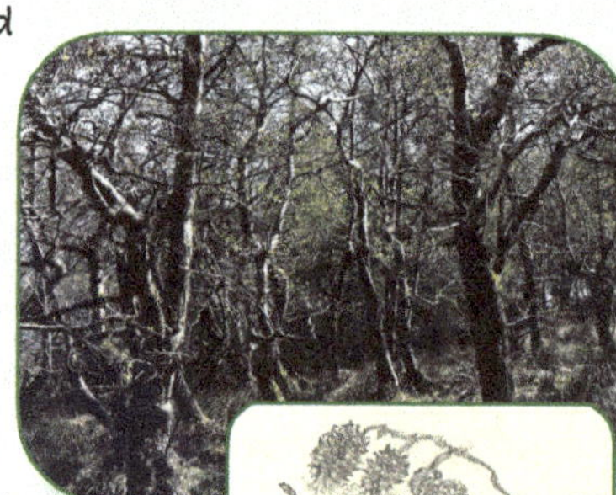

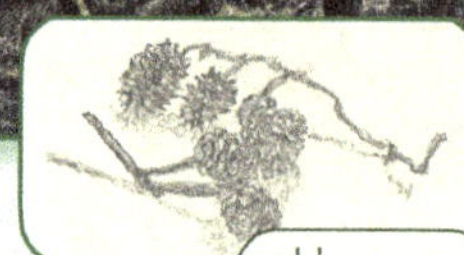

Alder cones

Ancient oaks, sycamores and alders crowd into these wet green cloughs, coated with moss on every branch and twig, some so old that they have fallen, crashing through walls, and demolishing smaller trees as they fell, green, furry roots high in the air.

On we go, downhill, through conifer and deciduous woods, retracing paths that seem steeper going down, as we reach the wide, grassy rides to the edge of the water, and walk back along the flower-verged path, starred with yellow, white and blue, with a rather tattered peacock butterfly emerged from hibernation to look for their nectar. We reach the car, relieved to find that there is no parking ticket on the windscreen.

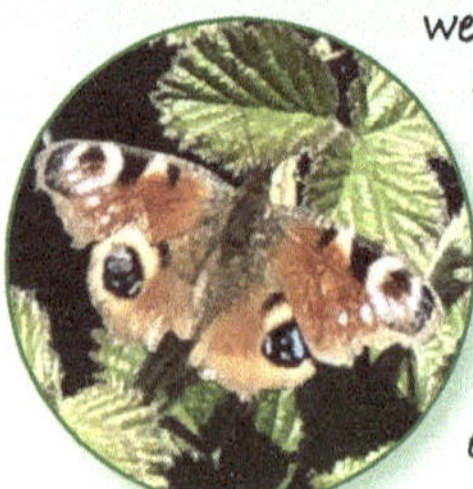

and meanwhile, as we climbed Win Hill: A further 823 deaths are recorded, taking the total to 17,337, a sharp rise on yesterday, but many of these relate to deaths previously not included, some dating back as far as March.

Although there are still few cars about and even fewer walkers, we are glad we came early in the day for such a wonderful and secluded walk, and cannot understand how this activity can possibly be considered even harmlessly criminal!

Another life remembered: Richard Nabieu; 65, Nurse; Croydon, South London.

23rd/26th April 2020 Confirmed Cases: 110,203 Total deaths: 26,258

25TH - THE FIRST HUMAN TRIALS OF A VACCINE BEGIN.

Remembered today:
Kevin Ronson;
Security guard;
Nottingham; UK.

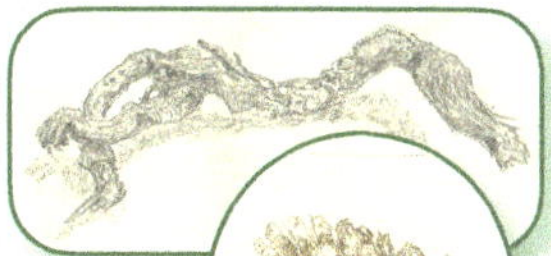

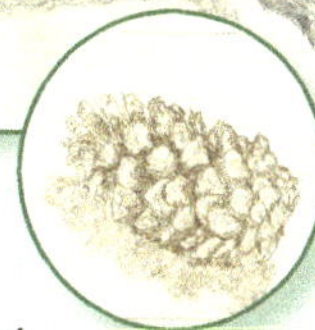

We now get the depressing, but not unexpected news that lockdown may continue until the end of the year, but even this sobering thought can't erase the calming solitude and natural Spring beauty of Ladybower.

24th - We empty our pockets of fir cones, bits of heather root, stones, catkins and twigs collected yesterday, and I spend part of the quiet day making drawings to add to the written account and photos. Writing the diary calms me, and makes me realise how lucky we are not to be at the forefront of the fight against the virus.

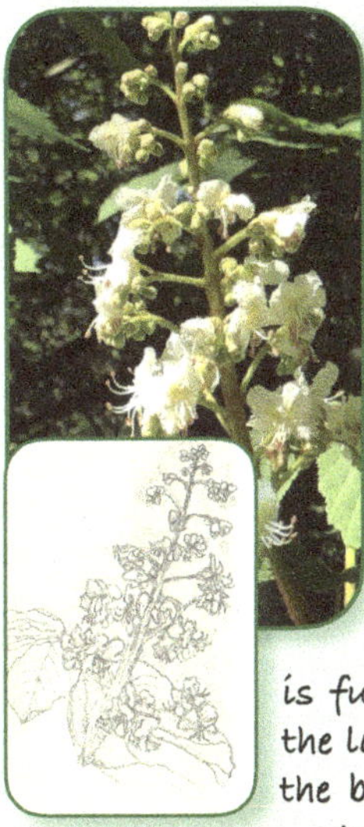

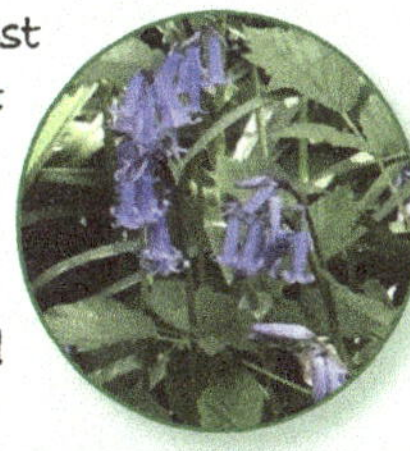

In the deserted Norfolk Park, bluebells bloom, wild garlic flowers fill the air with pungent perfume, fairy flowers of cow parsley shine against dark tree trunks and the first chestnut candles hold flowers aloft, surrounded by leafy hands. We walk round the Park as news comes that more than 100 health workers on the front line of the Covid battle have died from Coronavirus so far.

25th - UK TOPS THE GOVERNMENT'S 'WORST CASE SCENARIO' AS THE DEATH TOLL EXCEEDS 20,000.

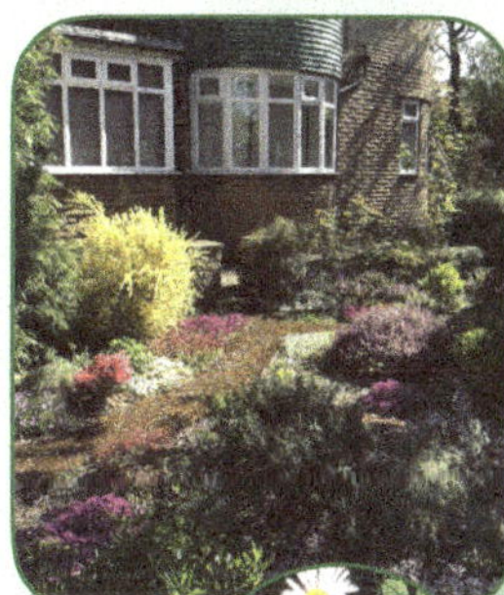

The garden at the Children's House is full of surprising Spring colour, and the lawn is full of daisies. We lean out of the bathroom window of the rental house to gaze at the pink and white blossom on next-door's apple tree.

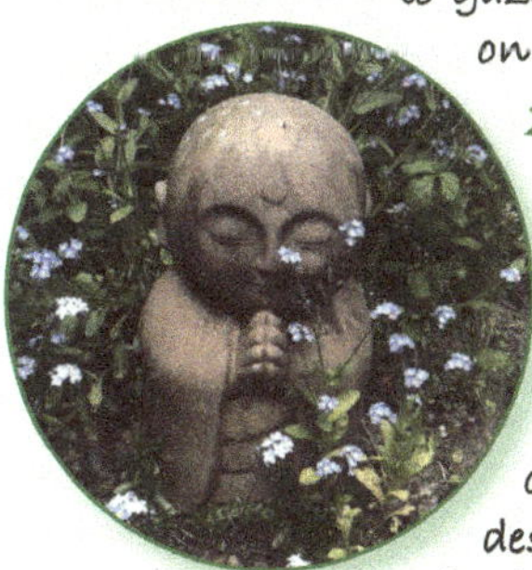

26th- THE PM RETURNS TO WORK.

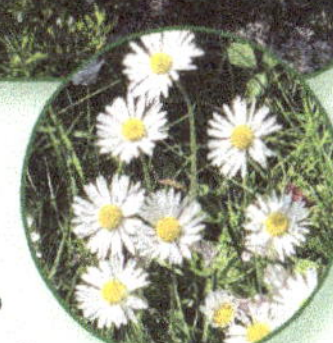

Sarah's garden is full of pink and blue forget-me-nots among the hairy, dew-covered leaves of lady's mantle. Last night a fox roamed up and down the road howling a haunting cry, like some lost soul wandering in this deserted city, where night-time activity usually disturbs wildlife exploration.

Pandemic Day: 43/46 Lockdown 1: day 29/32

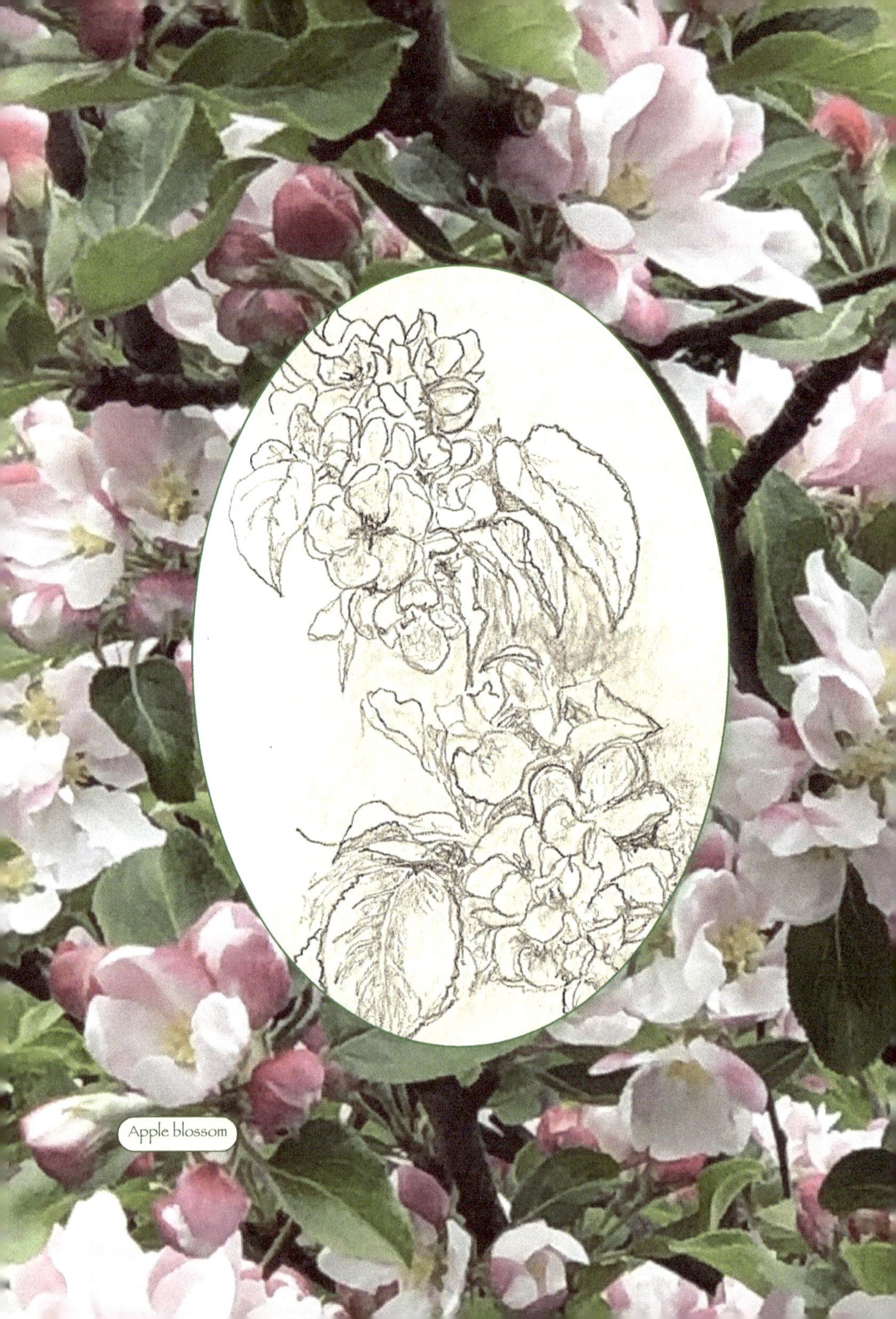
Apple blossom

28/30th April 2020 Confirmed Cases: 118,343 Total deaths: 28,535

28th - AN ONS REPORT INDICATES A THIRD OF COVID-19 DEATHS IN ENGLAND AND WALES ARE OCCURRING IN CARE HOMES.

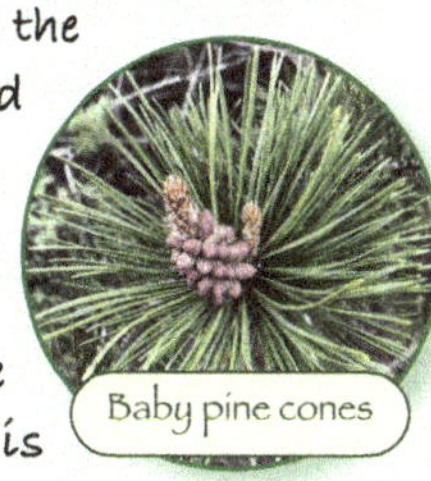

Baby pine cones

April ends, but there seems to be no end to the lockdown. All the PM's bombast and lack of realism comes to nothing, and although the death rate has fallen somewhat and is at the lowest since March, there is still a tense feeling of combined resignation and frustration. The benefit of social distancing is beginning to be felt, with stabilisation of the number of new cases, and fewer people in hospital. A nation-wide minute of silence is held to remember those who have died during the pandemic.

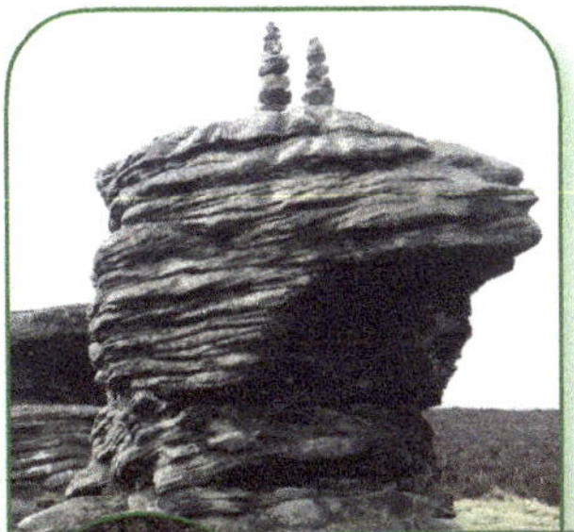

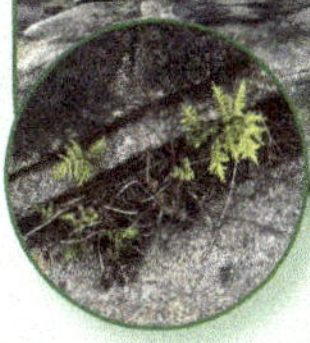

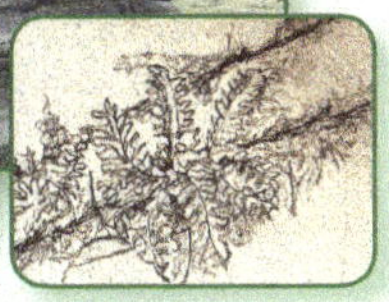

Finding the parks overcrowded, we drive to Lady Channing's Plantation on the outskirts of Sheffield, a small area of pine forest, which proves damp, deserted, trampled and disappointing. It is obviously heavily used by walkers and mountain bikers, carving their way through the woodlands, leaving deep muddy ruts and puddles.

We leave the woods to walk out onto the moorland, where well-trodden paths criss-cross the heather, and huge rounded rocky outcrops topped with cairns of stones dot the landscape, their cracks inhabited by tiny ferns. Despite the gloom and pale grey skies, the views from this spot are wide and wild, despite the nearness to the city.

29th/30th - MORE GRIM NEWS COMES, WITH EVER MORE COMPLEX STATISTICS, AND DIRE PREDICTIONS FOR THE ECONOMY. A SUGGESTED BLANKET BAN ON GOING OUT FOR OVER 70s IS MET WITH AN OUTCRY.

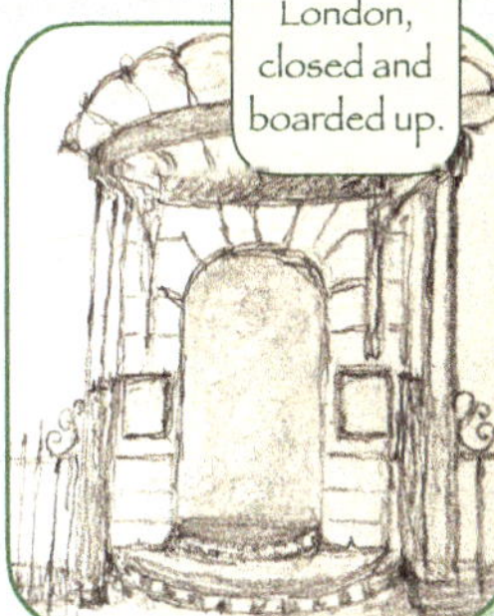

Kettner's French restaurant in London, closed and boarded up.

Tom Moore continues to walk after his 100th birthday. Deaths of people with learning disabilities in England have increased by 134%. No-one has established how much of this increase is due to Covid, and how much is due to restricted visiting by relatives and health care workers.

Many of the most famous and expensive restaurants in London are forced to close their doors, as lockdown restrictions hit even their most affluent customers.

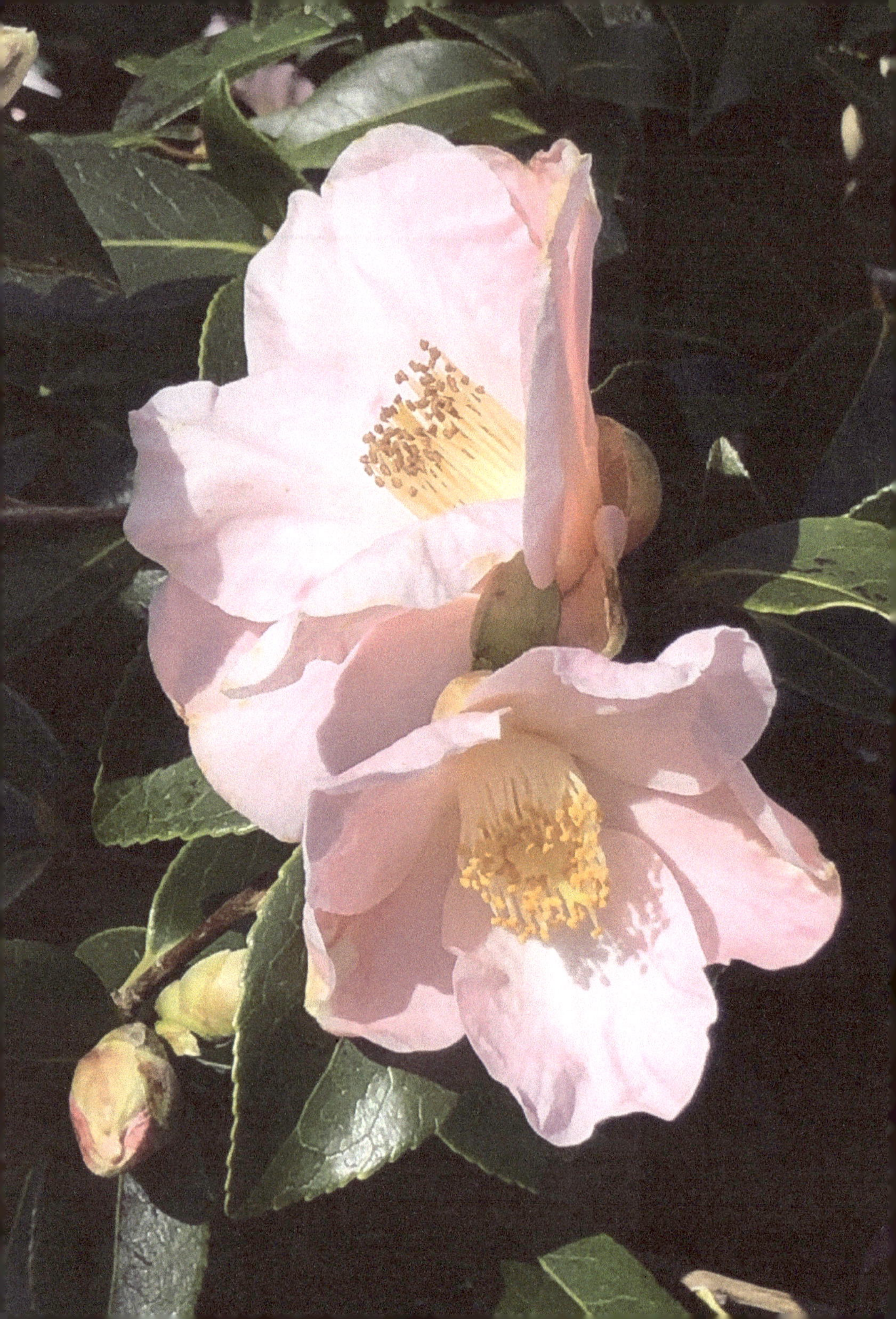

April 2020 ends

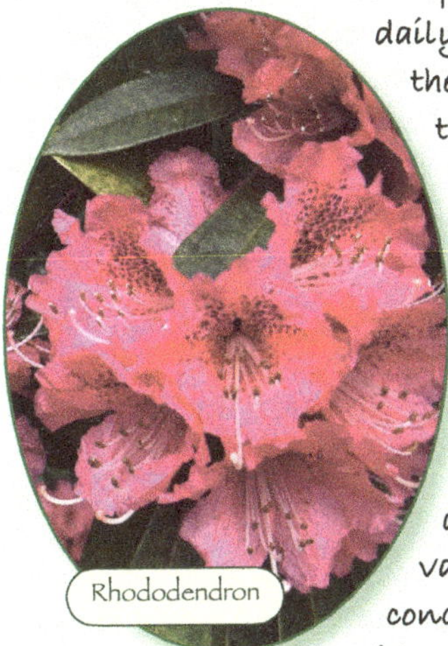
Rhododendron

As April ends, government announcements come via daily TV news conferences from Downing Street, when the PM, ministers and scientific advisers appear, talking the talk of confidence and knowledge, while their expressions and body language often tell a different tale of concern and difference of opinion.

Information is also channelled through the welter of social media, where denial, misinformation and bias often cloak the truth and influence opinion. Projections of all sorts prove to be underestimates. We are encouraged to worry about death rates, availability of PPE, development of vaccines, and most importantly, the increasing concern about care homes, where staff are coping without adequate PPE as residents are returned from hospitals to release beds for Covid patients. Matt Hancock, Health Secretary, makes the first of many promises on the number of tests available and the tracing of contacts.

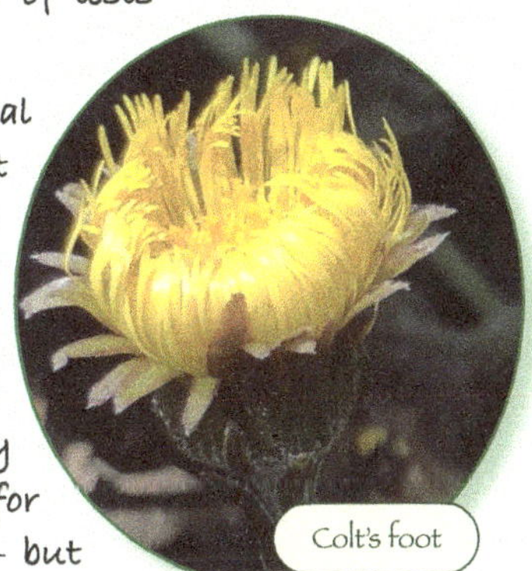
Colt's foot

The Prime Minister spends some time in hospital with a severe case of Coronavirus, apparently just avoiding the need for one of the ventilators he assures us are in plentiful supply.

In less than a month, we have become strangely accustomed to the lockdown, with its rules and regulations - masks, hand sanitiser, grocery deliveries or visits to supermarket car parks for collections, home schooling - but that doesn't mean we like it!

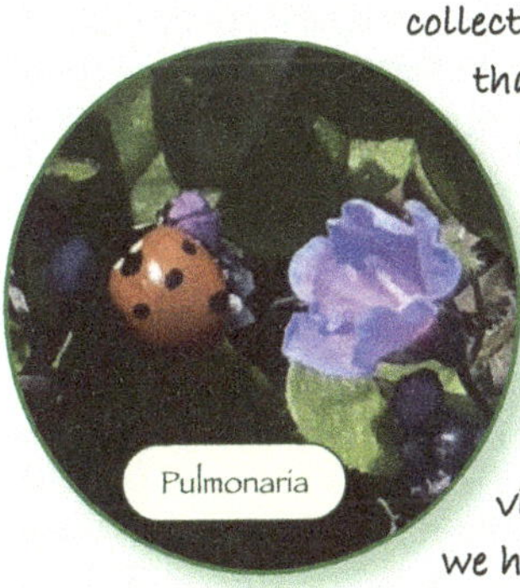
Pulmonaria

People who are old, or have 'underlying conditions', are urged to 'shield' - not go to work, shop or go out at all. As I am both older and have an immune system condition, I should take note of these regulations, and so should our daughter, Sarah, who is advised to avoid the risks of exposure to the virus during teaching. She is shielding at home, but we haven't seen her, or her family, in person this month.

As human life becomes more and more restricted, natural life continues its unstoppable progress into Spring. Planters and beds of bulbs bloom, and trees begin to open their leafy hands, as parks and public gardens provide a welcome space for our restricted exercise. The garden at the Children's House begins to surprise us with shoots and buds of hidden plants. We manage to extend our outings by the 'two plus one' of three long walks in the deserted local countryside of the White Peaks. Two of these walks are completed before the regulations become law, and we must stay within the City limits, our final 'legal' walk is on Day 1 of National Lockdown

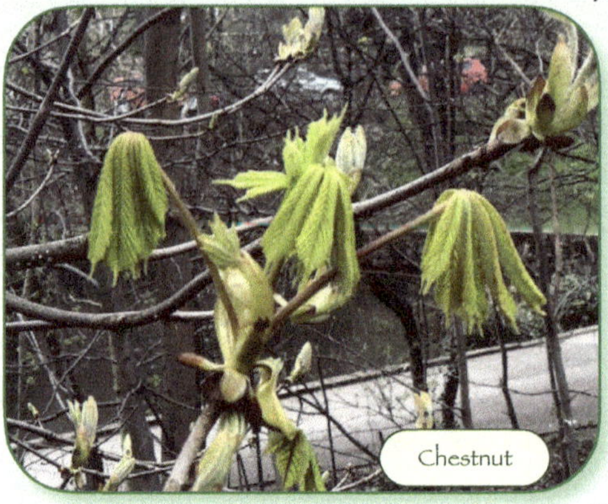

Chestnut

In the UK, there have been over 38 thousand reported cases, and more than four thousand people have already lost their battle with this virus, and Dominic Cummings seems free to go wherever he likes! As I continue to wonder how long this lockdown will last, I think about the many families destined to mourn those lost to the disease before its deadly stalking progress across the world finally loses its grip and it returns to its secret lair to prepare for another strike.

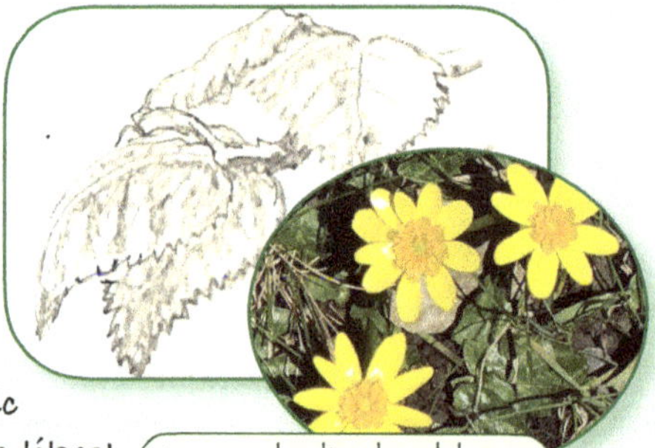

Lesser celandine, beech leaves

We are lucky that no-one we know has been infected, but we are evidently only at the beginning of this process, and no-one can assume that they are safe.

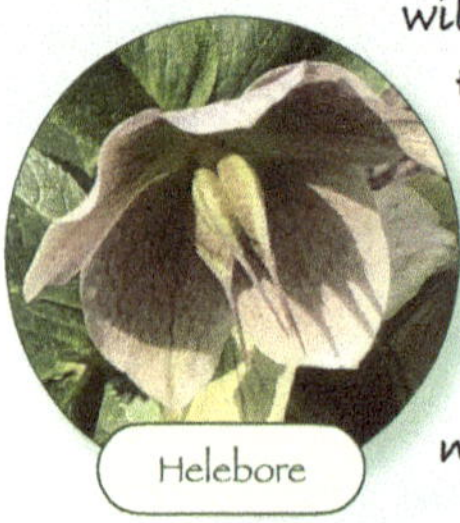

Helebore

MONTHLY UK CASES AND DEATHS: 30th April 2020

Total confirmed cases to date - 176,790 (up138,765)

Total deaths to date - 28,535 (up 24,105)

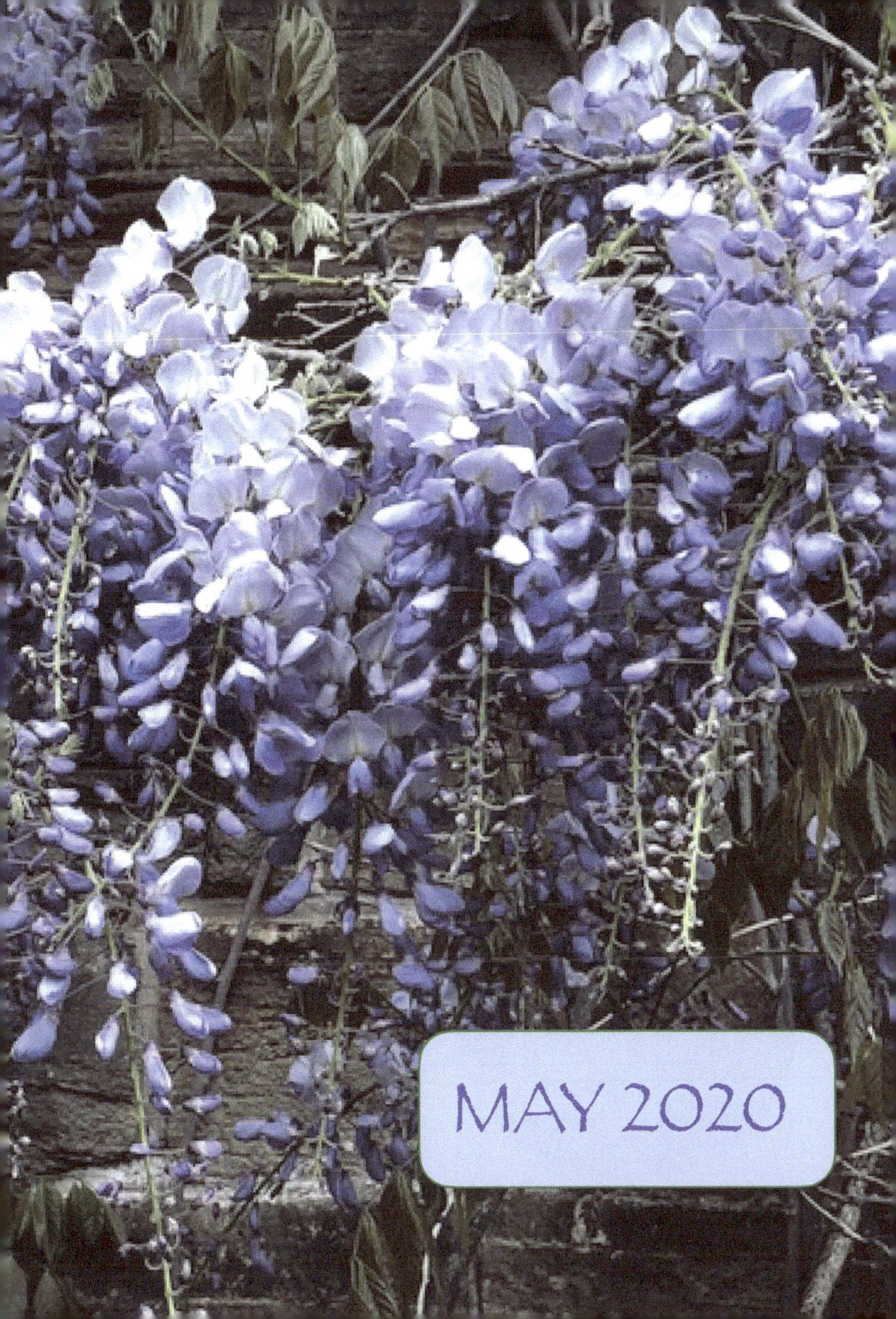

MAY 2020

1st May 2020 Confirmed Cases: 177,454 Total deaths: 29,597

DEATHS IN DEPRIVED AREAS ARE DOUBLE THOSE IN MORE AFFLUENT AREAS, AND THERE ARE WARNINGS NOT TO LIFT THE LOCKDOWN TOO SOON.

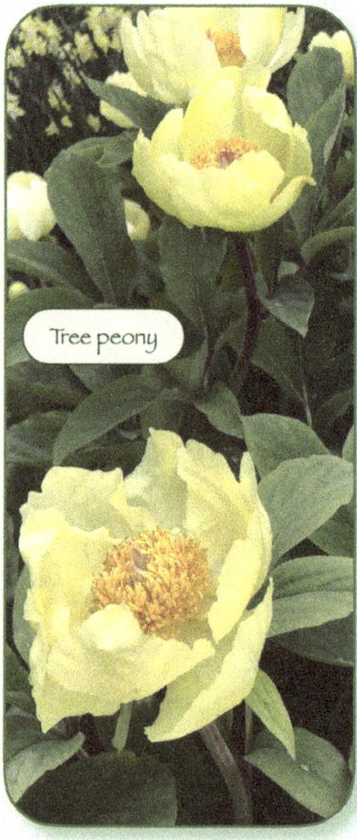

Tree peony

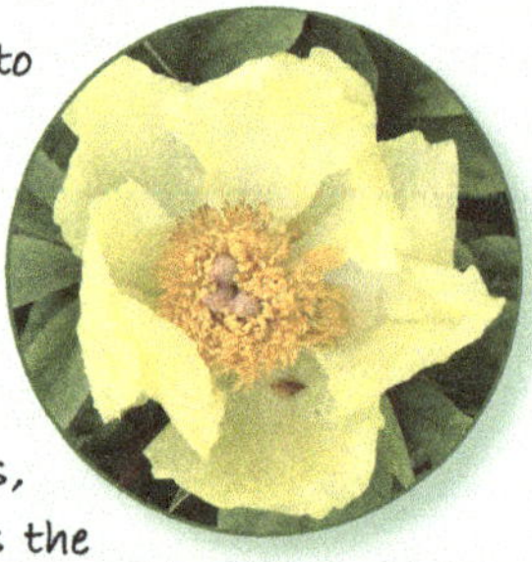

Our new month resolution is to go out walking more – today to the Botanical Gardens again, starting at the glass houses, past yellow tree peonies, pasque flowers and perfumed choisya bushes, whose leaves smell as good as the flowers. Botanical Garden staff are on the roof of the gatehouse, struggling in the wind to put up a flag in support the NHS.

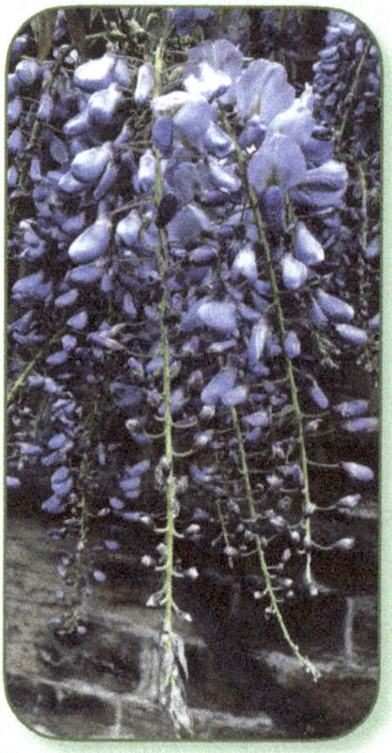

The wisteria by the closed café is in tumbling purple bloom, long plumes of flowers and waving tendrils of green decorating an old park building in pale mauve clouds and dripping from a grey network of branches.

Next we walk on pink petals, scattered by the cherry trees, blossoms now lying on the grass in carpets of gentle colour, almost too beautiful to walk on. Some children once called this sight 'pink snow'.

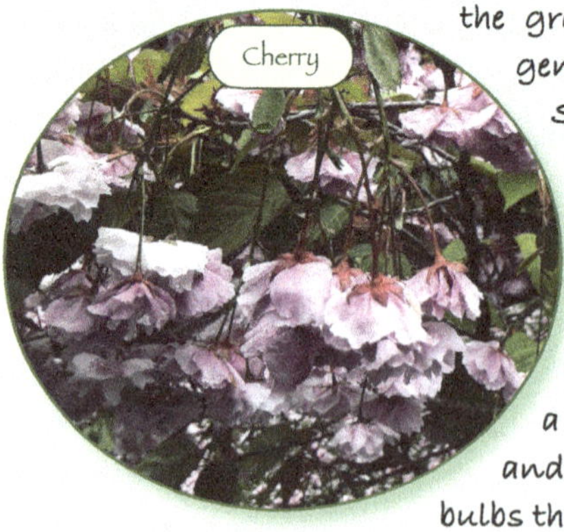

Cherry

At the top of urn-flanked steps in a newly discovered corner, we watch a female blackbird wrestling with the dead grasses for her nest building. These steps, hidden in a quiet corner of the gardens, are deserted and have a timeless air, with lilies and other bulbs thrusting their new leaves into the warm air.

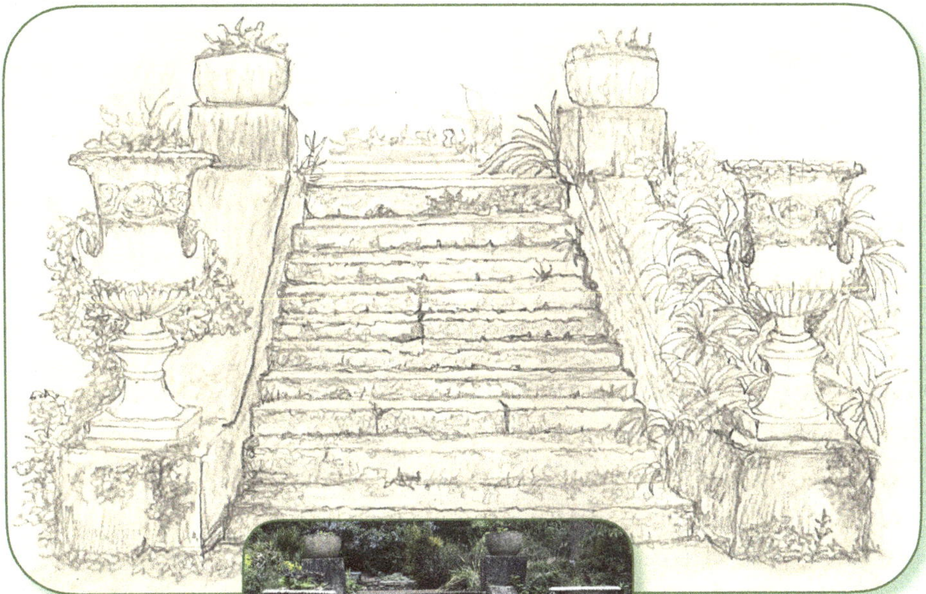

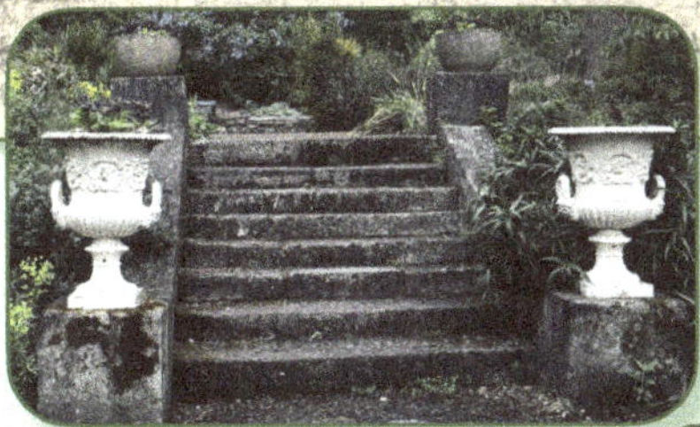

Our route next takes the path down to the fish pond (fish removed for lockdown safety), where yellow globe flowers and golden marsh marigolds bloom, and the greenish-white flowers of arum lilies line the banks with their feet in the water.

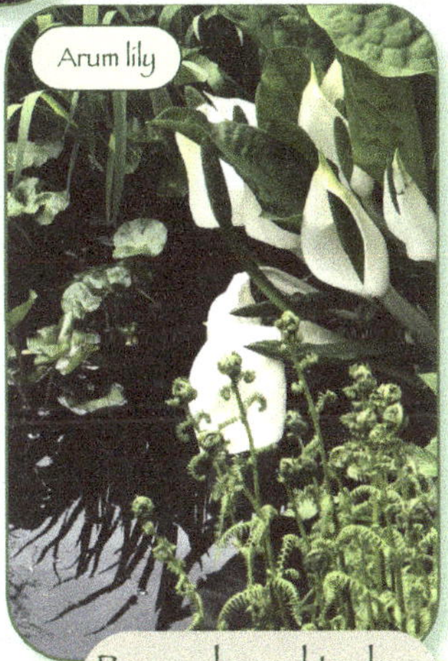

Arum lily

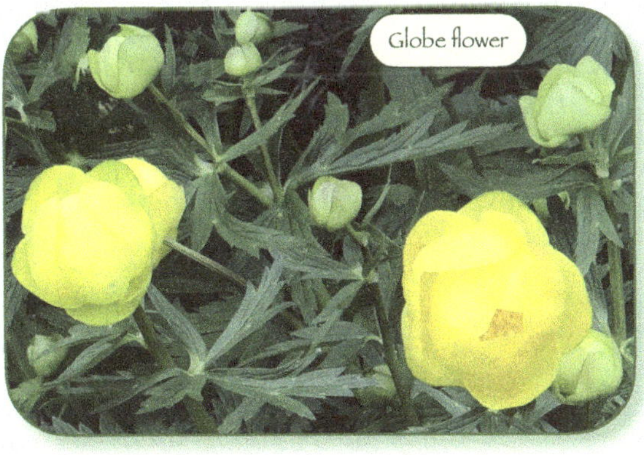

Globe flower

Remembered today:
Kevin Ronson;
Security guard;
Nottingham; UK.

Back up the hill next, past tall shuttlecock ferns, pink flowered dead nettles, and yellow archangel, and the strange 'vegetable curry' smell that we have noticed before on this slope, but can't locate the source!

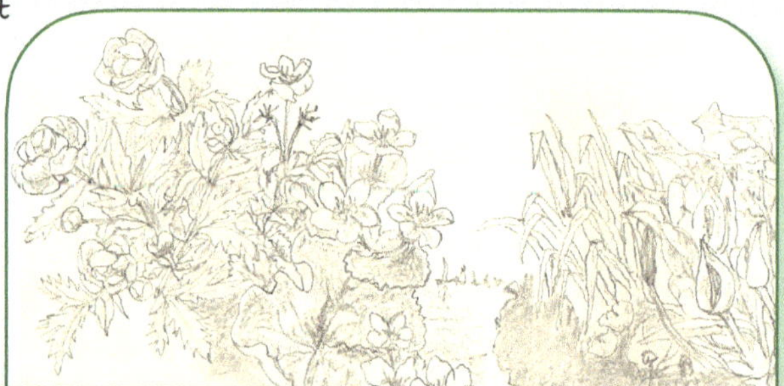

Chased by a sudden shower, we hurry home across the grass under the oak trees, covered with lime green oak flowers and leaves torn off and dropped by pigeons looking for bugs.

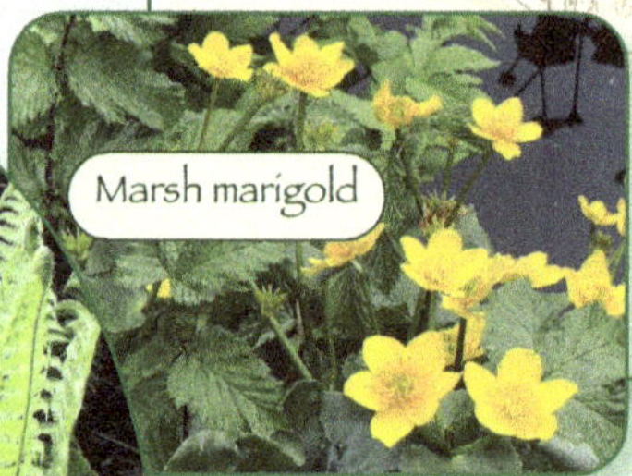

Marsh marigold

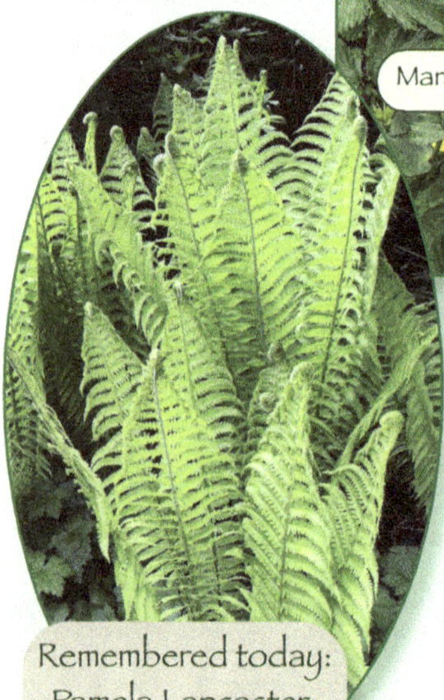

Crammed into the walls of all the roads here, and overflowing in miniature green and purple cascades, a little campanula is colonising and blooming in every crack and fissure, and flowering in bright purplish blue.

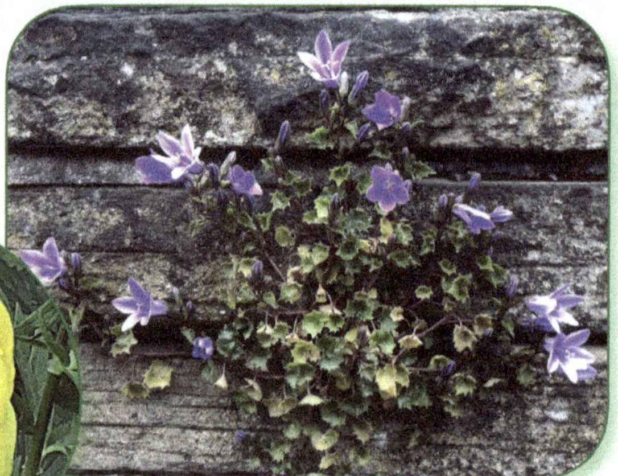

Remembered today:
<u>Pamela Lancaster</u>;
83; Retired auxiliary nurse; Doncaster.

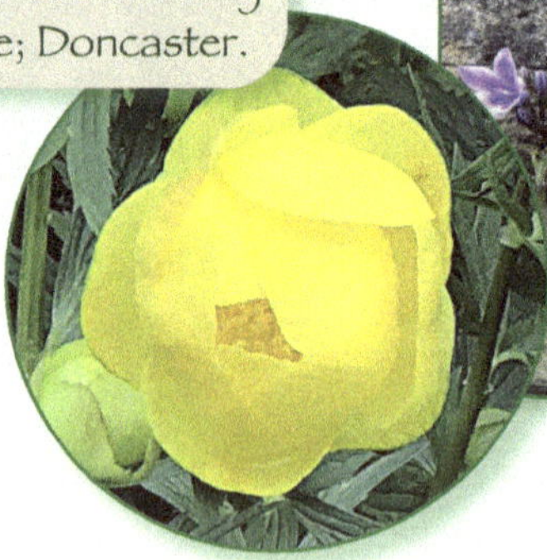

Pandemic Day: 51 Lockdown 1: day 37

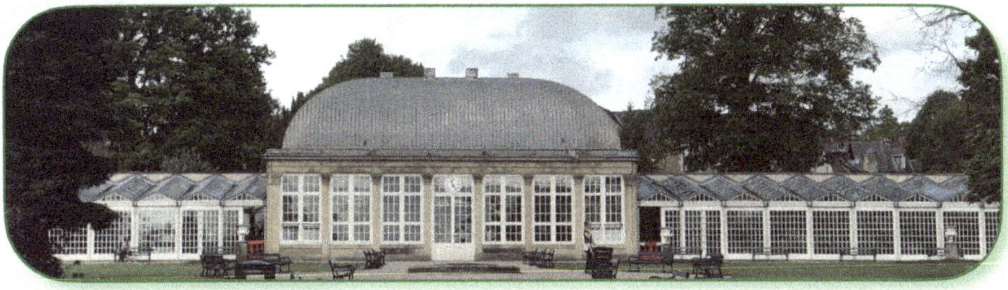

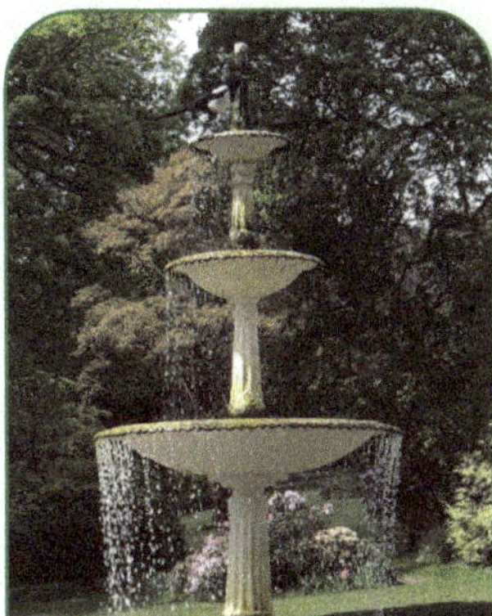

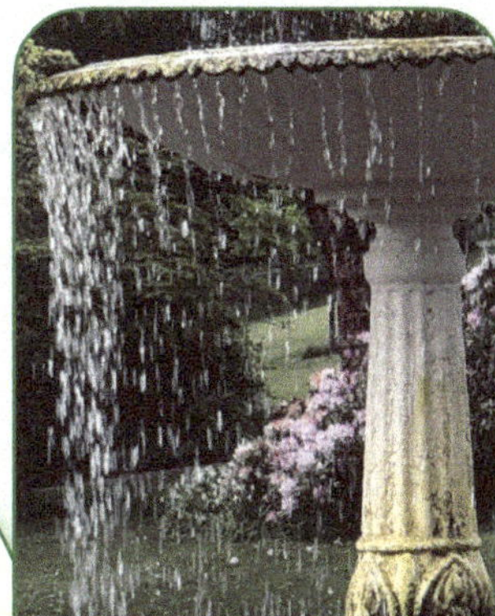

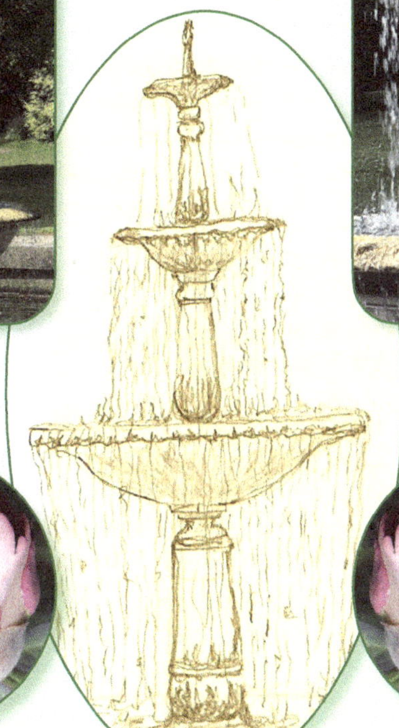

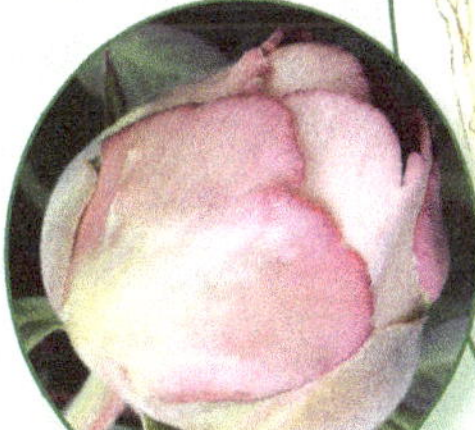

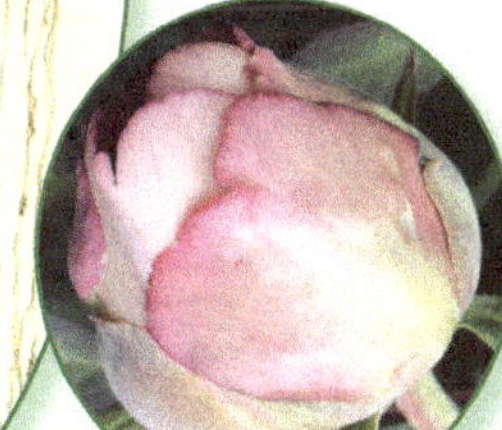

2nd - EVIDENCE EMERGES OF PEOPLE BREAKING THE RULES - NOT BY WALKING IN THE COUNTRY, BUT BY VISITING EACH OTHERS' GARDENS AND HOUSES.

We walk to Endcliffe Park, which is still full of parents with their small children, riding, running and batting about. I wonder how many children will be affected by the difficulty of learning to communicate in a world of mask-wearing adults?

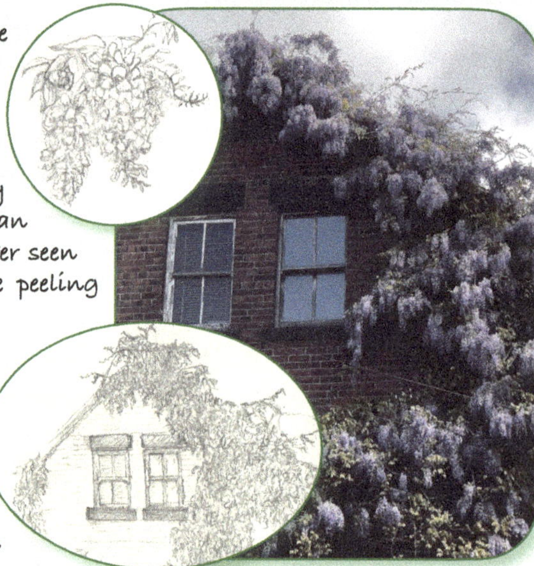

The 'Haunted', unkempt house on Brocco Bank has been a focus for family speculation ever since we moved here. It is apparently inhabited, because the hedge is very occasionally cut, and we have seen the postman delivering there, but we have never seen anyone leaving or entering the peeling painted front door.

However this strange house has one week of glory every May, when it is wreathed in wisteria, cascading down from the chimney, over the roof, down the walls and onto the unkempt trees and bushes below. This magical happening entrances us all, and turns the neglected house into something extraordinary.

3rd - SIR PATRICK VALLANCE TELLS THE HOUSE OF COMMONS SELECT COMMITTEE THAT EARLIER TESTING WOULD HAVE BEEN 'BENEFICIAL' BUT WOULD NOT HAVE PREVENTED THE SPREAD OF THE VIRUS.

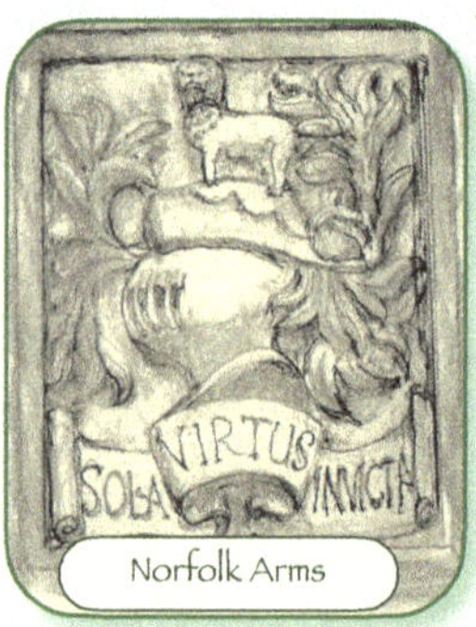

Norfolk Arms

We crossed the city centre to walk in the less busy Norfolk Park. We stopped to look at the carved coat off arms for the Dukes of Norfolk family, carved in the stonework above the gates. We are so lucky to have found this lovely space where so few people are visiting in the lockdown. I hope they will return when regulations are lifted, whenever that might be.

Lost shoe found on a wall

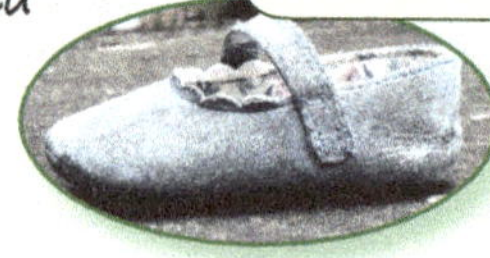

On this day we also hear about the preparations for our grand-daughter's wedding in September in Chicago. It is now unlikely we will be able to be there.

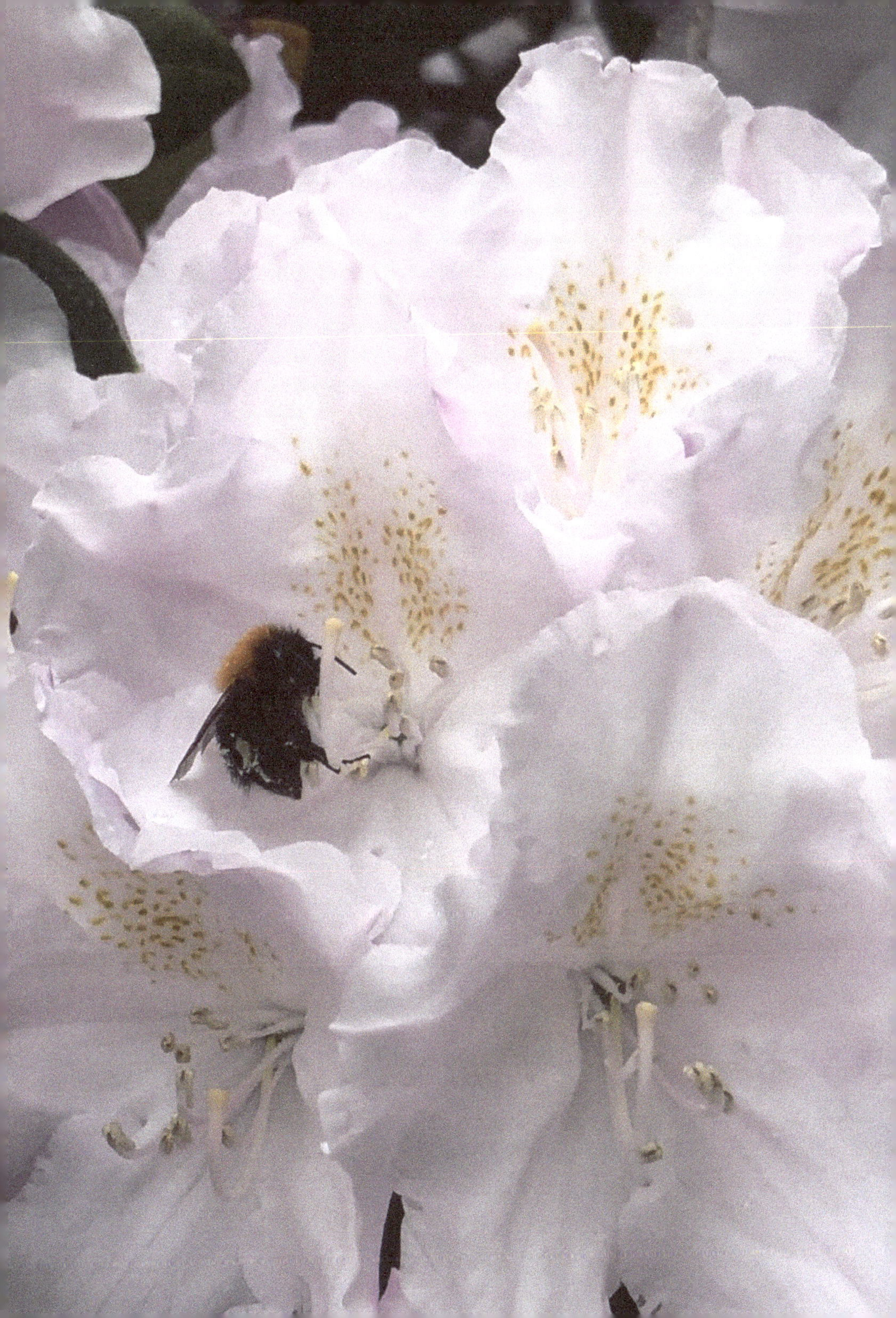

6th May 2020 Confirmed Cases: 132,234 Total deaths: 31,456

BARONESS DIDO HARDING, CHAIR OF NHS IMPROVEMENT, AND FORMER CEO OF TALKTALK IS APPOINTED TO LEAD THE GOVERNMENT'S PROGRAMME OF TESTING AND TRACING.

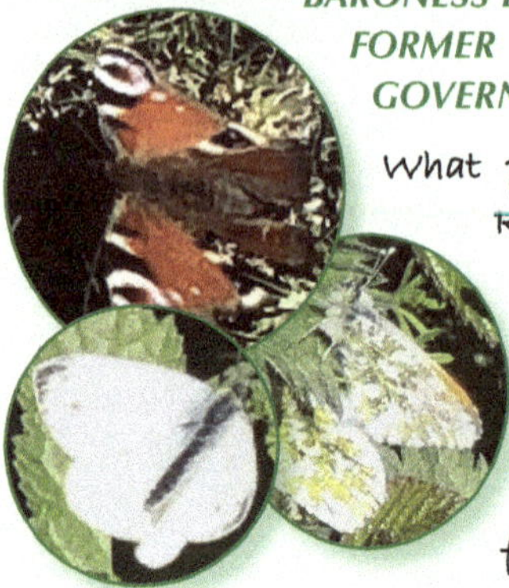

What proves to be a very long walk above Ladybower Reservoir is an early birthday gift for me, and we meet almost no-one among the new leaves, violets, blue speedwell and starry stitchwort. Orange-tip, small white, peacock and red admiral butterflies flirt and flutter, hover flies, bees and thousands of other small insects buzz and crawl. Birds, including a cuckoo, call from the trees as we walk along sandy paths though conifers and deciduous trees with the sun streaming between their trunks on emerald grass.

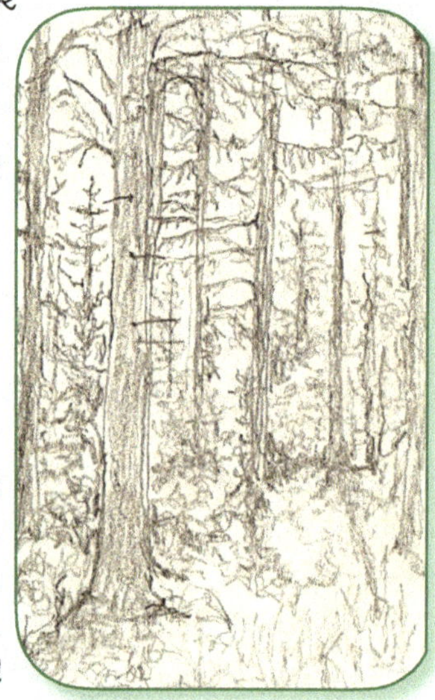

We take a new route, above but parallel to the water, through ancient pines, catching glimpses of tumble-down walls and buildings overgrown with plants, as under everything, the carpet of green grass, ferns and mosses spreads. The sandy soil drains well, so apart from some small streams and the occasional fallen tree, we meet few obstacles.

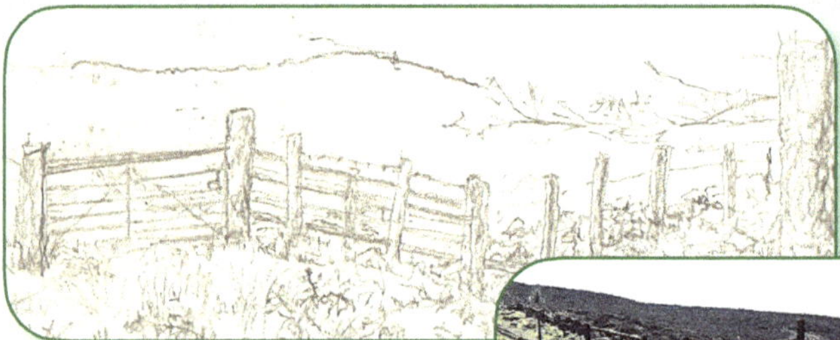

At the top of the plantation we are in the sunshine again, at the edge of the moorland under Win Hill.

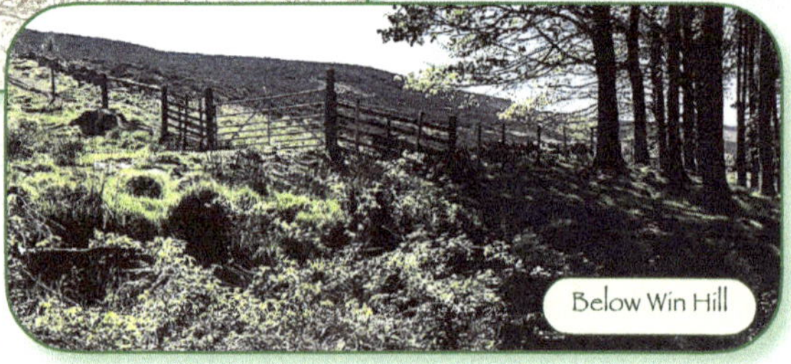

Below Win Hill

We stop for lunch in a grassy sunken hollow, where we rest and dream of a time when this sort of walk can be taken openly, rather than in shared, guilty secrecy.

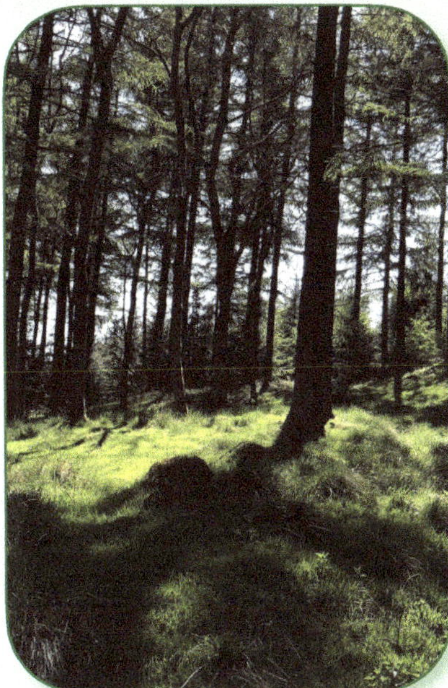

Climbing over the gate, we take the path towards the top of Win Hill, pausing at the signpost where we lunched last time.

Then, we turn onto the steep path downhill, through a newer plantation, where stones and gravel have been washed away from between the wooden steps by the winter rains, the work of volunteers curtailed by the pandemic. There will be so much to do when things get back to normal.

As we return through these quiet woods, the silence is shattered by vintage aircraft screaming over the reservoir. They must be practising for Sunday's planned remembrance of the end of World War 2.

Silence returns, and it is good to feel the sun on our faces and the air in our lungs, the sounds of the countryside and the delight of the little spring wildflowers – stitchwort, violet, bright speedwell, yellow pimpernel, dandelion and daisy, and ferns uncurling in tall green fronds with gingery orange hairs, like the legs of little orang-utans.

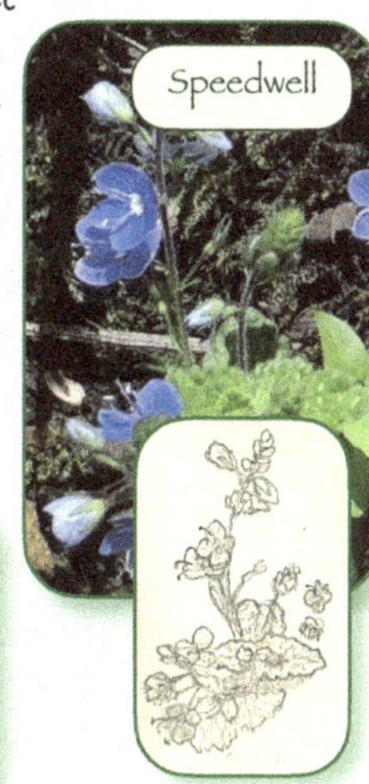

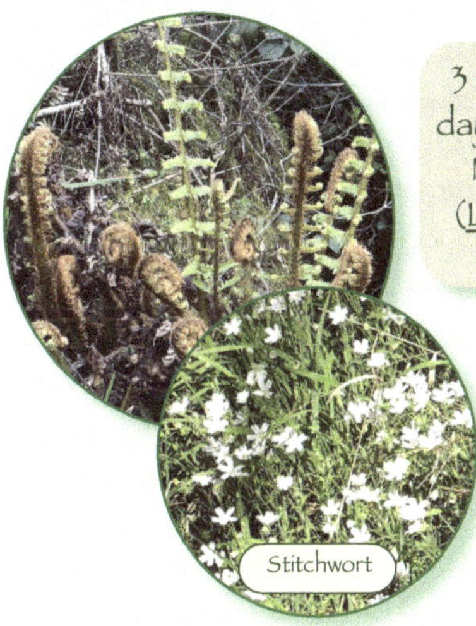

3 lives remembered on this day: Keith Dunnington; 54; Nurse; and his parents (Lilian, 81, & Maurice 85); South Shields: UK.

and as we enjoy the sunshiny woods:
At his first Prime Minister's Questions since returning to work Boris Johnson says he 'bitterly regrets' the crisis in care homes and is 'working very hard' to tackle it. He also pledges to reach a target of 200,000 daily tests by the end of May.

Pandemic Day: 56   Lockdown 1: day 42

7/8th May 2020 Confirmed Cases :134,108 Total deaths: 32,300

THE UK GOVERNMENT CONFIRMS 400,000 GOWNS ORDERED FROM TURKEY TO PROTECT NHS STAFF FROM COVID-19 HAVE BEEN IMPOUNDED, AFTER FAILING TO MEET THE REQUIRED SAFETY STANDARDS.

Remembered today:
Diane Hembury; 68;
Former emergency department assistant;
Nottingham

7th - My birthday. After so many birthdays, this is the strangest one ever. Sarah and her family come for an outdoor home delivery Indian meal – probably illegal, but I am prepared to take the risk.

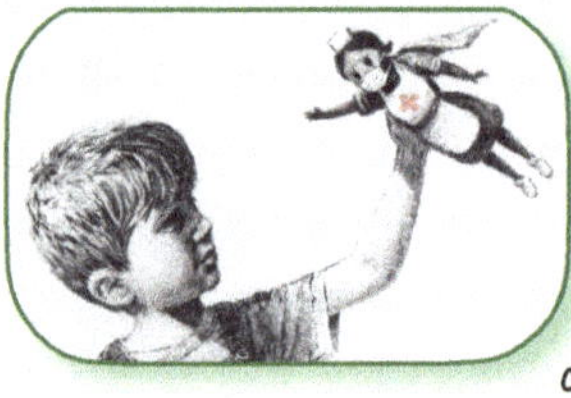

Our son John calls from Arizona – it's a comfort to have these calls, and we do miss him.

The death toll continues to rise, and it is now evident that allowing Cheltenham Races to go ahead led to a huge spike in cases. Banksy unveils a new work in London with NHS superheroes.

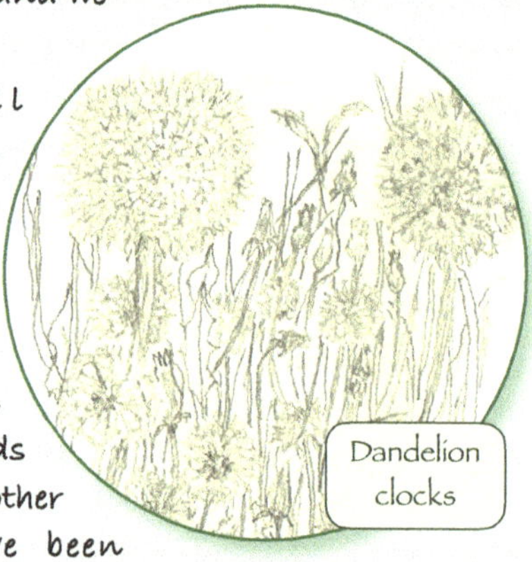

Dandelion clocks

8th - We continue to walk in the Botanical Gardens, and in Norfolk Park where hundreds of golden dandelions in a front garden of another deserted house by the park gates have been transformed into white globe seedheads, standing in still forests in the windless air. Just one breeze will lift them all to fly above our heads and escape this locked down life.

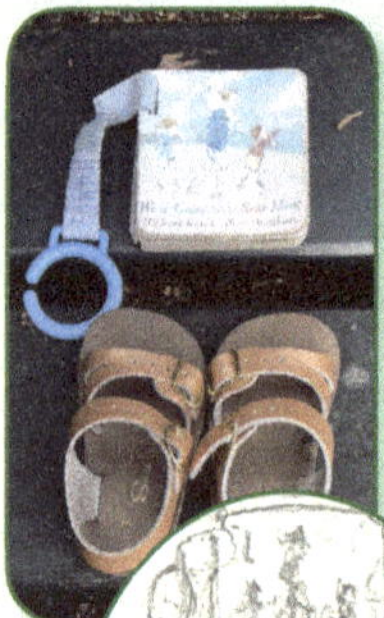

One morning, on a wooden bench in the Botanical Gardens we find an abandoned pair of child-sized sandals, and a book of 'The Bear Hunt'. These forgotten favourite items are a poignant reminder of current times when –

'We can't go over it, we can't go under it, we can't go round it, we just have to go through it'.

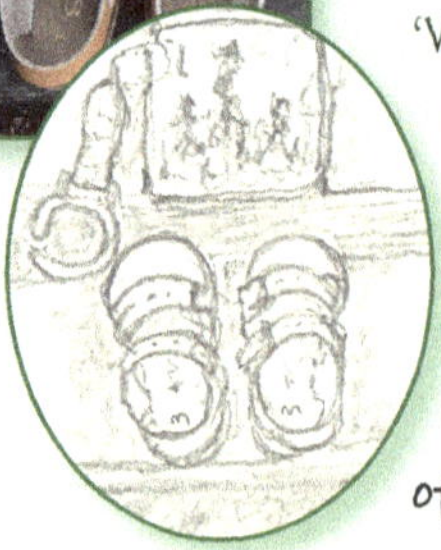

The book's author Michael Rosen remains in hospital recovering from a severe case of Coronavirus, which has left him with symptoms of emerging 'long covid'.

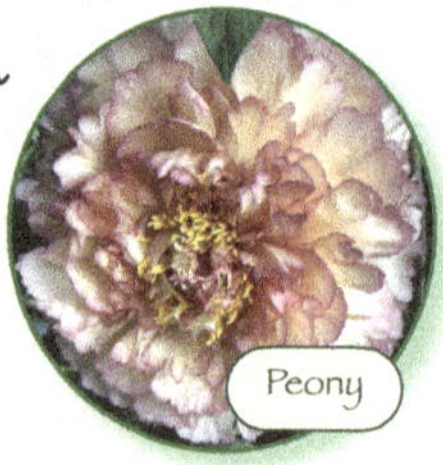

Peony

Pandemic Day: 57/58 Lockdown 1: day 43/44

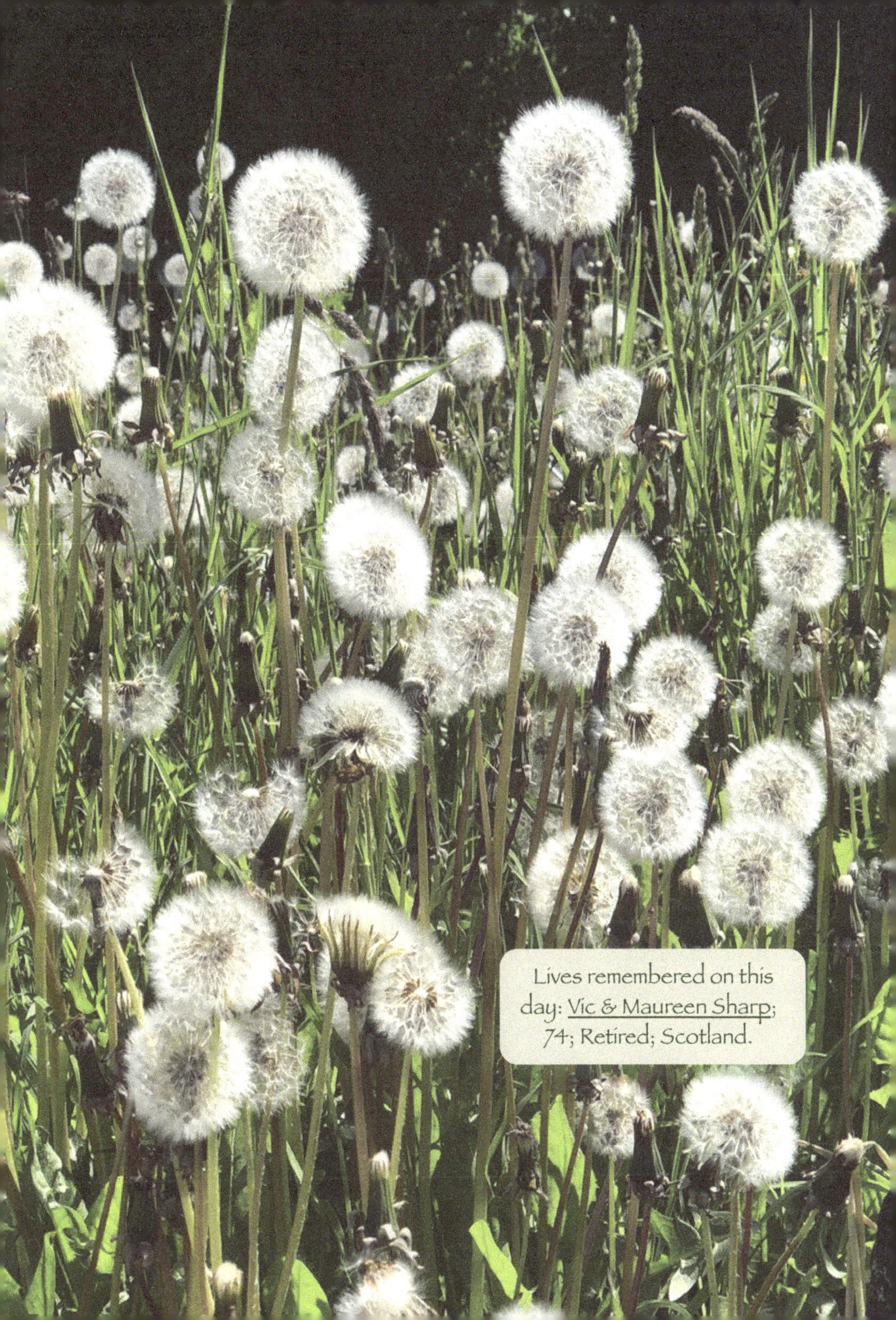

Lives remembered on this day: Vic & Maureen Sharp; 74; Retired; Scotland.

10th May 2020 Confirmed Cases: 137,265 Total deaths: 33,026

THE DEPARTMENT FOR DIGITAL, CULTURE, MEDIA & SPORT STATES 'IT IS ADVISED THAT LARGE GATHERINGS SHOULD NOT TAKE PLACE'.

The 'secret' garden at the Children's House continues to bloom. Cherry and crab apple trees are full of blossoms of white, pink and red, petals falling on paths and among the daisy sprinkled, neglected lawn. A golden waterfall of laburnum pours down the walls from the trees above, lighting up the dark hedges and ivy covered trunks of the big sycamore trees. Bright magenta and speckled white bunches of rhododendron flowers shine among the weedy borders,, and magenta azalea flowers adorn miniature varieties. In the flower beds and among the hedges, birds flutter and cheep as they visit their nests.

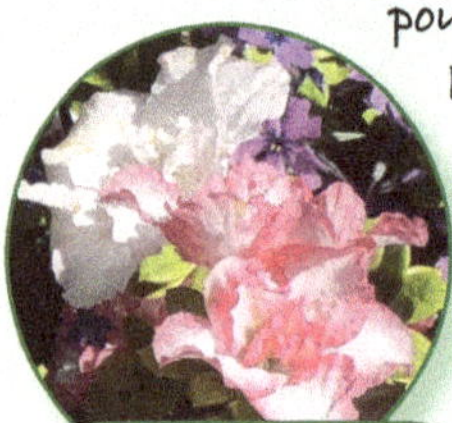

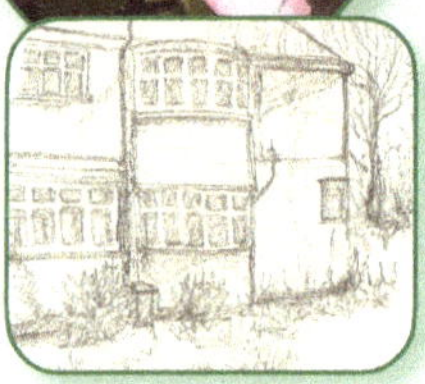

It is a real frustration that we can't get moving on our renovation of this sad and lonely house, and particularly the garden, which has been left in recent years to sink into disrepair, overgrowth and weeds. Daisies, violets and buttercups flower in the lawn among the fallen blossom, and the shrubs in the back garden flower untended, many of them unpruned for years. We are only grateful that someone has left the gate unlocked so we can share this sleeping place, as we wait for estate agents and solicitors to wake from lockdown.

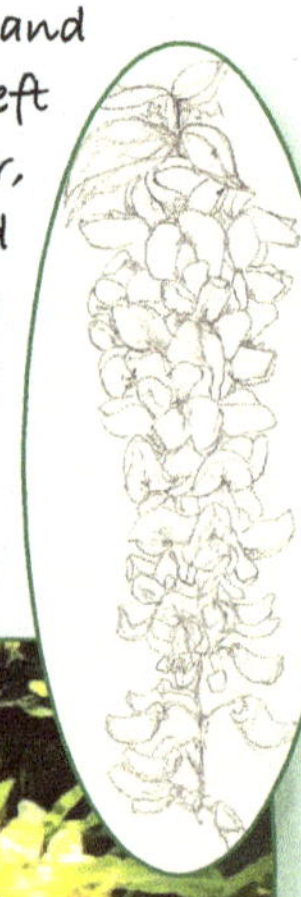

Remembered today: Mridula Nasreen Sarwar; 50; Civil servant; Glasgow.

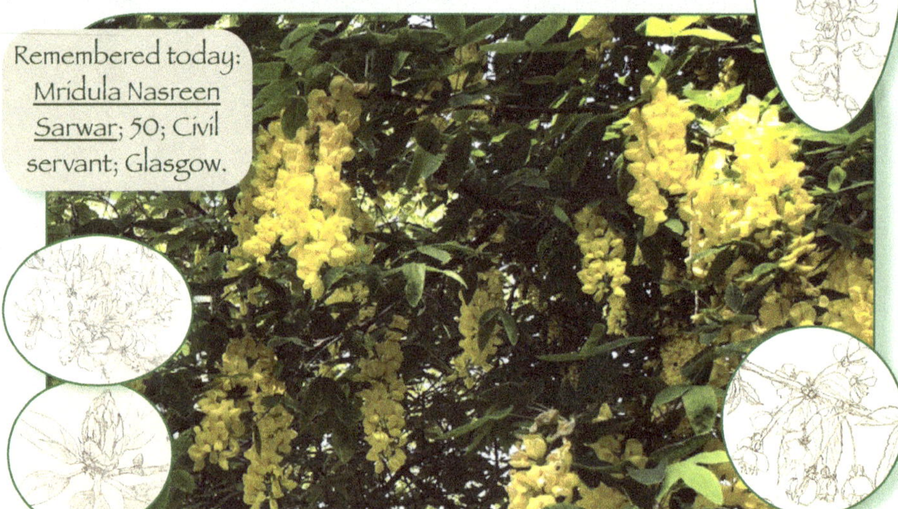

Pandemic Day: 60 Lockdown 1: day 46

11th May 2020 Confirmed Cases: 223,060 Total deaths: 33,335

A NEW ALERT SYSTEM HAS BEN ANNOUNCED, RANGING FROM GREEN (LEVEL 1) TO RED (LEVEL 5). EVERY CITY AND COUNTY HAS BEEN ASSIGNED TO ONE OF THESE LEVELS, THEORETICALLY FOLLOWING SCIENTIFIC EVIDENCE ON CASES AND DEATHS. HOWEVER, CHAOS REIGNS AS THE GOVERNMENT CONTINUALLY MAKES AND WITHDRAWS THE STATEMENTS AND CLARIFICATIONS, AND COUNCILS CHALLENGE CENTRAL GOVERNMENT RULINGS.

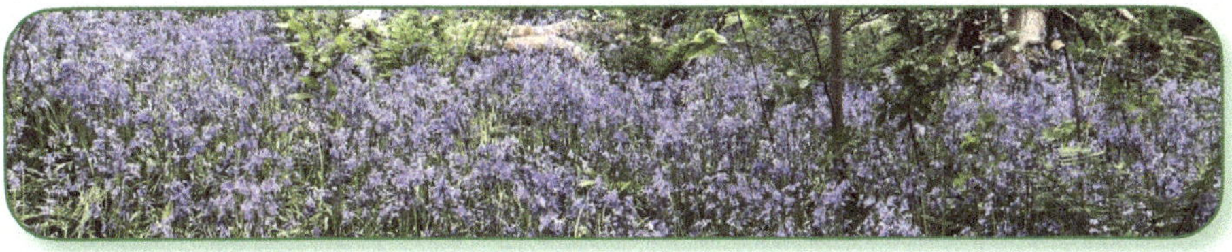

To take our minds off the national problems, we make a legal visit to Ecclesall Woods, the largest ancient semi-natural woodland in South Yorkshire, first enclosed in 1319 by Sir Ralf de Ecclesall as a deer park. 350 acres of mature semi-natural deciduous woodland are currently managed by Sheffield City Council 'for the benefit of wildlife and visitor access'.

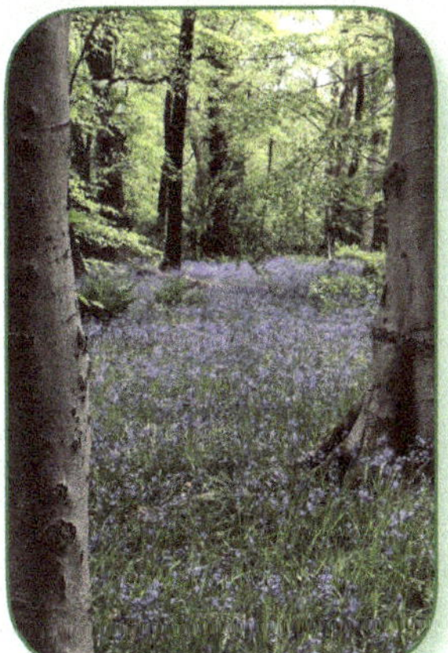

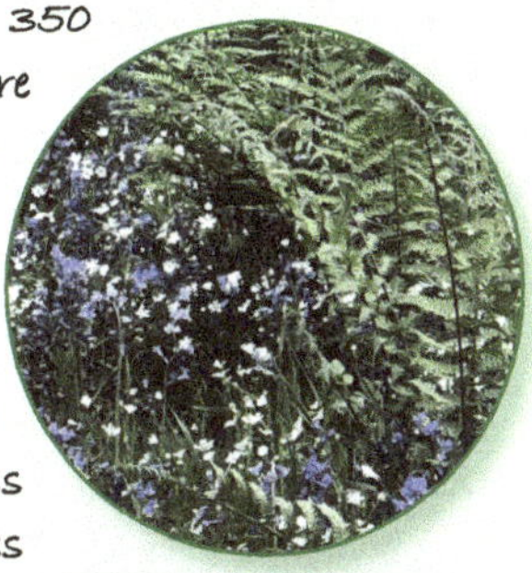

We are there to see the reputed carpets of English bluebells and the new green beech leaves fluttering above them. This is a new local walk for us, and we will surely return before their lovely blueness fades.

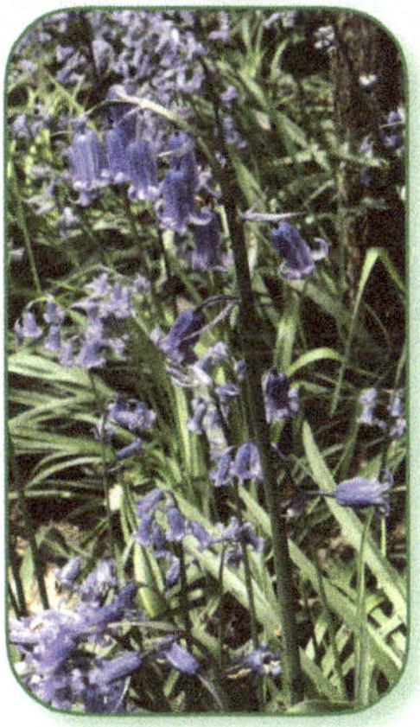

As we explore less visited parts of the woods, a deer walks slowly across our path, apparently oblivious of us, and is invisible seconds later. I wonder how many more deer there are in these woods, wandering unseen and I am reminded of the isolated, deer inhabited valley where we previously lived, full of bluebells soon to flower, and probably with no-one there to see their beauty as people stay in the safety of their homes.

A life remembered today: <u>Belly Mujinga</u>; 47; Ticket officer spat on by a passenger in London.

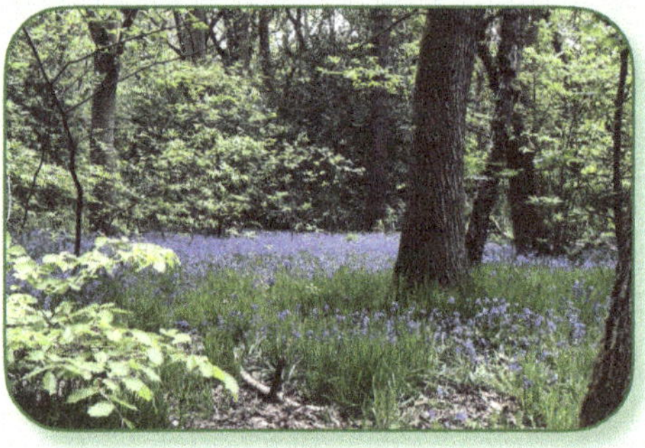

The massive blankets of English bluebells, appearing from nowhere, all over the country, and without any management, are a Spring wonder wherever they grow, and it's so good to have some here, just a mile or so away and protected for the future, so their magical blueness will be preserved beyond this dreadful time of Coronavirus deaths and lockdown.

The protection of Ecclesall and other bluebell woods is essential for our mental health as well as enhancing our natural environment. Every adult in Sheffield should take a child or two by the hand, and bring them here to enjoy this fleeting wonder of the natural world, and work to ensure its preservation.

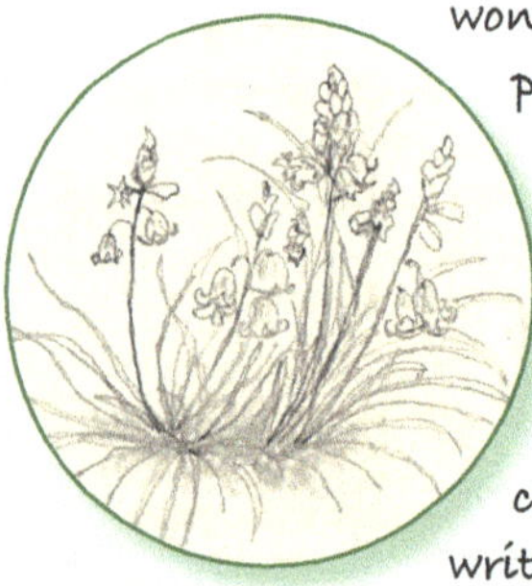

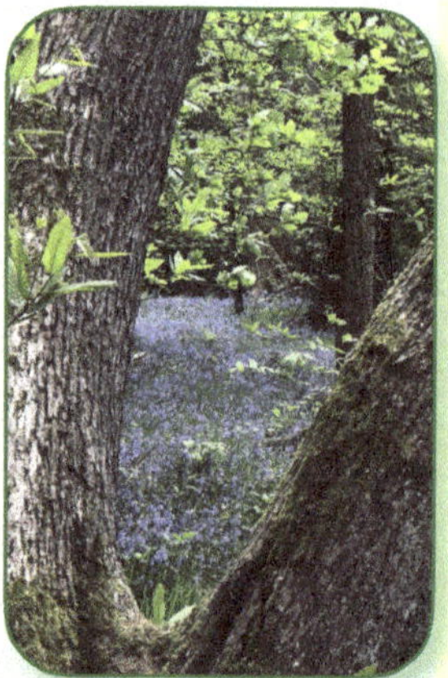

I am surprised at how quickly the time passes. I thought lockdown days would pass slowly, even with the respite of our visits to the deserted countryside, but we both enjoy writing, reading and listening to the radio, and legal outings 'within the city boundary' like today's, help in so many ways. But I really miss the wider experiences of art exhibitions, theatre, films and concerts, and the company of our friends, who we can only see through social media.

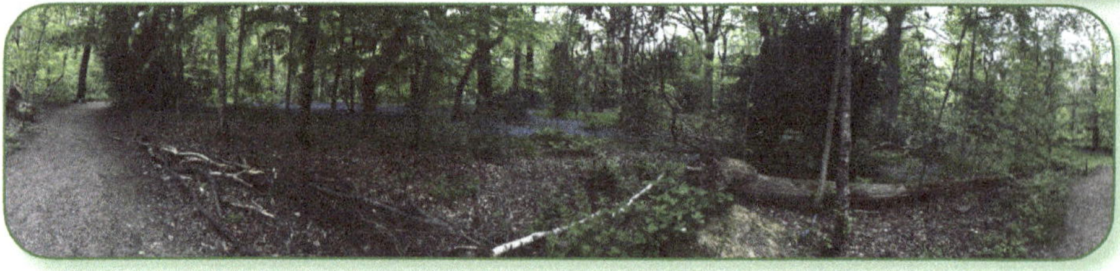

and meanwhile: *The government advises people in England to wear face coverings in enclosed spaces where social distancing is not possible, such as on public transport & in shops.*

Pandemic Day: 61 Lockdown 1: day 47

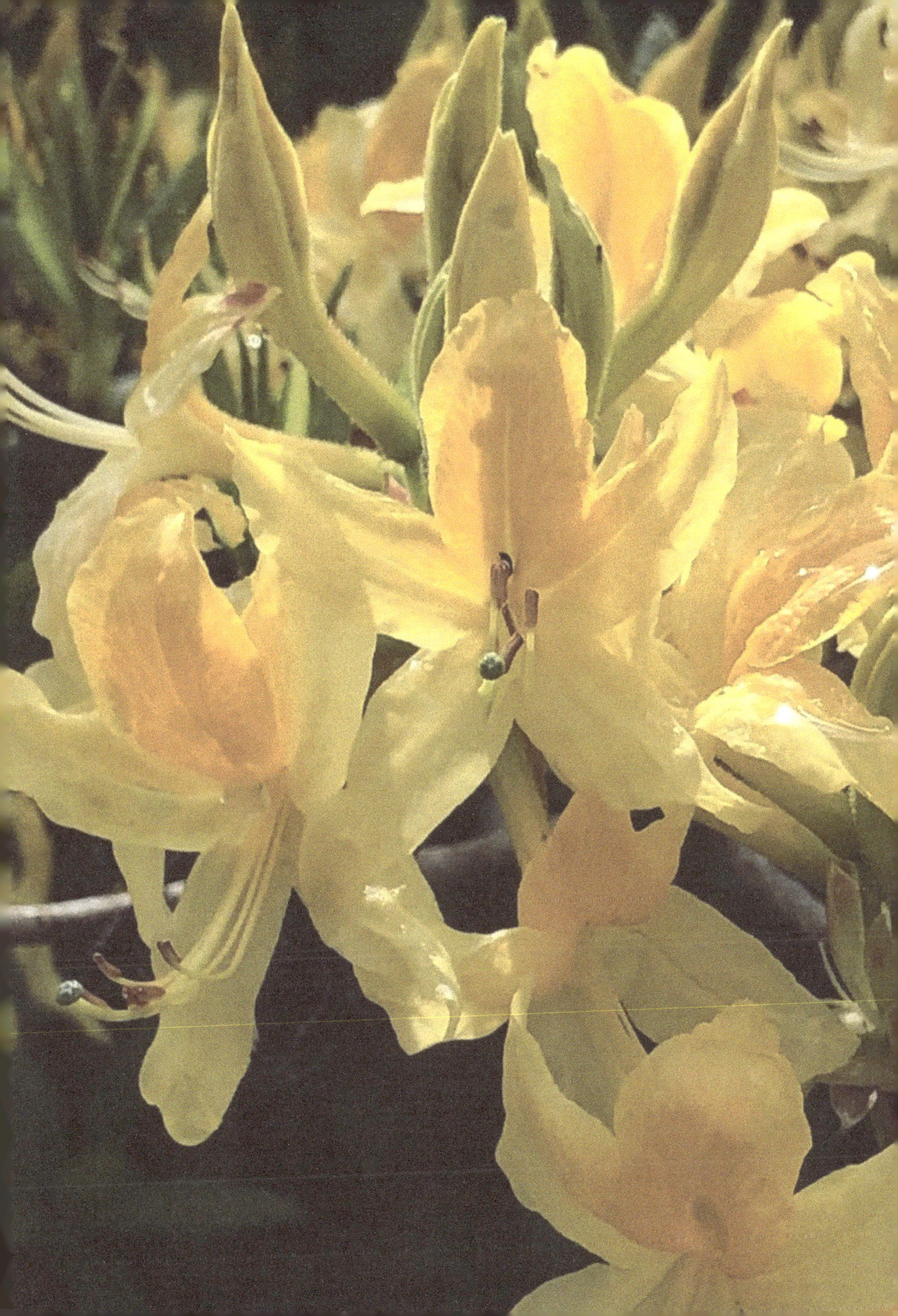

12/13/14th May 2020 Confirmed Cases: 139,478 Total deaths: 34,621

12th - FROM TODAY, AMENDED REGULATIONS MEAN WE CAN DRIVE FURTHER & WALK FOR LONGER.

A life remembered: <u>Dr Abdul Mabud</u> Chowdhury; 53; London - the doctor who warned the Prime Minister about PPE shortages.

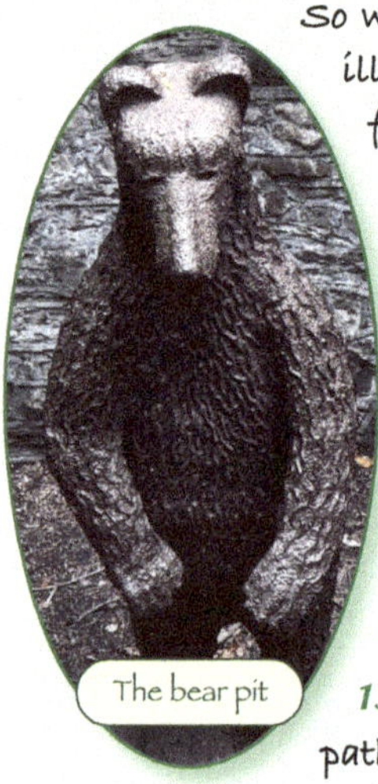
The bear pit

So we are released from the guilt of our illicit walks in the country! We go for a walk in the quiet Botanical Gardens where we greet the stone bear in the historic bear pit, a reminder of the time when this was also a small zoo. His imprisonment here, in the deep, locked pit is a fitting parody of our own locked down situation.

At last, house moves are unlocked as estate agents open, and our house purchase can go ahead.

13th - We revisit the bluebell woods, walking on less popular paths through green spires of Spring grass and the mists of bluebell banks.

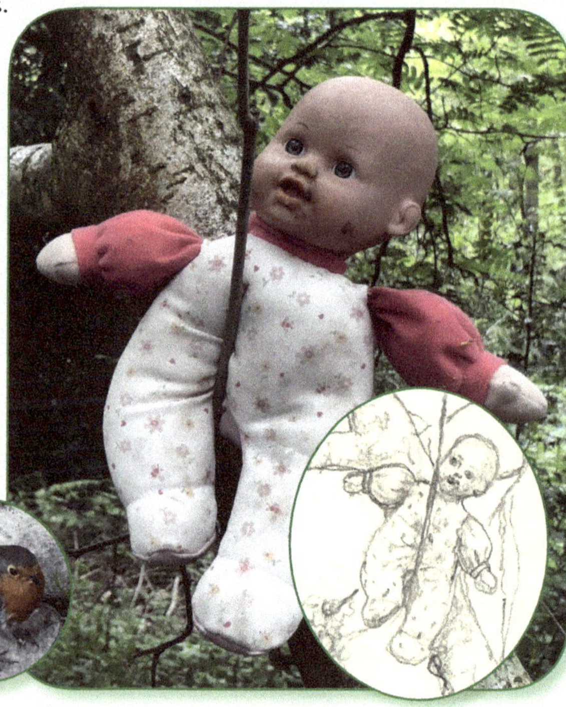

We find a lonely little lost doll perched in a tree!

14th - As we walk in Norfolk Park, two juvenile green woodpeckers clatter through the trees as they practise flying and landing. The lockdown has evidently made them much more tolerant of humans than usual.

May blossom blooms in white innocence in every hedgerow and a robin hangs around hopefully requesting crumbs.

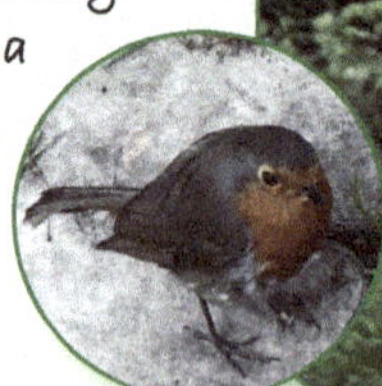

Pandemic Day: 62/64 Lockdown 1: day 48/50

A REPORT ON DEATHS IN CARE HOMES IN ENGLAND AND WALES FROM THE OFFICE FOR NATIONAL STATISTICS FINDS 9,039 ADDITIONAL DEATHS OCCURRING BETWEEN 2nd MARCH AND 1st MAY, AND A FURTHER 3,444 DEATHS OF RESIDENTS IN HOSPITAL.

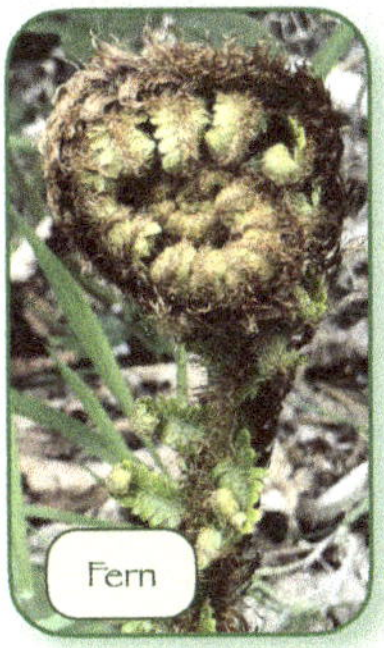

Fern

Today we take another welcome walk above Ladybower, and on a different route round the shoulder of Win Hill, we walk through the larch and spruce plantations to the open heathland. Up here are tiny flowers, like little jewels - bilberry flowers like miniature Christmas decorations, tiny versions of tormentil with shining yellow flowers, bright blue milkwort, violets, daisies and blue speedwell. In the woods, hairy dryopteris ferns raise their curled fronds with ginger hairs, slowly unfurling among the fading bluebells and creeping trails of brambles. Every conifer boasts bright shoots, now shedding a fragile, papery brown confetti of calyxes over paths and grasses.

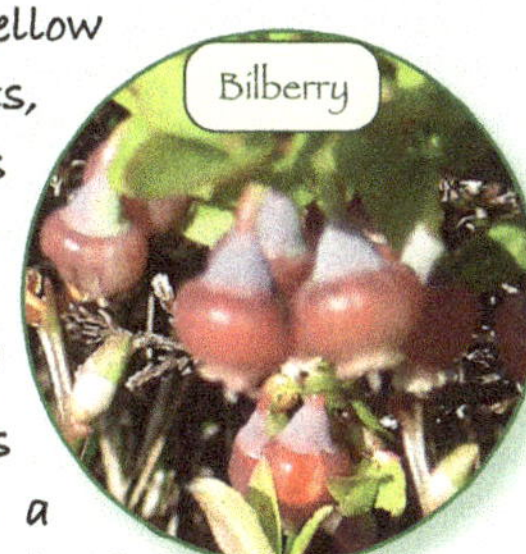

Bilberry

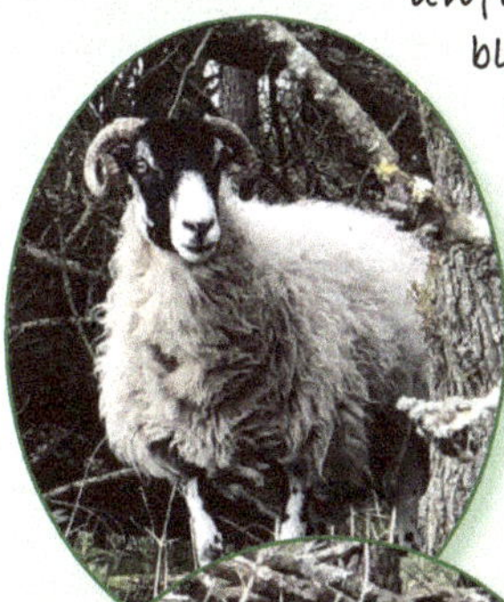

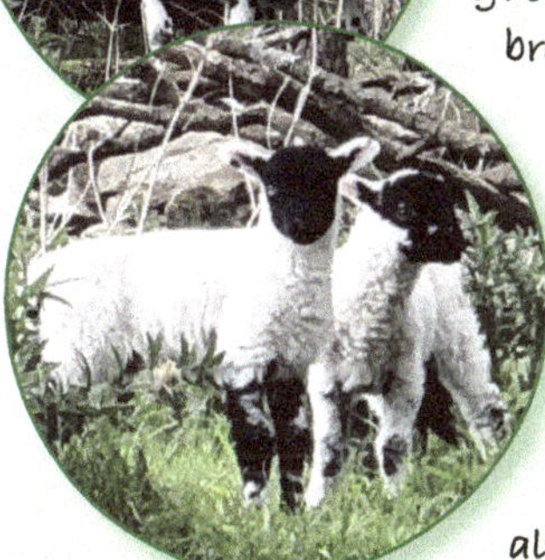

On the moor the wind is chilly, but in the woods it's green and mossy with breathless, moisture-heavy air, and a sheep with twin lambs, all black faces and helicopter black ears, shelters against an old wall. Skylarks soar and we think we hear twite whirring in the heather.

A life remembered on this day: Sheila Gompertz; 83; Computer scientist; Manchester; UK.

As lockdown rules become even more relaxed, although still not removed entirely, there are walkers, bikers, adults, children, dogs everywhere, cautiously emerging to enjoy the freedom and the last of the Spring sunshine.

A group of children are making a big 'Covid rainbow' in coloured chalks on the path by the dam.

and as a sign that even the Queen's budget is affected by Covid: *The two men in charge of the Queen's art collection have left and won't be replaced 'for the time being' because of Covid's impact on royal finances.*

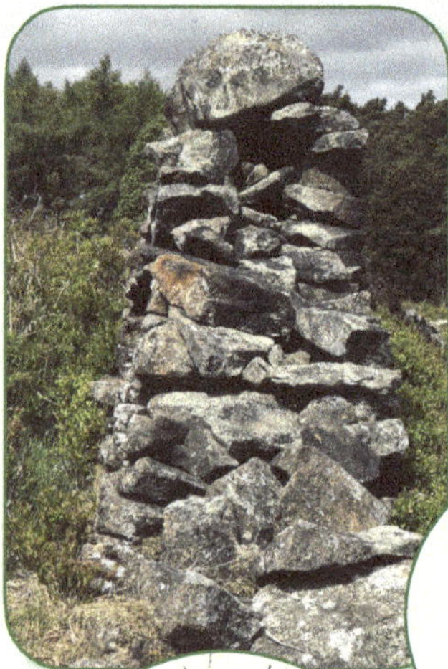

Down by the dam a fat toad is slowly crossing the road, its movements slow, as if it has just emerged from some stony, muddy hibernation.

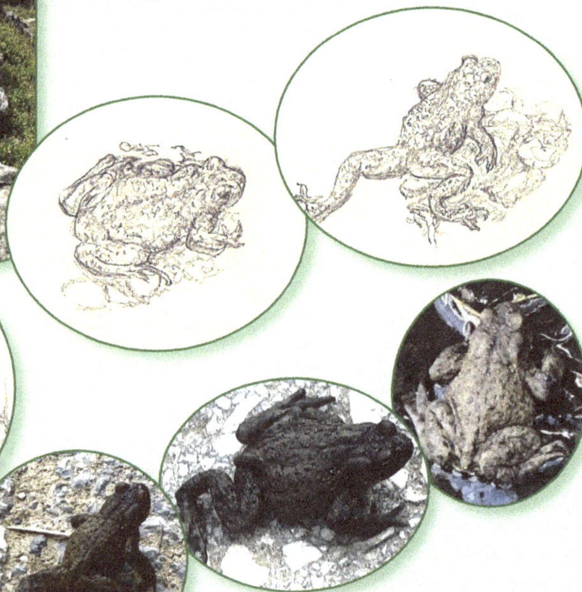

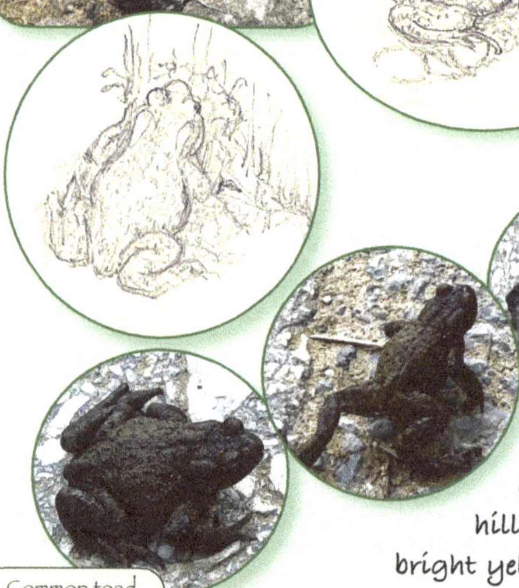

Common toad

On the way home, fields full of golden buttercups glow on every hillside, and even near the city, their bright yellowness shines through in the late afternoon light, gleaming between the trees and hedges.

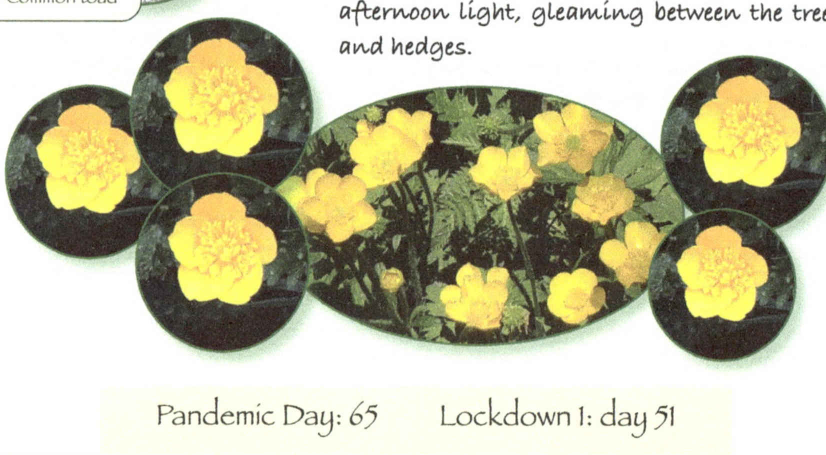

Pandemic Day: 65 Lockdown 1: day 51

16th - CONFLICT OVER SCHOOL RE-OPENING RAGES, AS DOCTORS AND TEACHERS AGREE THAT SCHOOLS SHOULD REMAIN CLOSED, BUT THE GOVERNMENT INSISTS, 'OPENING SCHOOLS GIVES CHILDREN THE BEST OPPORTUNITY'.

THE CHILDREN'S COMMISSIONER URGES THE GOVERNMENT AND TEACHING UNIONS TO 'STOP SQUABBLING AND AGREE A PLAN' TO REOPEN SCHOOLS, WARNING THAT THE CLOSURE IS NEGATIVELY AFFECTING DISADVANTAGED CHILDREN.

We are really beginning to plan for our move, although there is still a long way to go before the house will be ready for us to move in. But there are movements in the legal and financial process.

17th - AS WE MEET IN AND OUT OF DOORS, £84M IS INVESTED IN A COVID-19 VACCINE BEING TRIALLED BY THE UNIVERSITY OF OXFORD THAT SHOULD BE AVAILABLE BY SEPTEMBER. ASTROZENECA WILL MANUFACTURE THE VACCINE, AND DISTRIBUTE IT TO THE UK AS ONE OF THE FIRST CUSTOMERS.

For the first time since February, we visit Sarah's house. We admire the new workshop Jeff has built in their woodland garden, during Lockdown, when he was unable to teach at the university. Here among the damp leaves, slugs and snails now sits a Japanese inspired structure, already looking at home in the greenery. The lockdown has fractured all sorts of relationships, but many people, like Jeff have taken advantage of the time and space to create something unique.

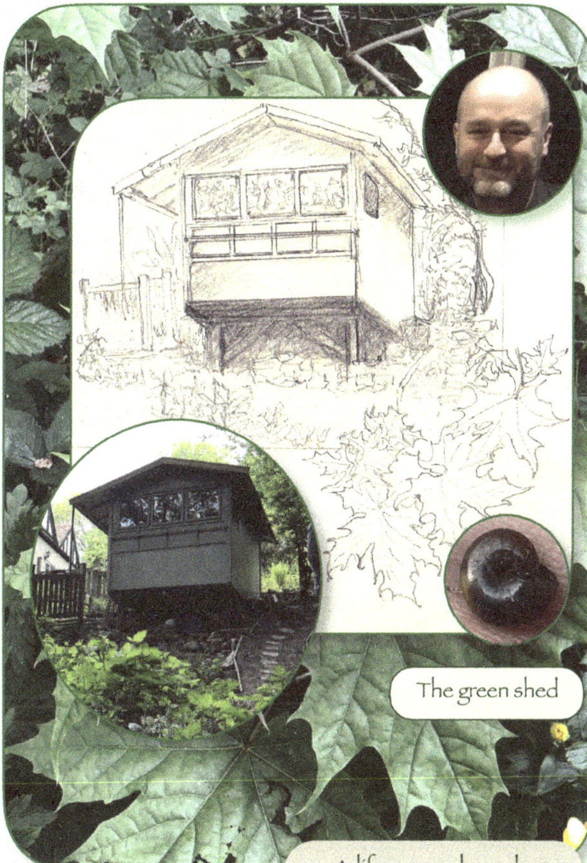

The green shed

A life remembered on this day: Ali Hadi; 53; Footballer; Iraq.

18th May 2020 Confirmed Cases: 143,703 Total deaths: 33,656

ANYONE OVER THE AGE OF FIVE CAN NOW HAVE A TEST, BUT THERE ARE LONG QUEUES AT THE TESTING CENTRES, AND PEOPLE ARE HAVING TO TRAVEL LONG DISTANCES TO GET APPOINTMENTS.

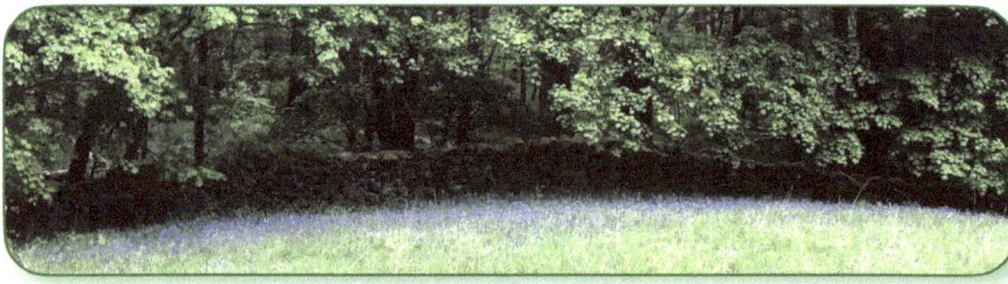

Over the green hills, and through country lanes, we drive to Huddersfield to collect medication from the hospital, a permitted journey. A case of shingles several years ago left me with damage to the retina in my right eye, and the steroid treatment to improve this continues.

A life remembered on this day: Martin Loveday; 62; Cellist; London.

This is my first lockdown experience of a big public building, and being so close to people who may be infected. But the NHS continues to meet patient's needs, and it is an efficient process, so I am quickly back in the car for a thorough hand sanitising. I didn't think I would be anxious but I am, even though the hospital is empty.

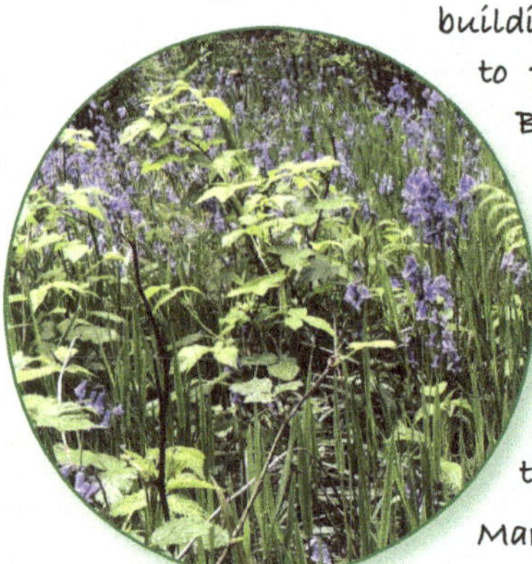

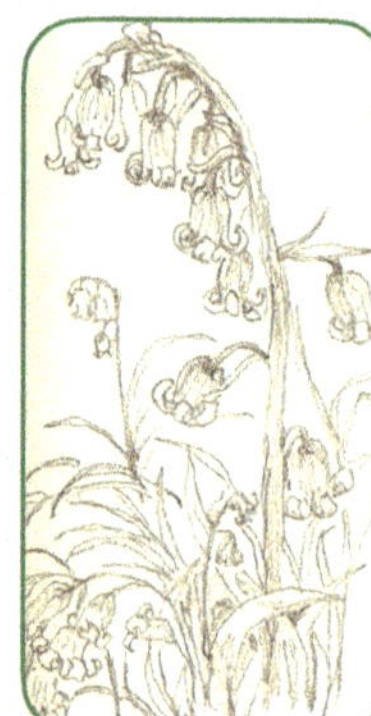

Marking more than 50 days of lockdown, we decide to visit Hebden Bridge for a walk in the misty woods at Hardcastle Crags, remembering our walks here over many years with family, friends and often on our own. The woods are empty of humans, with clouds above, mist caught in the topmost branches of the tallest trees, rain dropping from the Spring leaves, and the air full of the perfume of bluebells and the bright songs of birds.

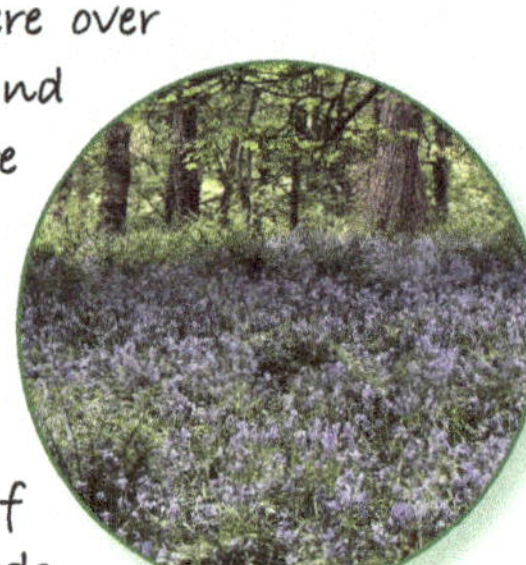

and as we revisit a favourite woodland: *The UK adds loss of smell and loss of taste to the list of COVID-19 symptoms that people should look out for.*

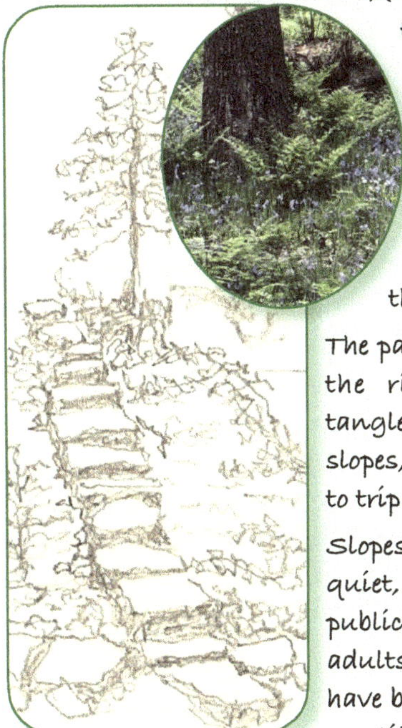

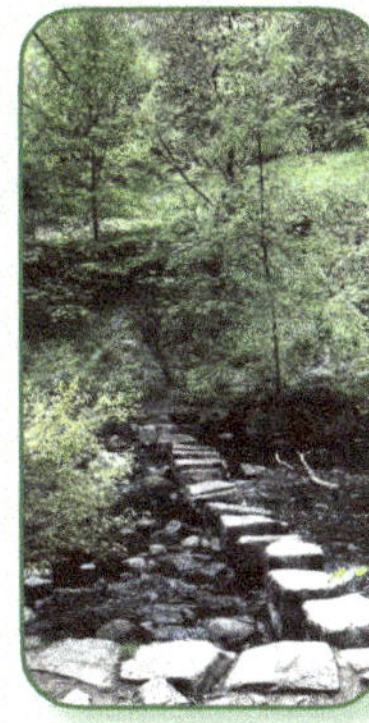

A heron silently circles over us, then lands on long grey legs to scout for fish before taking off again on the dark umbrella of its wings, to disappear like a ghost of itself, dangling long legs in the mist still caught among the treetops.

The path, deep in beech leaves, follows the river, often bordered by the tangled roots of great trees clinging on to the valley slopes, and making story-book patterns that conspire to trip the unwary.

Slopes and steep wooden steps are frequent in these quiet, deserted woodlands, still not frequented by the public, despite being long-time local favourites for adults, children and dogs. It is strange that people have become so cautious, and even though most schools are still closed, there are no children in this woodland playground today. The woods are dressed in their best Spring green, with bluebells, wild garlic, pink purslane and stitchwort among the straight green grasses and dark trunks of the beeches.

The roots of some trees, constantly washed by water rushing and trickling down the steep, leaf-mouldy land, are a tripping tangle, just waiting for a stumble or misjudgement to throw humans down those slopes and slippy steps towards the rushing brown, peat stained water.

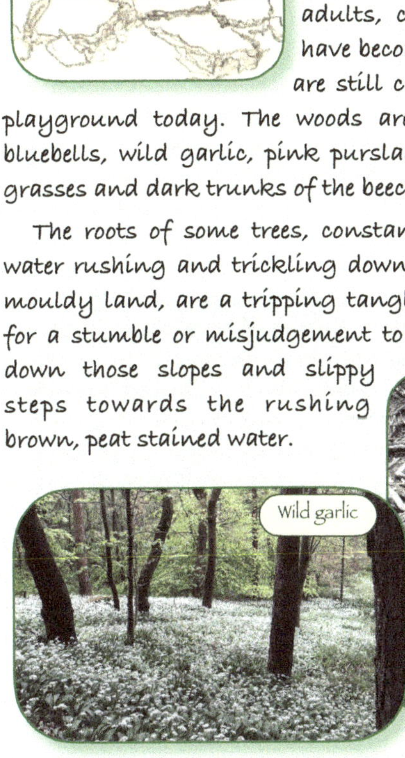

Wild garlic

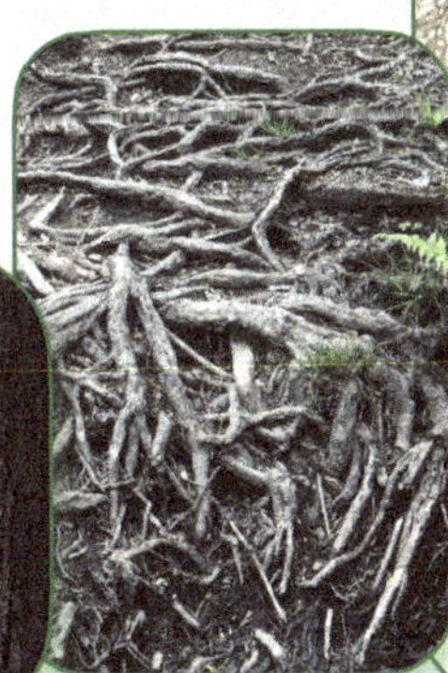

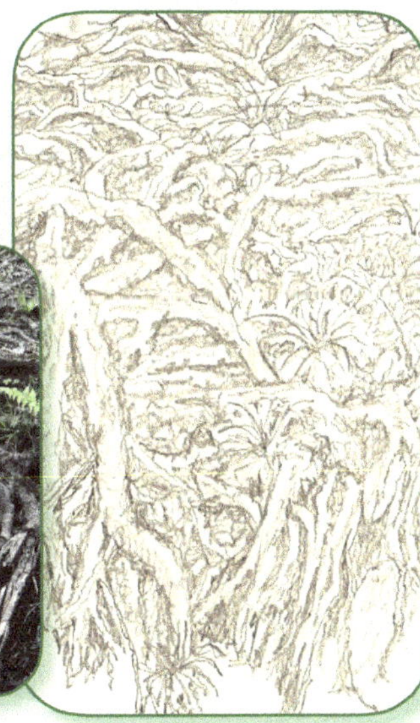

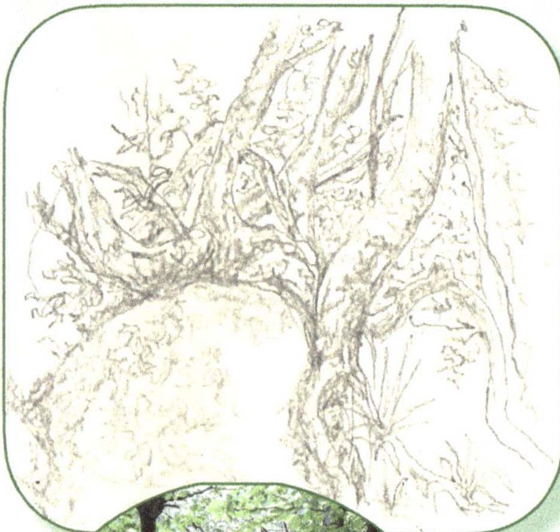

In the fast-flowing rivers of this area, great rounded rocks fill the water and line the banks, and some are topped by living trees, hanging on with their roots and risking being washed away when the river floods, as it frequently does in the wet Calderdale Valleys.

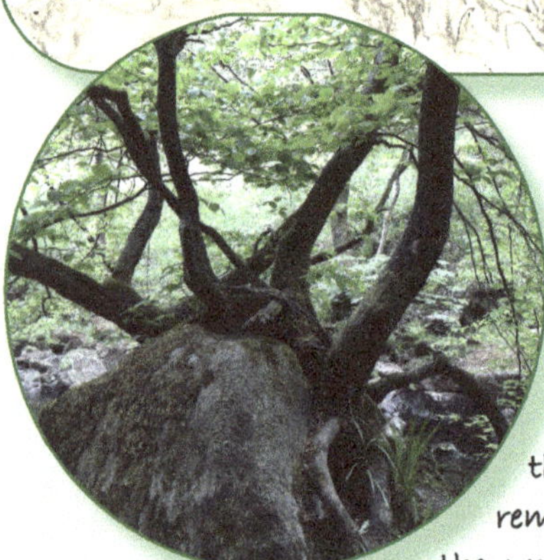

Leaving the river at the cafe (sadly closed), we abandon the watery woodland path to return down the white-stoned forest road. Here, the easier walking enables us to enjoy the last drifts of bluebells we will see this year, tumbling down the steep slopes, undisturbed by visitors - with no children or dogs making trampled paths through these beautiful, transient flowers, surrounded by the white clouds of wild, garlic-scented ramsons.

It is a real privilege to be here alone, exploring the Spring woodlands at their best. I will remember this day for many years to come, when the woods will once more be full of the voices of children and barking of dogs.

We choose to drive home down the M62 and M1 motorways, where there is little traffic and not one jam or queue - it's the first time we have been on a motorway for nearly eight weeks, and It seems just like being in a sci-fi apocalyptic film, until we remember that we are experiencing a frighteningly real apocalypse of our own making, as we return to our locked down home through the quiet streets of the locked down city.

A beech wood with bluebells

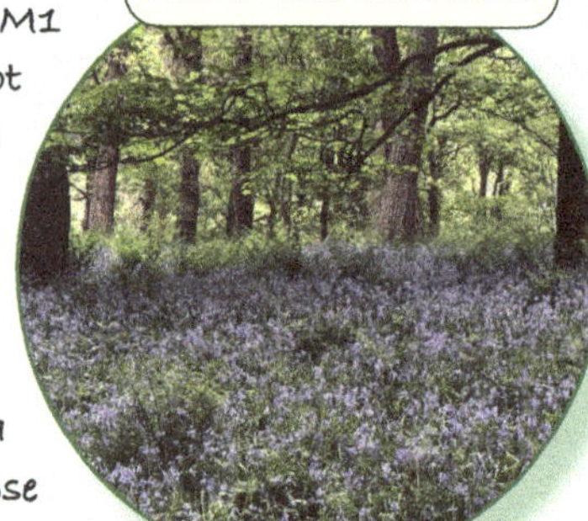

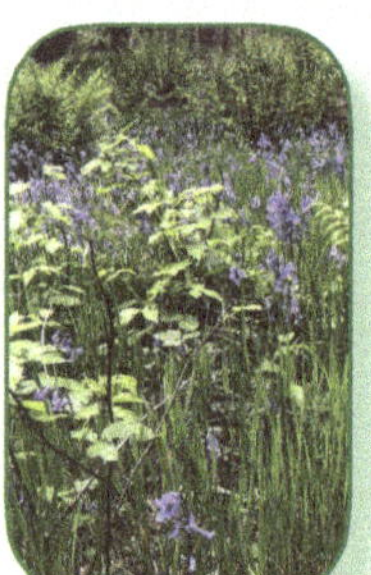

Two more lives remembered today: Twins Eleanor & Eileen Andrews; 66; Wales.

Pandemic Day: 68 Lockdown 1: day 54

19th May 2020 Confirmed Cases: 246,284 Total deaths: 35,770

THE OFFICE FOR NATIONAL STATISTICS REPORTS THAT OVER HALF THE DEATHS FROM CORONAVIRUS HAVE BEEN IN THE COMMUNITY (MANY IN CARE HOMES) – AND NOT IN HOSPITALS. FIGURES SHOW THERE HAVE BEEN 11,600 DEATHS IN CARE HOMES AS A RESULT OF COVID-19. PROFESSOR MARTIN GREEN, CHAIR OF CARE ENGLAND TELLS MPS THAT CARE SETTINGS SHOULD HAVE BEEN PRIORITISED FROM THE START OF THE PANDEMIC.

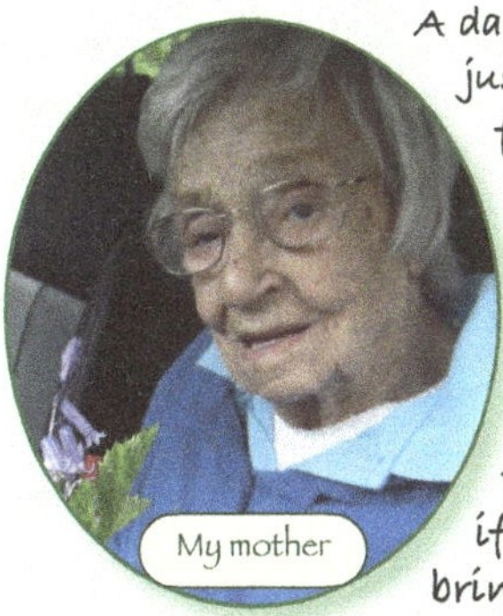
My mother

A day at home as the blame game grinds on. Sometimes the days just pass with no reportable events, no feelings of either frustration or fear, just tired resignation, often tinged with gratitude that we have managed to remain safe so far.

However, today is a day for real, deep anger on behalf of every person who has lost a parent, grandparent, aunt, uncle, other family member or friend, particularly if they died in a care home, and even more if they were returned to a care home from hospital, bringing the deadly virus with them.

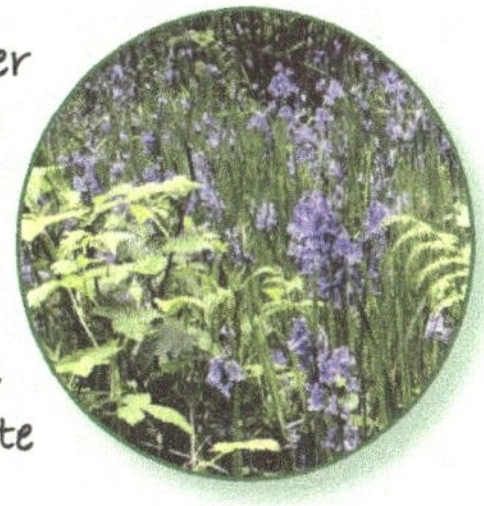

It appears that someone in a position of power deemed that many frail and elderly residents were disposable, did not deserve hospital treatment, and that the people who cared for them as they died didn't need proper protective equipment. It is probable that, when deaths in care homes and at home are added to the totals, will bring the real total of Covid deaths to 55,000, up to the date of the WW2 celebration weekend.

My mother suffered from dementia, and spent her last years in a very good care home, supported by kind and patient carers, even though dementia sometimes made her difficult to deal with. I am not sure how she would have responded to being told she couldn't go out or have visitors, because, like me, she loved being out of doors. I am just glad she didn't have to go through the dreadful experience at the end of her life that many others have suffered during this year.

The photo included here is of a day in May when I took her to the bluebell woods for the last time. Even holding a few blooms in her hand was some comfort to her when she was no longer able to walk among the bluebell woods in Spring.

A life remembered on this day: Neil Kraft; 69; Rabbi; London.

and as we fume about the awful death rate: *Experts identify major security issues with the NHS COVID-19 tracing app being piloted on the Isle of Wight, and call for new legislation to prevent officials using the data collected for purposes other than identifying those at risk from the virus.*

Pandemic Day: 69 Lockdown 1: day 55

20th May 2020 Confirmed Cases: 145,808 Total deaths: 36,038

THE GOVERNMENT IN ENGLAND FACES MOUNTING PRESSURE FROM COUNCILS AND TEACHING UNIONS TO RECONSIDER ITS PLANS TO REOPEN PRIMARY SCHOOLS FROM 1ST JUNE.

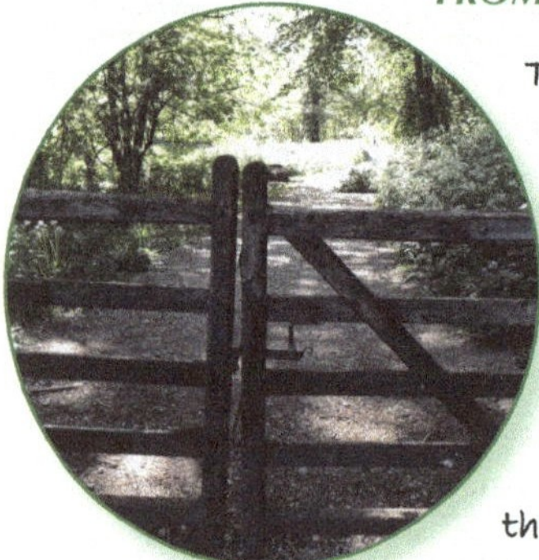

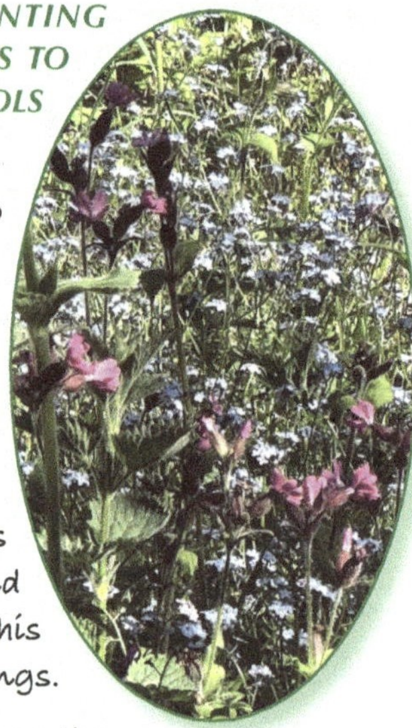

Today we drive to Lathkill Dale, on what will prove to be the hottest day of the year so far. We walk down the steep hill road from the village car park, past hedgerows thick with cow parsley and tall grasses, hoping that this new walk will be as enjoyable as our other spring outings.

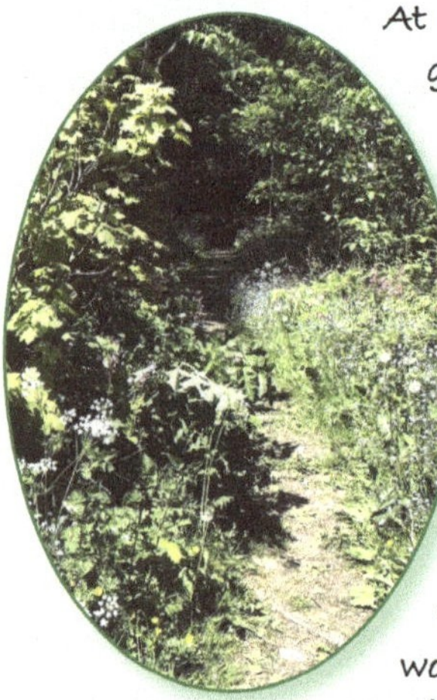

At the bottom of the hill, we open the gate to the nature reserve, and follow the footpath along the valley beside the beautiful, sparkling river. This is obviously a popular walk, well-trodden and signposted, but not too busy today, with everyone socially distant and polite, stepping aside, knee deep in the spring flowers to preserve their two metre, 'ironing board' social distance.

The paths are edged by floods of forget-me-nots, pink campion and ragged robin at their blue and pink best in swathes among the trees and on the verges. It is difficult to adequately describe the floral wonder of this walk. I have never seen wild flowers growing in such profusion, like a living Pre-Raphaelite painting everywhere you look.

A life remembered today: <u>Tim Brooke Taylor</u>; *79*; Comedian; London.

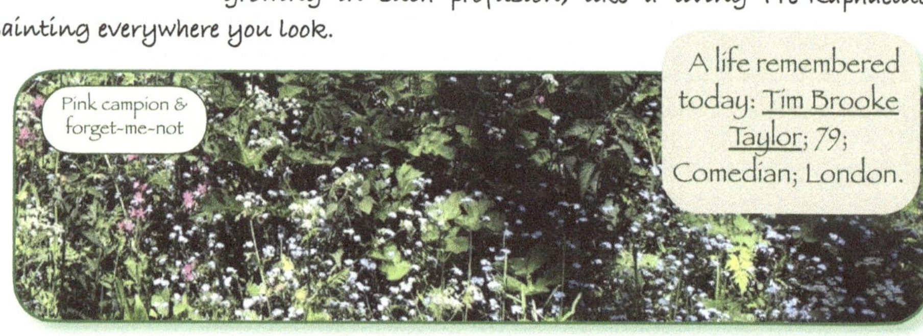

Pink campion & forget-me-not

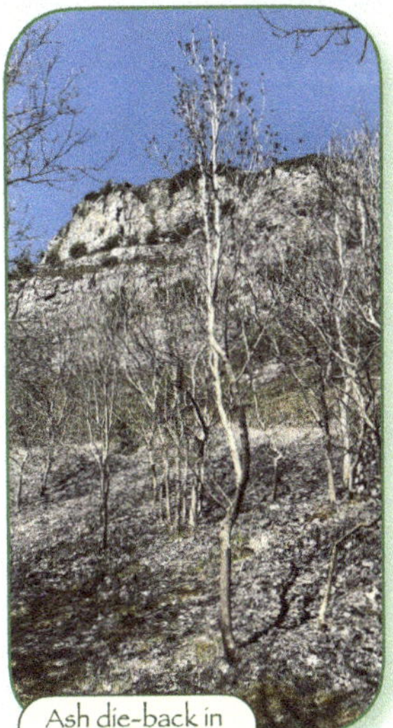

Ash die-back in Lathkill Dale

In contrast with its floral Spring glory, this valley is also a sad graveyard of dead and dying ash trees. There are thousands of them, victims of the Chalara virus which is destroying ash trees across the country. It is ironic that in 2020, communities of trees, like humans, are battling with their own virus, and losing many members in the process.

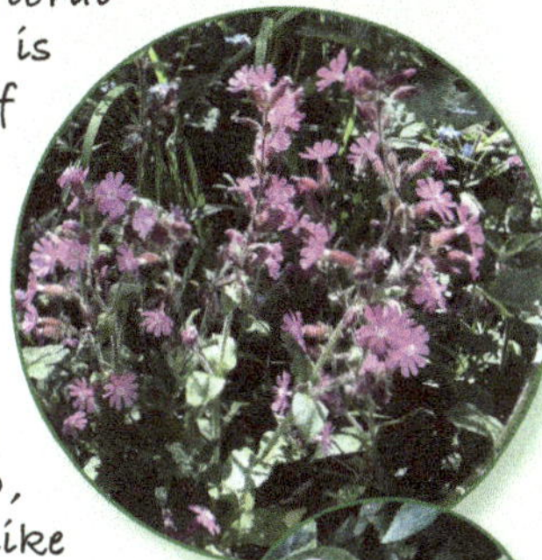

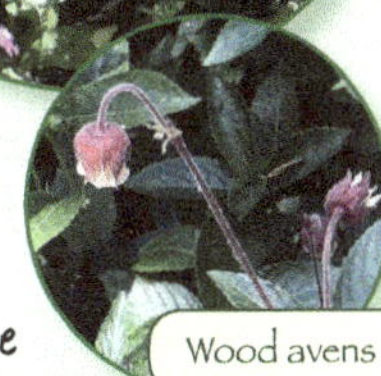

Wood avens

Odd bits of green leaves show on some trees as they struggle to survive, but death seems inevitable for all the trees in this and many other local valleys. However, their pale skeletons can't spoil the beauty of this deep limestone cleft, its steep sides white with rocks, sharp and unstable, rattling down with each winter's rain, often uprooting whole trees as they pass.

As well as containing a great fishing river, this valley is also littered with signs of lead and marble mining, now long abandoned. Deep shafts, protected by metal grids and gratings, are ghostly evidence of a community once living and working in this valley. Mysterious caves and mine openings, are made safe now, but still tempt children and adults alike.

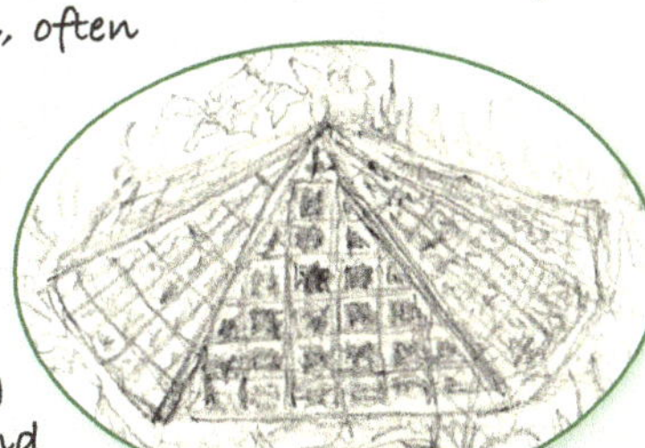

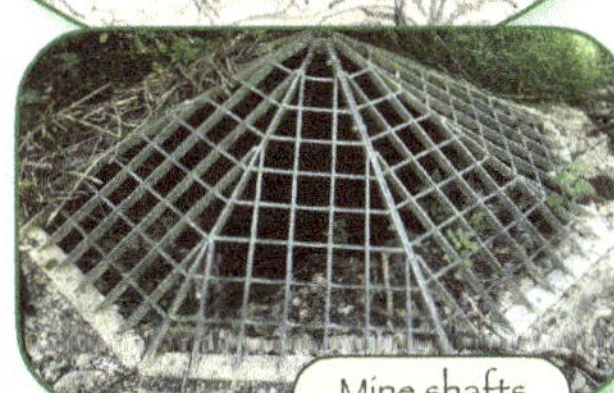

Mine shafts

Other relics line the river banks, evidence of the taming of water into locks, ponds and falls to provide power for mills and machines. Wooden structures and old bridges rot in the damp atmosphere, and huge millstone grit grindstones, once essential to the communities working and living here, now lie idle and cast aside, deep in the shadows, covered in moss and lichen and soon to be buried in flowers.

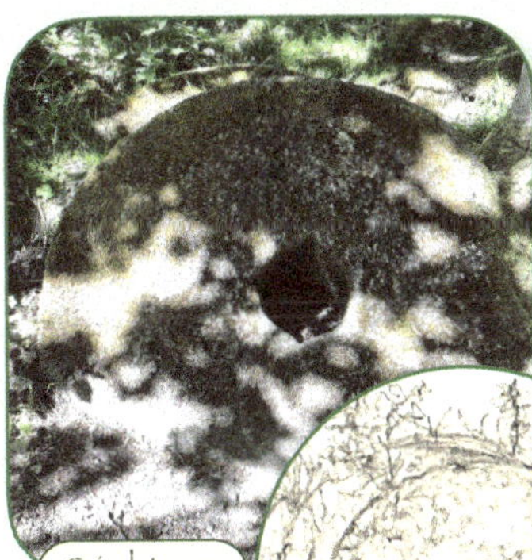

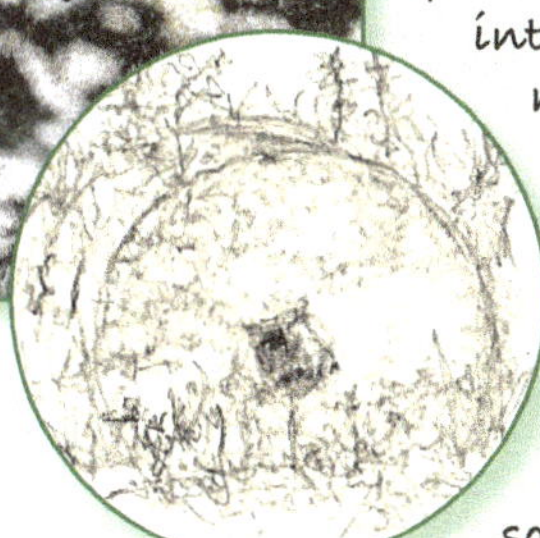

Grindstones

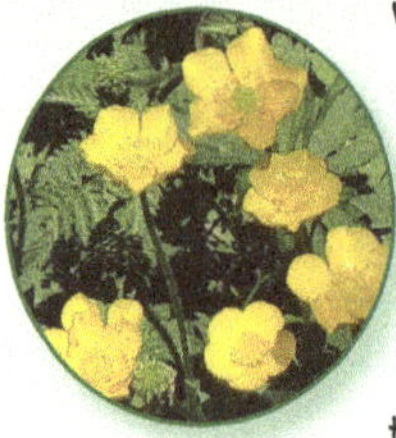

We pause for a rest by one of the wooden dams, gently rotting away in the sunshine and buttercups. The river is fast flowing but low today, glittering in the sun as it flows around and over the white limestone rocks and trailing green water weeds. Ducks dabble in this green stream and children paddle in the pools, with their clothes tucked in their knickers, or stripped to their underwear in the ever-increasing heat of this extremely hot day.

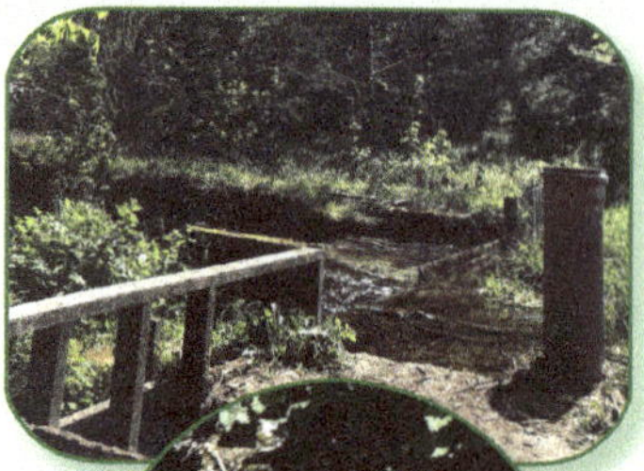

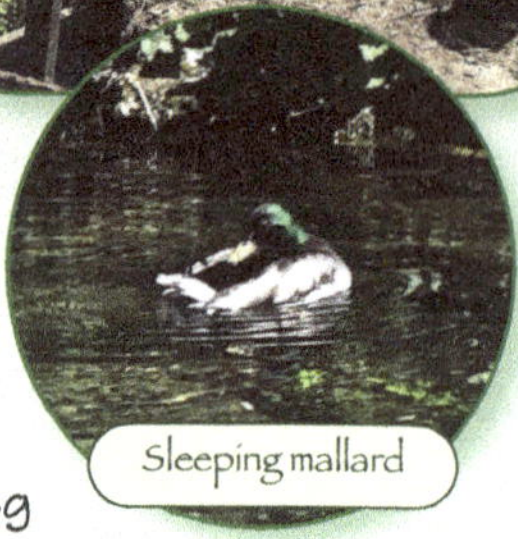

Sleeping mallard

A second life remembered today: <u>John Allison</u>; 76; Medication driver; Sheffield.

Further up the river, beyond the waterfalls and weirs that attract delighted, screaming children, we stop for a cool lunch, a long rest for reflection and for me to make a few sketches in the shade of the trees on the river bank. We then decide to retrace our steps rather than take the longer circuit of our intended but as yet unexplored route. Walking back along the banks, the afternoon sun becomes even hotter on our backs, captured thickly in the flower-filled valley. Passing the flowery verges, now wilting a little, and the ducks dozing with their heads tucked under their wings, we gently close the gate on this wonder of nature, only lightly managed to ensure the continued protection of this beautiful valley.

and as we enjoy the heat: *The number of people in hospital with COVID-19 drops below 10,000 for the first time since March.*

As we climb the steep hill back to Over Haddon I am almost overcome by the oppressive weight of the afternoon heat, and need to sit on a flower decked bench to cool down before facing the last part of the steep road back to the village, where the melting tarmac throws back yet more stored sunshine.

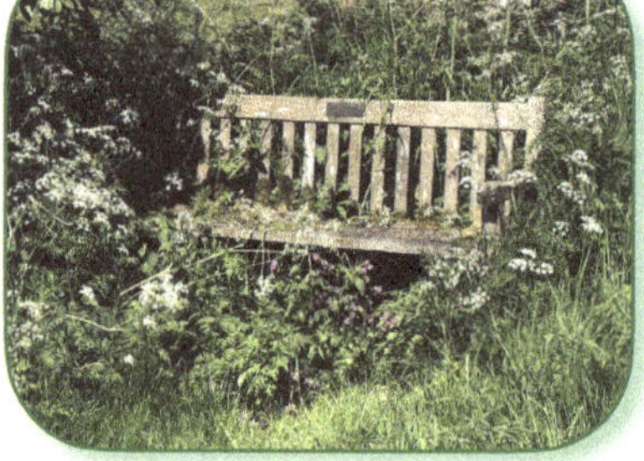

At last we reach the car park, the welcome coolness of an air-conditioned car, and a sunny, drive home, our heads full of memories of a flower-filled day.

Pandemic Day: 70 Lockdown 1: day 56

21st/22nd May 2020 Confirmed Cases : 146,662 Total deaths: 36,276

21st - OUTDOOR ACTIVITIES RESUME AND GARDEN CENTRES OPEN.

We venture out as a socially distanced family of six into Lady Spring Woods to see the deer by the golf course. We walk among the massive oaks and ashes of another of Sheffield's conservation woodlands where public access to these ancient wild, lightly managed woodlands is ensured.

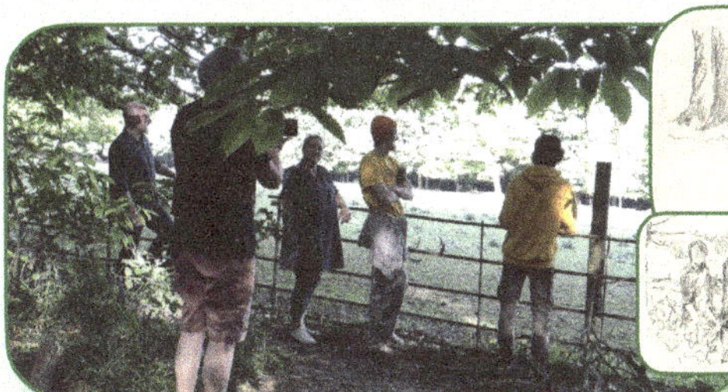

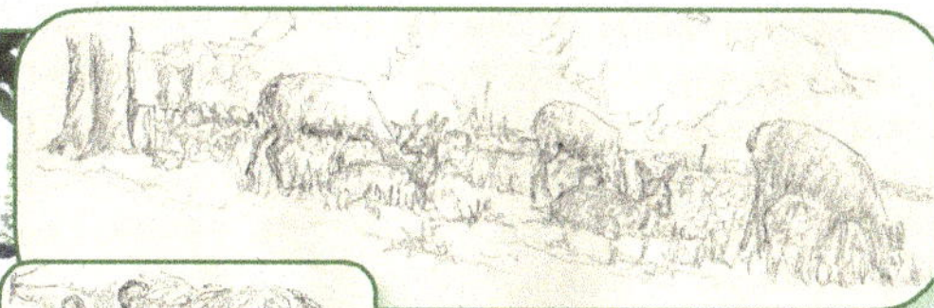

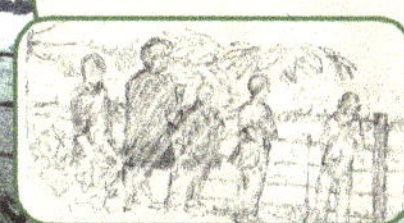

This first tentative family expedition into normality is so welcome, maybe we really are nearing the end of this terrible time of imprisonment. It is so good to be able to walk freely as a family, to see the deer in the ancient deer park of Beauchief Hall, as they too enjoy the sunshine, obviously well fed as local people resume their visits with pockets full of grain, carrots and apples. Birds and insects abound in this protected reserve, despite its popularity and location in the suburbs of the city.

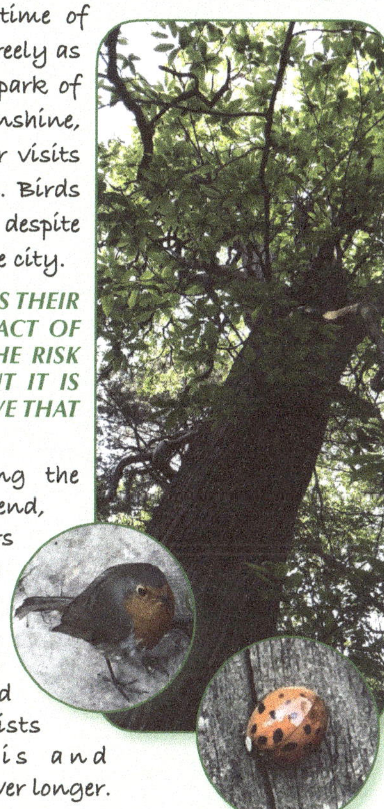

22nd - THE SAGE ADVISORY GROUP PUBLISHES THEIR EVIDENCE ON THE SAFETY AND POSSIBLE IMPACT OF REOPENING SCHOOLS ON 1ST JUNE. IT SAYS THE RISK TO SCHOOL PUPILS IS 'VERY, VERY SMALL, BUT IT IS NOT ZERO', THE RISK TO TEACHERS IS NOT ABOVE THAT OF OTHER OCCUPATIONS.

Annemarie Plas, credited with initiating the weekly 'Clap for carers', suggests it should end, and become an annual celebration for all carers and front-line workers. Last night was the ninth Clap for Carers, next week may be the last, although the NHS is still fully stretched and waiting lists for diagnosis and treatment grow ever longer.

A life remembered today <u>Sara Trollope</u>; 51; NHS Matron; Watford.

Pandemic Day: 71/72 Lockdown 1: day 57/58

23rd/25th May 2020   Confirmed Cases: 149,308   Total deaths: 37,115

23rd - DOMINIC CUMMINGS COMES UNDER MOUNTING PRESSURE TO RESIGN AFTER AN INVESTIGATION BY THE MIRROR & THE GUARDIAN NEWSPAPERS.

A life lost at this time: Mike Huckaby; 54; Musician; United States.

People are still very angry about Dominic Cummings' drive to Barnard Castle, but he has the Prime Minister's support, and he gives neither explanation nor apology. The injustice must make any sane person angry, when so many people have been unable to be near their dying family members in care homes or hospitals, they have not been able to attend funerals or show their respect in the usual way. Lonely singletons of all ages are locked in, and thousands are mourning family and friends.

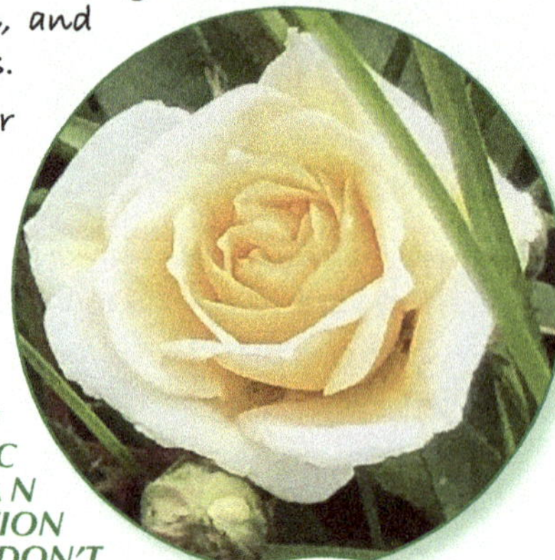

Although I sometimes feel guilty for breaking Covid rules, we never go far from the local area, and usually meet no-one, so my conscience is somewhat calmed.

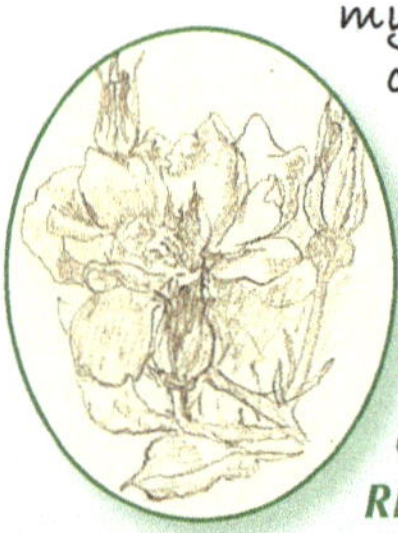

25th - AT A PRESS CONFERENCE IN THE ROSE GARDEN AT DOWNING STREET, DOMINIC CUMMINGS GIVES AN UNAPOLOGETIC EXPLANATION OF HIS ACTIONS, SAYING 'I DON'T REGRET WHAT I DID'.

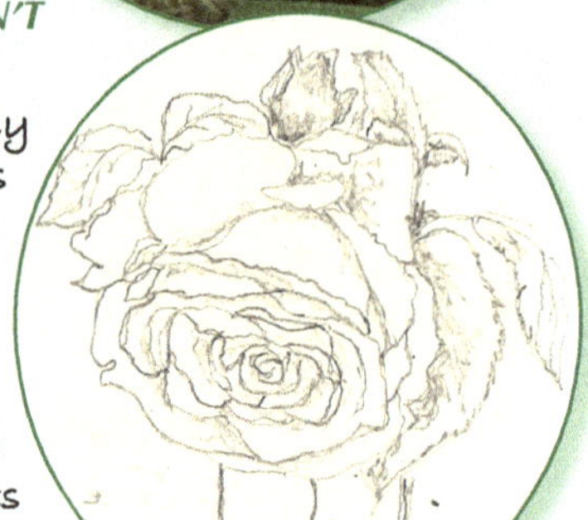

I'm not sure this statement, definitely not an apology, will convince anyone. It seems the matter is now closed, but I am sure that people will not forget!

Far away from the Downing Street rose garden, the roses in the Children's House garden still bloom, pale yellow, orange and white, with no-one to pick them and only occasional visits from us. I hope that when we eventually complete our purchase of this house, we can revive these ancient bushes.

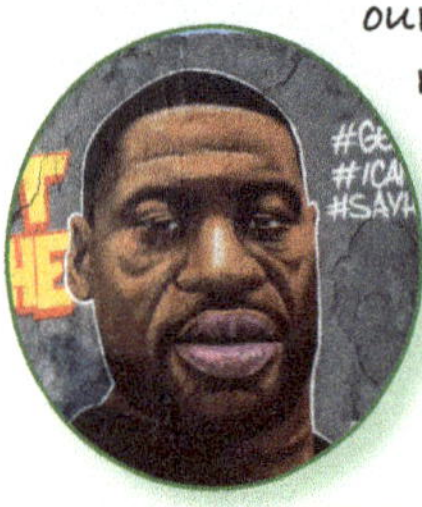

We hear today that an innocent black man, George Floyd has been killed by a white policeman in Minneapolis. This act of blatant racism, captured on phone cameras has triggered widespread protests in the USA and around the world.

Pandemic Day: 73/75   Lockdown 1: day 59/61

26th May 2020 Confirmed Cases: 150,294 Total deaths: 37,526

A life remembered on this day: Krishnapillai Yogan; age not known; Tower Hamlets, London.

A RARE BIT OF GOOD NEWS! REMDESIVIR, A DRUG THAT CAN SPEED UP THE RECOVERY TIME OF PATIENTS WITH COVID-19, IS MADE AVAILABLE THROUGH THE NHS.

Today we undertake another epic walk but without the previous heat anxiety. We start at Hulme End in Staffordshire, at Hulme Station, on the disused milk line that is now part of the Manifold Trail.

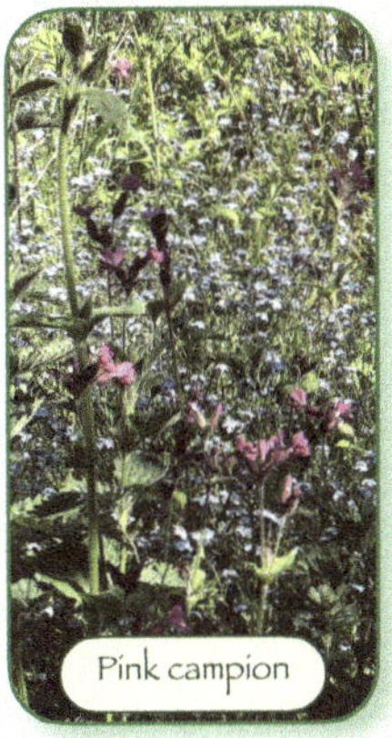
Pink campion

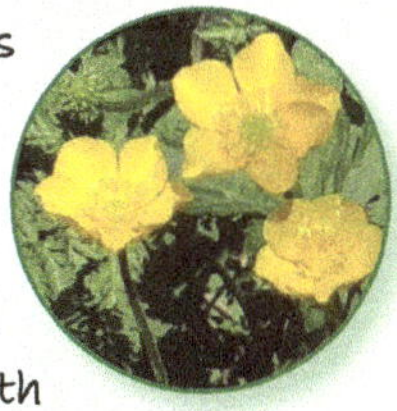

The coffee shop has reopened, so after snacks at the station cafe, we set off along the valley, crossing the river several times as it meanders through water meadows full of kingcups and other spring flowers, including great stretches of butterbur with huge rhubarb like leaves and strange dirty pink flowers – not the prettiest plant, but loved by butterflies!

Ash trees here have also suffered from chalara but everything else is in full spring leaf above the lacy cow parsley, dotted with ragged robin, speedwell, forget-me-nots and stitchwort. Winding along the valley bottom, we turn to walk up a shaded track, still following the river, but climbing consistently up the side of Ecton Hill, past caves, closed-off mine shafts and strange rock formations in the limestone walls. As we emerge into the sunshine again we stop for a picnic, sitting in a classic English water meadow, full of buttercups and long Spring grass, with May trees just beginning to bloom in the hedges.

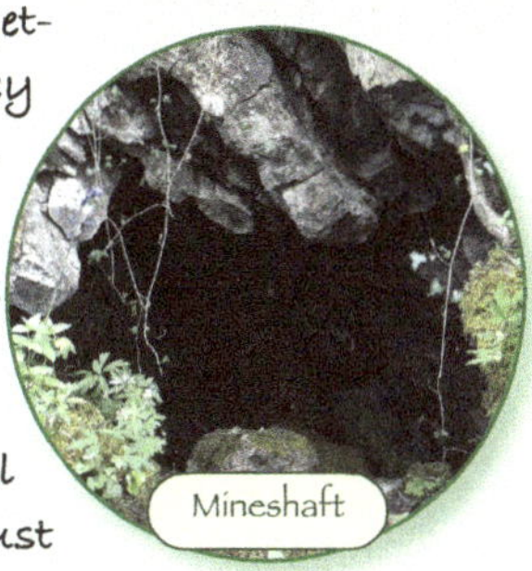
Mineshaft

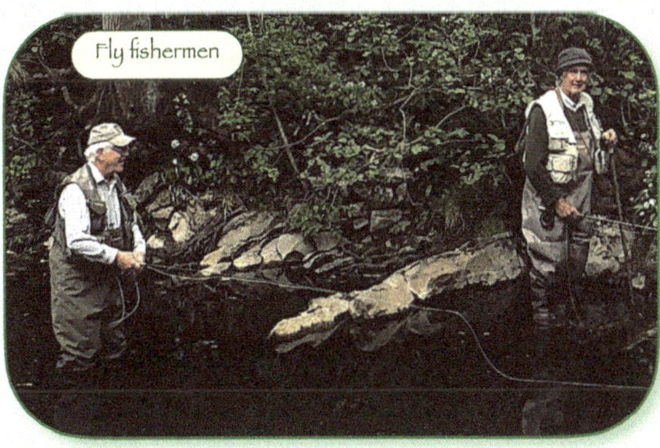
Fly fishermen

We stay in this sunny field, lazily watching two fishermen up to their thighs in the peaty brown water, unsuccessfully fly fishing for trout. We must find out more about this valley, with its strange buildings, ancient mine workings and evidence of an old, single track railway line.

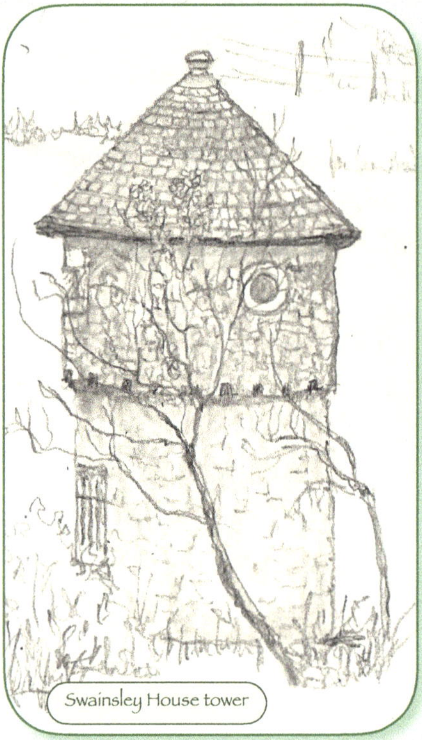
Swainsley House tower

A mysterious little round tower on the opposite bank reminds us of our own locked down lives, as we still spend most of our time locked in our own houses like characters in some storybook.

Leaving the meadow, the tower and the river, the track rises over sheep-grazed National Trust land, where 'stock' and their lambs wander freely across the limestone hills and vales or shelter, panting from the heat, in the shade of hawthorn trees.

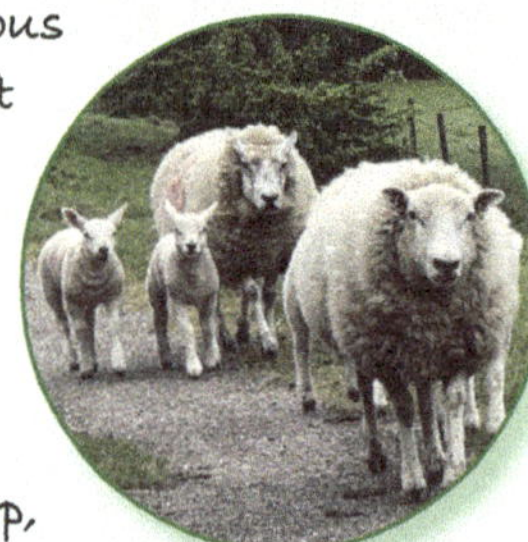

At Dale Farm, a quiet but evidently prosperous place, we turn left to climb through a shallow grassy valley towards the top of the low hills ahead, negotiating a steep, slippery, stony uphill path, washed away by winter rains rushing down from the Sugar Loaf Hill above. At the top, we are rewarded by flower filled upland hay meadows. Still climbing we cross land rich in mining history – stony heaps of spoil, fenced pits, and tunnels, trenches and dips in the hills.

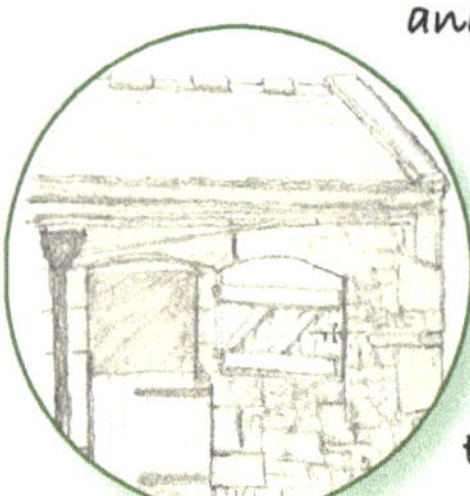

The well-marked but deserted path climbs over close-cropped grass, sprinkled with white-blossomed hawthorn bushes, and leads us to Broad Ecton Farm, where rare Longhorn cows and their calves lie about in the shady barn, too valuable to be outside in such hot, breathless weather!

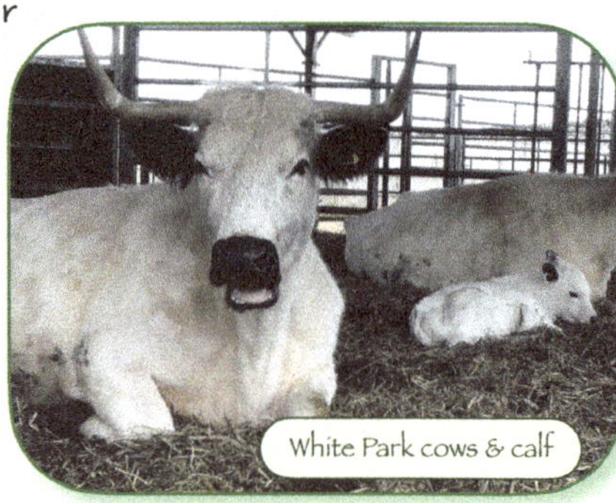
White Park cows & calf

Crossing another flowery meadow, reminiscing about the wildflower meadows in West Yorkshire, we enter a hill top field, home to sheep, lambs and swooping, croaking ravens.

At the summit, we are rewarded by a stupendous view over this oddly lumpy landscape, a mixture oof man-made soil heaps and natural formations.

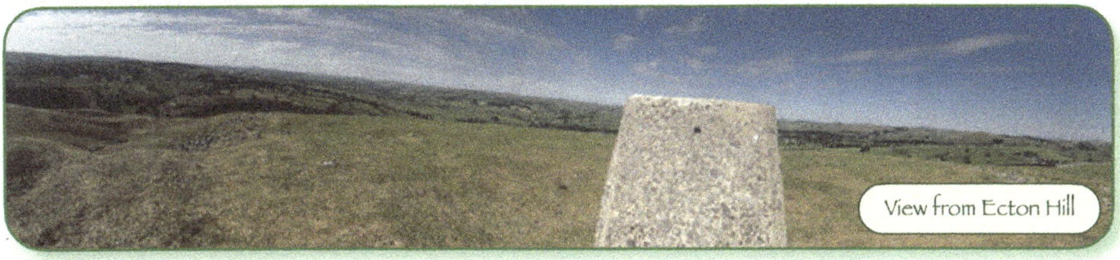

View from Ecton Hill

From the sheep-guarded trig point here we can see how far we have come, looking down into the valleys and distant villages where, somewhere, our car awaits us.

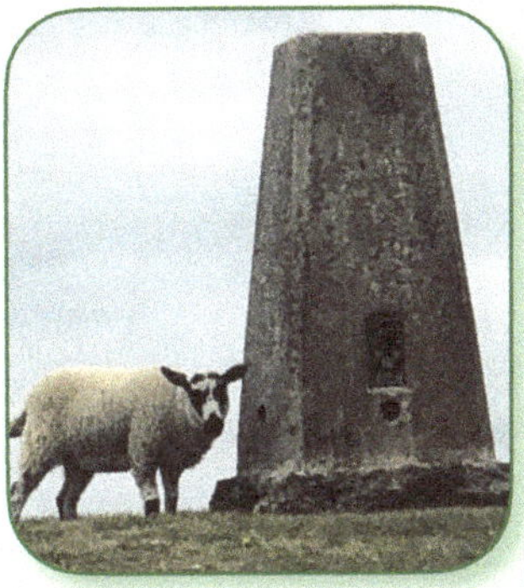

Finding a sign for Ecton, we begin our descent on a narrow, steep and slippery path, across flowery clearings of cropped dry grass, dotted with tiny yellow rock roses, and through thickets of shoulder-high, perfumed, yellow flowering, scratchy gorse.

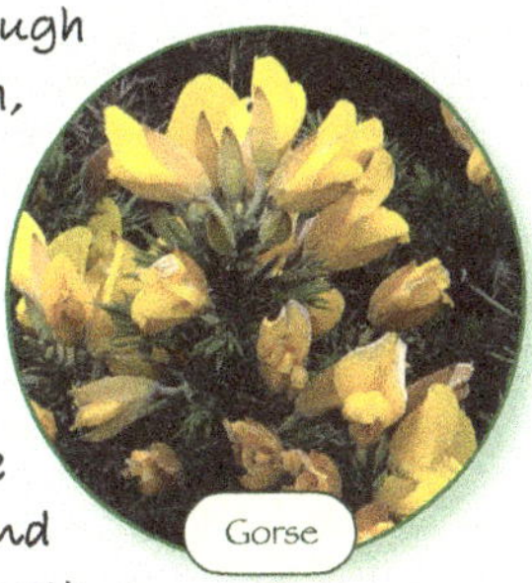

Gorse

From this high and steep path above the river, we can still see the whole valley spreading below us in the afternoon sun. This proves to be the most difficult part of our walk, and my knees and ankles begin to complain at the unusual angle of the path. I look enviously down into the shady trees in the valley, and the possibility of sitting on something without spikes!

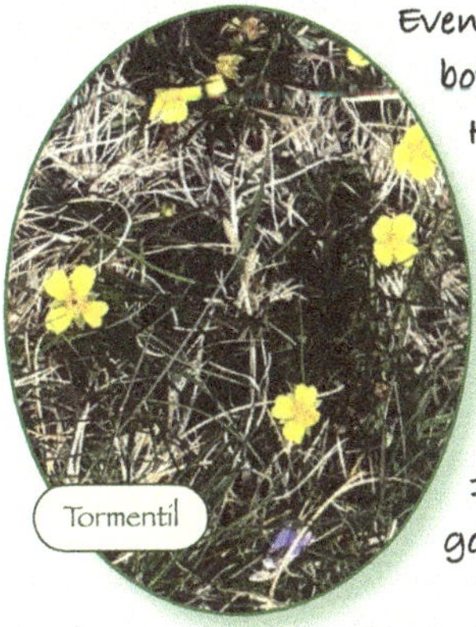

Tormentil

Eventually, scratched and tired, we are relieved to reach the bottom of the valley, climbing over the stile at Swainsley House, into the flowery river meadows and eventually along the hot river banks to the station car park.

We check our health app on the phone, and find we have walked 11.25km/7 miles - not bad going for two pairs of ancient legs!

and far beyond this remote valley: *Douglas Ross resigns as a junior minister in protest at the PM's defence of Dominic Cummings.*

Pandemic Day: 76 Lockdown 1: day 62

27/29 May 2020 Confirmed Cases: 151,826 Total deaths: 37,929

27th - THE PRIME MINISTER AGAIN PROMISES THAT A TEST AND TRACE SYSTEM WILL BE OPERATIONAL IN ENGLAND FROM TOMORROW (28th MAY). HE ALSO RULES OUT HOLDING AN INQUIRY INTO THE ACTIONS OF DOMINIC CUMMINGS.

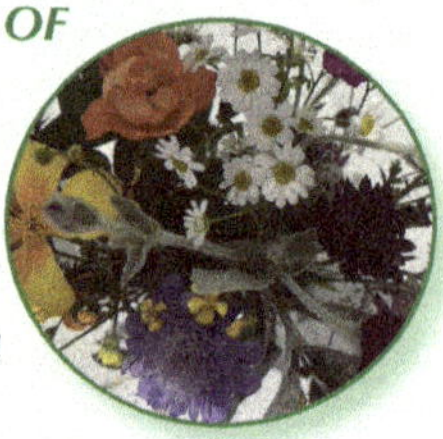

A quiet day at home recovering from yesterday's exertions. On these days I listen to the BBC, and maybe I am too much affected by the endless news stream, for I spend the morning depressed and angry. But then Sarah drops off a posy of flowers from her garden, which cheers me up.

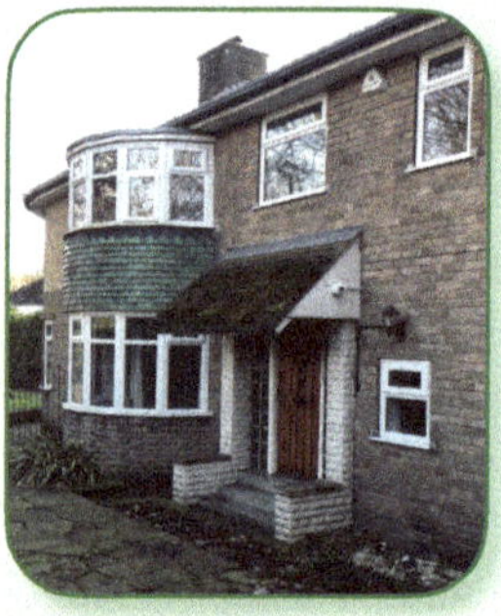

Then having decided to start looking at 'For Sale' boards again, we look at another possibility, and find a builder for the Children's House! This is very exciting!

28th - THE NEW TRACK AND TRACE SYSTEM FAILS TPO DELIVER AGAIN! DIDO HARDING TELLS MPS THE SYSTEM WILL NOT BE FULLY OPERATIONAL UNTIL THE END OF JUNE.

We join the tenth and final 'Clap for Carers' – a sad end to the idea, but the end of this salute to the NHS quite evidently does NOT imply that Covid is over!

29th - MEMBERS OF THE SAGE ADVISORY GROUP BREAK RANKS AND DISAGREE PUBLICLY WITH THE PROPOSED EASING OF THE LOCKDOWN.

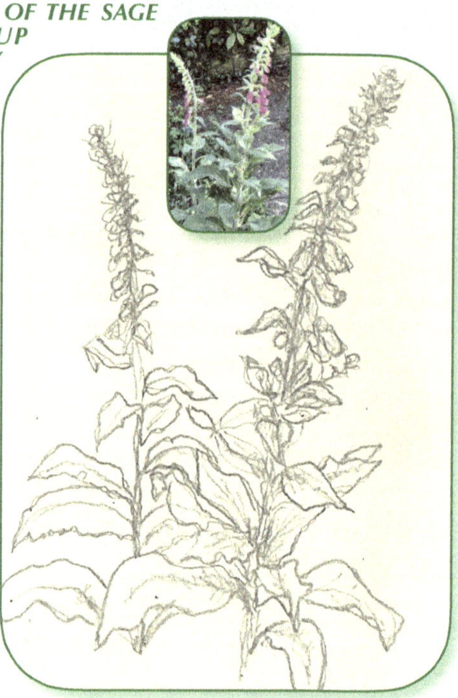

Foxgloves have seeded all over the garden, and are now blooming in spires of bright magenta.

We are now planning our tenth house move since we were married, and today sees a leap forward as we meet with the builder on site to discuss our plans for turning an institution into a home. He will start on Monday week!

A life remembered on this day: Julie Mott; 60; Recently retired Headteacher of a Special school; Rotherham.

Pandemic Day: 77/79 Lockdown 1: day 63/65

30th May 2020 Confirmed Cases: 151,856 Total deaths: 38,130

GOVERNMENT SCIENTIFIC ADVISERS WARN OF THE RISK ASSOCIATED WITH LIFTING LOCKDOWN RESTRICTIONS IN ENGLAND TOO EARLY, CITING THE STILL HIGH NUMBER OF CASES AND DEATHS. PROFESSOR JONATHAN VAN-TAM TELLS THE DOWNING STREET BRIEFING THAT BRITAIN IS AT A 'DANGEROUS MOMENT' AND PEOPLE'S RESPONSES MUST BE 'SENSIBLE AND PROPORTIONATE'.

A life remembered on this day: Rahima Bibi Sidhani; 68; Care Assistant; London.

It seems strange that as the SpaceX rocket takes off for the International Space Station, we are launching rockets into space when we can't even sort out problems on Earth! We enjoy an outside barbecue at Sarah's, and sit in the sun on her new terrace, watching the sunset over the Peaks, reflecting on this momentous time in our history. Later, I drive our two grandsons to meet a friend and hope they will stay safe as they depart for some desperately needed freedom.

Phill and I drive home in the moonlight, but with none of the promised sightings of the SpaceX rocket, although the sky is a clear, deep blue.

Our new wisteria frutescens is in full bloom, flowers purple or blue depending on the light. An impulse supermarket bargain, it seems to have been a good one, I hope it will be happy to be transplanted to the new house.

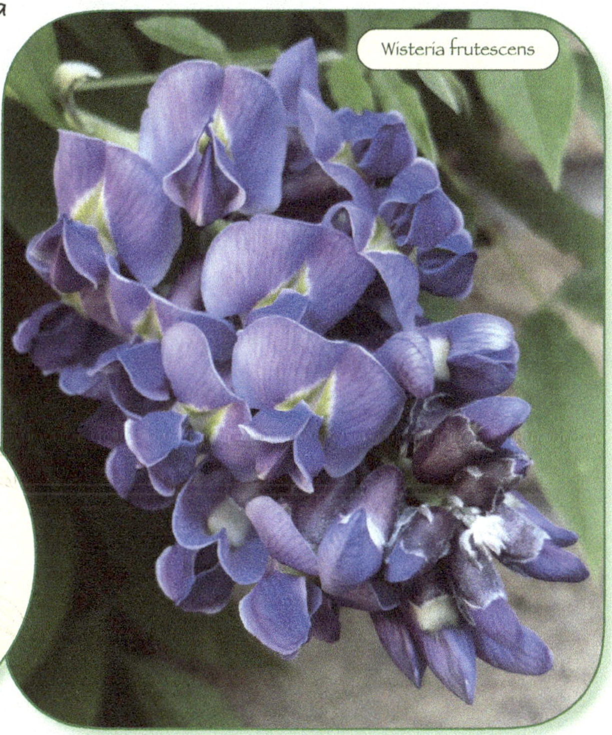
Wisteria frutescens

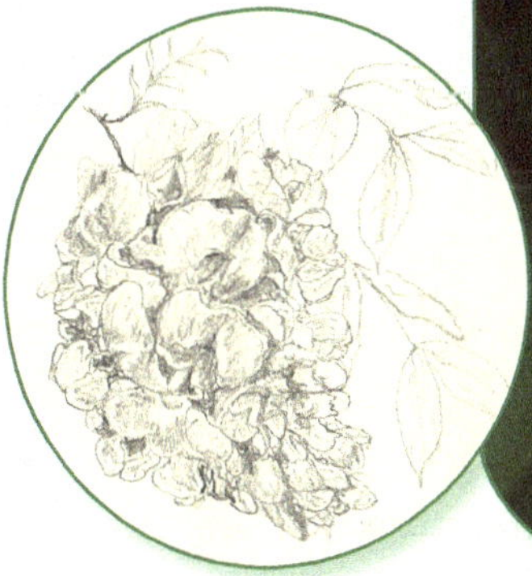

Pandemic Day: 80 Lockdown 1: day 66

31st May 2020 Confirmed Cases: 152,126 Total deaths: 38,219

ROBERT JENRICK TELLS THE DOWNING STREET DAILY BRIEFING HE IS 'REASONABLY CONFIDENT' CURRENT MEASURES ARE 'MANAGEABLE'.

On the last day of another month, we reflect on whether the decision to lift restrictions on travel and shopping is wise. The hot sunny weather continues, and everyone seems unclear about government advice on how to behave.

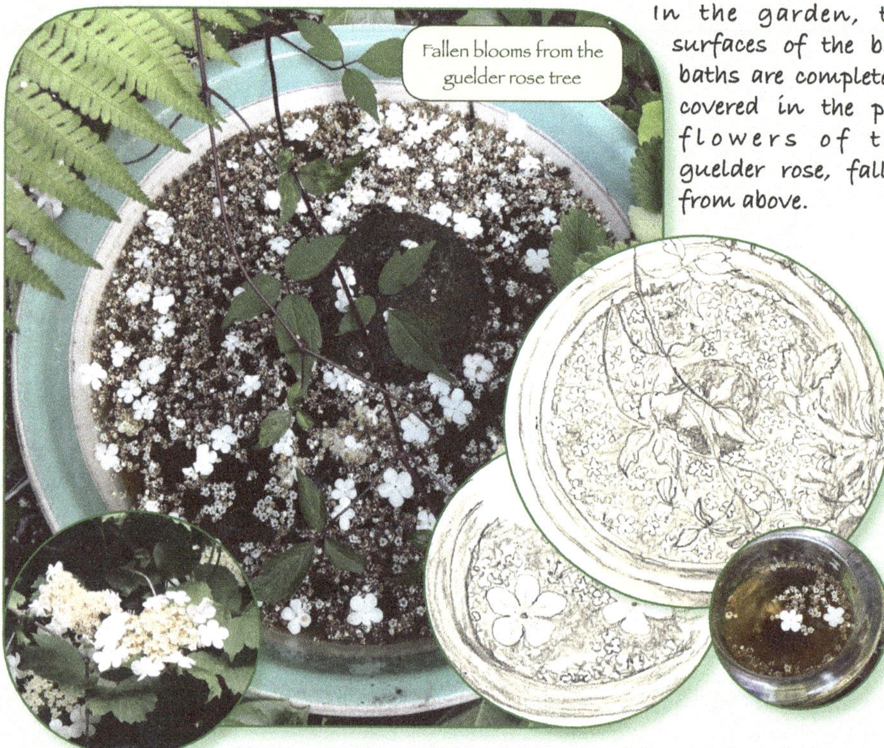

Fallen blooms from the guelder rose tree

In the garden, the surfaces of the bird baths are completely covered in the pale flowers of the guelder rose, fallen from above.

All morning, two big crows have been cawing loudly and flapping about just outside the house. Yesterday they were in next door's trees, and at 4am today in next door's garden – cawing so loudly that I have to get up and shut the windows. Eventually, as they settle down in the tree in the front of the house, the dawn chorus starts in earnest, and the house sparrows nesting in the gutter begin their monotonous cheeping just outside our bedroom window! I give in and get up, but may regret it this afternoon when I fall asleep in front of my computer!

It is a relief at last to be able to go out without feeling guilty, and by the end of the month, as rules begin to relax we really may be nearing the end of this unforgettable time.

Remembered today: Harry Toulman; 93; Retired; Manchester.

Pandemic Day: 81 Lockdown 1: day 67

May 2020 ends

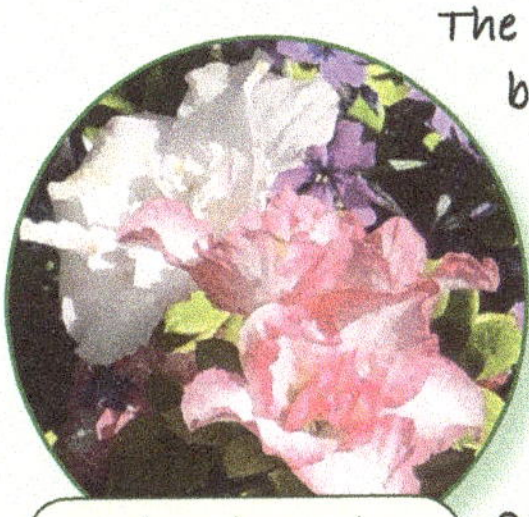

A pink & white rockery azalea in our new garden

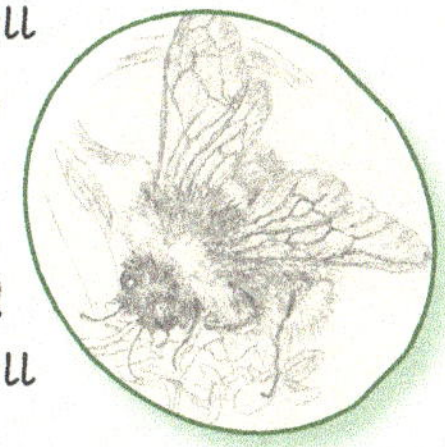

The weather continues to be good, a small bonus during this endless lockdown, and Spring reaches a flowery peak, with new leaves and bright blossoms on the trees, birds nesting, and insects buzzing and flapping, all unaware of human troubles.

Constant gloomy daily news about the virus, the alarming number of cases, and the unbelievable death toll have all brought home to everyone the tragedy underlying the stalking progress of this virus across the world.

At the beginning of May we are told to expect the lockdown to last much longer than we first expected, and by the end of the month there is little evidence of a slowing of the death rate. We know that people are getting tired and bored with their own company, teaching their own children, cooking their own meals, having limited exercise, and making their own entertainment.

Despite some relaxation of the rules, everyone is waiting anxiously to hear whether schools will re-open next month, and when we will be able to shop, go back to work, eat out or see relatives and friends after such a long time. It is no surprise that some people are beginning to push against the boundaries and bend the rules.

Despite the temptations, we do try hard to stay within the rules, and for the time being, to limit our outings to local parks and woods, and the now very busy Botanical Gardens.

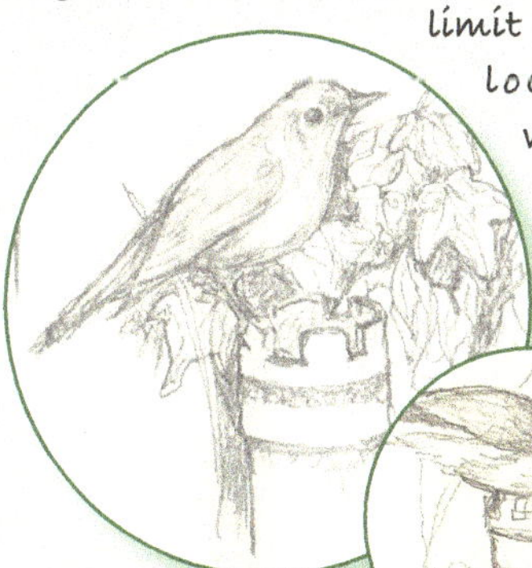

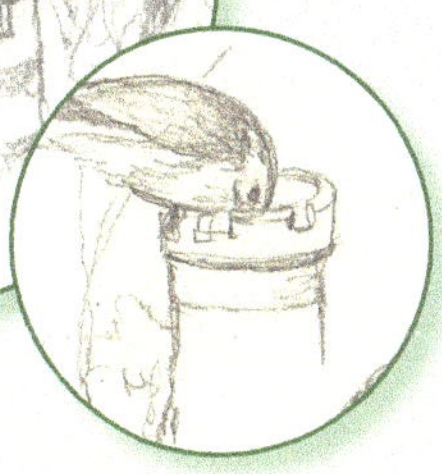

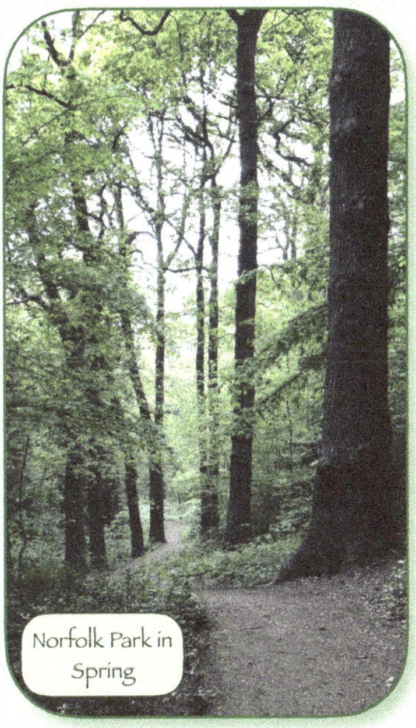

Norfolk Park in Spring

However, the call of the wild proves irresistible, and we follow a permitted hospital visit with the chance of a walk in the undisturbed blue seas of bluebells at a deserted Hardcastle Crags above Hebden Bridge. Emboldened by this day of nature, we then visit the woods above Ladybower Reservoir twice, watching as the trees and plants burst into leaf and flower. In this strange locked down time, we find more lost objects, children's shoes, books and what must be a favourite, much missed doll!

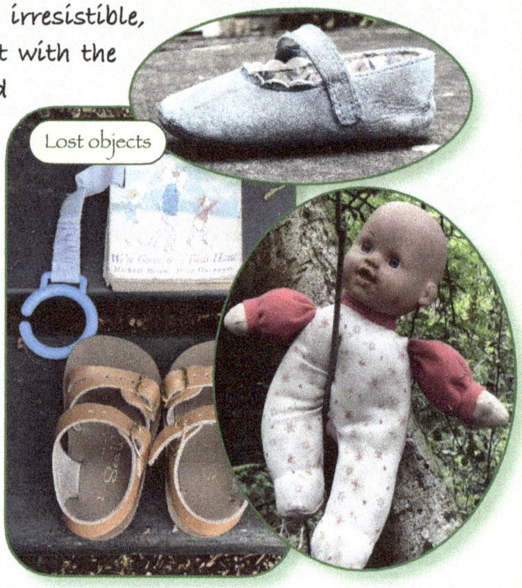

Lost objects

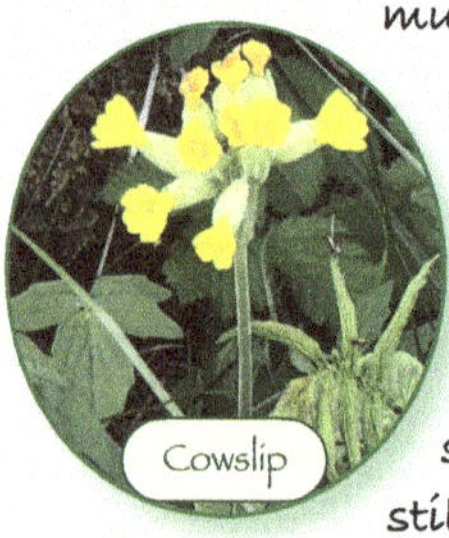

Cowslip

In the middle of this uncertain month, unlimited exercise and meeting up out of doors are allowed, garden centres are reopened, but schools are still closed and children are still taught (or not taught) at home.

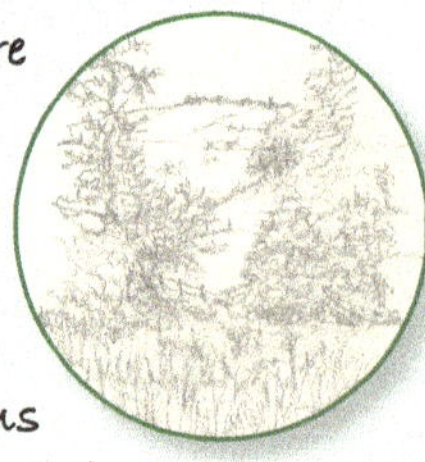

We follow our early May rule breaking with two legal long walks in the White Peaks of Derbyshire, as the Spring blooms decorate the verges and stream banks; Lathkill Dale is covered in flowers on one of a succession of the 'hottest days of the year', in 'socially distanced' company of families enjoying the spring heatwave. Next we explore the Manifold Valley and climb Ecton Hill above it, on deserted footpaths and through flowery meadows, although we do find that the very steep and slippery descent from Ecton Hill is surprisingly much more difficult than the climb to the top.

It is a relief at last to be able to go out without feeling guilty, and by the end of the month, as the rules begin to relax we feel that we really may be nearing the end of this lockdown which no-one will forget.

TOTAL UK CASES AND DEATHS: 31st May 2020

Total confirmed cases to date- 256,426 (up 79,636)

Total deaths to date - 38,219 (up 9,684)

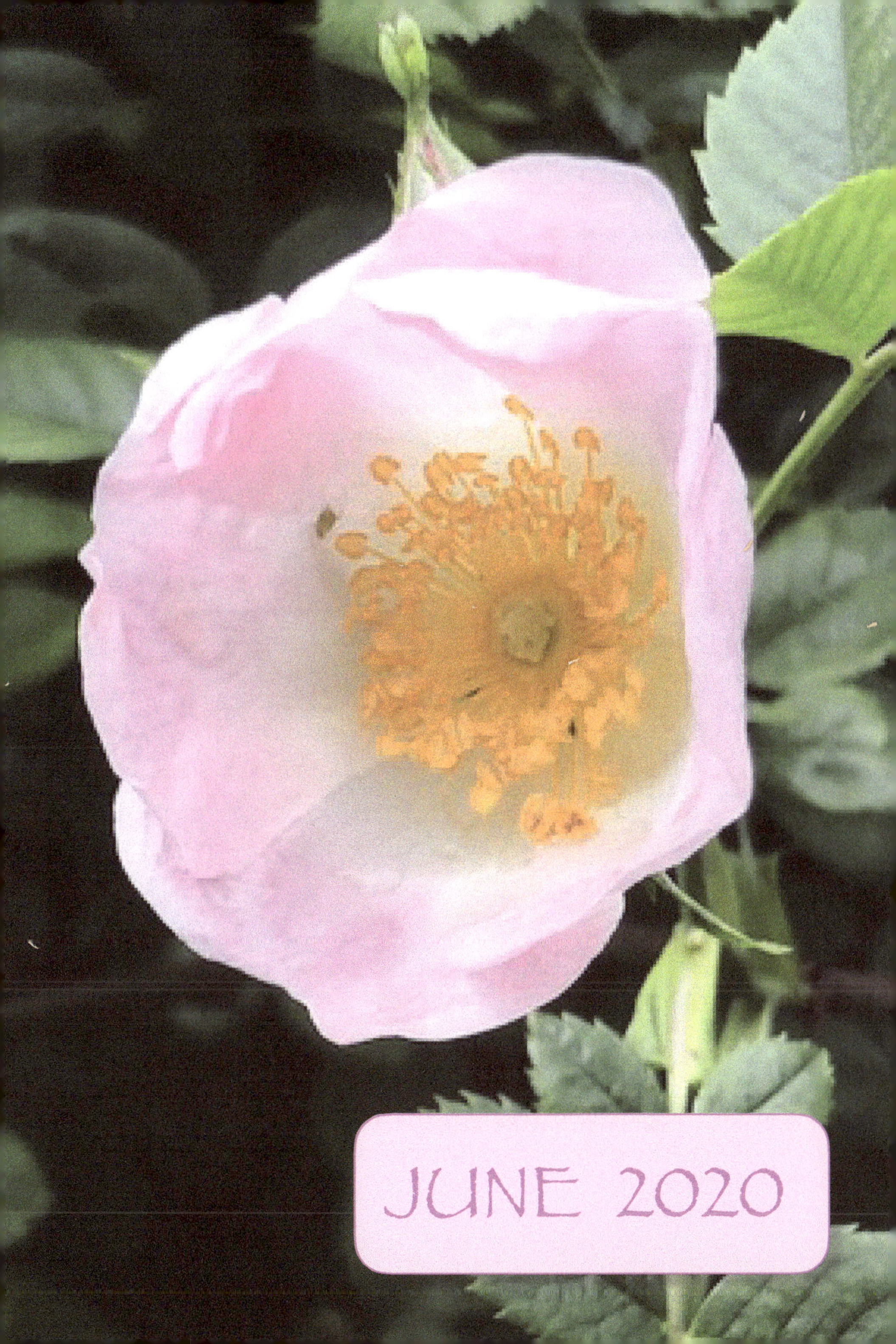
JUNE 2020

1st June 2020 Confirmed Cases:152,470 Total deaths: 38,354

THE PROHIBITIONS ON LEAVING HOME ARE REPLACED BY A LIMIT ON STAYING OVERNIGHT AWAY FROM HOME, WITH CERTAIN SPECIFIC EXCEPTIONS. GATHERINGS OF PEOPLE FROM MORE THAN ONE HOUSEHOLD ARE LIMITED TO 6 OUTDOORS, AND PROHIBITED ENTIRELY INDOORS, EXCEPT IN EDUCATION.

In the continuing sunshine, confusion and chaos reign. Lockdown measures begin to be eased, with children in England in Reception, Year 1 and Year 6 returning from home learning to sanitised and 'bubbled' classrooms.

However, during the seemingly endless heat wave, lockdown measures appear to have been neglected by many. Beaches are crowded, social distancing ignored, masks are abandoned and barbecues set fire to moorland and hillsides. Traffic seems to be almost back to normal, and the shielded are at last freed.

We go to Sarah's garden for alfresco coffee and to admire her amazing floriferous yellow tree peony, each perfect flower like a silky golden cup, a real contrast to the tree's leathery, hairy leaves.

A life remembered on this day: James Reid; 77; Retired electrician; Widnes; UK.

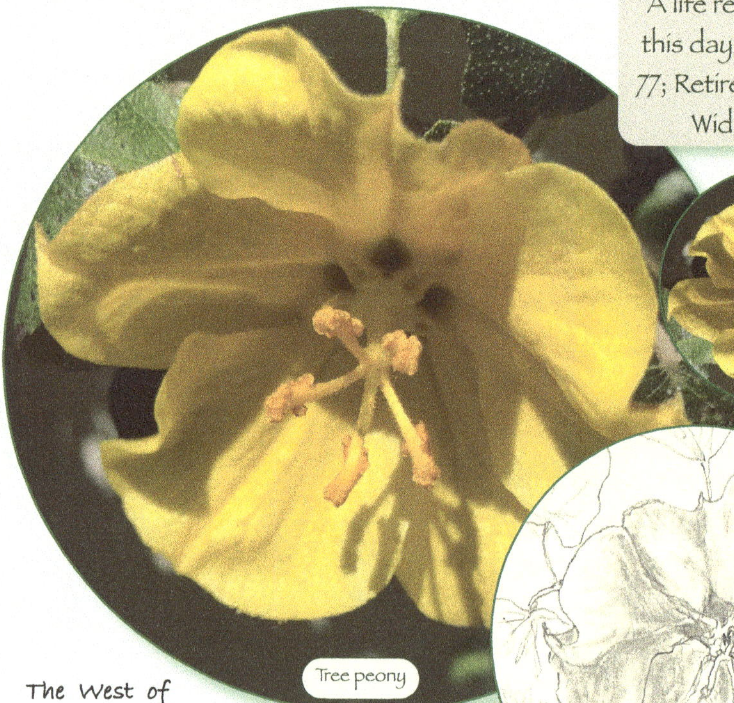

Tree peony

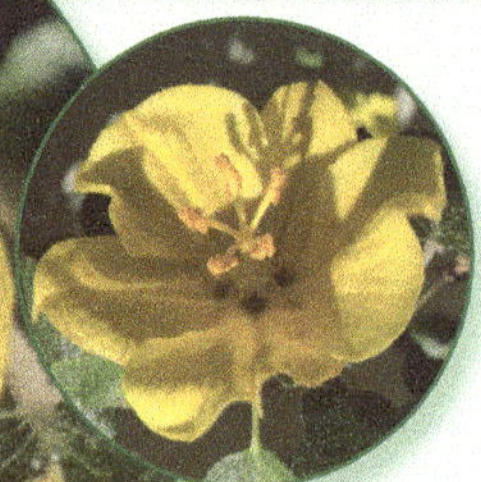

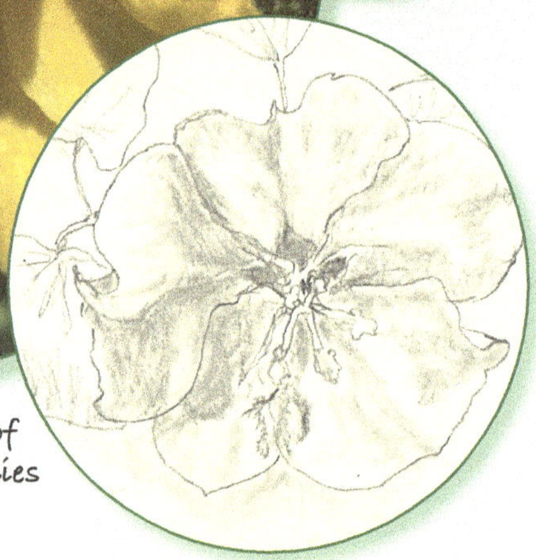

The West of the USA continues to burn in forest fires that are now out of control, while Donald Trump still denies climate change.

Pandemic Day: 82 Lockdown 1: day 68

2nd June 2020 Confirmed Cases:153,276 Total deaths: 38,522

THE CHAIR OF THE UK STATISTICS AUTHORITY REBUKES MATT HANCOCK IN A CONTINUATION OF HIS 11th MAY CRITICISM OF THE GOVERNMENT'S HANDLING OF TESTING DATA, SAYING THE FIGURES ARE 'STILL FAR FROM COMPLETE AND COMPREHENSIBLE' AND APPEAR TO BE AIMED AT SHOWING 'THE LARGEST POSSIBLE NUMBER OF TESTS, EVEN AT THE EXPENSE OF UNDERSTANDING'.

We decide to try another version of last week's long walk over the Ecton Hills, having consulted OS maps and local guide books.

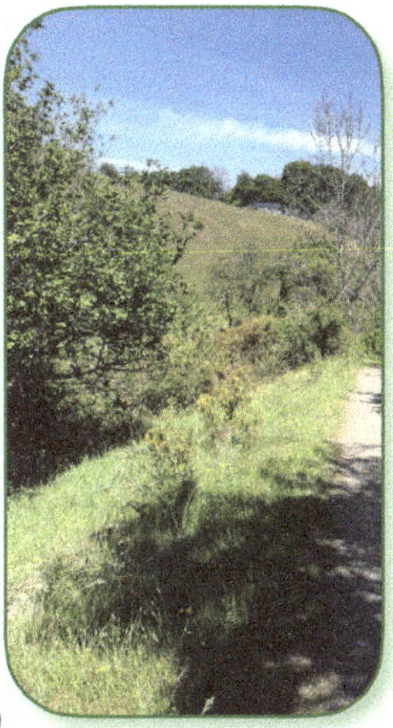

It is extremely hot and sunny, so we have cool clothing, hats and plenty of water with us. Sadly, when we reach Hulme End, we find the café closed, so we return to Hartington for coffee and biscuits, corncockle and marigold plants, then drive back to Hulme End station for the walk, following the river path along the disused milk line track (parched) and the water meadows (wilting) in a final burst of campion, buttercups and forget-me-nots. Hogweed flowers burst from their papery coverings, ox-eye daisies are floods of white, and spiky thistles rear their green fuzzy heads, soon to break into purple flowers. Bugle and speedwell make a blue haze in the verges among the waning foam of cow parsley, and some fields are still yellow with buttercups.

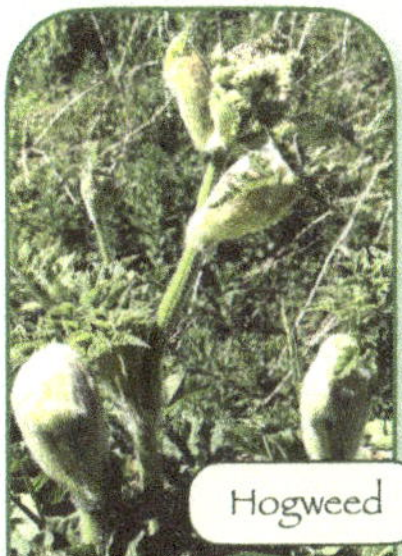

Hogweed

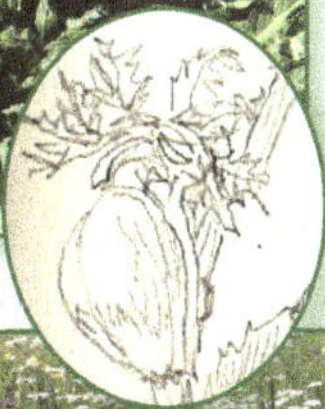

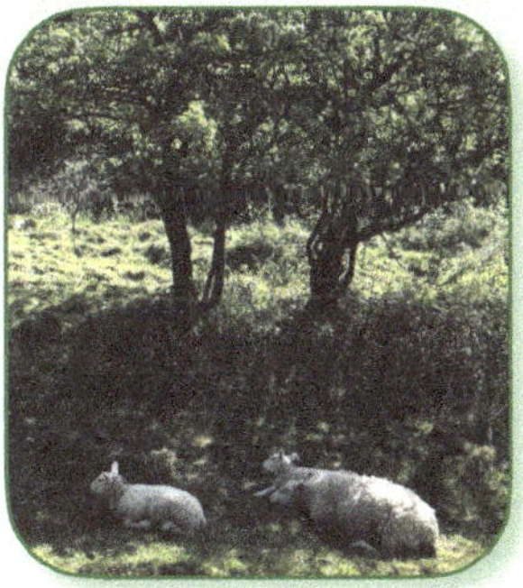

On we walk, along the road and up the sloping hillside path which passes under hawthorn, hazel, maple and sycamore, and more and more dead ash trees, some paint-marked for felling.

Emerging onto the close-cropped meadows, sheep and lambs lie panting in the shade of the May trees, but we decide to continue walking to the top of the hill before stopping for a mid-day rest and picnic in the hottest part of the day.

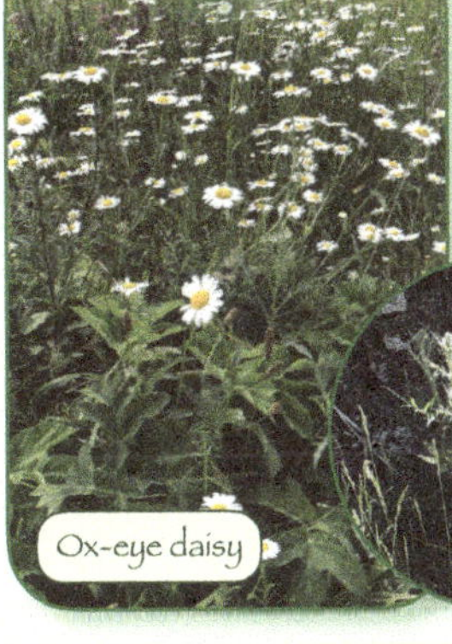

Ox-eye daisy

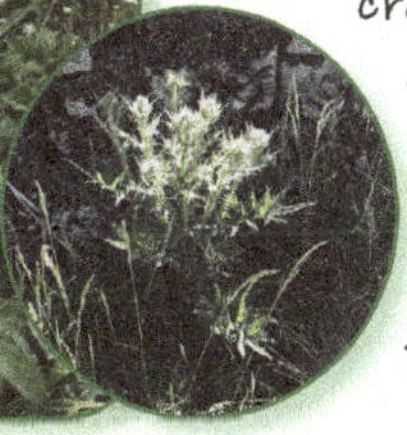

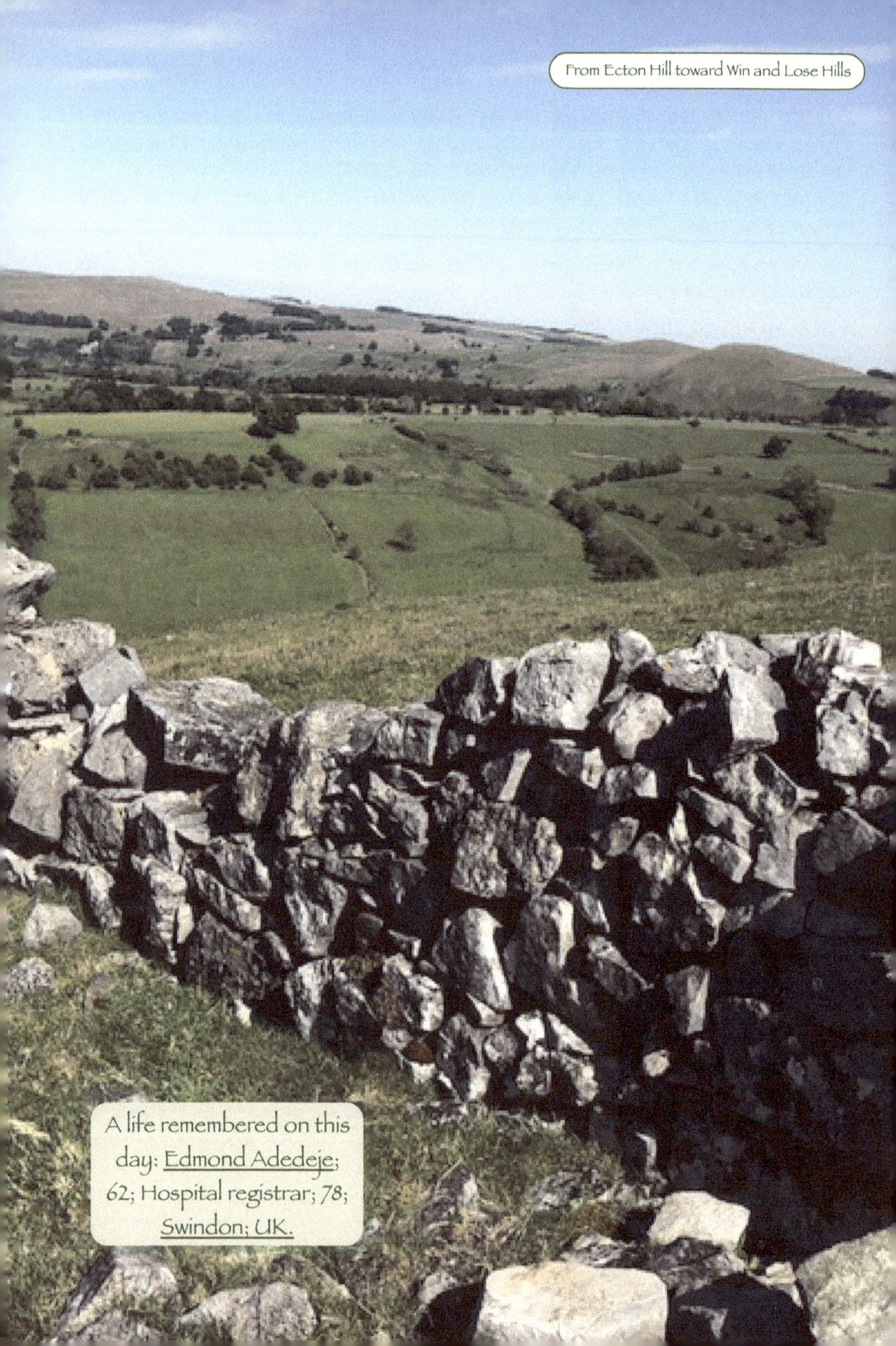

From Ecton Hill toward Win and Lose Hills

A life remembered on this day: Edmond Adedeje; 62; Hospital registrar; 78; Swindon; UK.

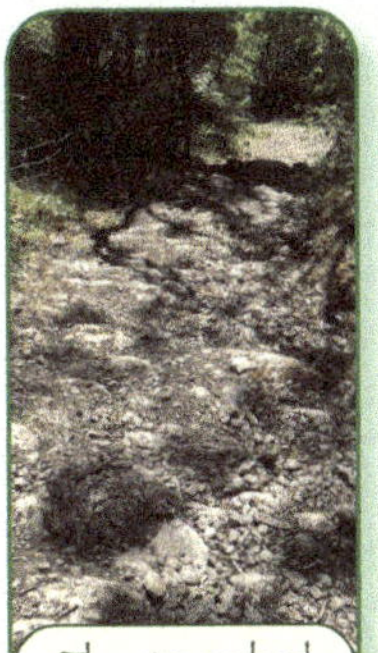

The stream bed

Passing Dale Farm once more, we climb the sheep studded valley and negotiate the rolling, white, sliding-stone stream bed of a path to pass the Sugar Loaf. The meadows above this point are temptingly shady, flower-bedecked and green, but we keep going along hot sheep tracks, where invisible lost lambs call for their mothers and hopeful crows wheel in the cloudless sky. All the way we are accompanied by trills, chirps, cheeps and squawks of wild birds in the bushes.

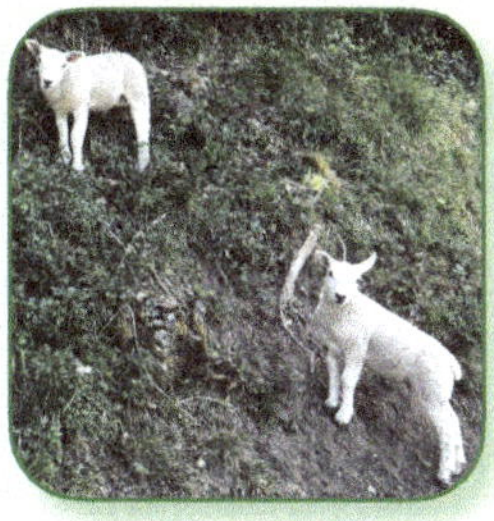

At the top of Ecton Hill, we find a shady tree on the skyline where we can rest for a couple of hours, serenaded by magpies, and once, by the faint croak of a distant raven high above the hills beyond the trig point. At about 3:30 we resume our walk, determined to find a better way down the steep north-eastern side of the Ecton Hill. We climb up above Ecton Farm to the trig point, and using map, guide book and compass, we find what appears to be a better, less slippery way down, although we are soon proved wrong!

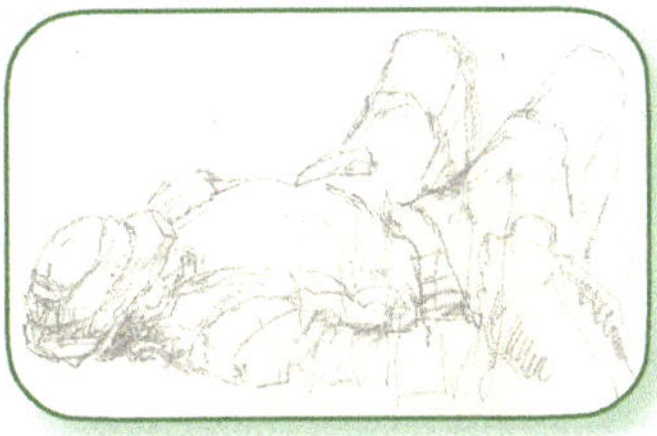

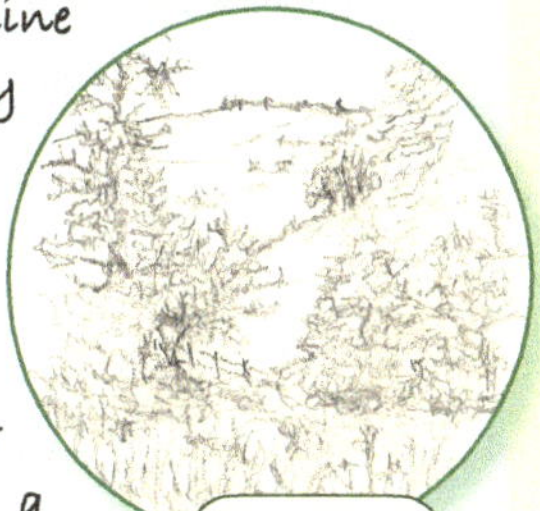

Picnic view

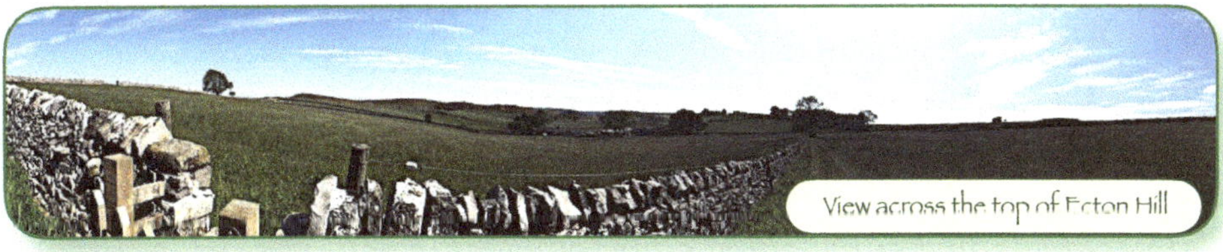

View across the top of Ecton Hill

The upland grass path crosses slopes starred with purple thyme, rock rose, milkwort, blue speedwell, and tiny yellow vetch, proves an easier, certainly less prickly route than the last time, but still very steep, dry and slippery. Even the grass slides from under our boots, threatening to cast us rolling down the hot, steep slopes as we carefully slip and balance our careful way down.

This long and imposing hill has a mining history, not just in the carefully fenced mine openings and spoil heaps, but in the buildings still standing and maintained by enthusiasts.

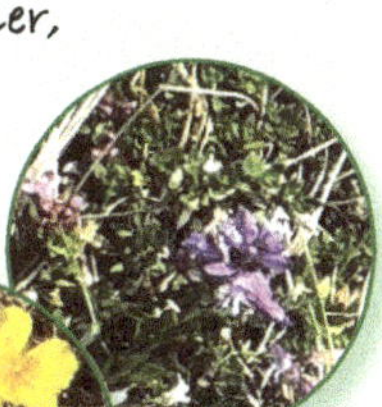

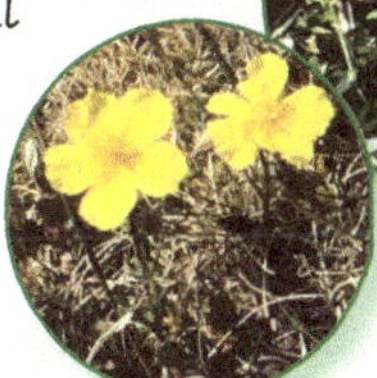

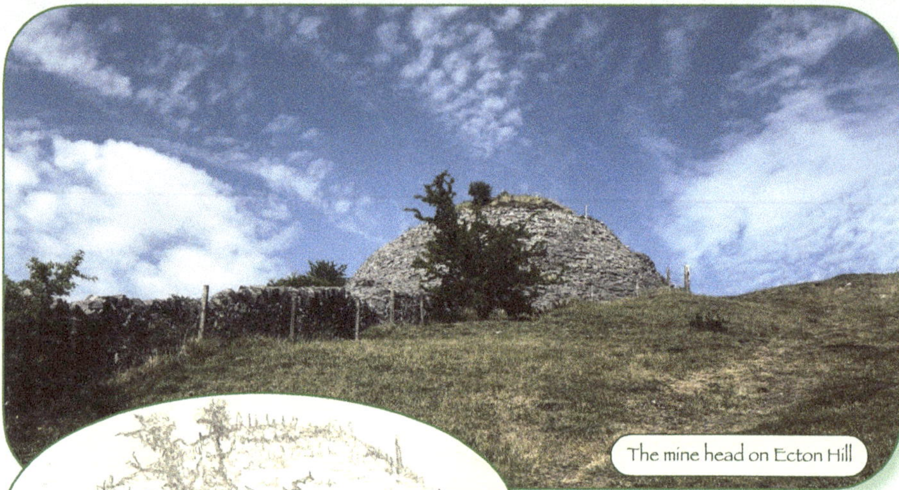

The mine head on Ecton Hill

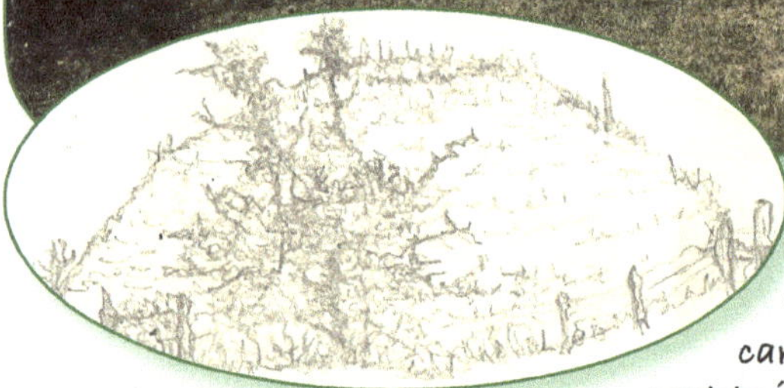

We continue down, past the historic copper mining works, Ecton Engine House, and the carefully constructed stone dome next to it, which must have been part of the structure, possibly housing the original winding shaft. This site merits another visit at a later date, but certainly on a cooler day.

A life remembered: Leonard Gibson; 78; NHS Sheffield; UK.

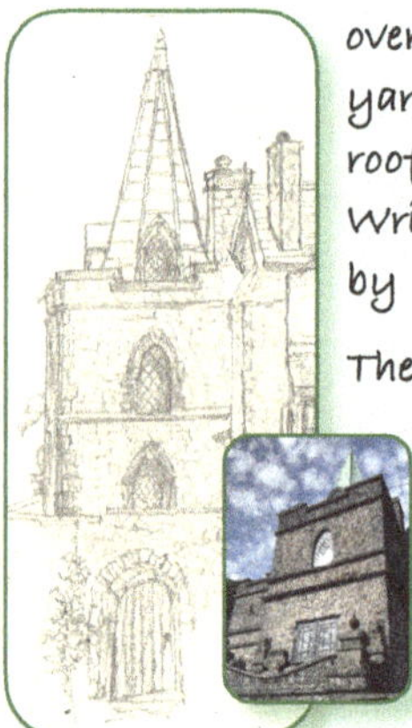

Lower down this slip-sliding slope we climb over a mossy wall to find ourselves in the yard of Castle Folly with its copper-clad roof – a cross between Frank Lloyd Wright, Hogwarts and a Disney castle, originally built in 1933 by a local MP, and now home to a mining history group.

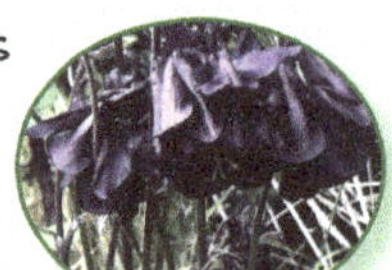

There is no sign of anyone awake on this baking hot, drowsy afternoon, so we continue down the rough, white stoned road, nicely reflecting the afternoon heat, and lined with bee-filled purple columbines and the blue-eyed flowers of greater forget-me-nots.

Along the sweltering milk line path to the car park, we return home from our walk through the evening sun, having met not one human for the whole of this sunny green day.

Pandemic Day: 83 Lockdown 1: day 69

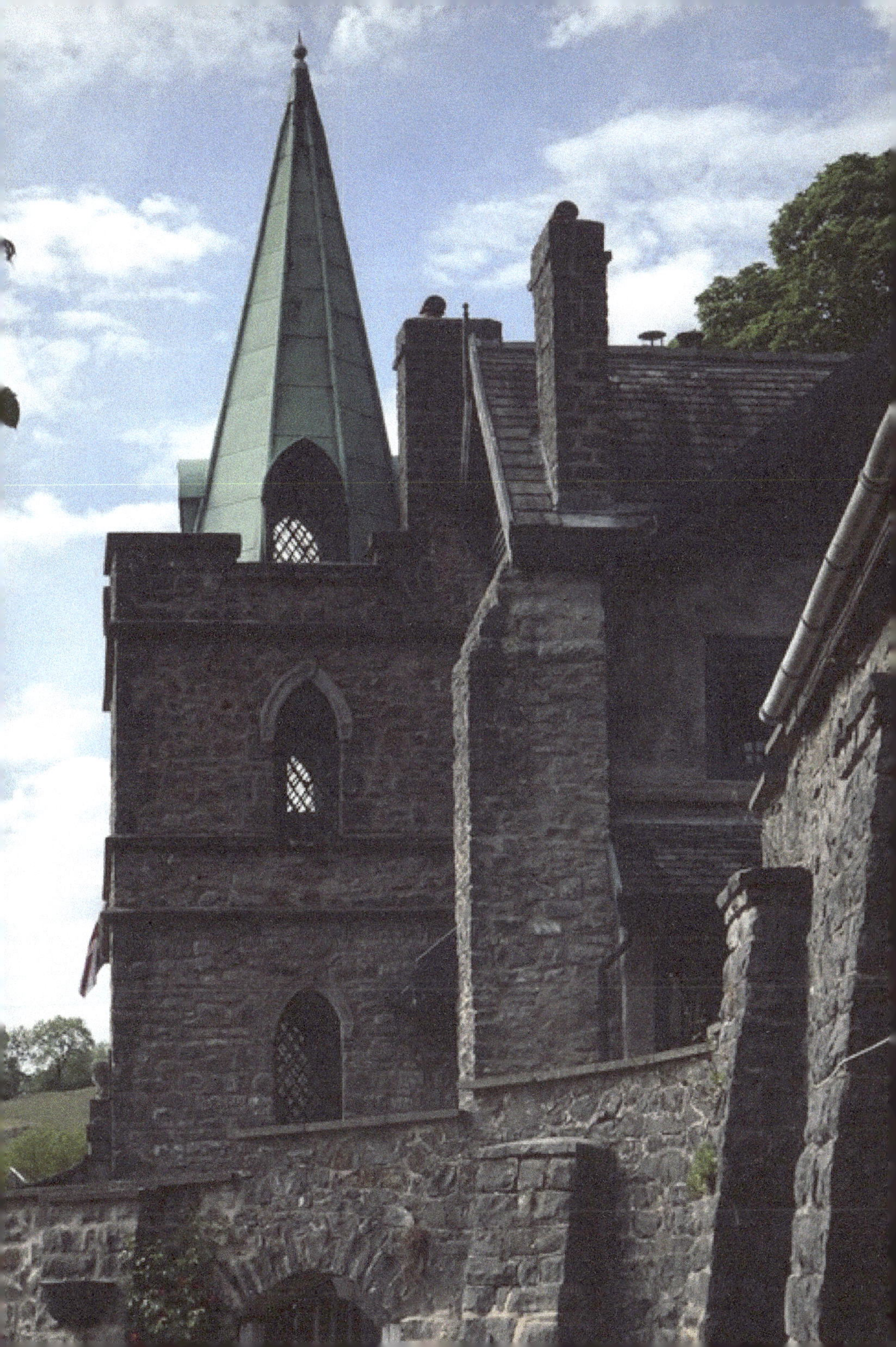

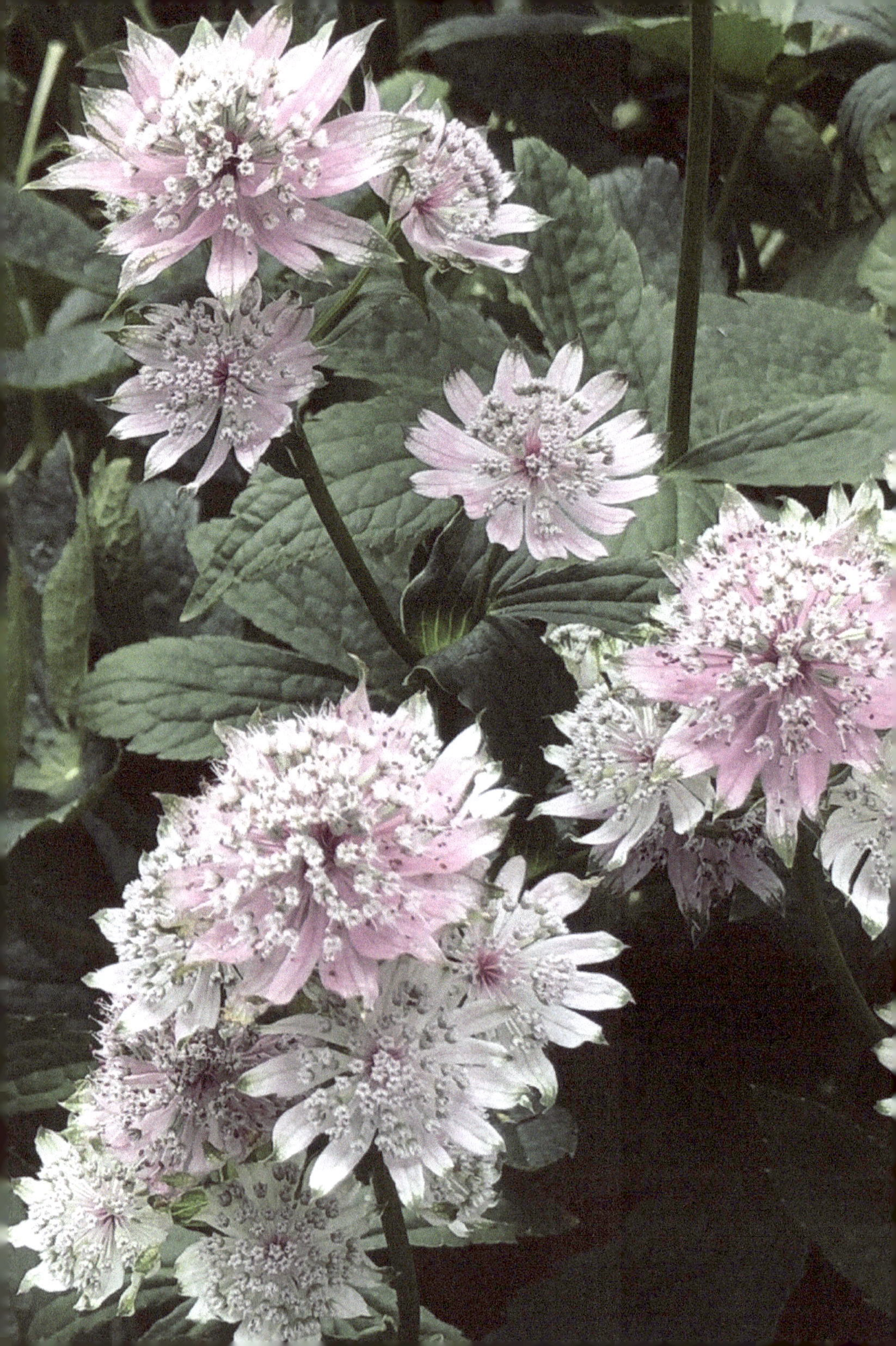

3rd/5th June 2020 Confirmed Cases: 154,258 Total deaths: 38,934

3rd - THE HOME SECRETARY CONFIRMS PLANS TO INTRODUCE A 14 DAY QUARANTINE PERIOD FOR ARRIVALS TO THE UK.

The recent heatwave is coming to an end. Our walk yesterday was a real 'head clearer', but our feet are now firmly back on the wet ground, refreshed but still frustrated by the pace of everything we want to do. I begin to think about the practicalities of the move.

Our daughter Sarah still comes and goes like a friendly elf, with gifts of food and flowers. Other visitors are not just infrequent, they are non-existent.

4th - We walk to the bank to transfer funds for the purchase of the new house. Deserted school playgrounds and quiet gardens indicate the national reluctance to send children back to school.

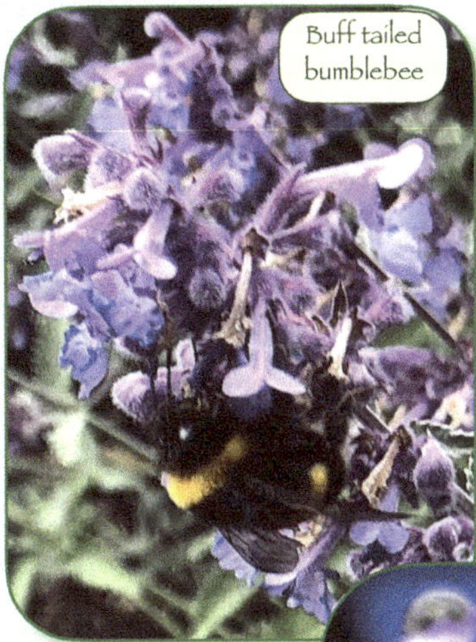

Buff tailed bumblebee

On the way home, I venture into a supermarket for the first time in 70 days. I feel anxious but also keen not to waste a 'shopportunity'.

5th - COVID DEATHS IN ENGLAND PASS 30,000. ORIGINALLY, THE GOVERNMENT SAID 20,000 DEATHS WOULD BE 'A GOOD RESULT'.

This day has great significance for us. We exchange contracts and complete on the purchase of the house.

Bees visit the thyme flowers, and raindrops balance on the tall purple heads of Verbena .

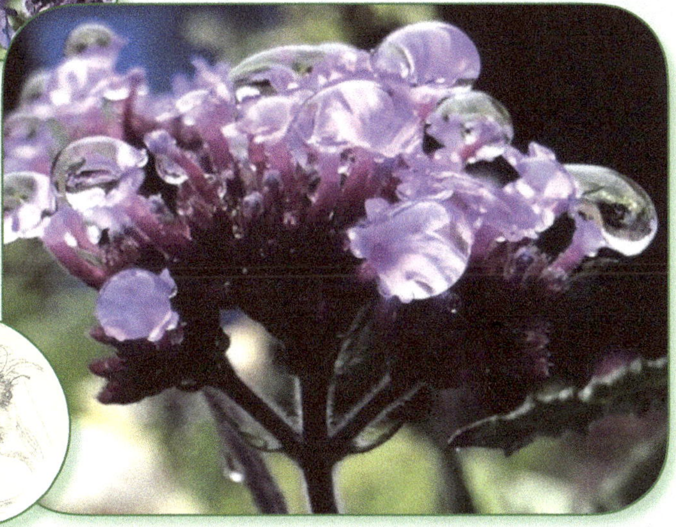

A life remembered today: Noach Dear; 66; Supreme Court Judge; New York.

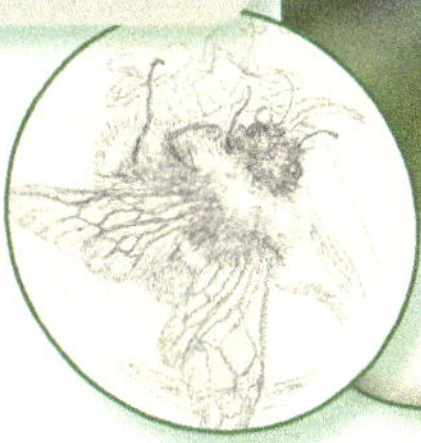

Pandemic Day: 84/86 Lockdown 1: day 70/72

MANCHESTER COUNCIL ADVISES SCHOOLS NOT TO OPEN NEXT WEEK. THE GOVERNMENT DECIDES, WITH NO CONSULTATION, THAT ALL NHS STAFF MUST WEAR MASKS.

Meanwhile, we meet with Tom the builder at the Children's House, to discuss major structural alterations to the house, both inside and out.

The lawn is full of orange flowering fox-and-cubs, much loved by our resident bumble bees.

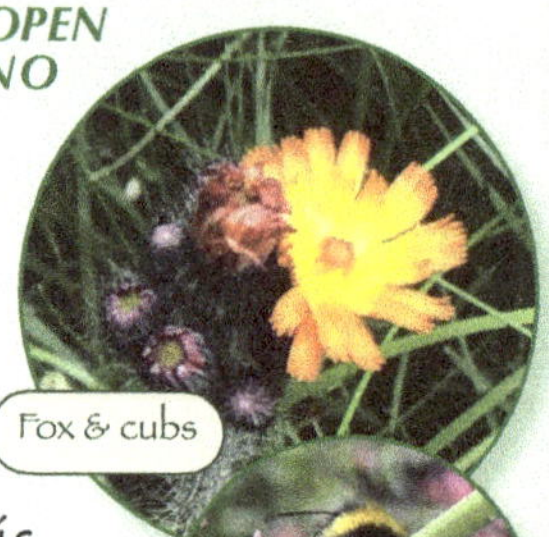
Fox & cubs

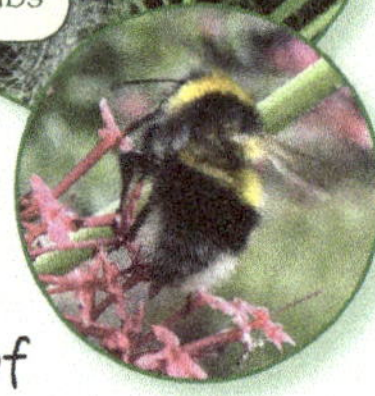

7th - The death rate is not coming down, and the virus is now mutating. The R rate is rising and is already over 1 in the North West and South West of England. Health chiefs say there should be no further easing of restrictions before test and trace has been proved to work. It now seems possible that face coverings will be mandatory in all public places; schools will remain closed, and universities may delay their start until 2021.

Two brothers remembered: Ghulam & Raza Abbas; 59 & 54; Newsagents; Newport.

7th - At a Black Lives Matter demonstration, a statue of Edward Colston, the slave trader, was pulled down and thrown into Bristol Harbour. In his life, he trafficked a shameful 80,000 men, women and children to work in the southern states of America.

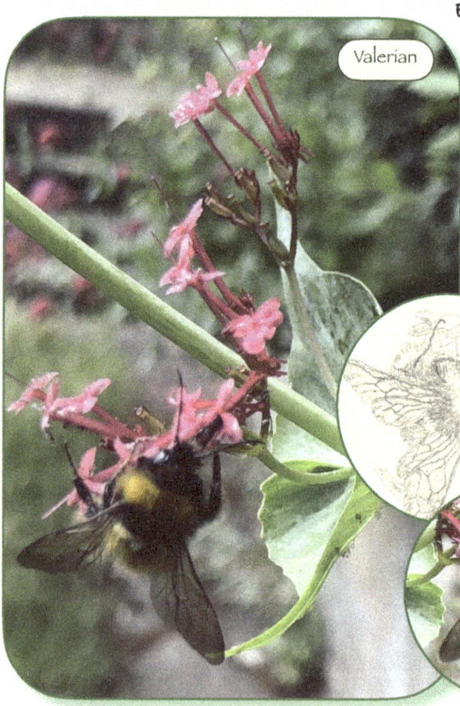
Valerian

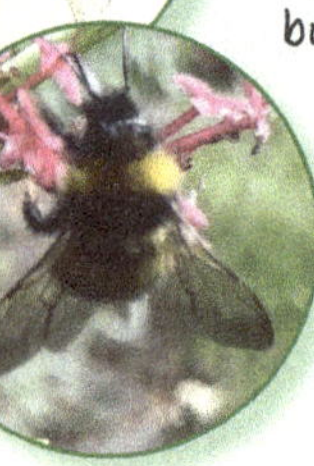

In a parallel universe, the bees work late, visiting the last few bright pink flowers of valerian sprouting from the cracks in the garden wall at the Children's House. This plant is one of the varieties that is both a garden plant and a weed. It grows wild in the 'stone hedges' of Devon and Cornwall, but is also sold in garden centres. It holds a great attraction for pollinators in the late summer, and seeds freely in any soil, sometimes becoming a bit of a nuisance.

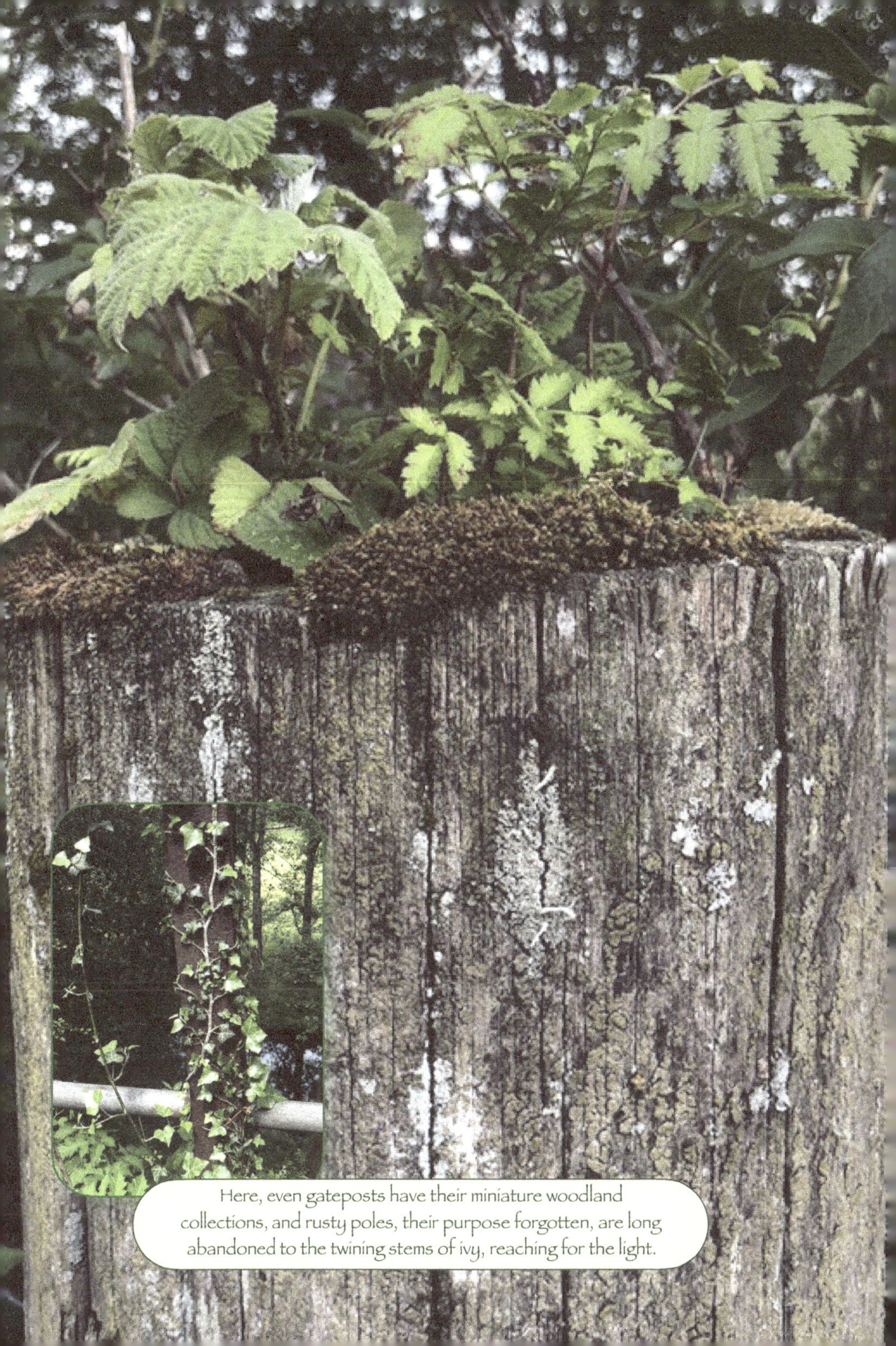

Here, even gateposts have their miniature woodland collections, and rusty poles, their purpose forgotten, are long abandoned to the twining stems of ivy, reaching for the light.

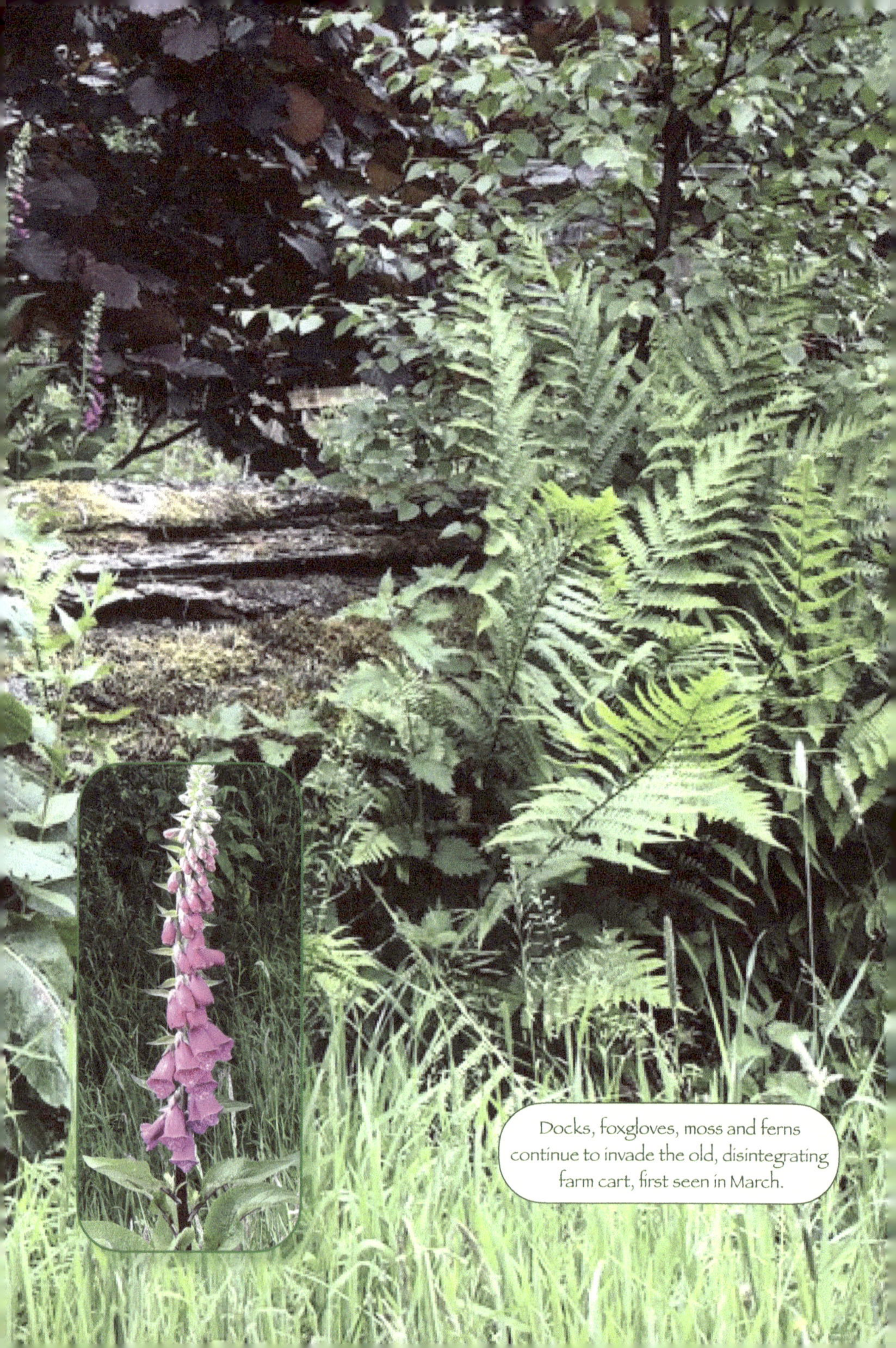

Docks, foxgloves, moss and ferns continue to invade the old, disintegrating farm cart, first seen in March.

9th June 2020 Confirmed Cases: 155,714 Total deaths: 38,387

THE UK GOVERNMENT DROPS PLANS FOR ALL PRIMARY SCHOOL CHILDREN TO RETURN TO SCHOOL BEFORE THE END OF THE SUMMER TERM, DEEMING IT UNFEASIBLE.

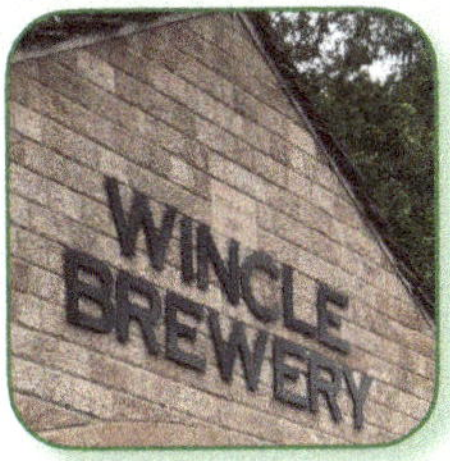

As continuing 'harmless criminals' we return to the Dane Valley and the walk we last made on 19th March, before lockdown and as one of the very first entries in this diary.

There are small signs of life in the village, but everything is still shut down, including the pub and the trout farm by the river.

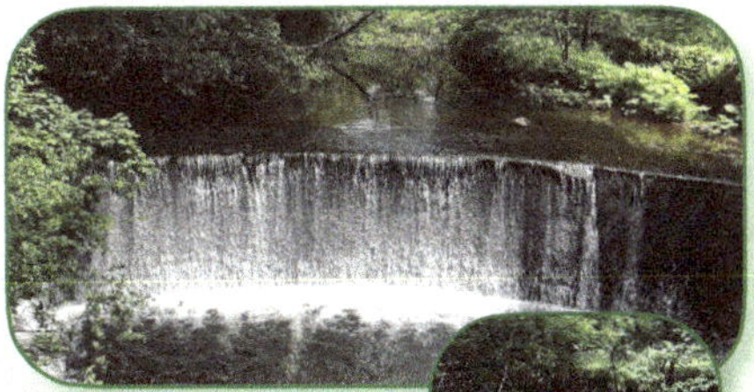

Since our last walk in the valley, the whole countryside has burst into pink, gold and green, fields by the river are dusted with buttercup yellow and campion magenta, and after lockdown closures, the brewery is open again, but just for take-away sales. Concerned that we may not return before closing time, Phill puts a crate of beer in the boot of the car.

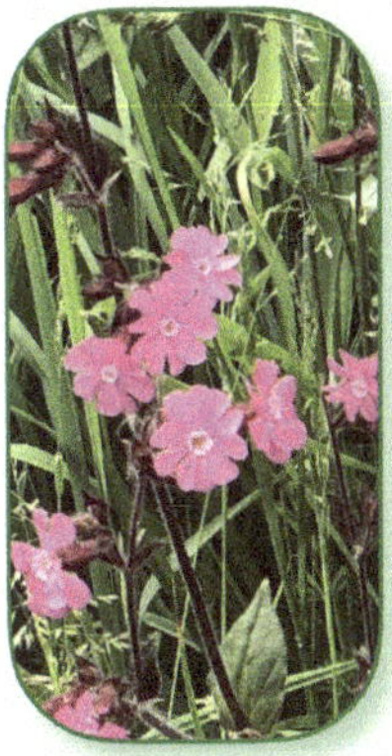

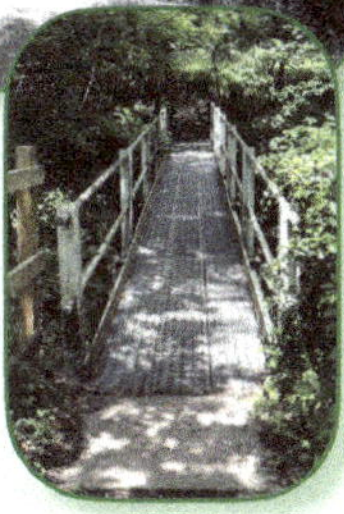

The weather is cloudy but not cold, ideal for a long-ish walk, and we set off through the water meadows to the old canal. The birds are singing everywhere, and we are accompanied by a wide range of insects, bees, flies, midges, wasps, hover flies and others, taking advantage of the flowering of early summer. Bright pink campion, pale pink ragged robin and blue-eyed speedwell punctuate the banks of buttercups. Tall heads of pink hogweed flowers are decorated with the iridescent wings and bodies of insects.

Ragged robin

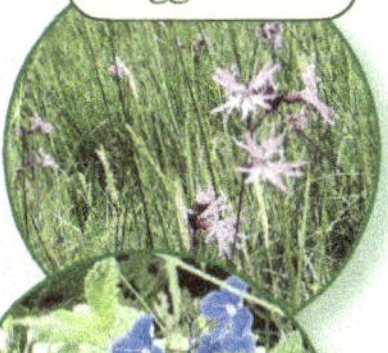

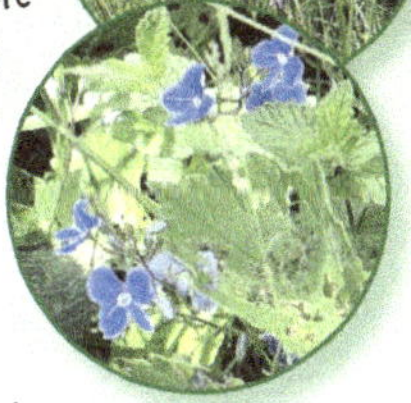

This valley and the hills above are home today to hundreds of tall foxgloves in uniform, white-spotted magenta, growing and flowering in every hollow, by every gatepost, as well as here by the disused canal. They are beginning to open their tubular blooms for the bumblebees, which are struggling into each flower and reversing out again in buzzing business.

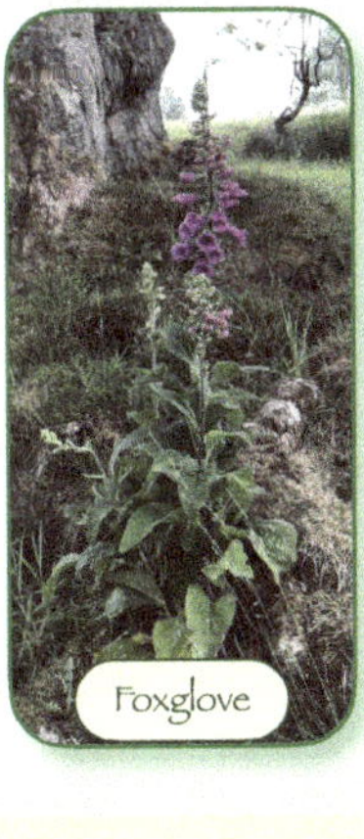
Foxglove

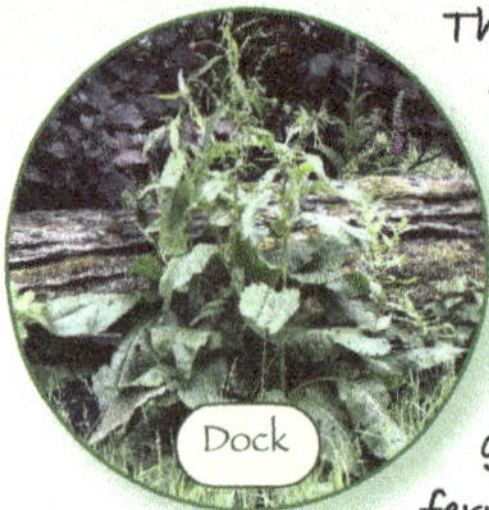
Dock

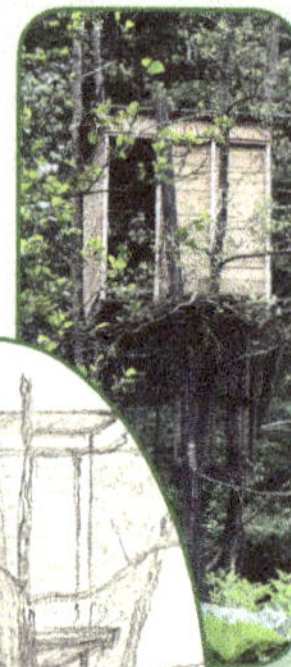

The disused canal is now a river of green plants. Meadowsweet, bulrushes, and the invasive trio of Himalayan balsam, horsetail and knotweed are evident among the riot of green. The old cart that I drew last time is now completely covered in green plants - great docks, lacy ferns, foxgloves and even little tree saplings - as it gently disintegrates in the breathless air.

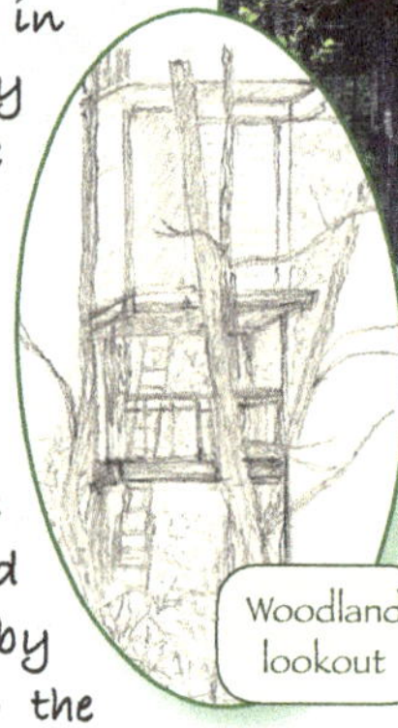
Woodland lookout

The invisible human inhabitants of this remote valley have planted potatoes, beans and other vegetables in the dark, rich, soil by the track, and they are flourishing in what feels like a greenhouse atmosphere. Below the tree house/hide, hidden among the trees, there are slides and prints in the mud on both sides of the water, surely made by badgers and deer coming down to to the water to drink.

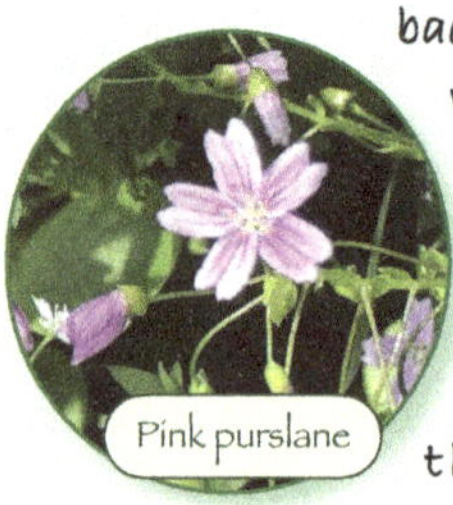
Pink purslane

Blackberries flower in the leafing green humidity, pink purslane spiders its thin stems among the tall grasses, and the endless parade of tall foxgloves adorn the verges of this hidden path, and ivy twines among the trees, colonising every opportunity to reach for the light. This valley seems to have been left to grow almost entirely untamed, except for clearing a path for the invisible and unheard vehicles that obviously use it.

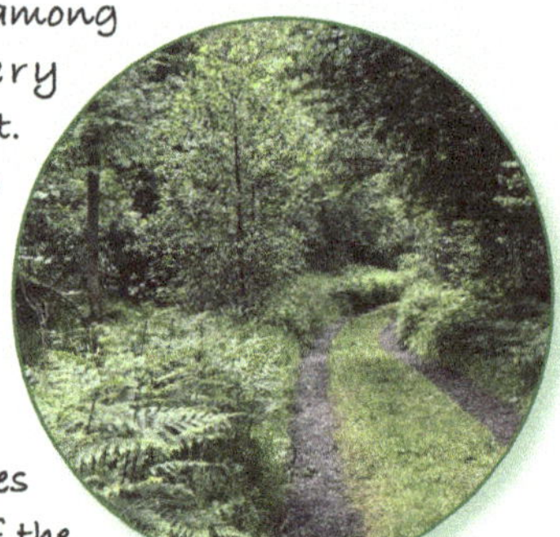

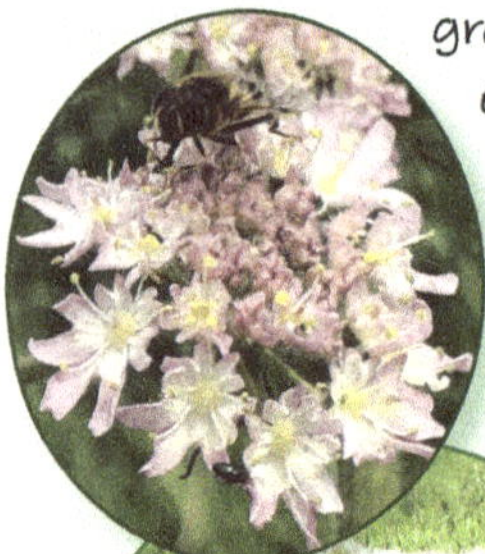

Leaving the old stone bridges and the wonky iron gates of the canalside path, we join the concrete road out onto the open fields where cattle graze and birds of prey wheel and cry over the hilltops above us.

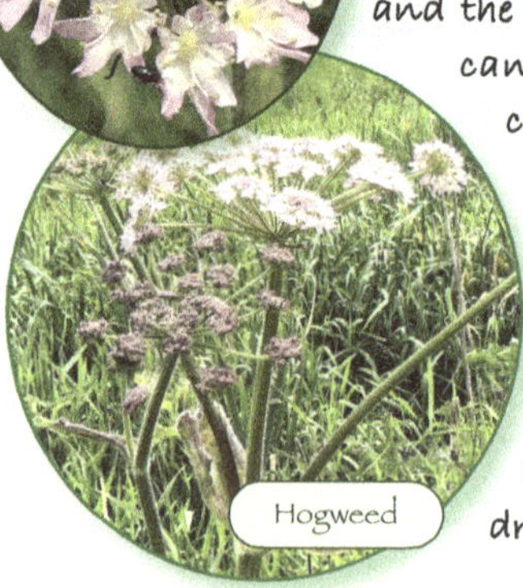
Hogweed

We climb to the Gritstone Trail, past more lowing groups of cattle, and slopes full of flowers, ancient hawthorns and abandoned farmsteads where endless streams flowed on our last visit, now dry and lumpy with deep bovine hoofprints.

We stop at a picnic viewpoint on a grassy slope under ancient sycamores, watching the clouds as they break into warm sunshine, then bring an occasional chilly shower.

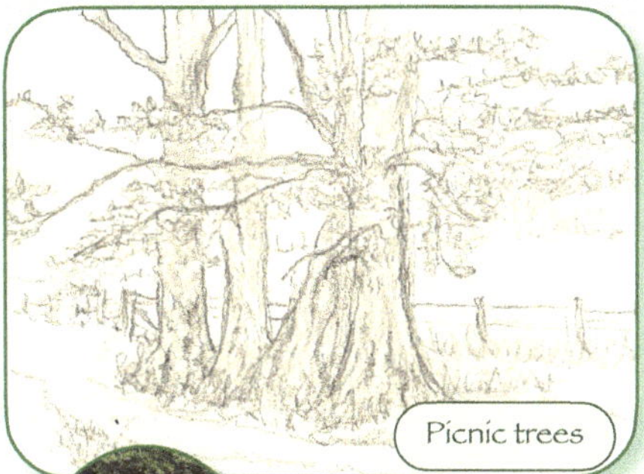

Picnic trees

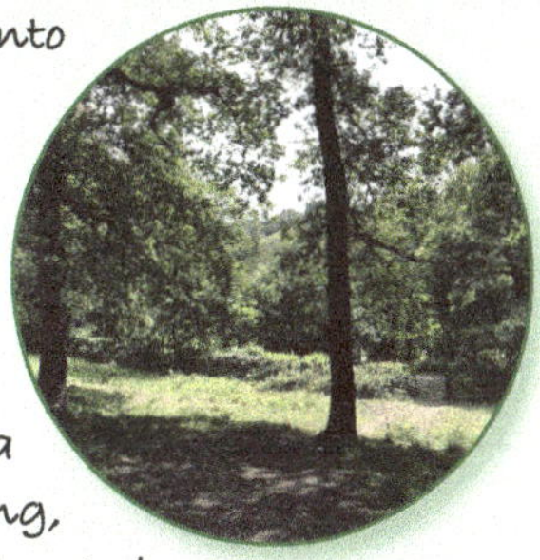

Later we pass through the plantations of new saplings, doing well after a warm, wet spring, and past the deserted farm, even more tumbledown under a towering old sycamore, gently disappearing beneath the advancing green of tree saplings, ivy and foxgloves.

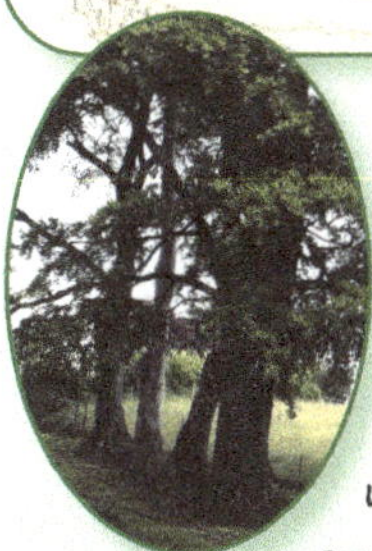

We continue on our way, through the soft, sunken paths with their ghosts of Medieval travellers, and here find the little body of a velvet mole, unmarked by any predator, perfect as it lies on the path.

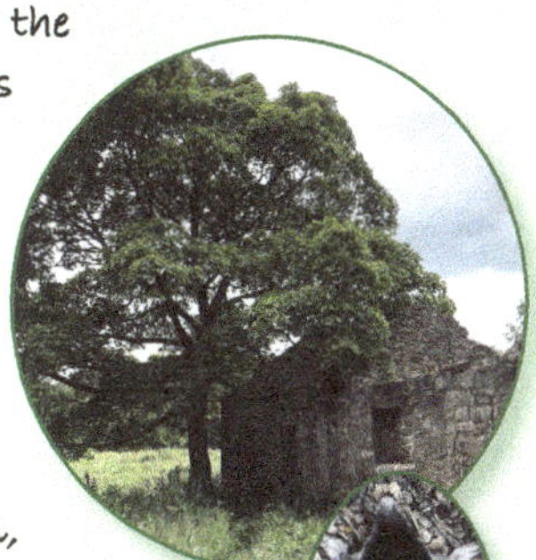

Next through the top fields scattered with black-faced sheep, where we begin the downhill part of the walk. The grasses in the hay meadows are at their green, waving best, reminding me of those in the high meadows of West Yorkshire.

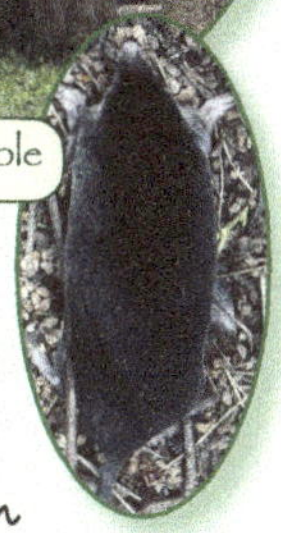

The mole

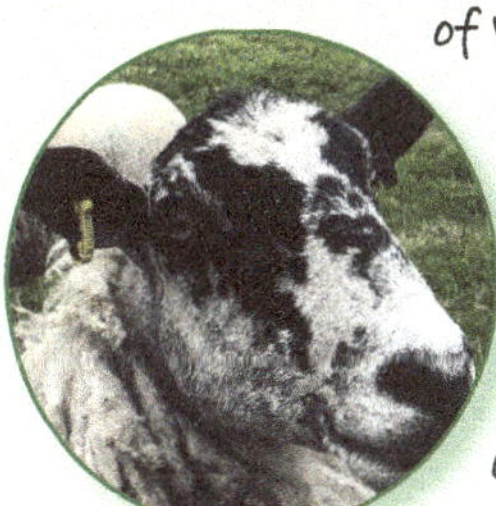

Towering banks of foxgloves are everywhere, filling the dips and ditches, decorating stiles and gates, even waving from the tops of walls as we walk the final downhill stretch between pale stone walls to the car, and the end of another day away from this never-before experience.

Once again we meet no-one at all until we reach the village where we pass a masked grandmother and grandson on their way home from the village school.

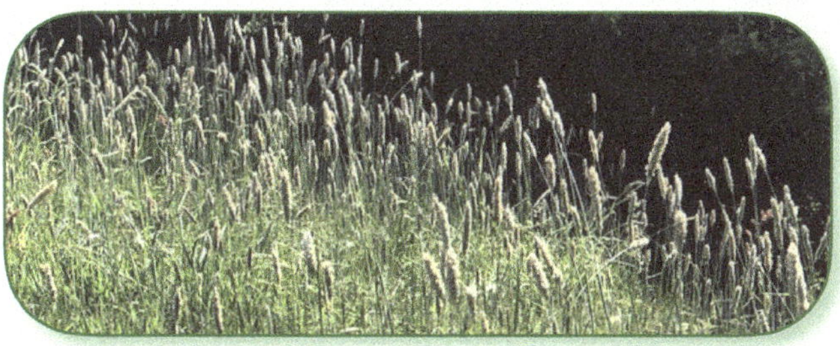

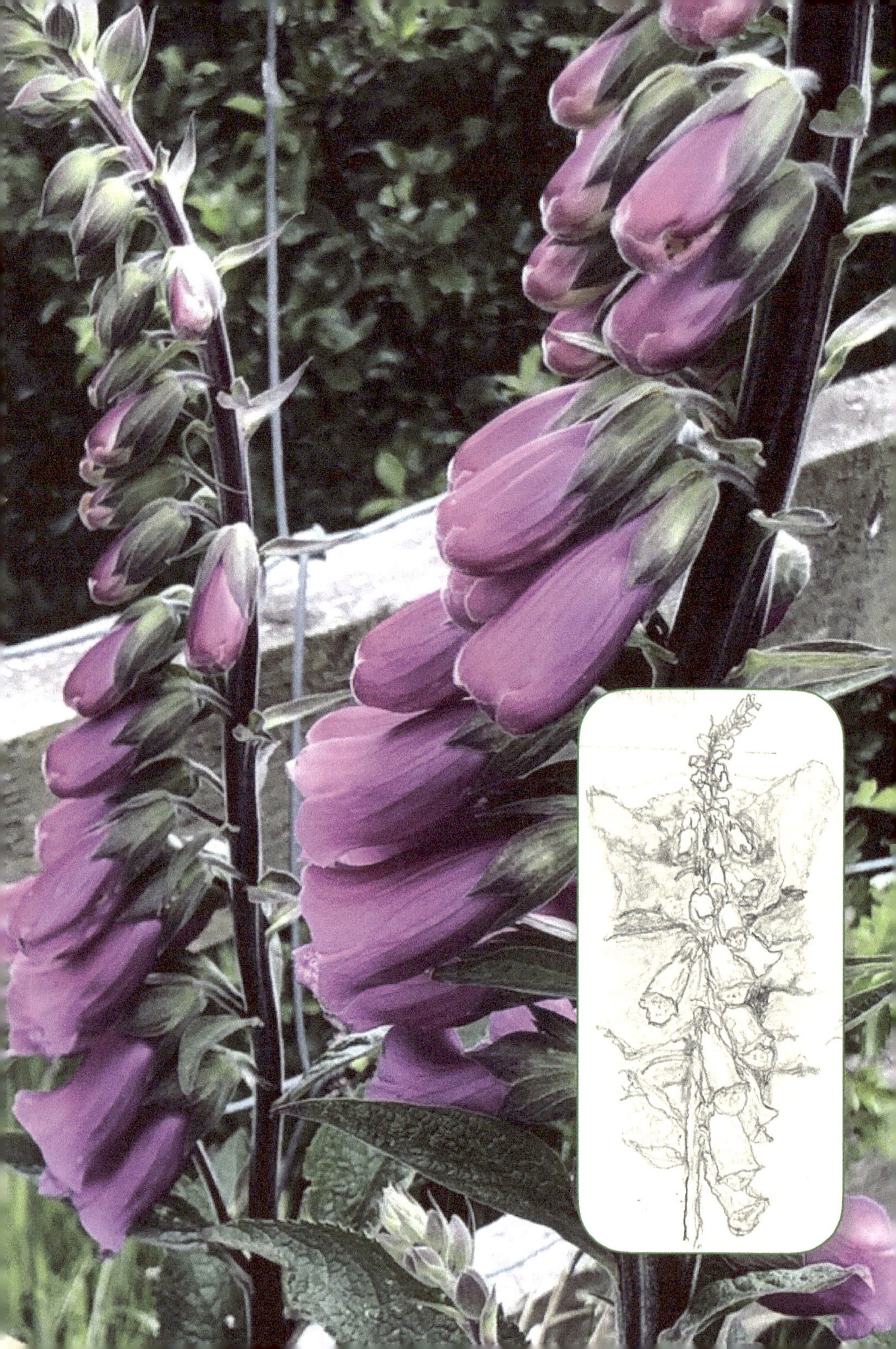

We pause on our drive home to admire the fan window of the old Buxton Station, preserved when the new station was built.

This glass wall is the sole survivor of two windows, built as part of the original station, opened in 1863. The window was restored and repaired in 2019, following vandalism which had broken many of the glass panels.

A life remembered on this day: Seraphim; 51; Russian Orthodox Bishop of Anadyr and Chukotka; Russia.

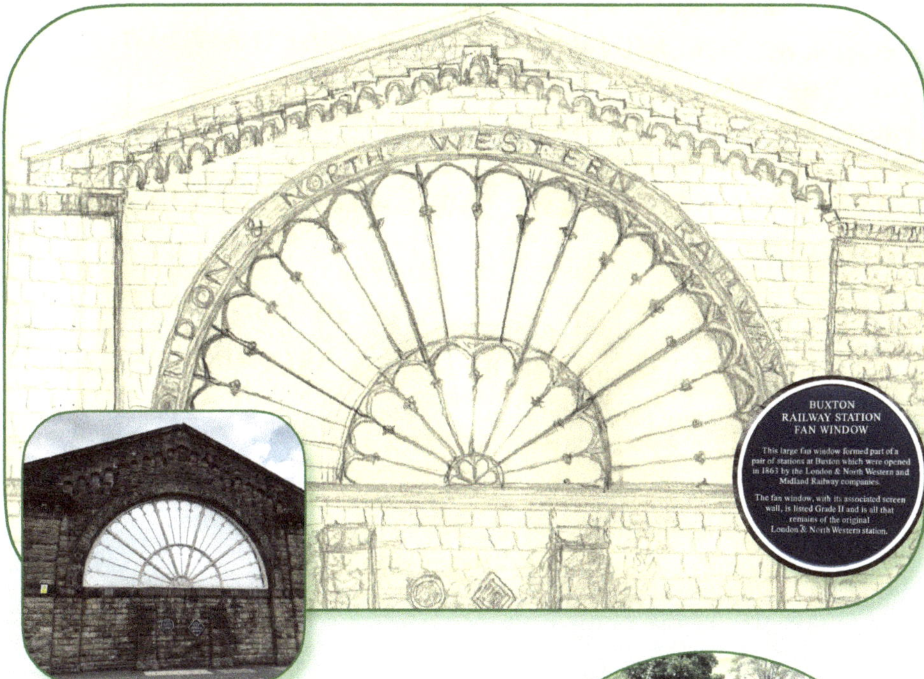

and as we return from calming nature and a very different solitude: *The Business Secretary confirms that all non-essential retailers, zoos & safari parks can reopen on 15 June, and pubs, bars, restaurants and hairdressers on 4 July.*

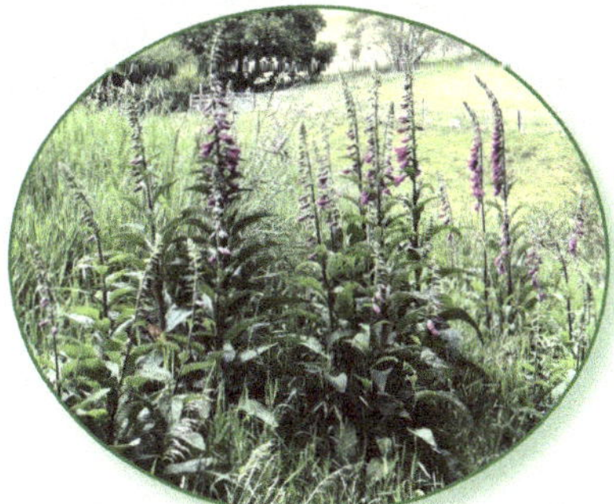

Pandemic Day: 90 Lockdown 1: day 76

10th - NEIL FERGUSON SAYS HALF THE LIVES LOST TO COVID COULD HAVE BEEN SAVED IF LOCKDOWN MEASURES HAD BEEN INTRODUCED A WEEK EARLIER.

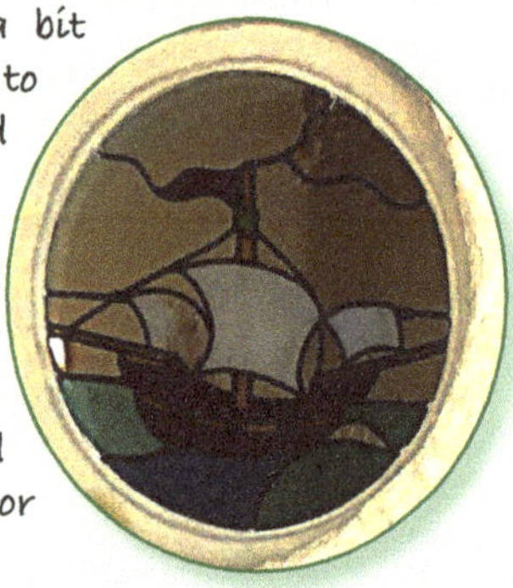

There is so much to do at the new house. It's a bit daunting, but exciting too. We meet the builder to discuss ground work outside, and the demolition and rebuilding of internal walls. There is so little that we want to keep inside this strange shell of a house, that the few internal features such as the little round stained glass window in the kitchen have become very important, and will influence the interior design.

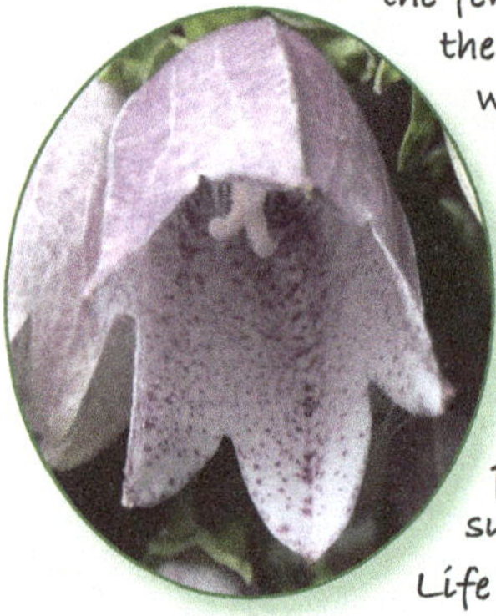

A surprise, pink, spotty campanula is flowering in the rental garden! I had quite forgotten buying it at the Botanical Gardens' Spring plant sale. I must remember to transplant it so it can surprise us again.

Life continues to be played out against a backdrop of blame and recrimination, but no-one in the government has been sacked. Housework, shopping, cooking and packing continue between the constraints of lockdown. We can remember what was once normal, but this memory is fading.

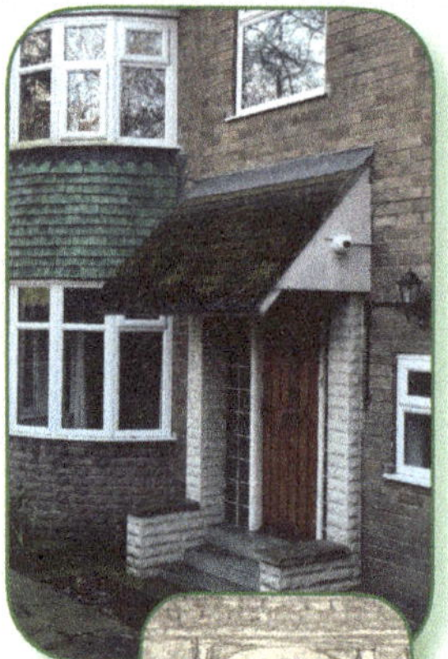

We avoid contact with others, hiding always behind our masks. We look on a simple shopping trip or even, for me, sitting in the supermarket car park as Phill collects the on-line shopping, as a treat. Release from lockdown is receding into the future, and we begin to realise that life will probably never be the same after this experience.

It's strange to be working at the new house with other people after so much time in isolation. Of course we need to be careful, but the doors are open, and we have meetings with the builder in the garden to avoid close contact.

Two lives remembered today: Sharon (Care Assistant) & Malcolm Bamford (Bus driver); 63 & 73; Swansea.

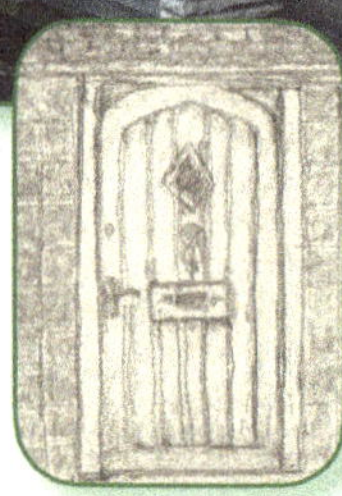

Every night we leave unwanted items on the pavement outside, and by the morning they have all quietly disappeared.

Pandemic Day: 91 Lockdown 1: day 77

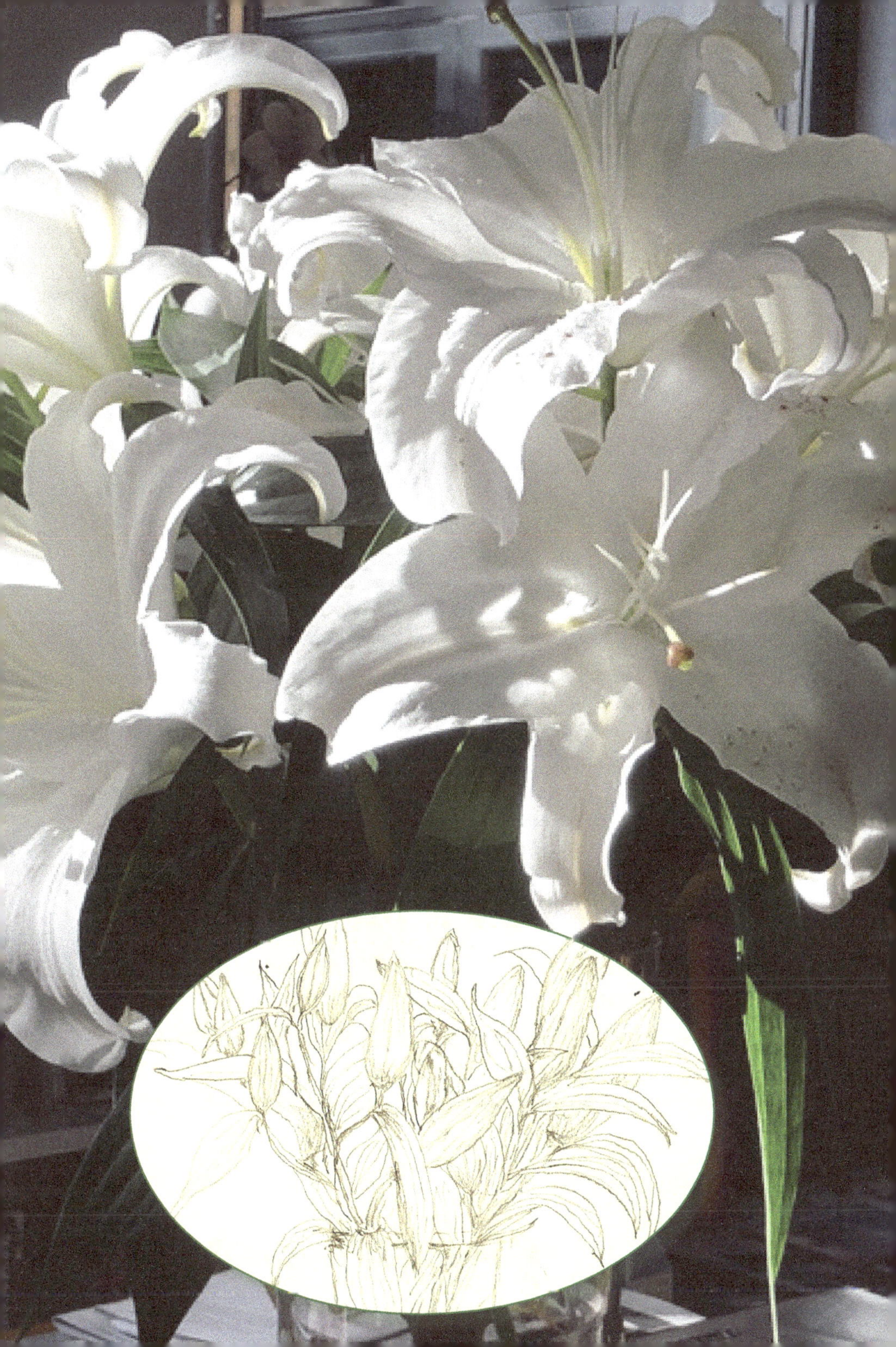

11th - ONS FIGURES INDICATE THAT DEPRIVED AREAS HAVE BEEN HIT TWICE AS HARD BY COVID AS AFFLUENT AREAS.

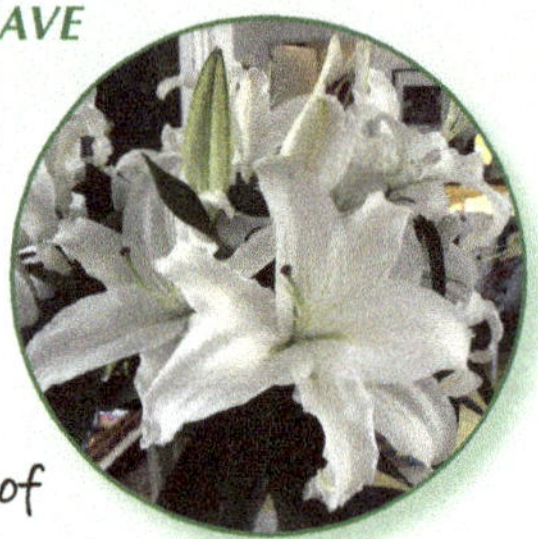

After rain all night and a misty wet morning we go to the house to meet our kitchen designer. It's really hard to make decisions with a blank canvas, and choices can be difficult when no-one has asked my opinion about anything for months!

I make the first of a series of drawings of a vase of perfect white Asiatic lilies, which are cheering up the house with their light and perfume. Its is so comforting to still be able to buy flowers!

13th - 'SOCIAL BUBBLES' ARE IMPLEMENTED FOR PEOPLE LIVING ON THEIR OWN.

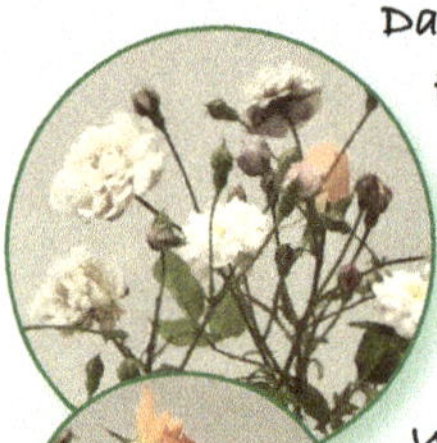

Days are becoming worryingly similar, and the danger is that, like many others, we will continue this sinking into lethargy and drift, watching movies on TV and eating and drinking too much as we put on the much publicised 'Covid stone'.

A life remembered: Eileen Landers; 67; Hospital cleaner; Burton on Trent; UK.

We go over to the Children's House and spend Sunday afternoon clearing the old flower beds in the front garden, ready for work on the driveway. We pick the last of the little rose blooms and dig up their roots, keeping some for the back garden, and put bluebell bulbs in a bucket for Sarah's woodland area. This is the first real piece of work we have done at the new house, and it feels good to be starting on the garden, although at the moment it is just a clearance job.

14th - MANY POLITICIANS AND THE MEDIA AGREE THAT THE GOVERNMENT HAS LOST CONTROL OF THE STREETS AND OF PUBLIC RESPECT.

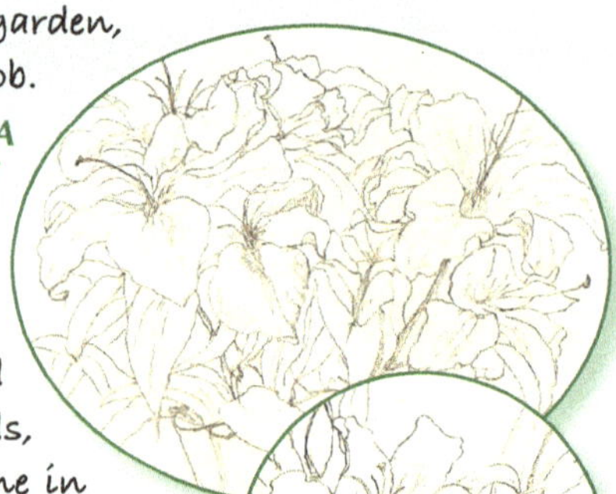

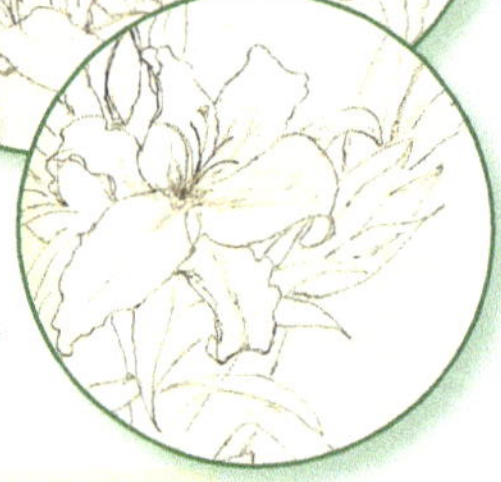

Sarah's friend, NHS consultant, drops by for a doorstep chat. She looks pale and exhausted from working on the Covid wards, supporting front line staff, and says everyone in the NHS is worried about a second spike later in the year if people don't continue to adhere to social distancing rules. I make further drawings of the lilies before their petals finally fall.

Pandemic Day: 92/95 Lockdown 1: day 79/81

15th - HEADTEACHERS SAY THAT A THIRD OF PUPILS ARE NOT ENGAGING WITH THE WORK SET FOR THEM BY THEIR TEACHERS, AS THE GOVERNMENT TALKS ABOUT SUMMER SCHOOLS AND CATCH-UP CLASSES. FACE COVERINGS BECOME MANDATORY ON PUBLIC TRANSPORT. NON-ESSENTIAL SHOPS REOPEN AND ENGLAND'S RETAIL PARKS, HIGH STREETS AND SHOPPING CENTRES WELCOME CUSTOMERS. ZOOS AND SAFARI PARKS OPEN THEIR DOORS FOR THE FIRST TIME SINCE MARCH, AND PLACES OF WORSHIP OPEN FOR PRIVATE PRAYER.

The doctor says I should continue with strict social distancing - unwelcome news! But on our shielded way to the builder's merchant, we are delighted to see scarlet poppies on wiry stalks, scrambling heaps of yellow vetchling, dainty ox-eye daisies and other wild flowers blooming in the unused, locked down car parks of the locked down factories.

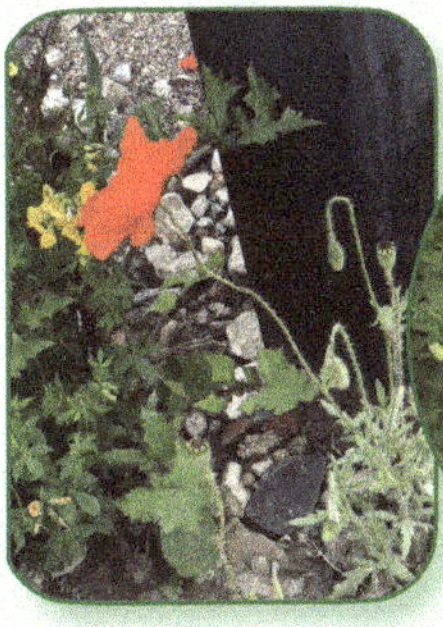

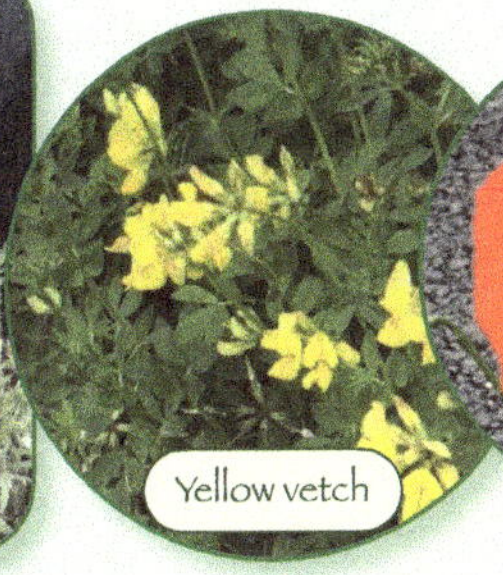

Yellow vetch

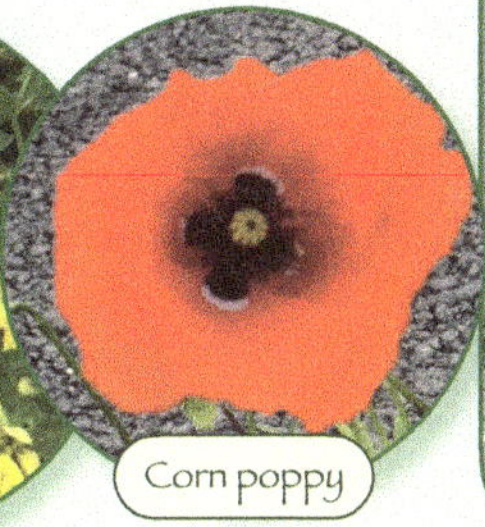

Corn poppy

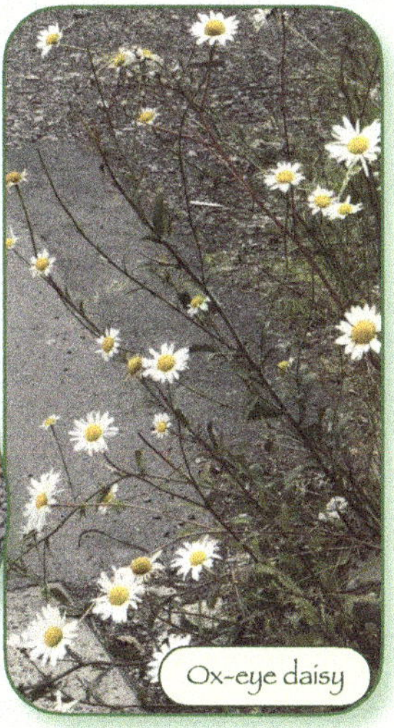

Ox-eye daisy

16th - THE TESTING TARGET IS MISSED AGAIN; AND THE MAJORITY OF VOTERS THINK LOCKDOWN WAS IMPOSED TOO LATE. IT EMERGES THAT ALLOWING CHELTENHAM RACES GO AHEAD LED TO A HUGE SPIKE IN CASES AND DEATHS.

Remembered today:
Jermaine Wright; 45;
Senior Pharmacy
Technician; London.

We fetch samples of units, worktop, flooring and wet wall, and set them up on the yellow step ladder in the kitchen, where they look very pleasing in their shades of grey with the bright yellow splash-backs we have chosen. I really find making decisions of this magnitude difficult, after so much time isolated from the world, so I am pleased with the result.

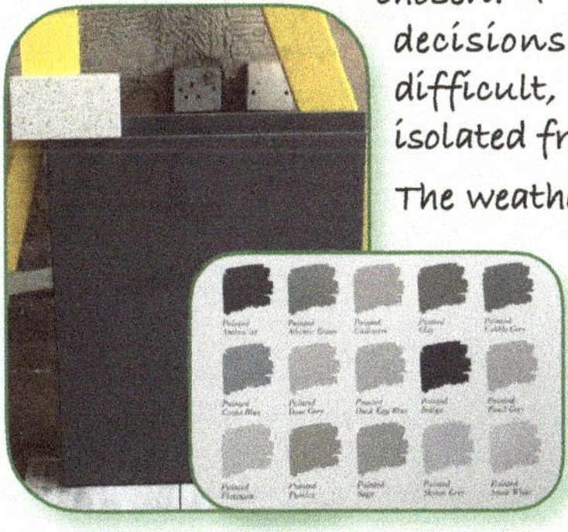

The weather finally breaks with storms of huge raindrops splashing and splattering down on every surface and at last wetting the parched earth in the gardens. I hope this does not mean the end of the warm and sunny weather that has helped us all to cope with this long and stressful summer.

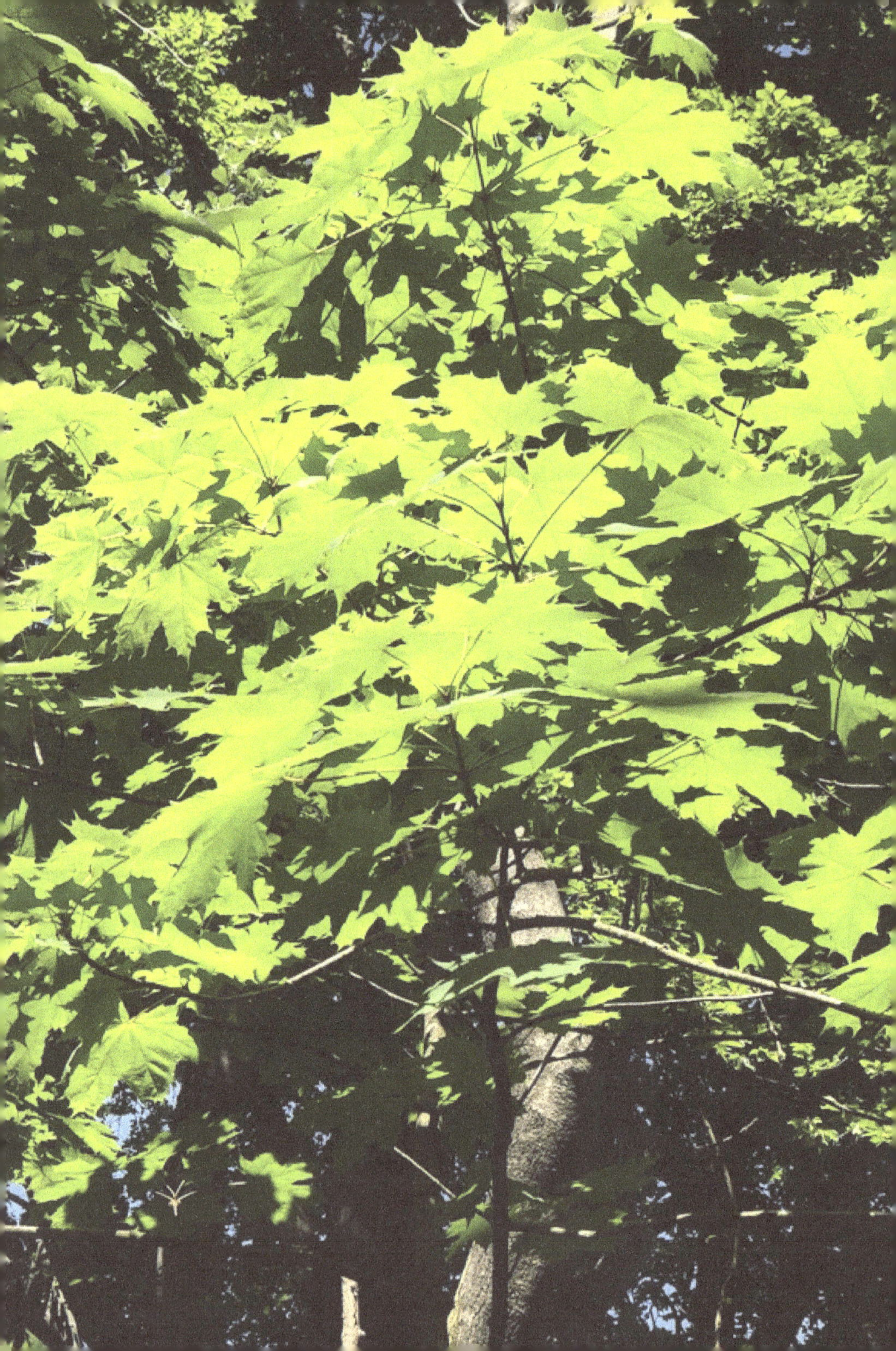

17th June 2020 Confirmed Cases: 158,401 Total deaths: 40,020

THE PARTIAL LOCKDOWN CONTINUES, AND WE DECIDE TO EXPLORE A NEW WALK AS INTERPRETING THE LATEST GUIDANCE IS DIFFICULT.

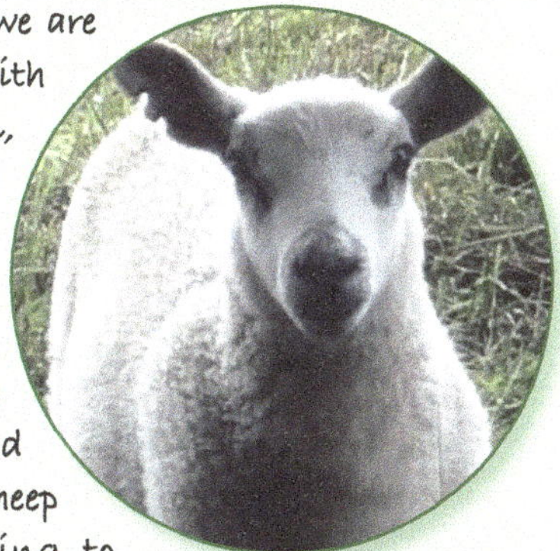

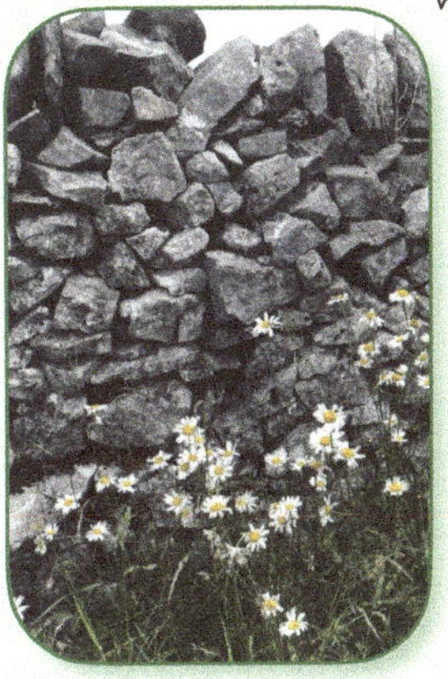

A walk where there is virtually no-one, and we are alone all day, seems very tempting to us. With sunshine again today, we park in Hartington, where we buy California poppies, then set off up the hill out of the village to grassy hilltops edged with pale stone walls and dotted with cows and calves, sheep and lambs, some coming to the walls to see us, but most happier to lie panting in the shade.

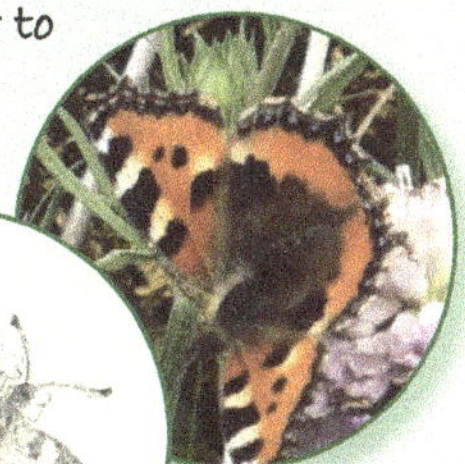

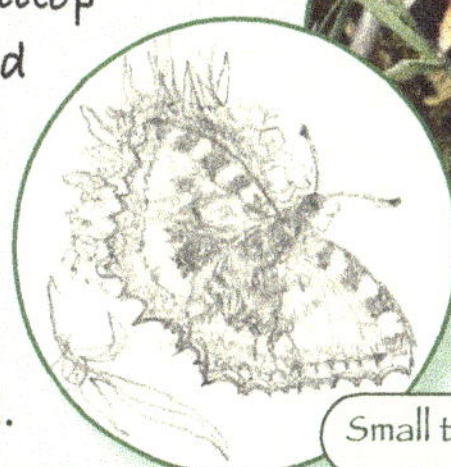

Small tortoiseshell

The double-walled hilltop paths are deserted and well-manicured, with help from Natural England to restore barns and rebuild walls. The verges are lined with flowers – ox-eye daisies, campion, blue wild geraniums, lacy cow parsley and hogweed. Purple and yellow vetches and pink scabious are alive with visiting butterflies, bees and other insects.

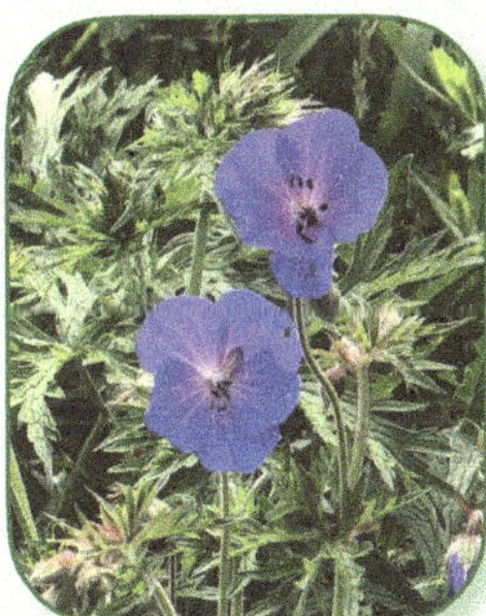

As we descend into Biggin Dale, we begin to meet other people, but still no groups or crowds. Confused by lack of signs, we ask help from a lone local walker to find the next part of our route, and receive some useful advice, including directions to more local trails for us to explore.

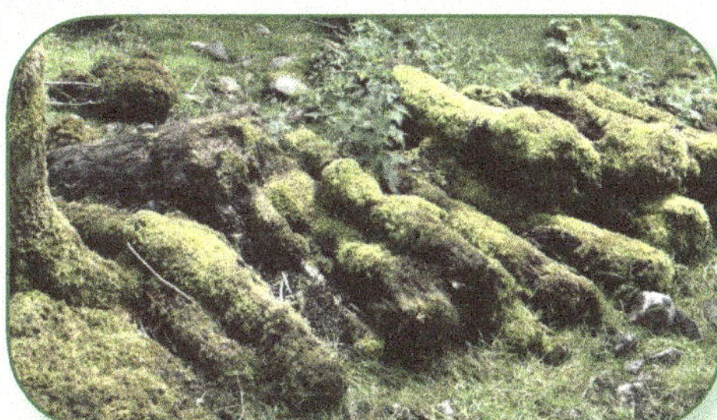

Biggin Dale, is a long, moss-covered, ankle turning, stony, currently dry river bed leading to the tranquil River Dove, and a newer, most welcome flat path along the wide, slow flowing river.

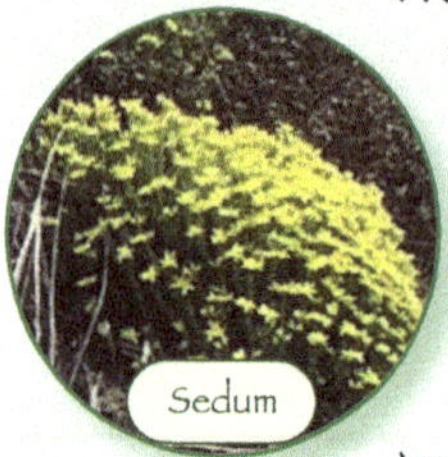
Sedum

We sit on the grassy bank of the river for our picnic lunch, where ducks dive, sheep wander and few walkers pass. The white walls of rock here hold little gardens of thyme, rock roses and a tiny yellow sedum, and the paths are lined with great purple musk thistles, their heavy heads beaten down by last night's violent thunderstorms.

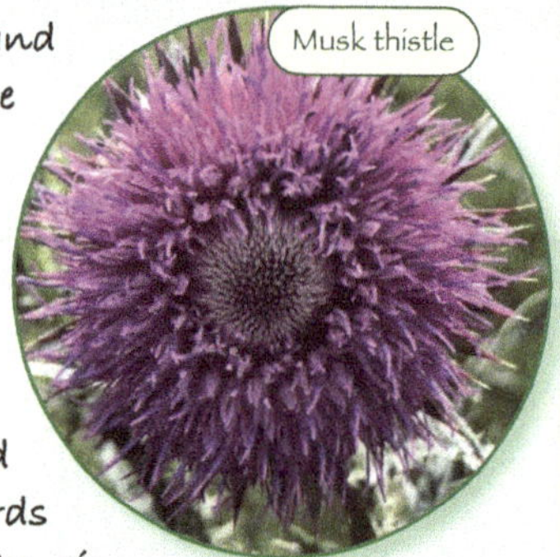
Musk thistle

Our walk continues along the river bank, and through the gorge of Wolfscote Dale, where it is said wolves once lived among the limestone caves. Birds soar and sing, and fish rise to grab flies from the air above the river. On our right, more great slips and slides of rock like white waterfalls run round stately old sycamore trees, hanging on with their roots deep in the ground under the stones, waiting for the day when the weight of rain and stone finally takes them down.

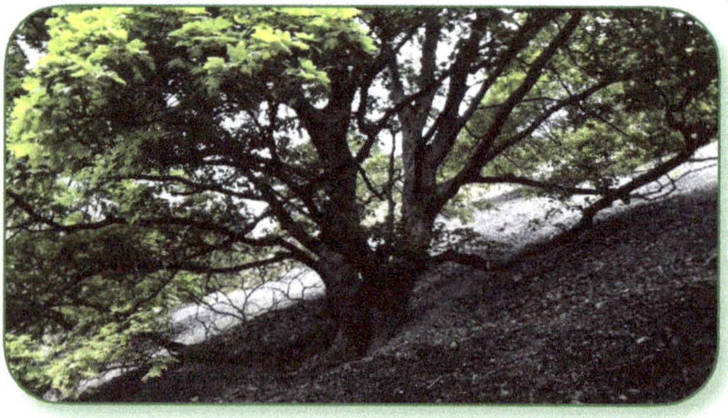

We listen to a pair of tuneful songbirds, invisible as they call and follow each other from tree to tree, up and over the steep valley sides and into the fields above. A hawk cries repeatedly high above us, whether hunting or just calling we will never know.

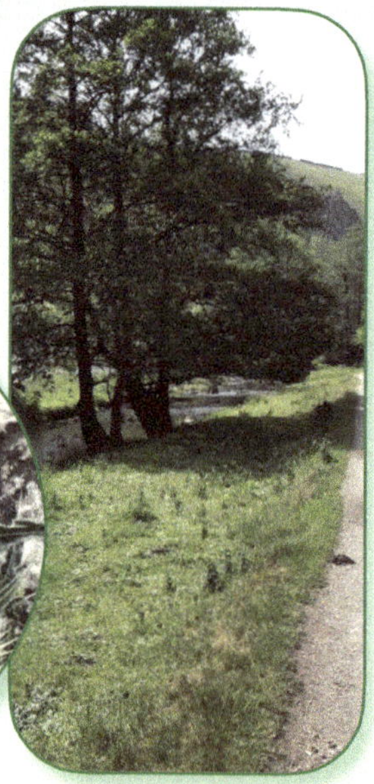

A life remembered on this day: Antonio Gonzalez Pachecco, 73; Political-Social Brigade inspector; Madrid; Spain.

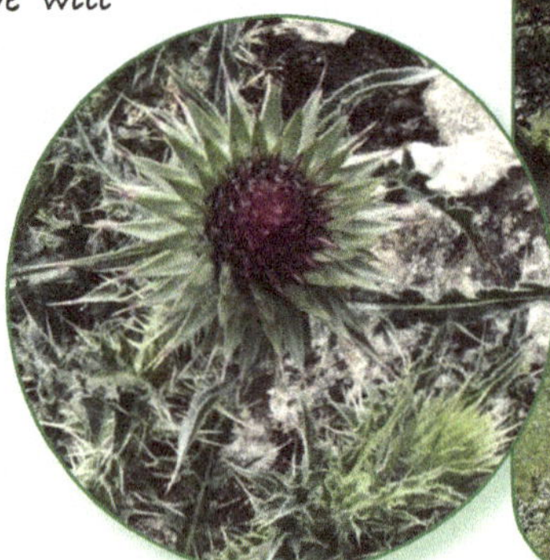

A life remembered:
Ray Paternoster; 78;
Factory supervisor;
Ipswich; UK.

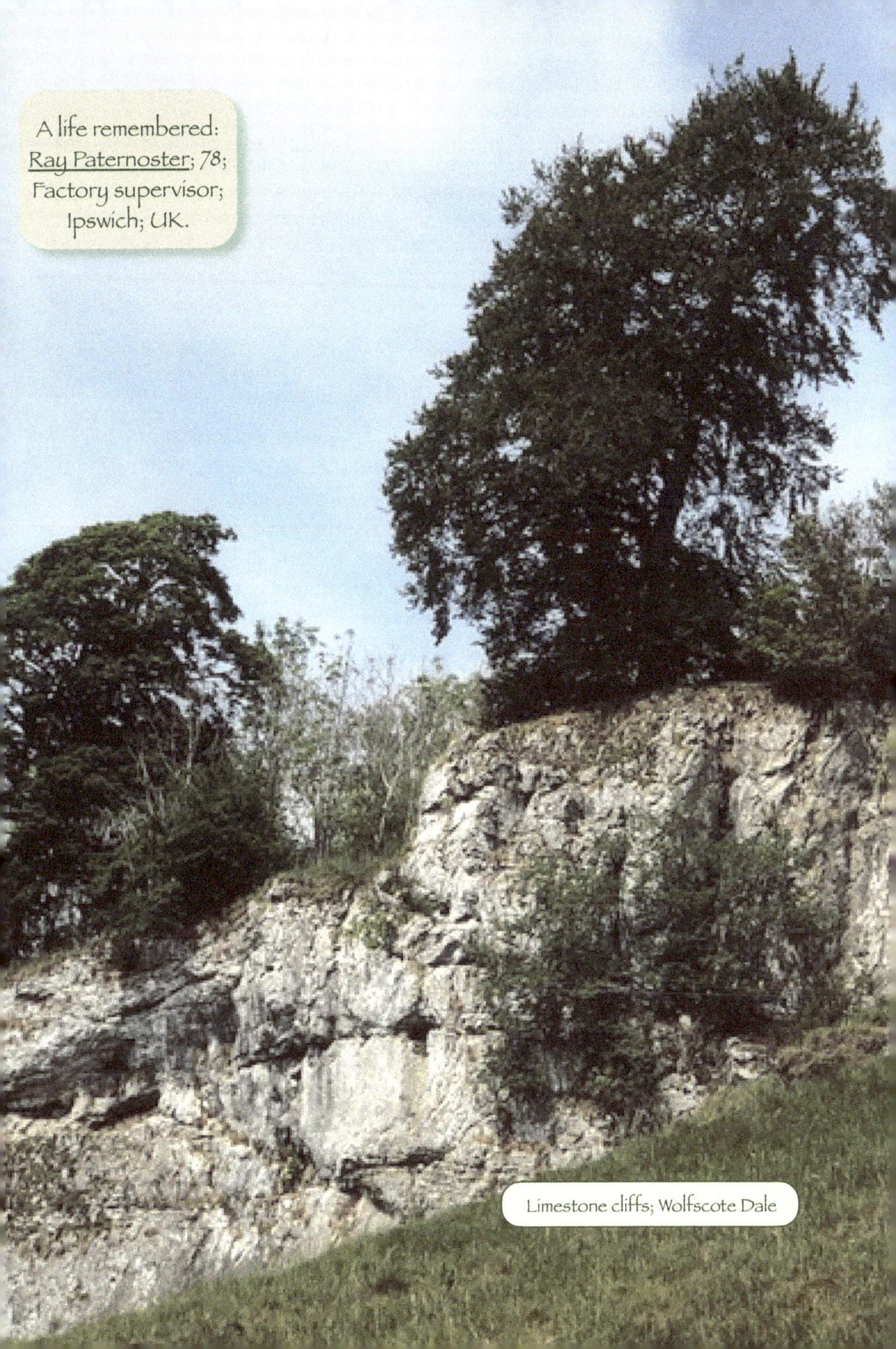

Limestone cliffs; Wolfscote Dale

Further along the valley, the landscape changes, becoming one of water meadows and flatter, even calmer water in Beresford Dale. We cross the river here, leave the butterflies and flowers, and enter into the gloomy woods of the grounds below Beresford Hall, now destroyed, where Isaac Walton stayed to fish with Charles Cotton. The damp and rampant summer growth under the trees here hides a possible sighting of the remaining tower, as the path climbs through woods to the edge of the valley, emerging at last onto the meadows skirting Penilow Hill.

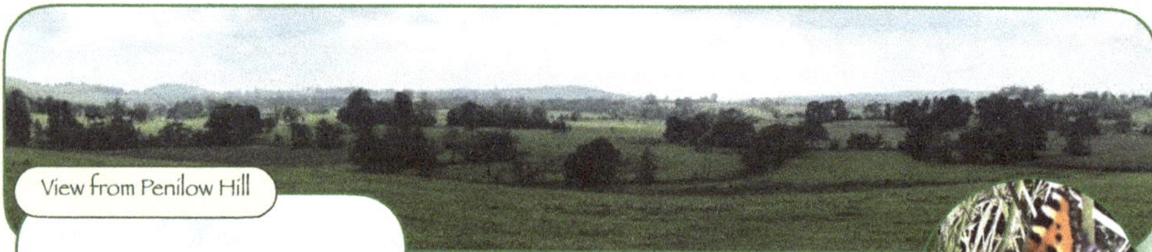

View from Penilow Hill

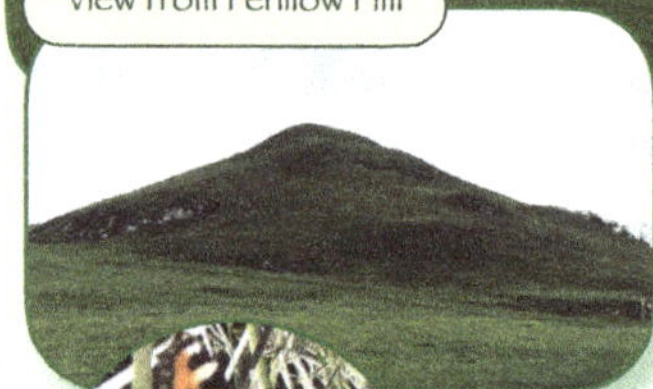

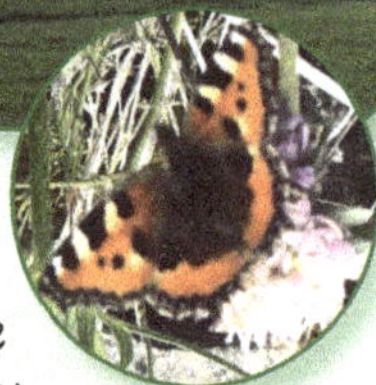

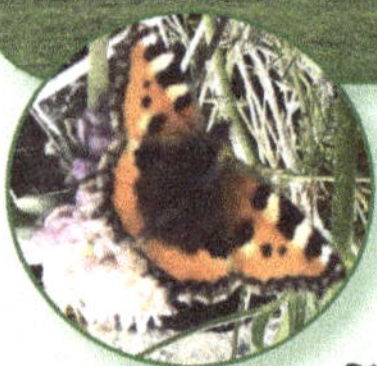

The footpath here runs through sheep-cropped meadows, and we pause to sit on the edge of the white stone path to look out at the hills and valleys below, laid out like a patchwork quilt in the hazy afternoon sun.

Flapjack eaten, and the wide view appreciated, we complete our circular walk, returning to Hartington village across the meadows and down the road for a visit to the specialist cheese shop for local Stilton, and a warm, sunset-rosy drive home.

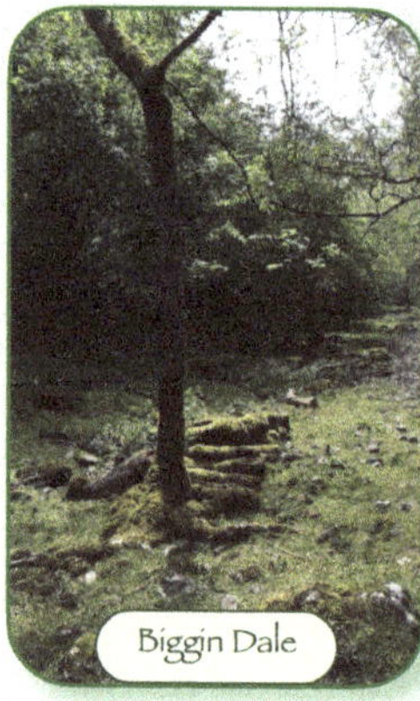

Biggin Dale

and as we walk the Dales, *Matt Hancock is pictured slapping a colleague on the back as they arrive at the House of Commons, apparently totally forgetting social distancing.*

I AM AT THE END OF MY FIRST LOCKDOWN SKETCHBOOK, AND I HOPE THAT THINGS REALLY WILL GET BETTER, AND THAT 'ALL THESE THINGS REALLY WILL PASS'.

I OPEN THE SECOND VOLUME OF OUR LOCKDOWN DIARIES, WONDERING WHETHER I WILL STILL BE WRITING ENTRIES AT THE END OF THIS NEXT SKETCHBOOK, AND IF THE WORLD WILL EVER BE THE SAME AGAIN.

Pandemic Day: 98   Lockdown 1: day 84

***18th* - THE UK DELAYS THE LAUNCH OF THE CONTACT TRACING APP AGAIN, AND CHANGES ITS FORMAT TO ONE BASED ON TECHNOLOGY BY APPLE AND GOOGLE.**

A life remembered; <u>Malcolm Pridmore</u>; 56, Residential home maintenance man; Shotley; UK.

I start a new sketchbook as the nation remains confused, with many now ignoring the guidance. After our long hot walk yesterday, we make a quick visit to look at progress on the Children's House where a skip has arrived and demolition of the upstairs walls is well under way.

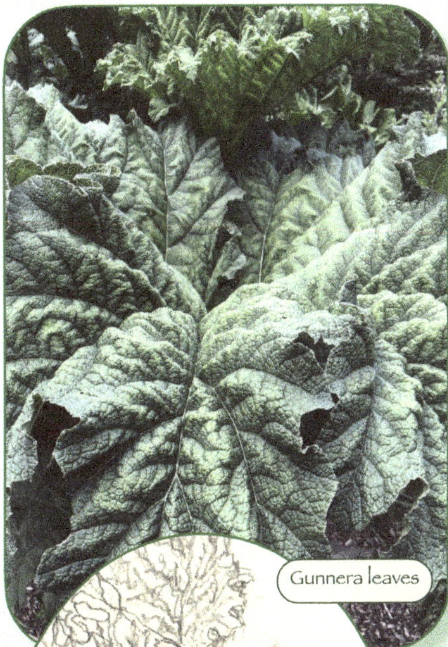

Gunnera leaves

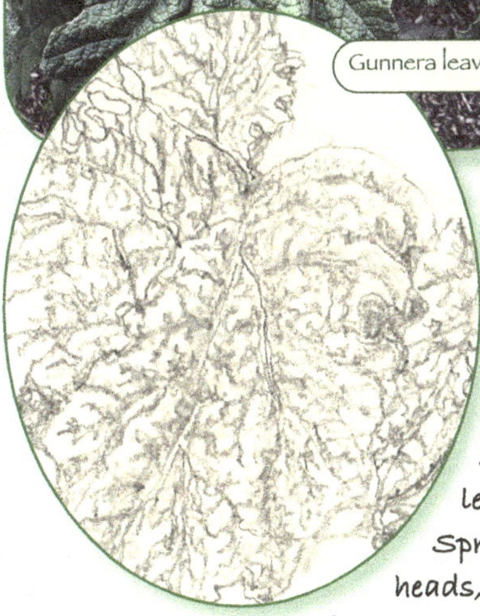

***19th* - MATT HANCOCK ANNOUNCES THAT ASTRA-ZENECA WILL BEGIN MANUFACTURING AND STOCKPILING A VACCINE, PENDING CLINICAL APPROVAL.**

In the garden of the Children's House, the dark leylandii conifer tree growing too close outside the back door, and shading the kitchen windows, has been felled and chopped into logs.

***20th* - THE CULTURE SECRETARY CONFIRMS THAT THE REVIEW INTO 2M SOCIAL DISTANCING RULE IN ENGLAND WILL REPORT WITHIN THE COMING DAYS.**

A random knife attack in a Reading park leaves three dead and more injured, but the reason is unclear.

Still anxious about going into shops, we are told to expect more easing of restrictions, but the tragic stabbing in Reading may cause a rethink.

We walk to the Botanical Gardens, where the gunnera spreads giant, prickly leaves over the pond, and Spring flowers are just seed heads, now replaced by towering foxgloves.

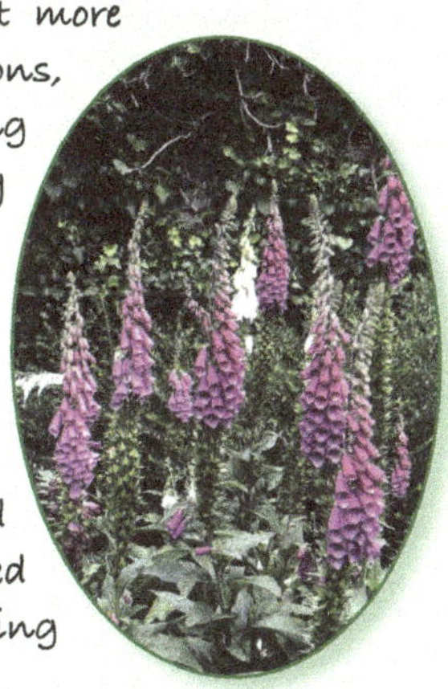

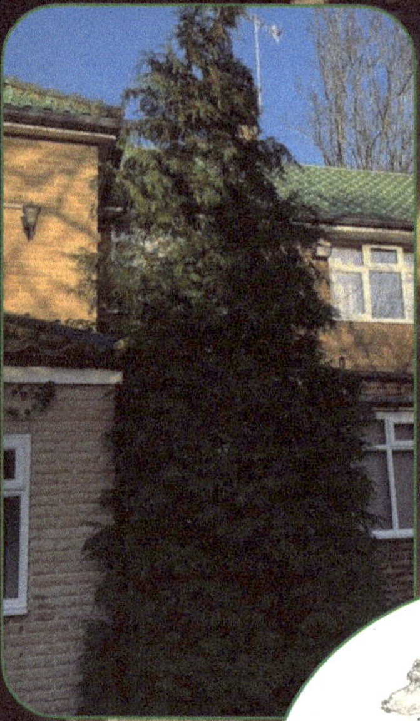

Farewell to the tall Leylandii tree in the back garden of the Children's House, remembered here in my drawings of logs and roots.

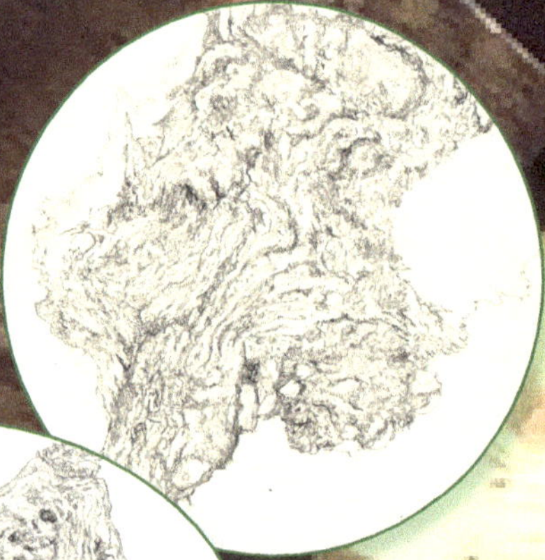

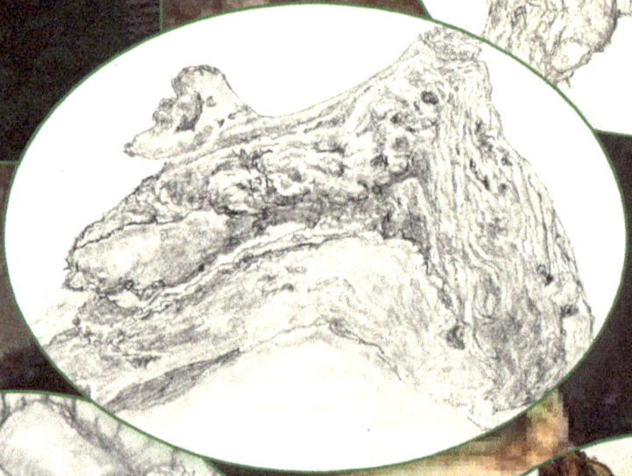

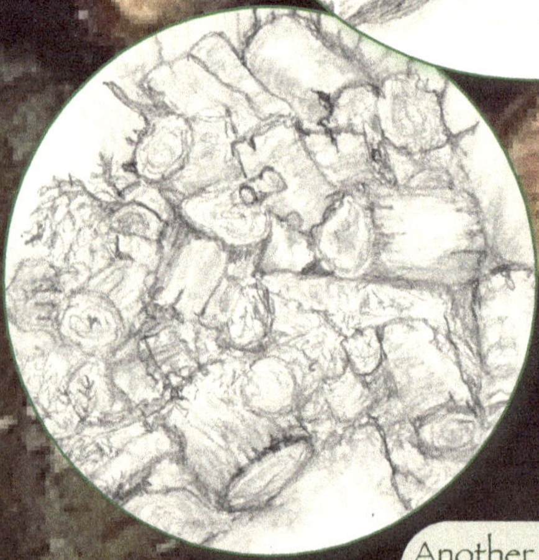

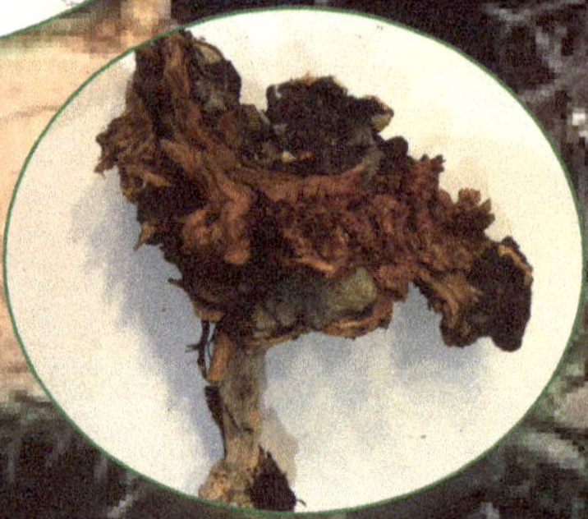

Another life remembered; <u>Dave Stanford</u>; 72, Retired landscape gardener; Walsall.

21/24 June 2020   Confirmed Cases: 158,238   Total deaths: 40,450

21st - MORE GOVERNMENT INDECISION AND LACK OF CLARITY, WITH ANNOUNCEMENTS SUCH AS, 'THE NATION'S HIBERNATION IS COMING TO AN END.'

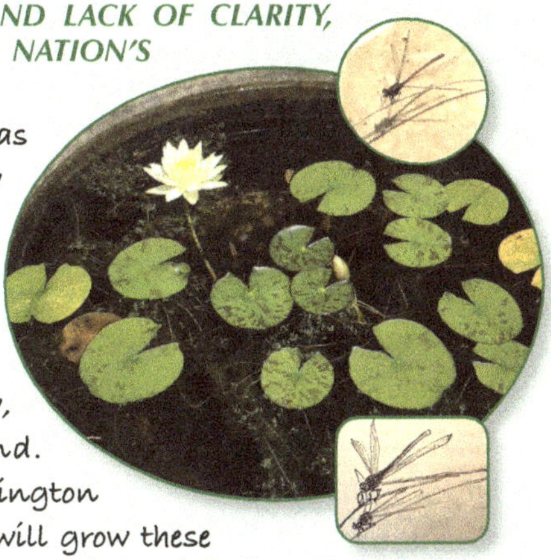

Information seems to have dried up, as ministers decide what to do next. How wonderful it would be, to relax, visit a pub or an exhibition, entertain friends, or go for a walk without feeling jumpy and guilt-ridden.

The water lily blooms in lemon yellow, and damsel flies visit the lily pond. California poppies, bought at the Hartington village stores flower all over the garden. I will grow these again!

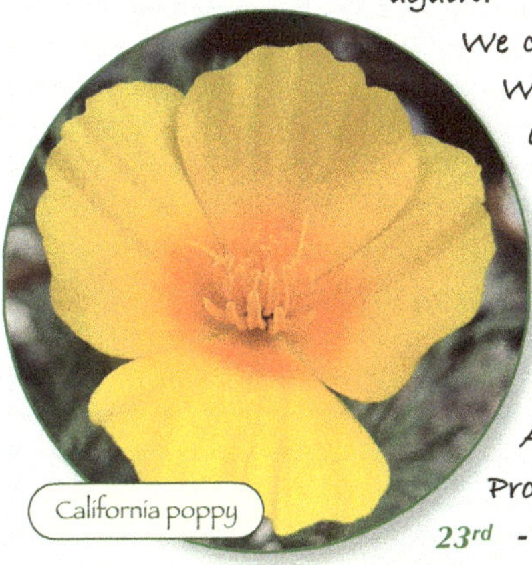

California poppy

We console ourselves by watching the last part of Wolf Hall, and later, hear repeated 'news' that we are 'past the peak'.

22nd - THE UK RECORDS ITS LOWEST NUMBER OF NEW COVID-19 CASES SINCE THE BEGINNING OF LOCKDOWN, 958 POSITIVE TESTS.

In the real world outside lockdown, the highest temperature ever is recorded above the Arctic Circle.

Progress at the new house gains momentum.

23rd - THE PM SAYS SOCIAL DISTANCING WILL REDUCE FROM 2m-1m.

There is a vague promise of lifting of lockdown, and a feeling of relief. We walk in Norfolk Park, down the sunny fields and back up the hill. Sunshine pours down through a canopy of leaves.

24th - DOCTORS WARN OF 'LONG COVID', AND SCIENTISTS WARN OF A 2nd WAVE OF THE VIRUS.

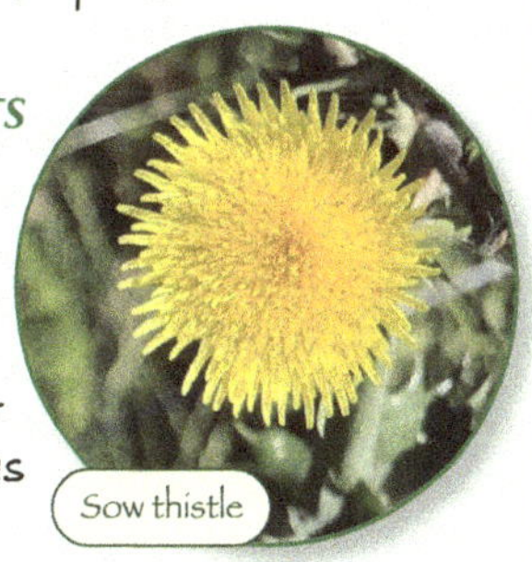

Sow thistle

I can't bear to pull out the bright yellow flowers of the thistles growing in the front garden path of our rental house. Their bright blooms cheer me up just as much as the poppies.

A life remembered:
Alan Finder; 72 ;
Journalist;
Ridgewood;
United States.

Pandemic Day: 102/105   Lockdown 1: day 88/91

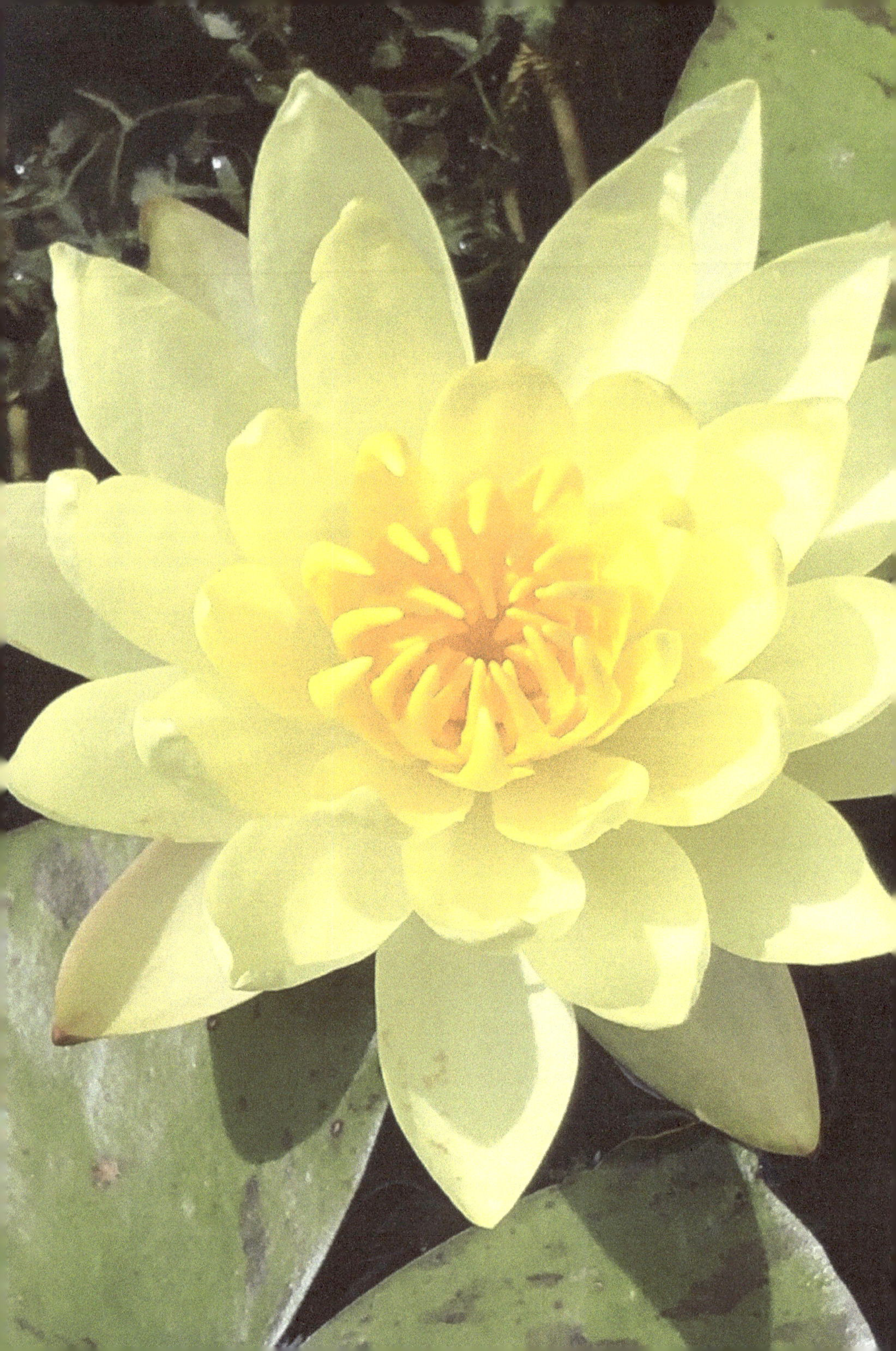

25th June 2020 Confirmed Cases: 159,626 Total deaths: 40,559

SCIENTISTS AT IMPERIAL COLLEGE LONDON BEGIN HUMAN TRIALS OF A COVID-19 VACCINE AFTER TESTS ON ANIMALS INDICATE AN EFFECTIVE IMMUNE RESPONSE; 300 VOLUNTEERS WILL TAKE PART IN THE PROGRAMME. DOES THIS SIGNAL A POSSIBLE END TO THIS TERRIBLE SUMMER?

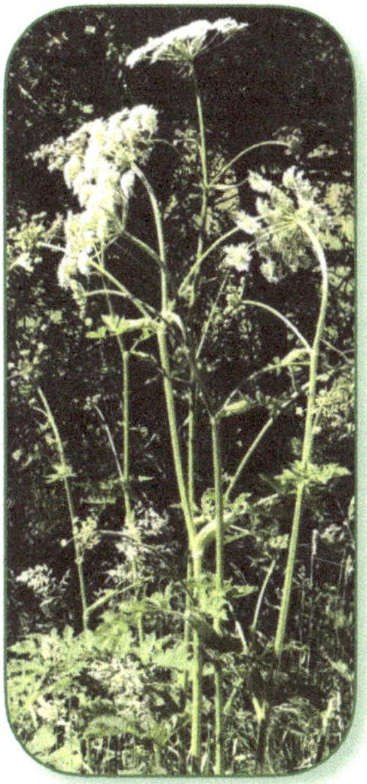

We decide to leave the city and take refuge in the country on what promises to be another 'hottest day of the year', even hotter than the last 'hottest day' in May when we walked in the sweltering Lathkill Dale.

A life remembered on this day: Julia Sigmond; 90; Puppet actor & Esperantist; Italy.

Driving down the Manifold Valley along familiar roads through the summer meadows, we find many already pale and mown for hay, with lazing cows, and sheep looking thin and small in their short coats after shearing.

A stop at Hartington for coffee results in the inevitable loading of more plants, then on to Hulme End Station, to repeat what is currently our favourite walk, through the water meadows, where pink campion and shining buttercups still bloom, now under towering umbels of meadowsweet, hogweed and cow parsley. The huge leaves of butterbur, like giant rhubarb, are now invading large areas of these previously varied habitats.

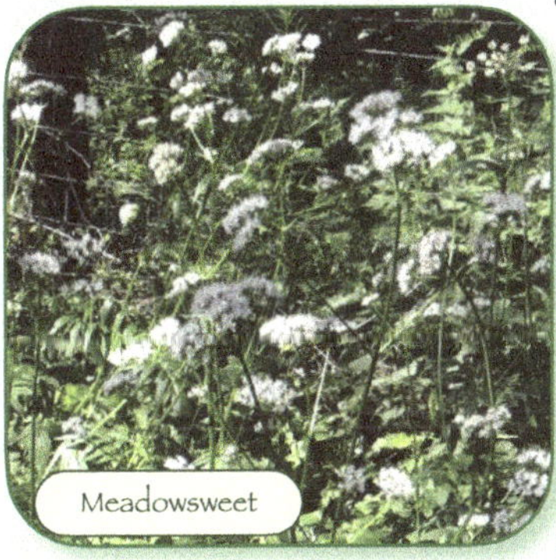

Meadowsweet

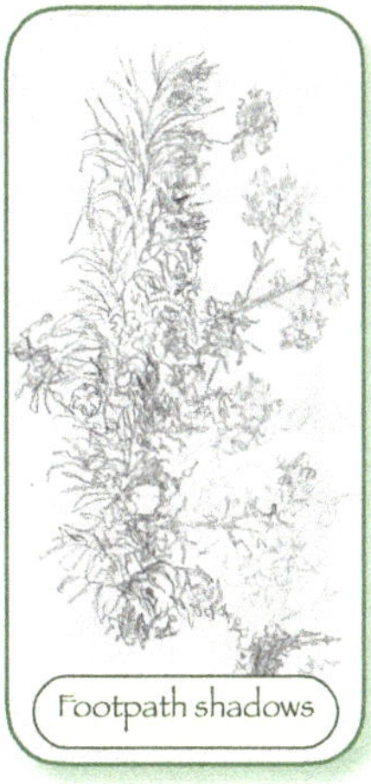

Footpath shadows

The valley is hot and humid, full of pollen and smelling damp from the river. We meet more people than ever before along this stretch, on foot and on bikes, and we begin to feel almost resentful at sharing this previously deserted place, where the sun makes shadows of the wild flowers lining these usually quiet paths.

Above us, the long hill of Ecton lies sweltering in the sun, but we have already decided not to attempt the steep and rocky paths to the top in todays extreme heat.

We plan to stay by the river where it might be cooler and shadier, so, passing Swainsley House, we start the usual path uphill towards Dale Farm, beneath the leafy shade of the trees, catching frequent glimpses of the river, now brown and peaty and much lower, following the dry weather.

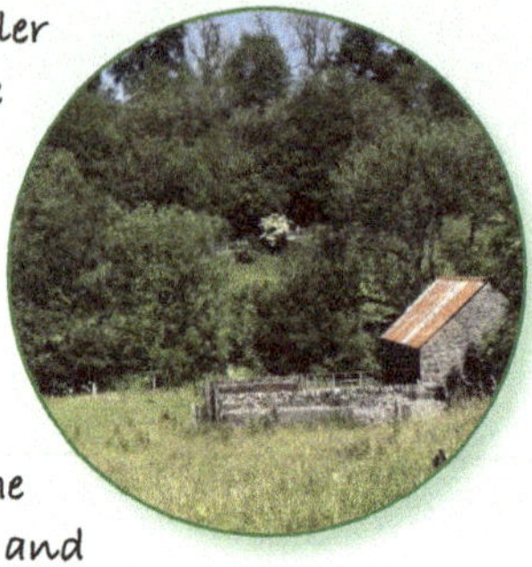

After a stop for oranges by the ruined barn with the view of the old stone tower beyond, hidden now by the leafy trees, we continue across familiar hillsides and woodland above meadows, full of buttercups on our last visit, now in cricket pitch flatness after hay mowing.

At Dale Farm we take a turn onto a new path, which continues along the Manifold Way to Wetton Mill. Here, at the bridge, we are surprised to find a car park full of motorbikes and family cars. There are queues at the cafe, and 'unlocked' families wading and paddling in the river with dads' trouser legs rolled up and children stripped to their underwear, and only the occasional nod to social distancing. Barbecues smoke, and the ice-cream van is very busy.

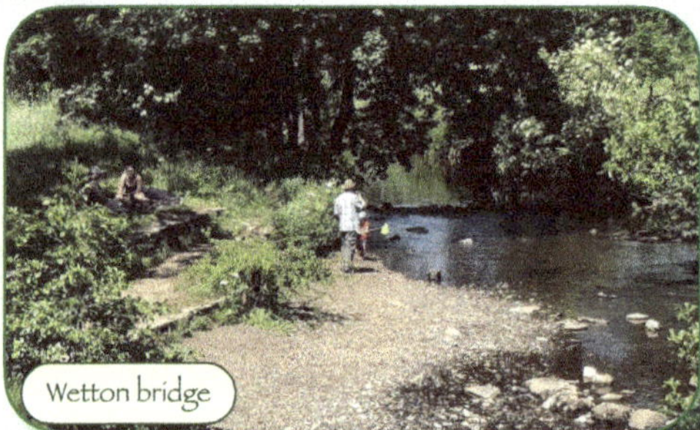

Wetton bridge

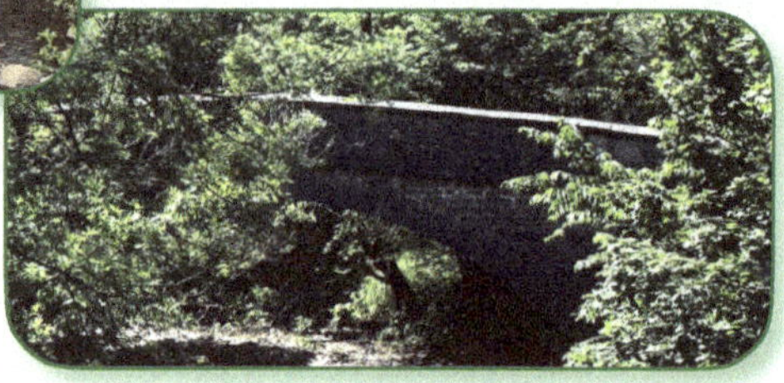

I don't know where these families are from, but they have come in crowds to what is obviously a well-known beauty spot in what we previously thought to be a quiet valley, known only to a few people - an easy mistake to make during illegal lockdown visits!

Remembered today:
Sue Hill; 74;
Retired; Exmouth.

Crossing the bridge, we continue on the opposite bank of the river, where beyond a historic stone bridge, and more hay meadows and barns, we are surprised again to find yet another full car park, complete with yet another ice-cream van.

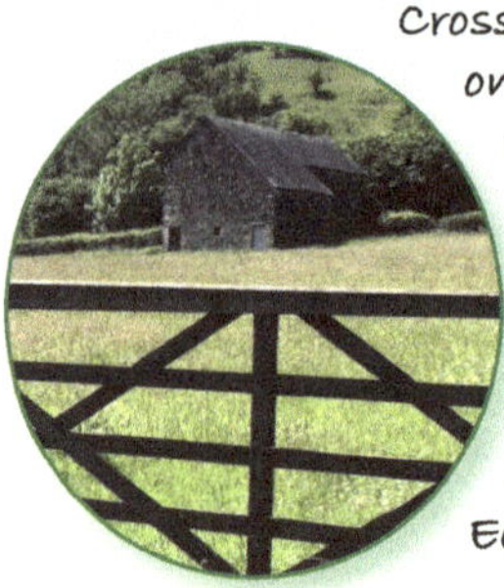

Concerned that we might not find any solitude today, we consider retracing our steps, or even climbing up Ecton Hill.

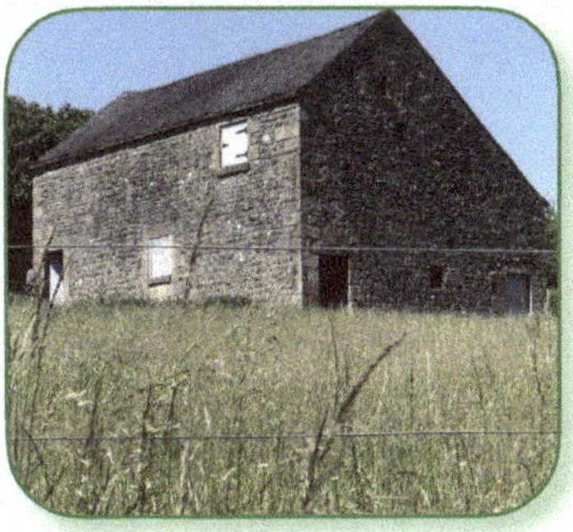

However, we decide to turn through a gate into one of the steep-sided grassy valleys so typical of this landscape.

Out of sight of the car parks, a twisted and scratchy old hawthorn tree gives us shelter for a hot picnic, a rest and an undisturbed snooze. Hawks soar over us, and lemon yellow brimstone butterflies flitter like shards of sunlight through the shady woods by the river, searching for just the right young nettle plant for their eggs.

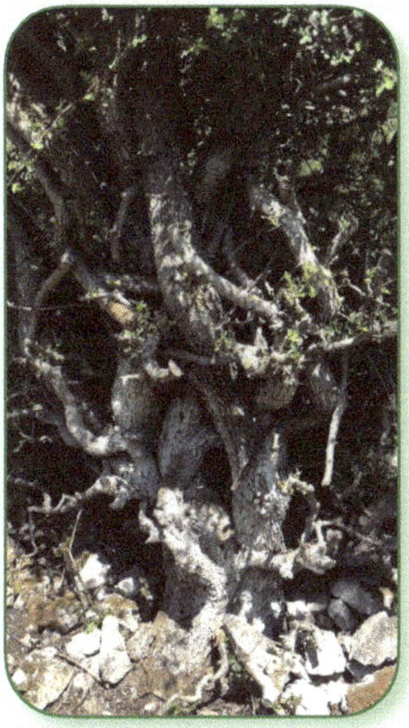

Refreshed, and with map in hand, we walk on, with above us the green slopes of Wetton Hill and the Sugar Loaf shimmering greenly in the afternoon heat. This deserted valley is full of little yellow rock roses and tiny thyme plants, and is such a contrast to the hubbub by the bridge. Although we wonder if we are just being unsociable not to remain there, we are glad of the peace and quiet of nature, and happy to leave the ice creams, paddling and riverside barbecues to others.

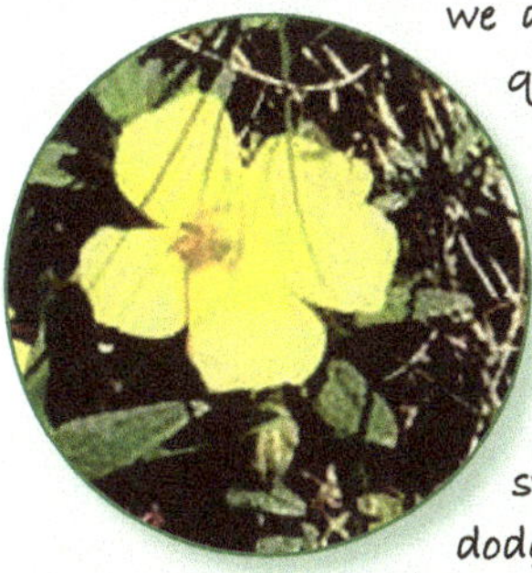

Following the map and guide book we climb the shoulder of the hill, returning to Wetton Mill down a steep field path and through the garden of a farmyard, dodging the flapping washing hung across the footpath.

The return walk is unbelievably hot, avoiding motor bikers and young bathers intent on drinks and ice-creams, until we reach the shady trees of the familiar paths through and beyond Dale Farm.

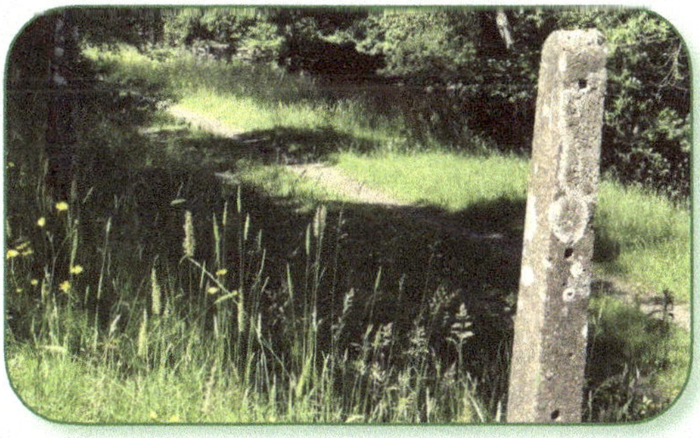

At last we come down through the river valley, walking alternately in and out of baking sun and cooling shade.

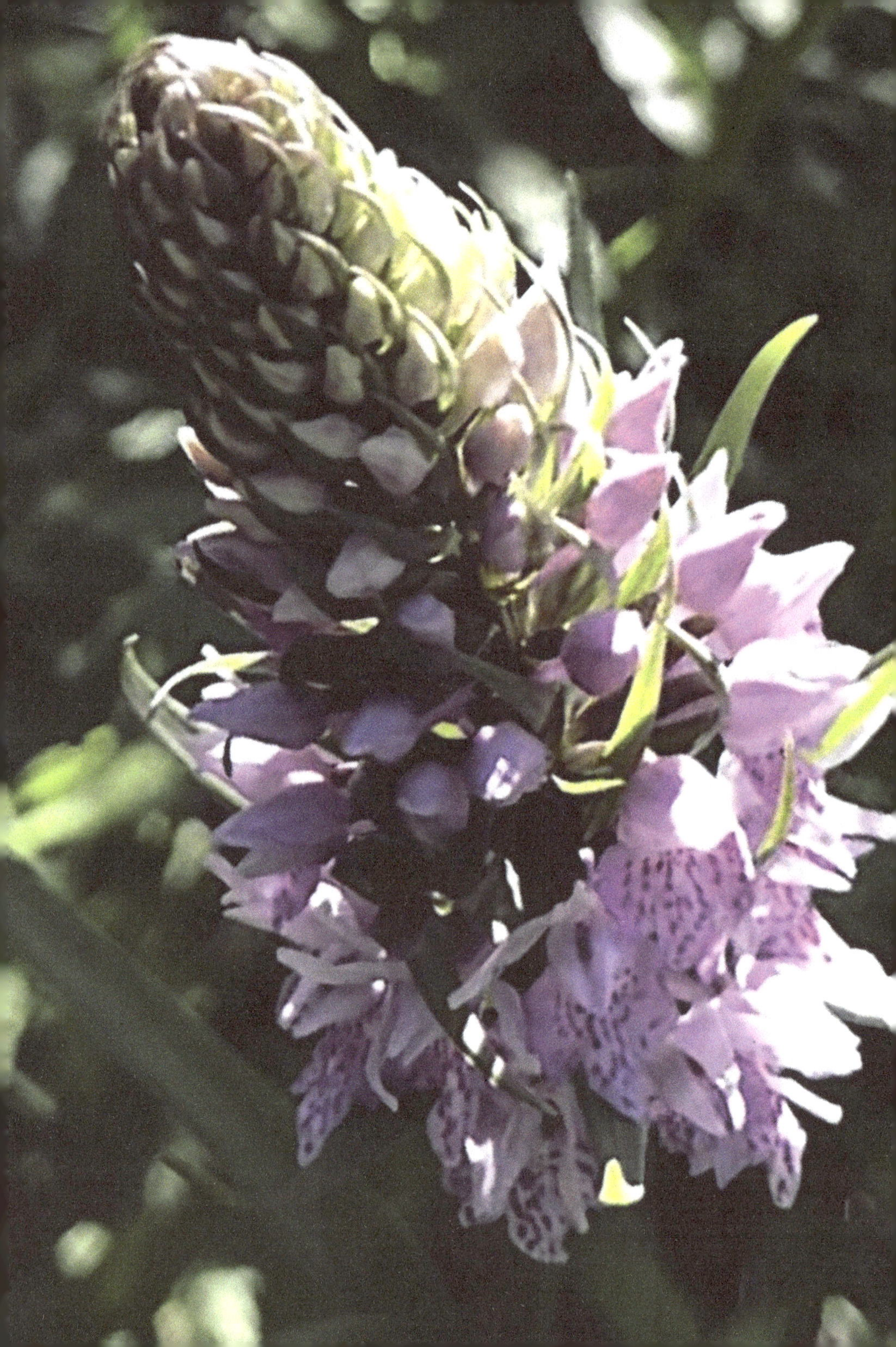

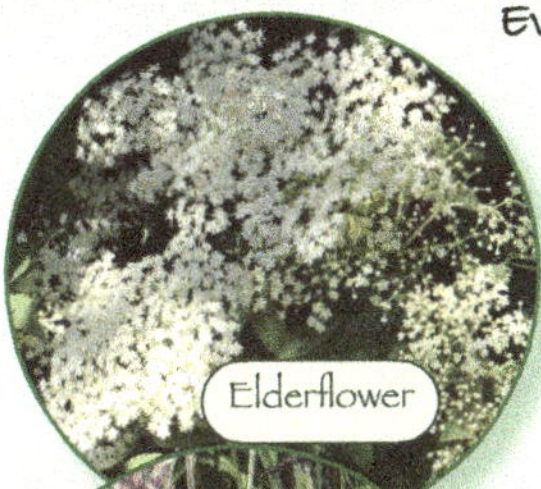
Elderflower

Everything seems further away, and distances much longer as we tire in the hazy, windless summer air of the river valley. Every surface reflects the sun's heat - the hillsides, the riverside track, the black tarmac road in the afternoon sun, even the water meadows high-lit by still-flowering spring blooms are shimmering with heat.

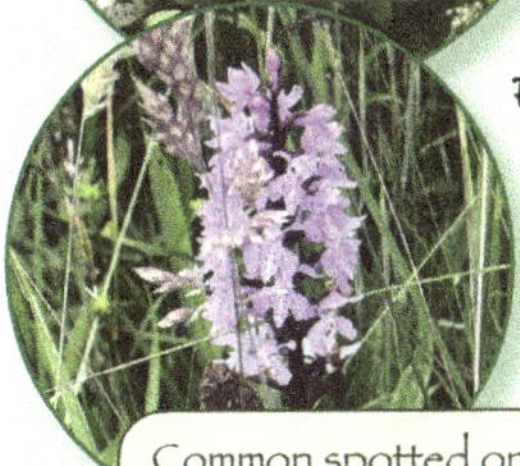
Common spotted orchid

Pale elderflowers shine brightly in the shady hedgerows, towering hogweed casts dainty shadows across the path, a single dark pink wild rose blooms in the shadowy hedge, and a surprise – a perfect pink orchid growing in the long grass of the verge.

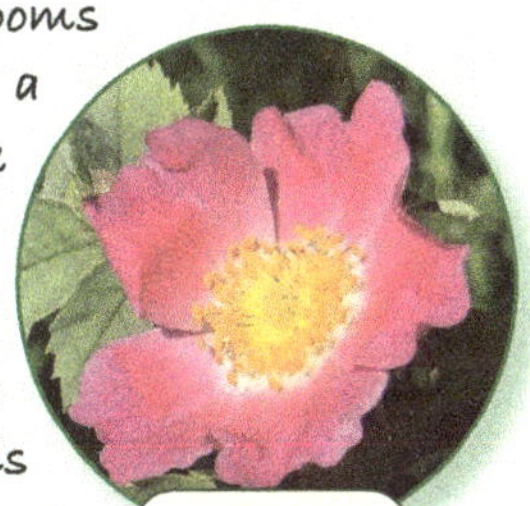
Wild rose

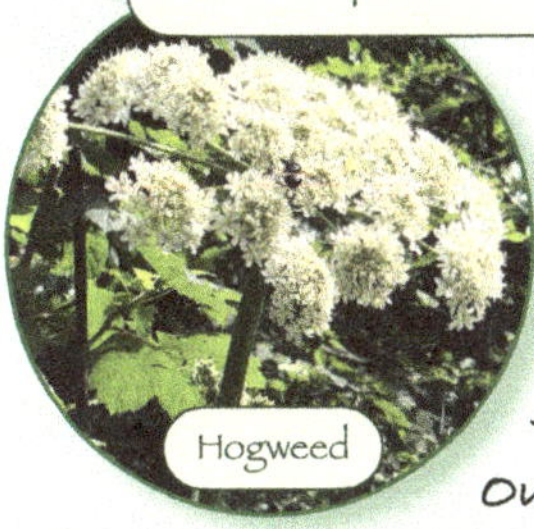
Hogweed

Our expedition on a very hot day and relatively flat terrain is completed, and we eventually reach the hot car – to find we have walked 9.7 kilometres/6.25 miles.

Our return drive is through summer country lanes and hot meadows full of panting sheep and cows sheltering in the leafy shade of the ever-present tangled hawthorn trees.

and it should not have surprised us that: *We were not the only people to visit crowded beauty spots! As the UK experiences a heatwave, Bournemouth, Christchurch & Poole Council declares a major incident after nearly half a million people travel to the Dorset coast.*

Professor Chris Whitty, the UK's chief medical officer, warns people to respect social distancing guidelines while enjoying the weather or the number of COVID-19 cases 'will rise again'.

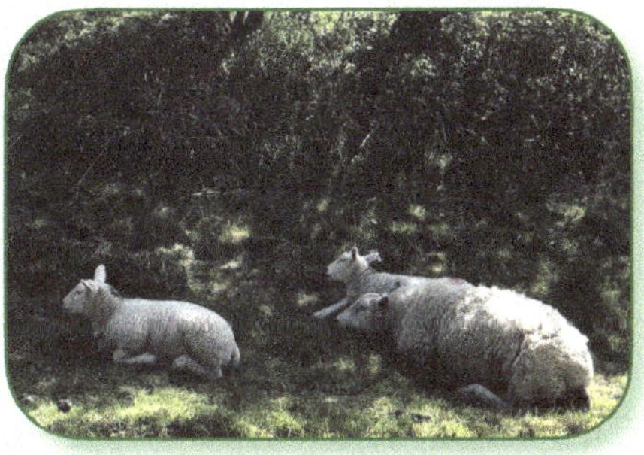

Five friends from Birmingham, all remembered on this day: Nazir Awaan, 67, Choudhary Aslam Wassan, 67, Miah Zaffer, 80, Umar Afzal, 71, & Jawad Iqbal, 50.

Pandemic Day: 106 Lockdown 1: day 92

26/27th June 2020 Confirmed Cases: 160,150 Total deaths: 40,658

26th - THE PM WARNS THAT THE UK COULD BE SET BACK IF PEOPLE CONTINUE TO IGNORE SOCIAL DISTANCING.

We are back to decisions about the house, which we think will now start to take up more and more of our time. Even though the builder should be managing the work every day, he seems distracted by a much bigger contract waiting in the wings. It will become more important for us to be here every day, and we may have to curtail our walks, despite the lifting of regulations.

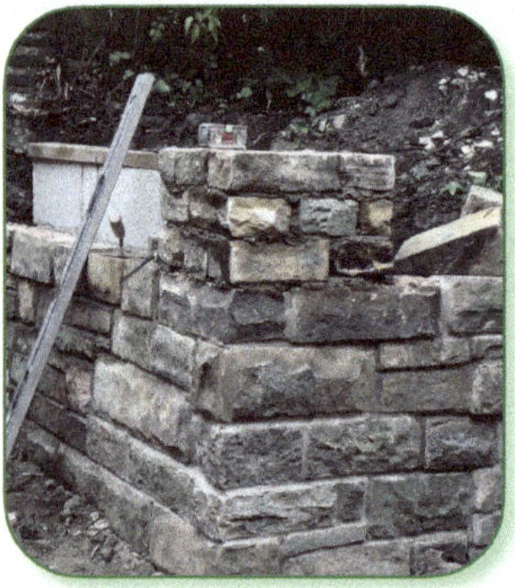

27th - TRAVEL COMPANIES REPORT A BOOM IN BOOKINGS SINCE THE EASING OF QUARANTINE.

After long days of sunshine, thunderstorms rage everywhere as Phill and I go shopping together for the first time in three months. Down local streets, middle class families wander without a care, behaving as though the virus and lockdown have never happened, walking too close to us, not wearing masks, calling forward on the pavements, as if there is no problem. To risk a second spike seems just insane. Order seems to be fraying at the margins, even in this area where people should know better.

A couple remembered: Rameshchandra Bhailalbhai and Suryabala Patel; 88 and 90; Retired civil servant & Housewife; Harrow.

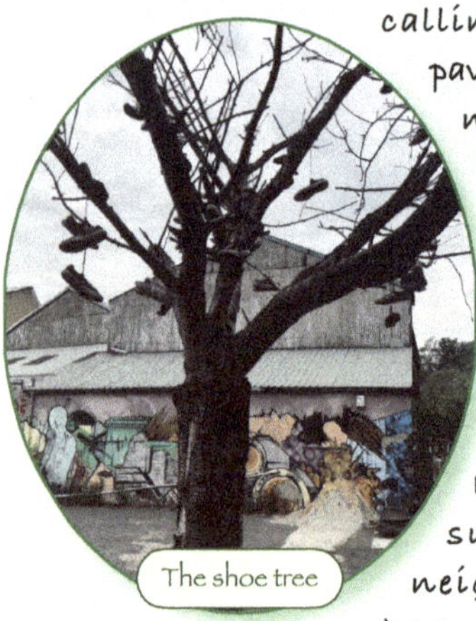

The shoe tree

On our way home we pass a tree decorated with pairs of training shoes - a cheerful creation in a kids' skate park.

I photograph the sunny flowers in neighbours' gardens where Spring has moved brightly into Summer, with Oriental poppies and orange marigolds now invaded with wild geraniums and pink campions, all glowing brightly after the rain.

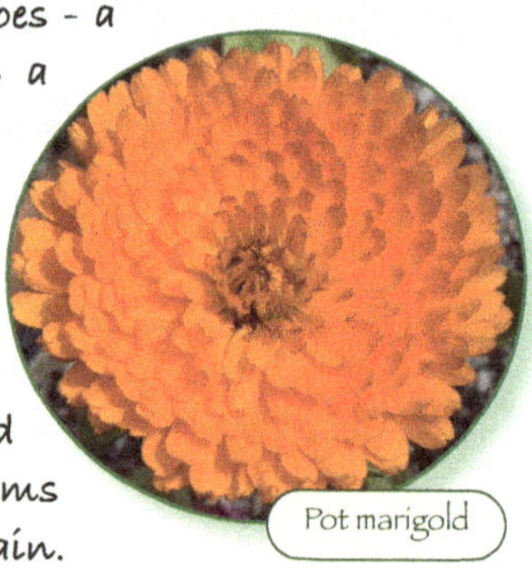

Pot marigold

Pandemic Day: 107/108 Lockdown 1: day 93/94

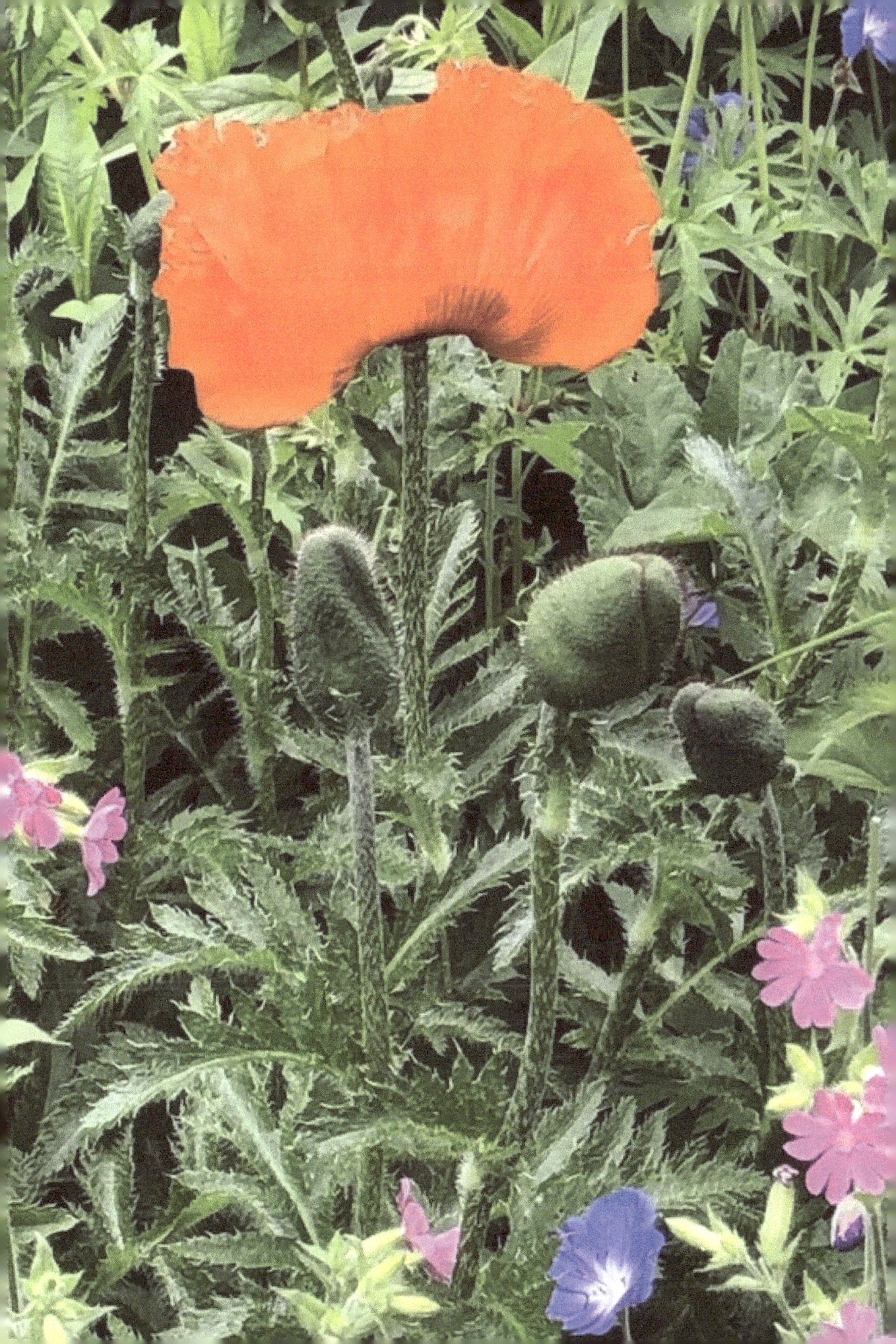

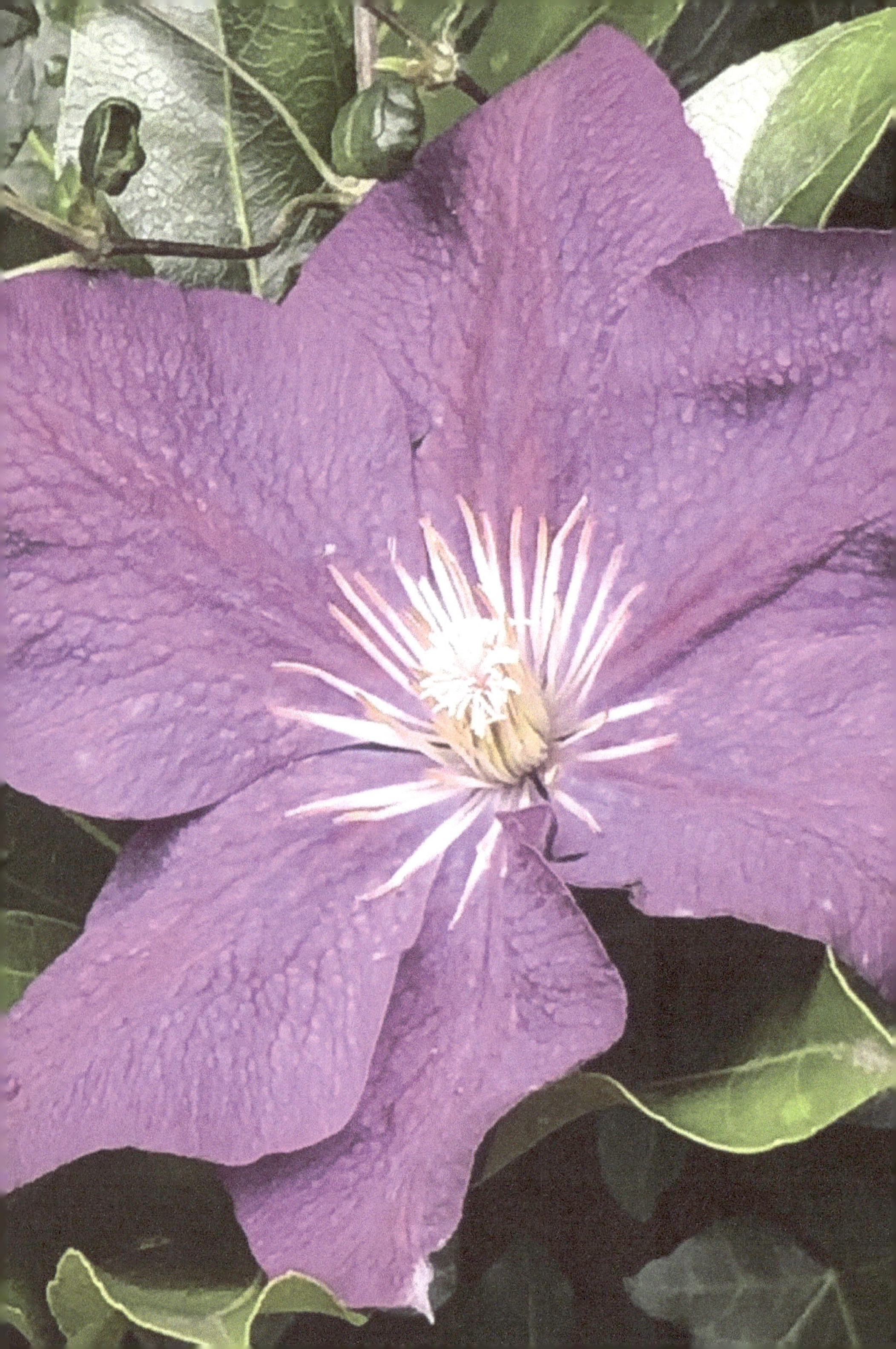

28/30th June 2020 Confirmed Cases: 160,587 Total deaths: 40,739

28th - THE GOVERNMENT IS CONSIDERING A LOCAL LOCKDOWN FOR LEICESTER CITY, FOLLOWING AN ALARMING INCREASE IN CASES.

We have Sunday evening 'family lunch' at our house, our first meal together indoors for 3 months, we have cooked meals for each other, exchanged biscuits, cake and flapjack, and shared snacks out of doors, but never inside.

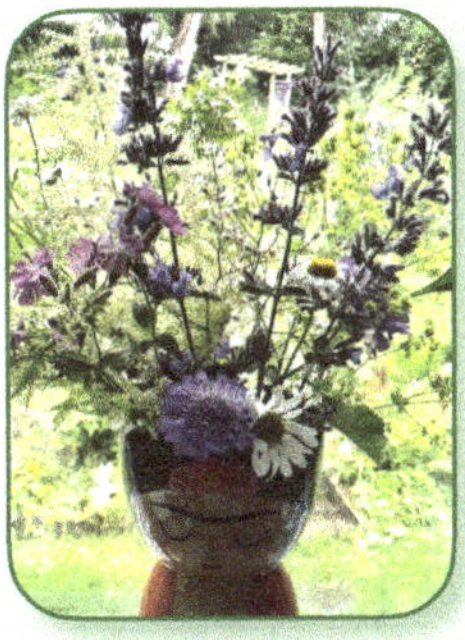

On this momentous day we sit carefully distanced round the dining table, with doors and windows open, politely passing things to each other. I don't know how long it will be before this sort of event will feel normal again, but this wonderful evening is enough for me for now!

29th - AS EXPECTED, THE HEALTH SECRETARY ANNOUNCES STRICTER LOCKDOWN MEASURES FOR LEICESTER - SHOPS & SCHOOLS THERE WILL CLOSE FROM 2ND JULY.

All but essential travel should now be avoided. The local lockdown of Leicester begins as the rest of England hopes for easing of restrictions from 4th July.

30th - THE PM SETS OUT A £5 BILLION POST-CORONA RECOVERY PLAN FOR THE UK.

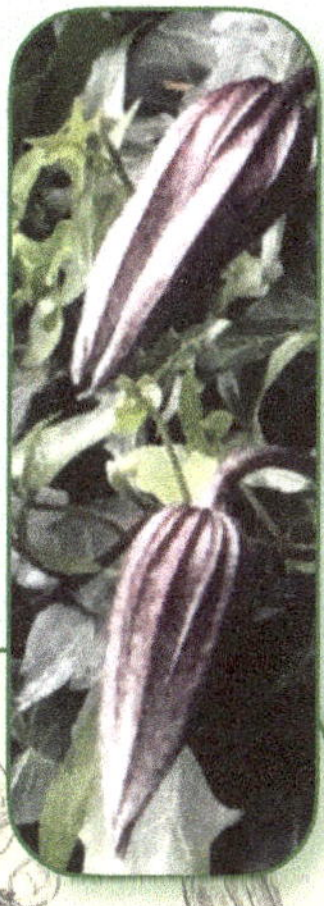

The clematis we planted last year has burst into purple glory, with so many flowers and buds shining among the ivy on the back wall.

It's almost 100 days since lockdown began, but we still don't feel confident enough to think about going to restaurants. Although hairdressers open next week, and despite a desperate need for haircuts, we won't go until we are sure of safety.

A life remembered: Ken Kayani; 73; Market trader; Chorlton, Manchester; UK.

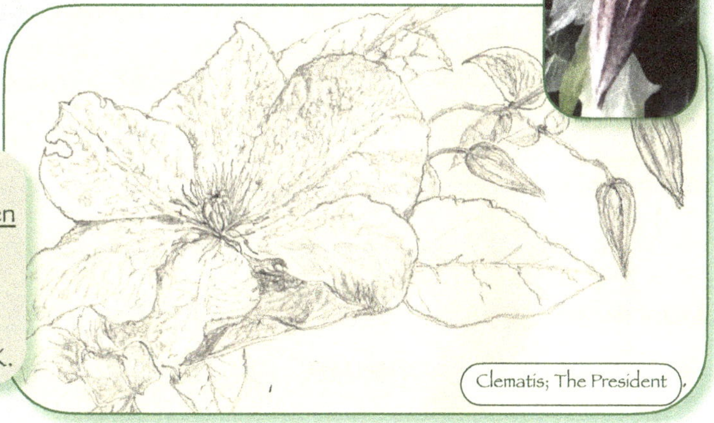

Clematis; The President

Pandemic Day: 109/111 Lockdown 1: day 95/97

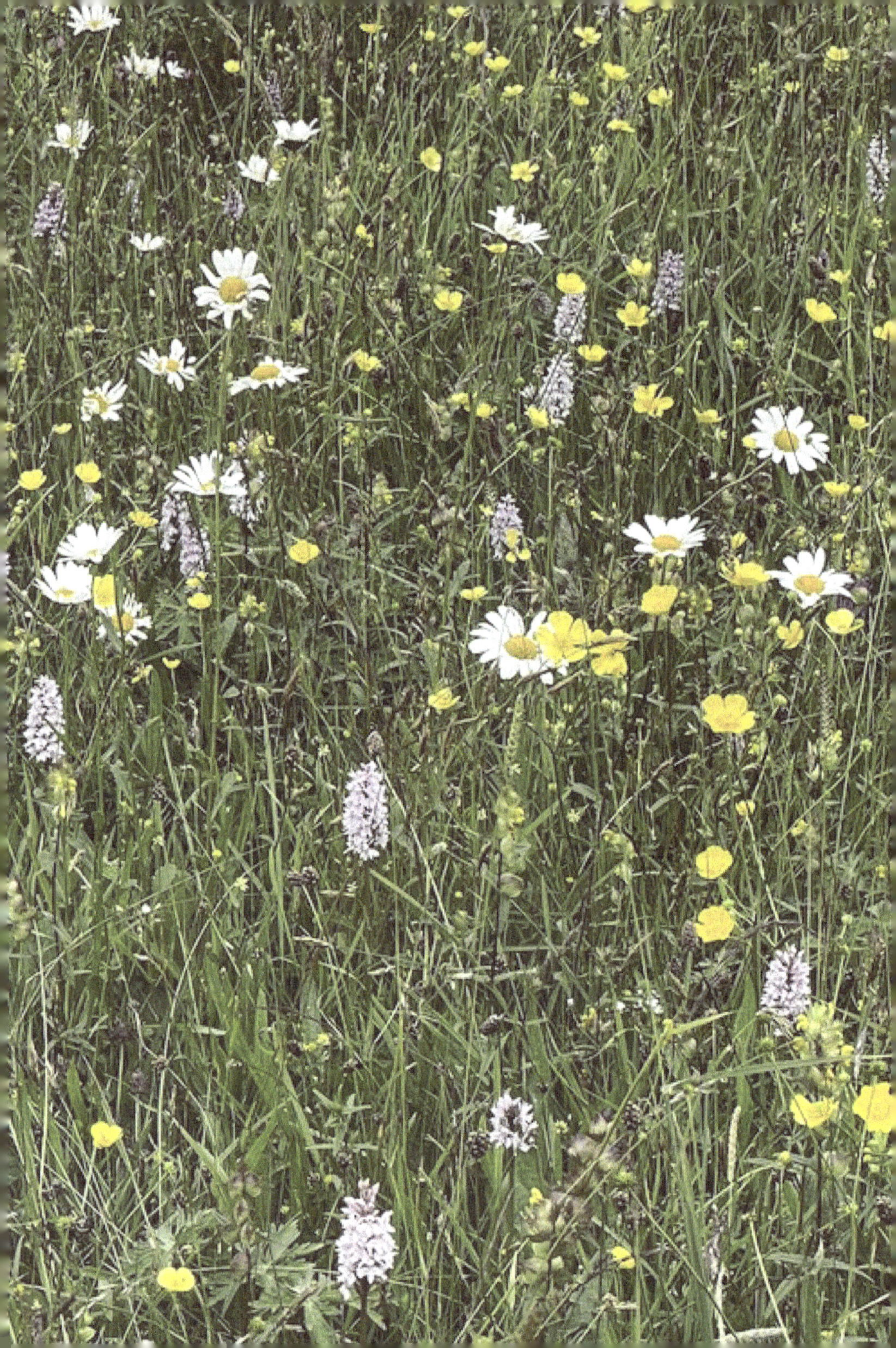

June 2020 ends

Lockdown continues during June, gradually easing, but with such complex arrangements that it is no wonder people can't keep up - 'Rule of Six','Meet outdoors but not indoors', and then different rules in different cities and areas. Mid month we are plunged back into the Black Lives Matter debate, another global issue for discussion and demonstration as, triggered by the news of the death of George Floyd, the statue of Edward Colston is torn down and pushed into Bristol Harbour,

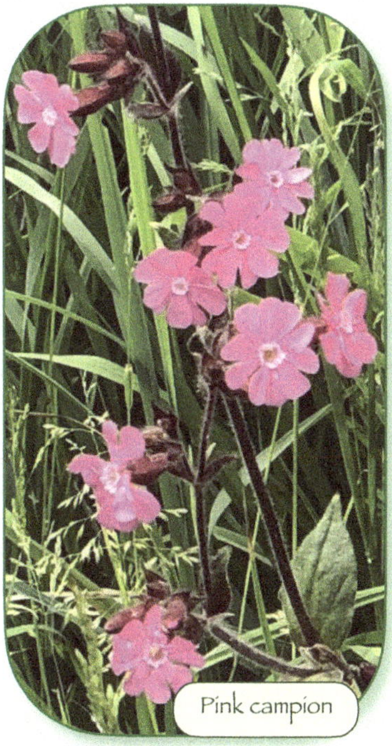

Pink campion

For most of the month, the fine weather continues and we make more escapes in June than in any previous month, particularly at times when restrictions are eased.

During a third visit to Ecton we explore mining heritage and scramble up and down the hot slippery grasses and over tiny alpine versions of hillside flowers in the early summer sun. On another very hot day we extend our knowledge of the Manifold Trail by walking further along the valley below the steep slopes of Ecton Hill.

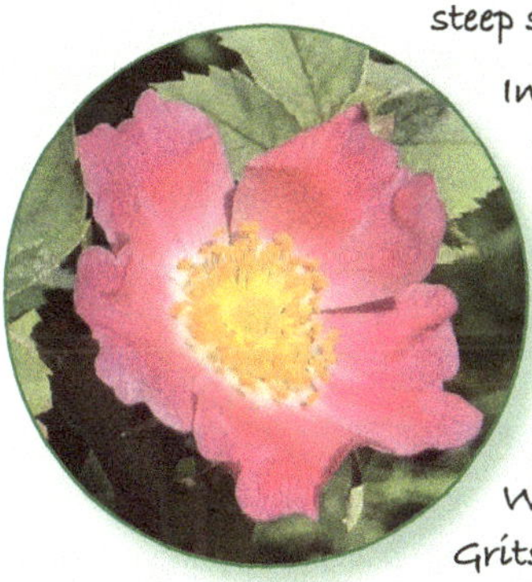

In June, we also try a new walk from Hartington, through Biggin Dale and Wolfscote Dale, meeting very few others, even on what is apparently a very popular trail, giving evidence of people's hesitance to return to their normal behaviour.

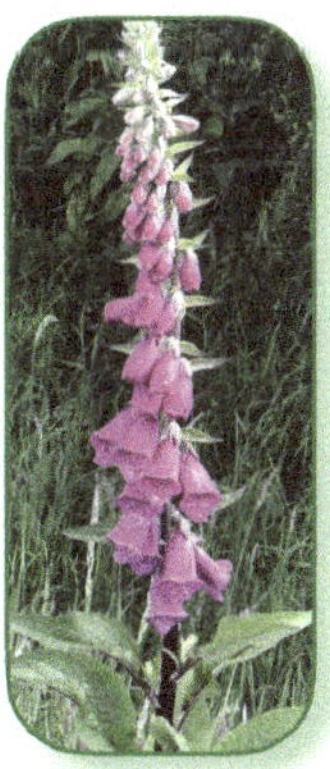

We return to Wincle to walk the Gritstone Trail again, this time over hills covered with magenta foxgloves on walls, beside paths, under trees and in floods on sunny banks. Sitting under a huge sycamore tree, it is hard to believe what has happened to us all in the hundred days since 19th March, when we walked over these hills as lockdown began.

Locally, we continue to revisit the Botanical Gardens and the garden of the Children's House, where work eventually starts on 10th June.

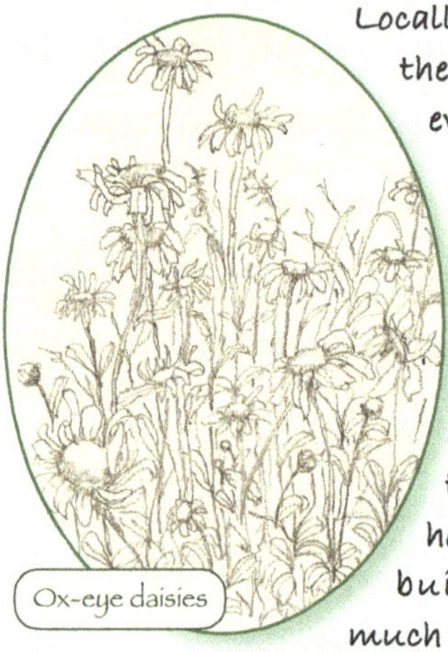

Ox-eye daisies

I am surprised that building work in the city appears to be going on almost as normal, except for the shortage of some materials, and we are promised completion of the work in six to eight weeks, bringing us to the beginning of September. We hope this is accurate, but by the end of the month, as the work team invades the house and garden and the builder himself becomes much less evident, we predict that we will only meet the completion if we give up all our own time to the project. We will need to restrict our undercover visits to the country to concentrate on ensuring we meet a September deadline.

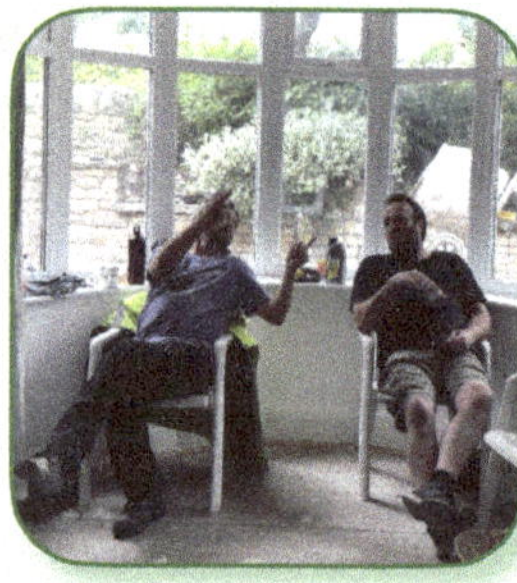

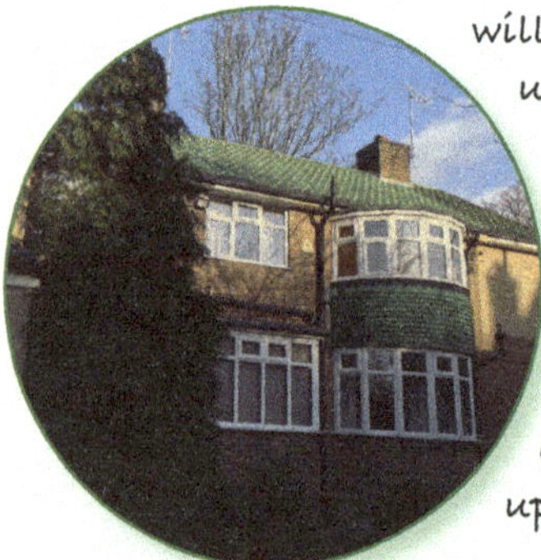

By the end of the month, work on the front yard has begun and the recycled stone is used to make a new pillar and low wall. Work indoors is concentrated on stripping out, rebuilding walls upstairs, and thinking about the kitchen.

As the hundredth day of lockdown approaches, I go shopping for the first time since March, and come to the end of my first sketchbook - both weirdly disconcerting experiences.

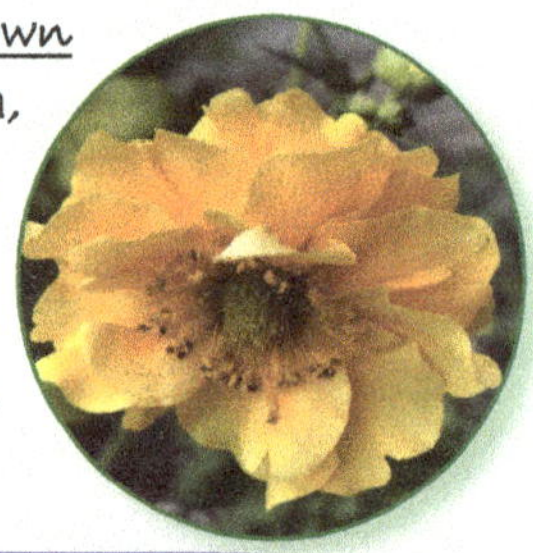

And although the Covid increases have slowed, still the number of cases and the dreadful death toll across the UK continue to rise.

TOTAL UK CASES AND DEATHS: 30th June 2020

Total confirmed cases to date - 284,759 (up 28,333)

Total deaths to date - 40,739 (up 2,520)

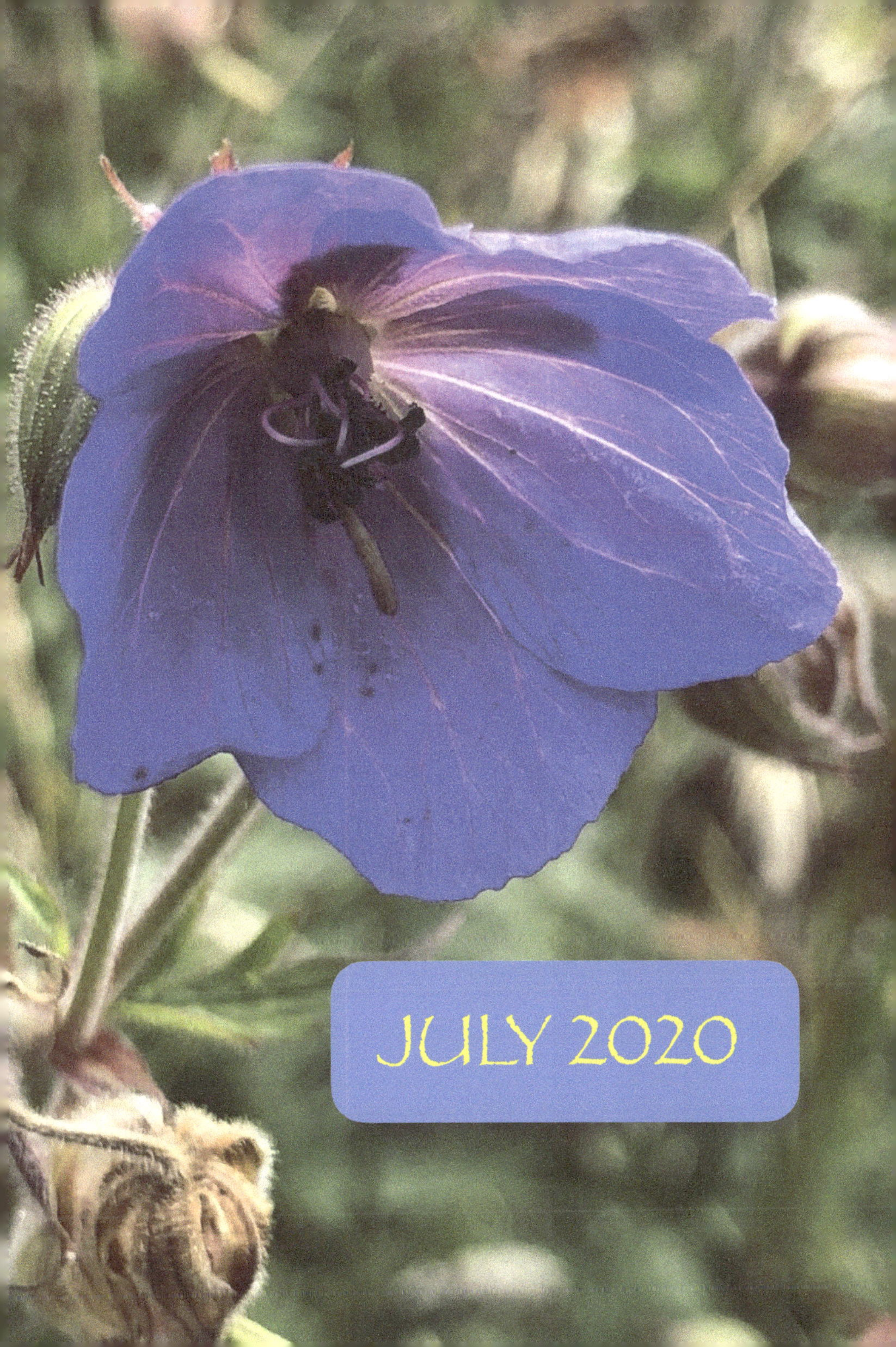
JULY 2020

1st - ON THE FIRST DAY OF A NEW MONTH, SCIENTISTS EXPRESS CONCERN ABOUT THE PROPOSED 4TH JULY OPENING OF PUBS AND RESTAURANTS.

It now seems that if testing at airports had not been stopped in March, and entrants to the country had been effectively quarantined, 15,000 deaths could have been avoided. England is now among the most severely affected countries in Europe.

2nd - THE OWNERS OF CAFE ROUGE AND BELLA ITALIA PUT BOTH INTO ADMINISTRATION WITH THE LOSS OF OVER 1.000 JOBS.

A life remembered; Augustine Agyei-mensah (Gus); 78; Learning disability Nurse; Northampton; UK.

New infections in England are occurring at a rate of 25,000 per week. We go to B&Q and the Co-op! it's like a dream - so much still the same, but significant things very different, with plastic gloves, masks, perspex screens, arrows, footprints on the floor. Shoppers clutch plants, bananas or special offers as they scuttle about wondering if they should be one or two metres apart – an arm's length, an ironing board length, or as the milkman says, 'a cow's length'.

3rd - POLICE GAIN THE POWERS TO ENFORCE THE LOCAL LOCKDOWN RECENTLY IMPOSED IN LEICESTER. 100 DAYS OF LOCKDOWN.

On this 100th day of lockdown, we decide to extend the utility room into the old garage space by knocking down the wall between it and the current utility room and bricking in the garage doors to match the front of the house.

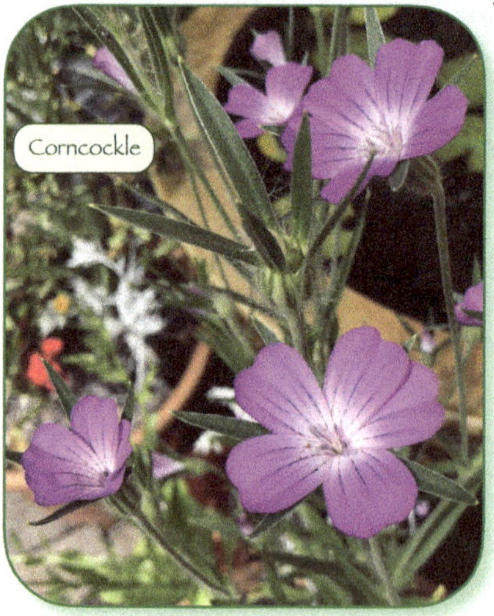
Corncockle

The lovely but possibly lethal magenta corncockle plants we bought in Hartington are blooming. Corncockle is an ancient plant that originated in the Iron Age and spread through cornfields, where it was often included in flour and eaten by mistake. Their flowers and seeds do contain mild toxins, but many plants are poisonous, including such popular blooms as daffodils, hellebores, lupins and particularly foxgloves, so growing this rare and pretty plant really doesn't present a risk to us, and is another plant for pollinators in the garden .

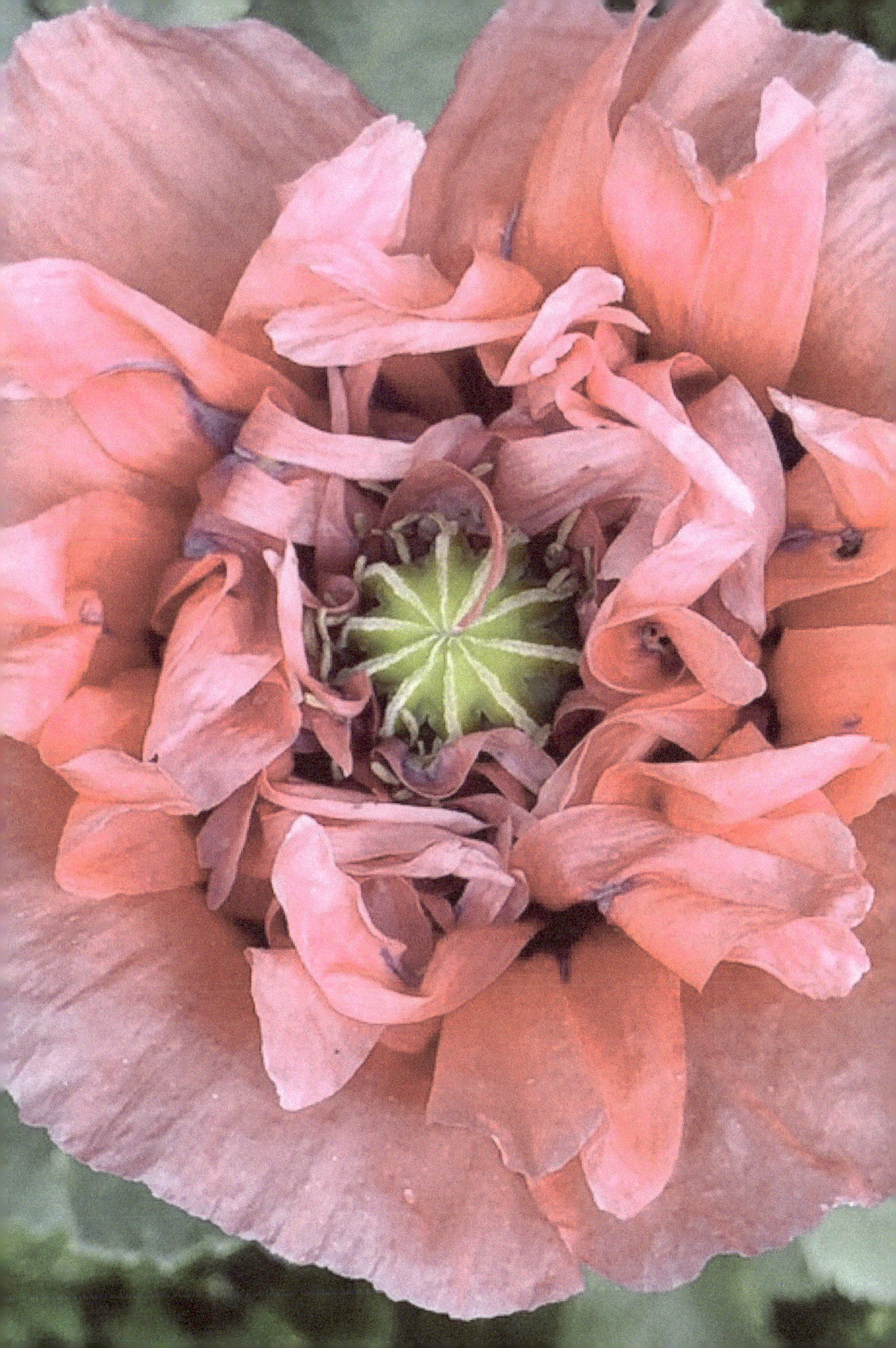

4/6th July 2020 Confirmed Cases: 245,814 Total deaths: 40,934

4th - RESTAURANTS, PUBS AND HAIRDRESSERS OPEN, AND SOME OF THE ORIGINAL LOCKDOWN RESTRICTIONS ARE LIFTED.

A life remembered on this day: Ranjith Chandrapala; 64; Bus driver; Ealing.

The Ecclesall Road is scarily just like before lockdown. Everywhere is open and groups of 30-somethings drink all afternoon in their evening finery with no masks or distancing. The UK's first local lockdown comes into force in Leicester City.

5th - THE UK MARKS THE 72TH ANNIVERSARY OF THE FOUNDING OF THE NHS WITH A NATIONAL ROUND OF APPLAUSE. THE NATIONAL GALLERY WILL REOPEN ON 8TH JULY.

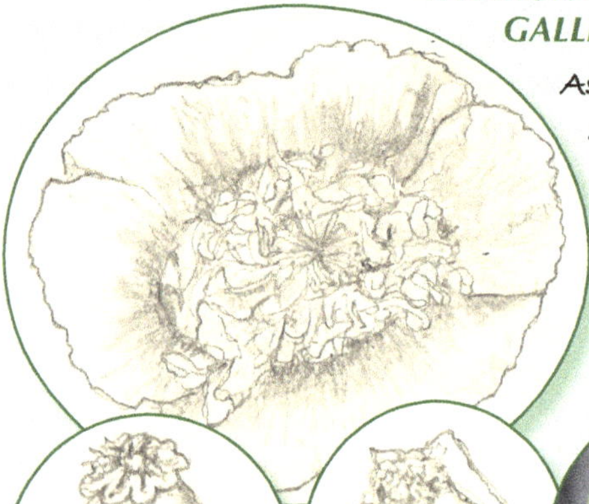

As usual on Sunday, we cook a meal for six, then take four portions to Sarah so we can at least share the same food, even in two separate houses. We receive cake in exchange, and as we leave, we admire the frilly pink peony poppies that have seeded by their garages, and are blooming bravely in the poor soil and competition from docks and dandelions.

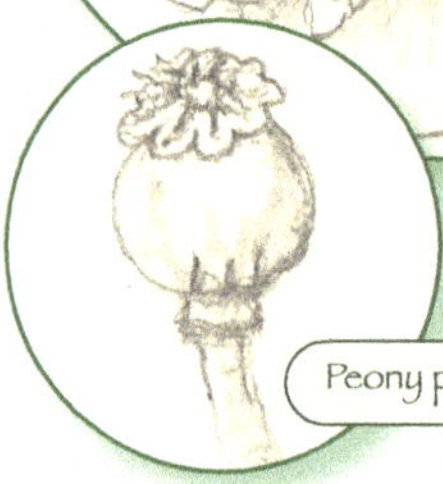

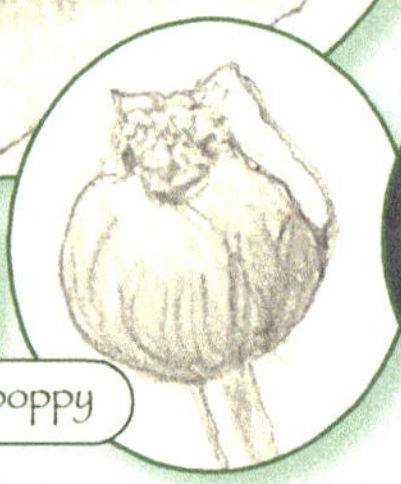

Peony poppy

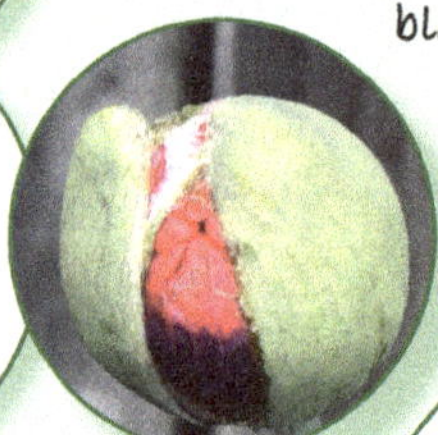

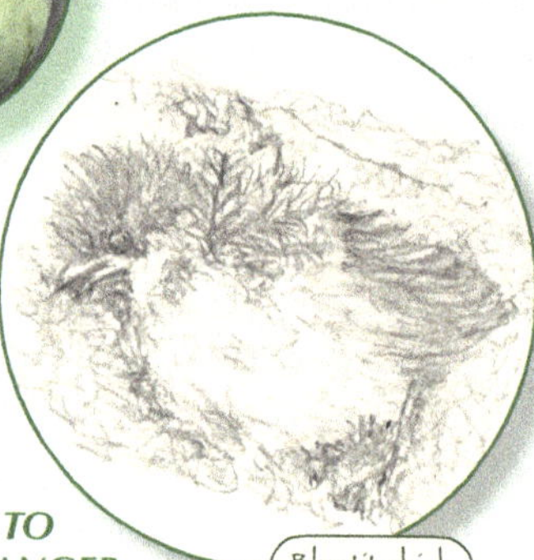

Bluetit chick

As Phill removes a smokers' box on the wall by the back door of the Children's House, he discovers a little nest inside with two tiny, but sadly long dead bluetit chicks, that must have grown too big to escape this formerly safe nest.

6th - WAITING LISTS AND CANCER DEATHS ARE SET TO INCREASE DUE TO PRESSURE ON THE NHS. PRET A MANGER PLANS TO CLOSE 30 OUTLETS.

I research places to walk, looking for wild flower meadows, and find reference to Hartington Wildflower Meadows. Despite the risks, we will go and try to find these tomorrow, as we feel really cooped up.

Pandemic Day: 115/117 Lockdown 1: day 101/103

7th July 2020 Confirmed Cases: 246,386 Total deaths: 40,985

DOWNING STREET REJECTS CALLS FOR BORIS JOHNSON TO ISSUE AN APOLOGY AFTER COMMENTS THE PREVIOUS DAY THAT 'TOO MANY CARE HOMES DIDN'T REALLY FOLLOW PROCEDURES' OVER COVID-19, BUT SAYS WHAT HE WAS SAYING WAS THAT NOT ENOUGH WAS KNOWN ABOUT THE VIRUS IN ITS EARLY STAGES.

A life remembered on this day: Cecilia Fashanu; 63; Nurse; Carlisle; UK.

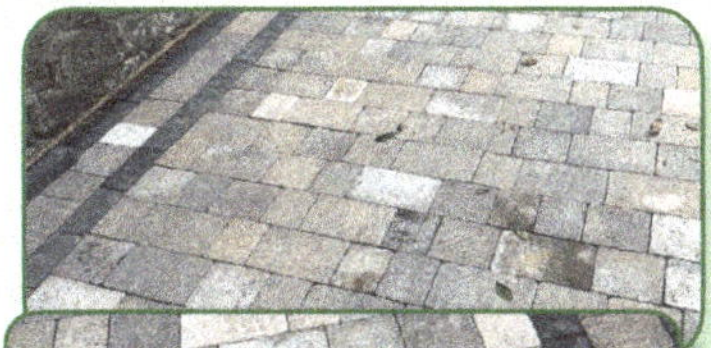

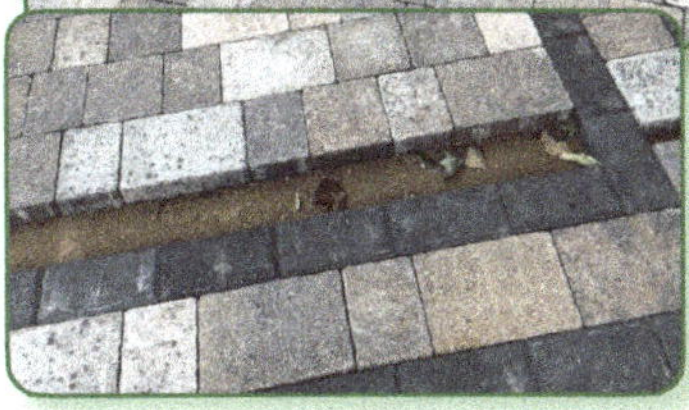

Many restrictions have now been lifted, so, after a brief visit to see progress on the front paving at the Children's House, we can set off for Hartington to look for the local flower meadows without a shred of guilt - no longer 'harmless' or even 'harmful criminals'!

We drive to Hartington Station, but just as we leave, a permeating drizzle begins to fall, and continues to fall for the rest of the day!

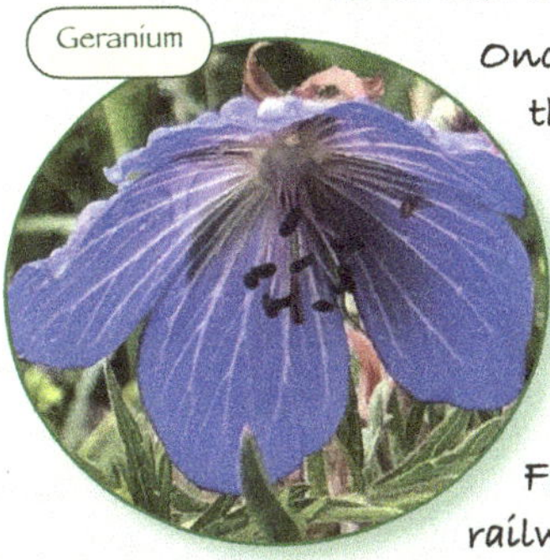

Geranium

Once you get to the station car park, the directions to the meadows are clear, but even though there are people on the footpath, none seem to be interested in exploring the nature reserve. This seems strange, but no signs or notices could prepare you for the natural wonders to come, once you enter this peaceful haven of nature.

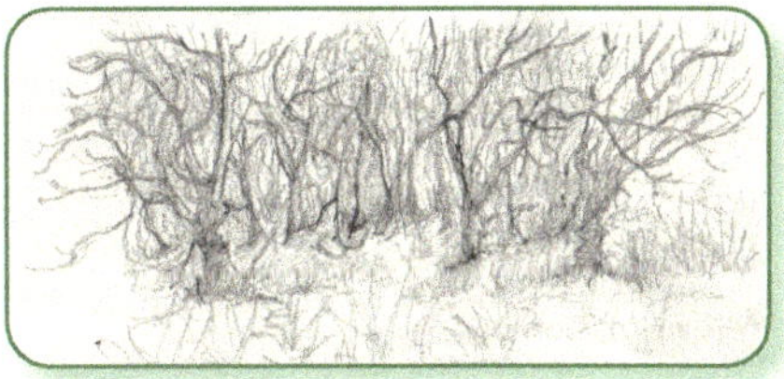

From the old railway line we climb up an uneven wooden stair hidden in the greenery under the trees, and through a gate in a tall, moss-covered stone wall. The path weaves through an ancient wood full of moss-coated field maples and brambles, opening onto the wide scrubland where the first wildflowers begin to show themselves - lavender scabious on waving stems, rosebay willowherb in pink bud, and raspberry canes bearing free red fruits. But these are not the real flower meadows, just old mine workings left to re-wild - the true meadows are yet to come.

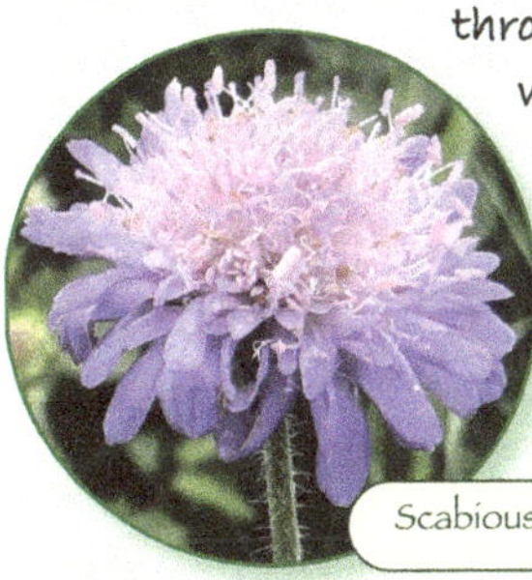

Scabious

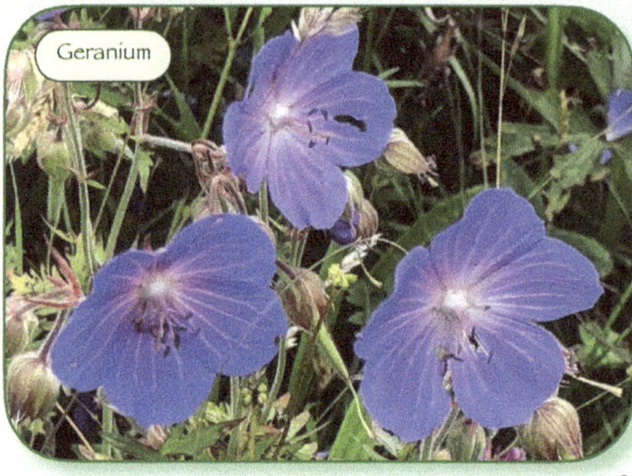
Geranium

Squeezing through a little wooden gate we enter a floral haven, where, even under the increasingly heavy drizzle, the flowers are in glorious bloom. Several fields on this south sloping hillside have been left to flower in natural wildness, looking just as meadows did between the First and Second World Wars, before intensive farming in English meadows almost completely eliminated the wildflowers.

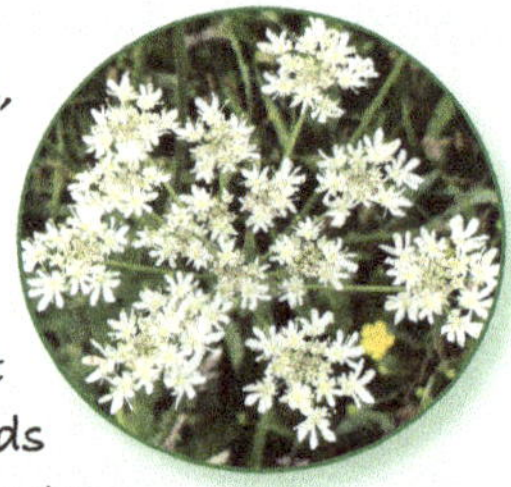

Across these fields, thousands of wild orchids, their tall, complex, patterned, pink and white flower pyramids, calmly stand in the rain, and nestling among them in the long grasses, hundreds of knapweed blooms with punk magenta haircuts, and blue meadow cranesbill lift their heads. Tiny yellow sparks of black meddick heads and the last buttercups shine with raindrops, and everywhere the green spears of plantain leaves give evidence of earlier floods of these plants with their starry, firework flowers.

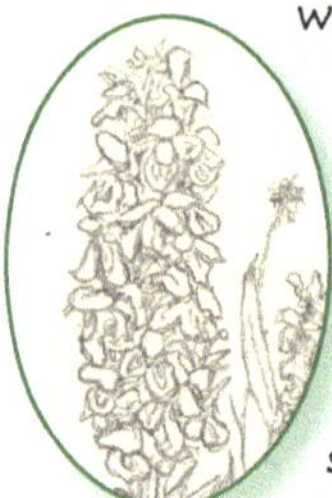

Great patches of cranesbill and knapweed dust the field, contrasting with clouds of white ox-eye daisies, feathery pignut and the wide, pale umbels of pignut, all dripping with raindrops. As we continue up the hill, we see golden clumps of catsear about to seed, the strange drumstick heads of red bistort standing darkly dripping, and under everything the glowing colours of red and white clover, yellow lady's bedstraw, and yellow rattle, with its rattly seed heads just beginning to ripen. Among them all, despite the rain, bees and butterflies continue to make nectar forays on their wet wings.

These meadows are the most flower-filled we have ever seen, since managing our own flower meadows for ten years in the Pennine hills.

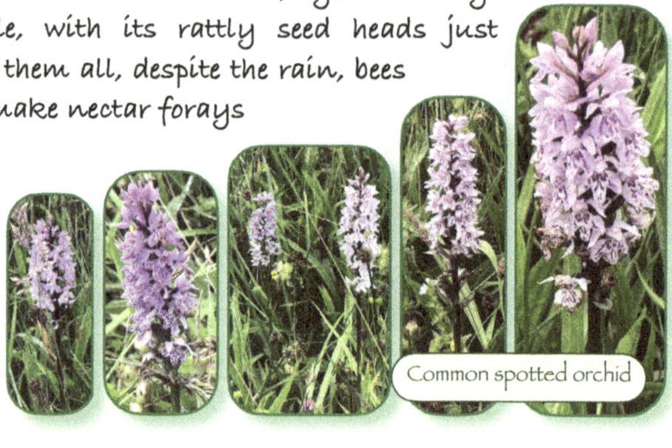
Common spotted orchid

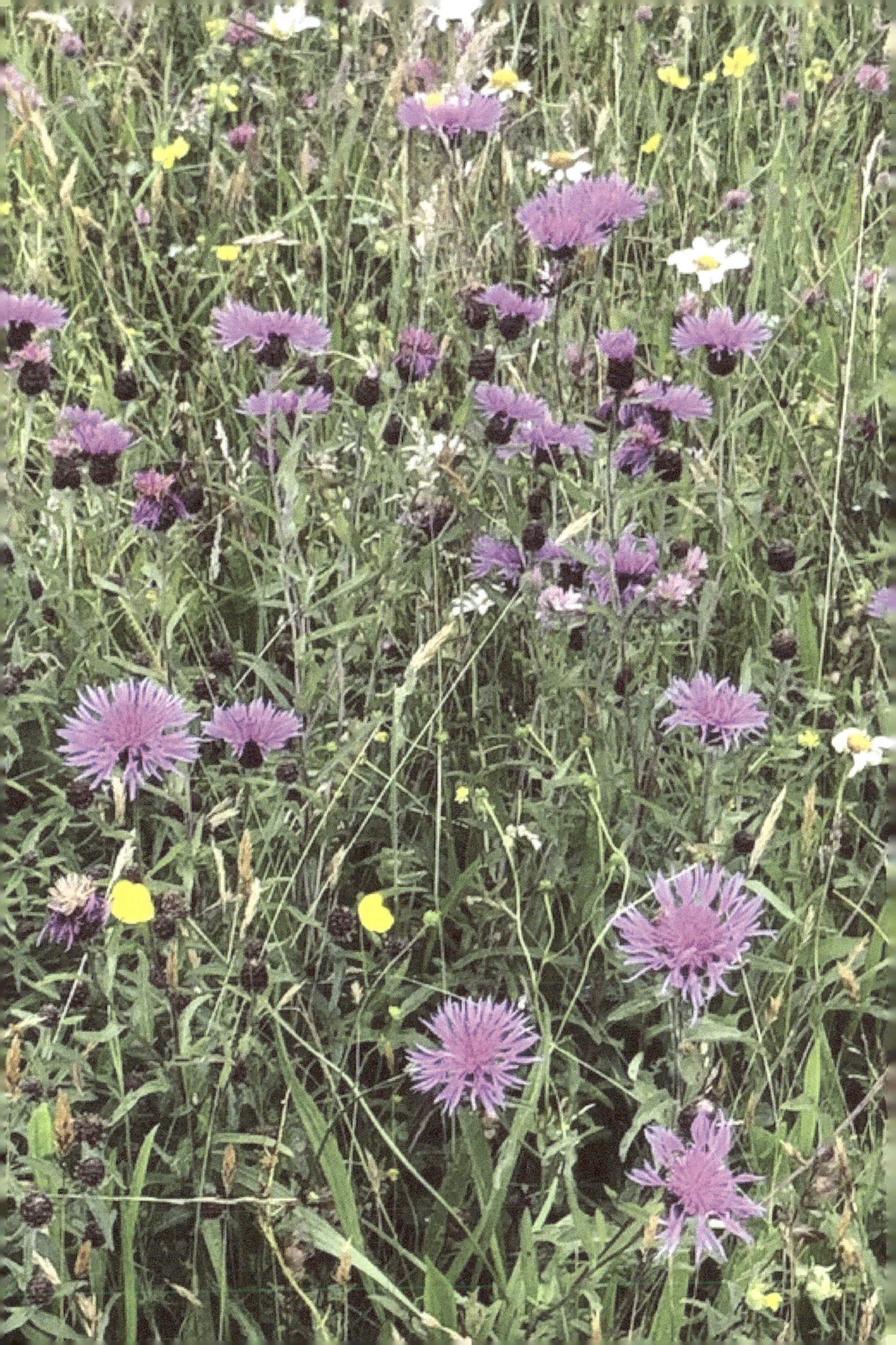

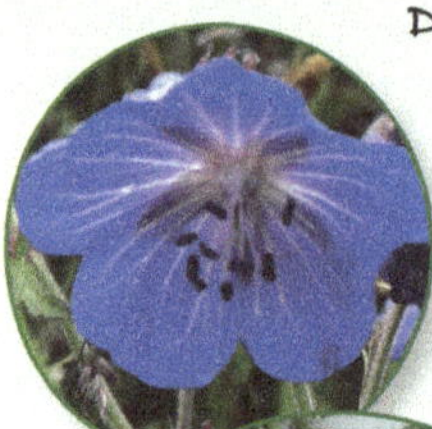

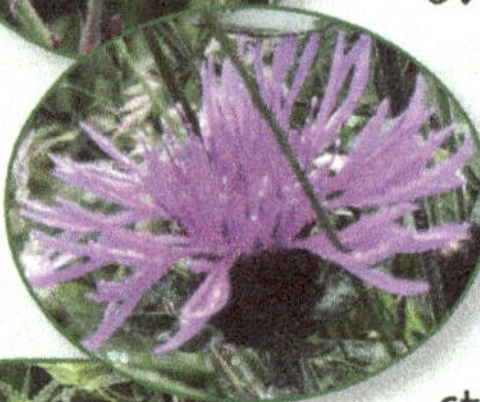

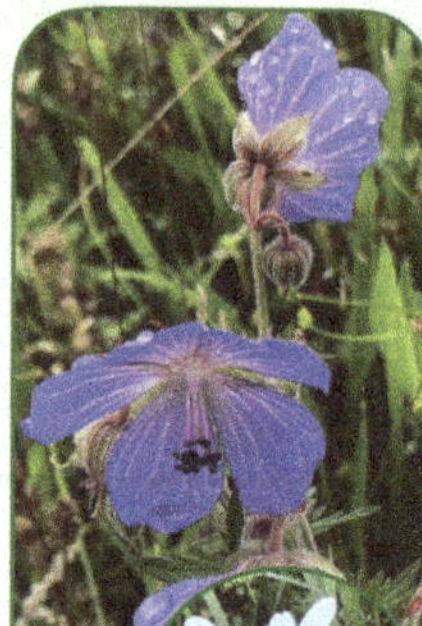

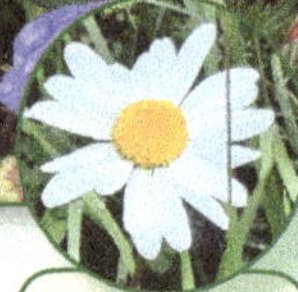

Despite the rain, we walk to the top of the fields, to stare in amazement at such a privileged sight, stretching down the hill like a tapestry created by the finest needlewomen.

Eventually, the soaking, straight down rain drives us back, down through the long grass and wet flowers, nodding gently as the raindrops fall in the still air. Past the wet bees and butterflies, still valiantly working, through the dripping gates and past the dripping woods until we reach the car park

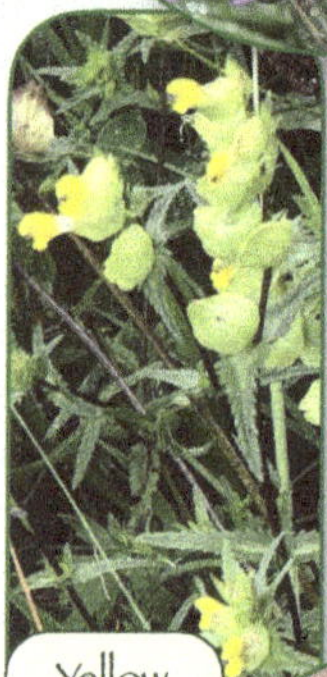

Yellow rattle

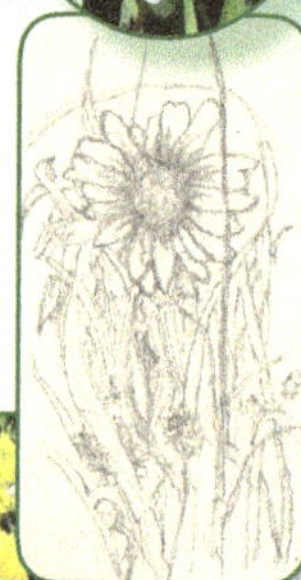

We eat our picnic in the car, return to Hartington to pick up our new plants from the village store, and drive home, somewhat stunned by what we have seen, and determined to return soon to this lost world, unchanged since the 1940s when such fields were commonplace.

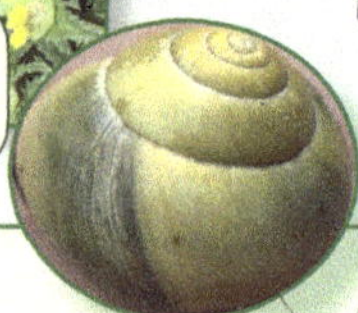

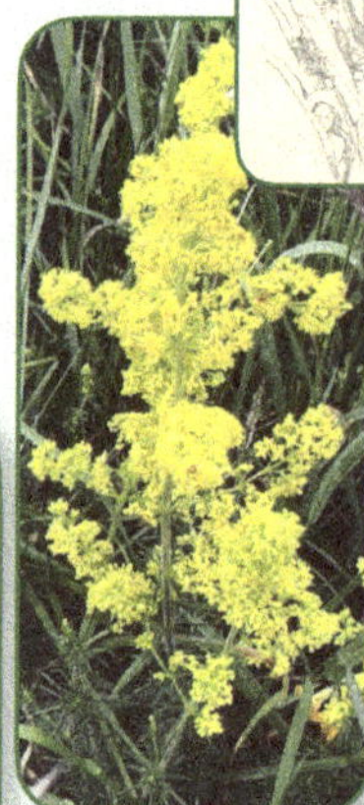

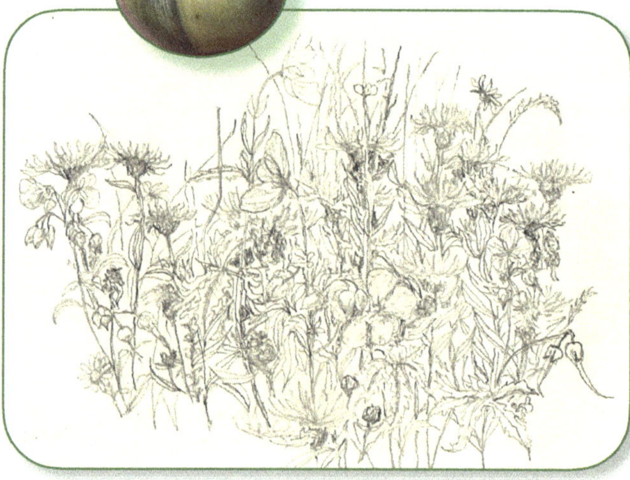

and as we drive out of the city: *Circus performers call on the UK government to include their industry in the arts rescue package unveiled recently.*

Pandemic Day: 118 Lockdown 1: day 104

8th/12th July 2020 Confirmed Cases: 248,895 Total deaths: 41,079

8th, 9th, 10th - LOCKDOWN RESTRICTIONS ARE FURTHER EASED, PINTS ARE POURED IN PUBS AND COUPLES FINALLY SAY 'I DO'.

Rain falls incessantly every day, and we are spurred into action by the pressure to do something about packing. So with help from our two teenage grandsons, we make good headway over these three days. I do little else, not even drawing, constantly worrying that the flowers in the Hartington meadows will fade unseen.

11th - FURTHER RELAXATION OF LOCKDOWN ALLOWS OUTDOOR SWIMMING POOLS AND WATER PARKS TO RE-OPEN - OWNERS SAY THE SEASON HAS BECOME 'UNVIABLE'. UNUSUALLY, PRIME MINISTER JOHNSON IS SEEN WEARING A MASK IN PUBLIC.

Another lost young life remembered: Lauren Jones; 25; Doctor's Administrator; Wales.

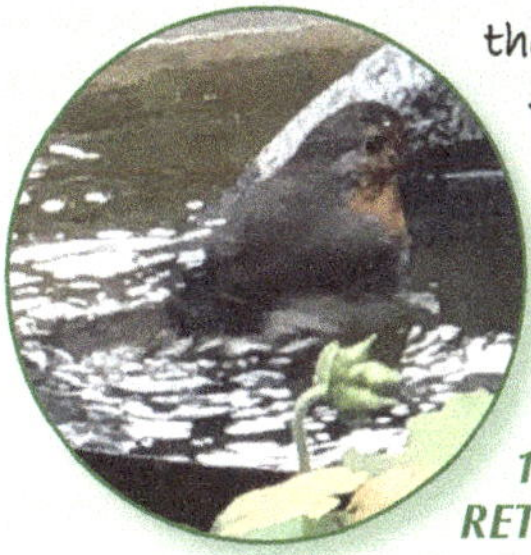

It is our son John's birthday, and there is no hope that we will be able to visit him in Arizona now or even later this year, when our grand-daughter's wedding is planned. Despite the relaxation of regulations, a transatlantic flight seems as far away as ever.

A robin comes every day to bathe in the bird bath.

12th - PRIMARK WILL NOT TAKE ADVANTAGE OF THE JOBS RETENTION BONUS OF £30 MILLION.

Our walks to the Botanical Gardens have been a salvation for both of us. Today families, sit on the grass and benches in the summer sun. Fantastic Turk's Cap lilies glow spotted orange in the sunlight, and acanthus blooms stand tall and spiky in the summer borders.

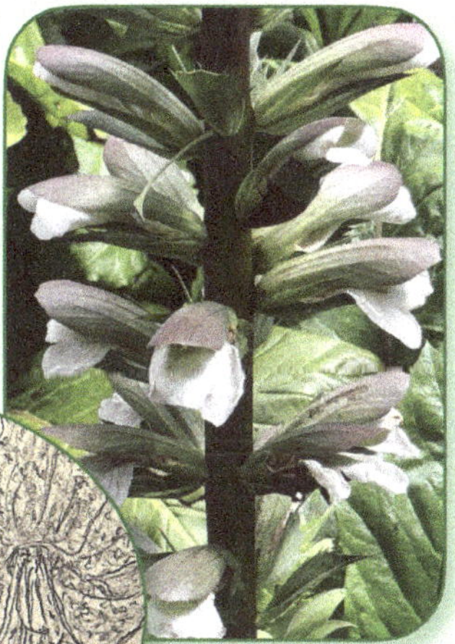

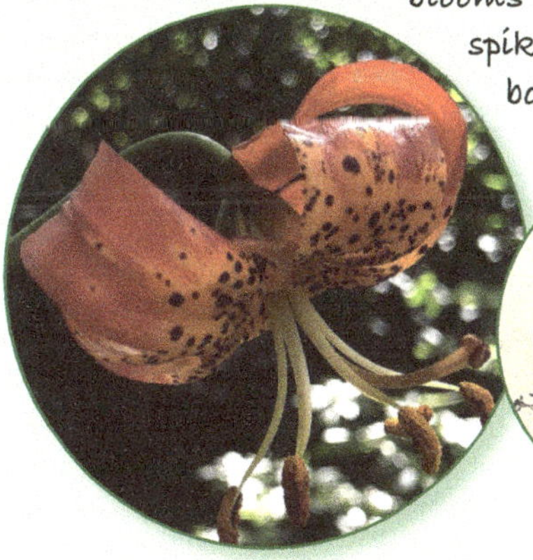

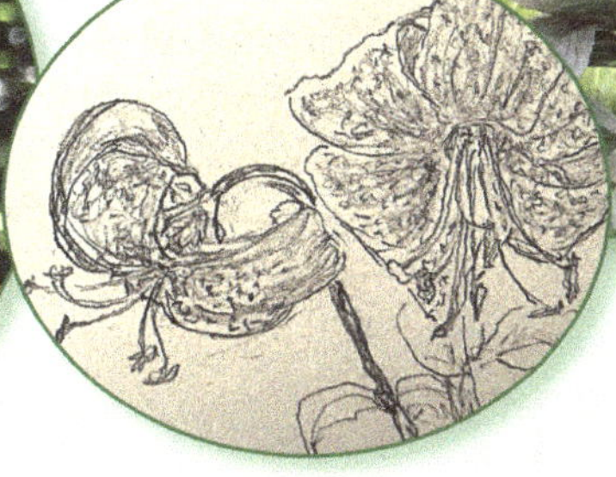

Pandemic Day: 119/123 Lockdown 1: day 105/109

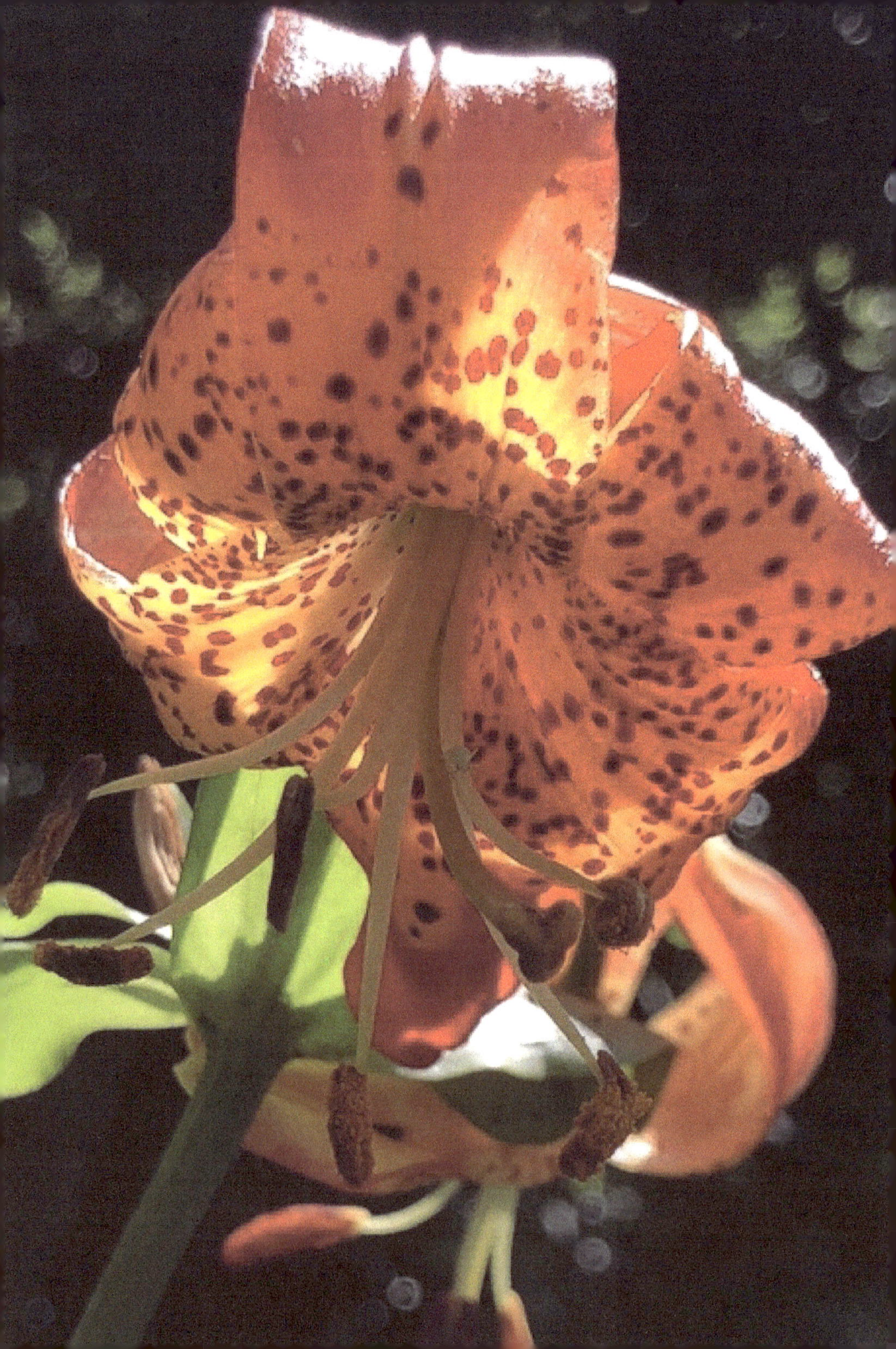

13th - FACE COVERINGS WILL NOW BE COMPULSORY IN SHOPS AND SUPERMARKETS FROM 24TH JULY.

I am up early today after a disturbed night, a frequent problem since lockdown. When I do wake, it is often to the eerie silence, only broken by the night sounds of foxes, owls and cats, until the earliest birds begin the dawn chorus.

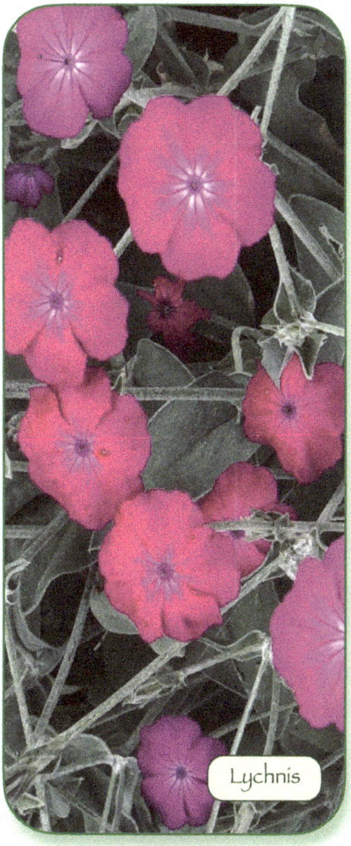
Lychnis

We visit the Children's House, where magenta lychnis grow almost wild in the unkempt borders, brightening the gloom. We return home through a grey morning to spend a grey day contemplating a grey future. The new rules are unclear and change all the time. Beauty salons, nail bars and tattoo shops in England welcome customers for the first time in four months, following the relaxation of social distancing.

14th - A REPORT BY SIR PATRICK VALANCE ESTIMATES BETWEEN 24,500 AND 251,000 POSSIBLE HOSPITAL DEATHS IN A DEADLY SECOND WAVE THIS WINTER.

At the new house, the final parts of a massive and ancient sycamore tree root, excavated from the front garden, are loaded into the skip among the old radiators and endless wiring.

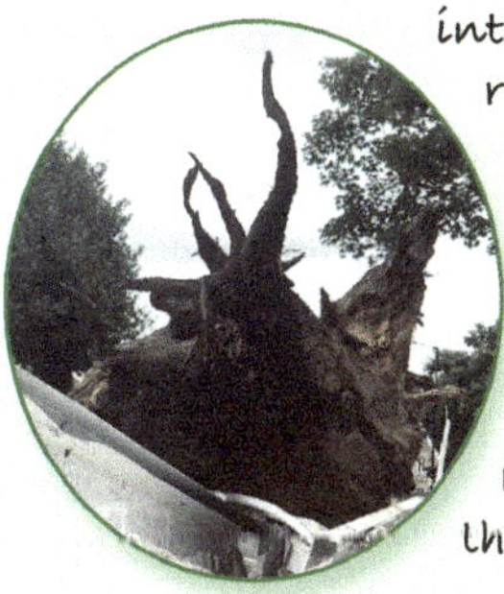

The paving is almost complete, and we can begin to think about the back garden.

In spite of the constant rain, the robin still comes every day to bathe splashily in our water feature. It is a delight to see it, and always makes us smile, even on the bleakest days of this bleak time.

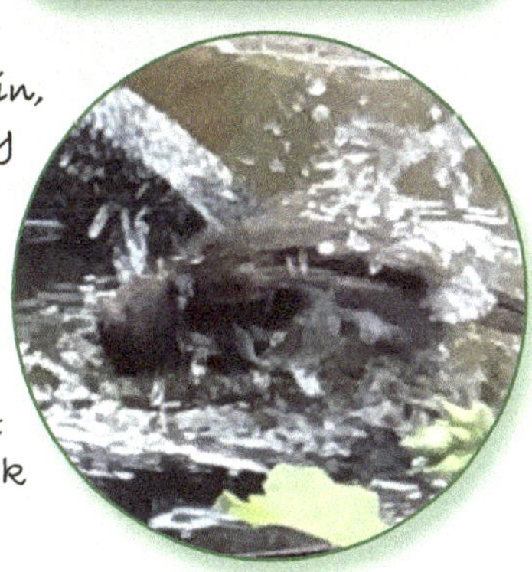

Lives remembered on this day: Karamat Ullah Mirza; 84; GP; Clacton. John Prine; 73; Country singer, Nashville.

15/16th July 2020 Confirmed Cases: 251,482 Total deaths: 41,145

15th - THE PM CONFIRMS THAT AN INDEPENDENT INQUIRY WILL BE HELD INTO THE HANDLING OF THE PANDEMIC, BUT SAYS IT WOULD NOT BE RIGHT TO DEVOTE 'HUGE AMOUNTS OF TIME' TO AN INQUIRY WHEN THE PANDEMIC IS ONGOING.

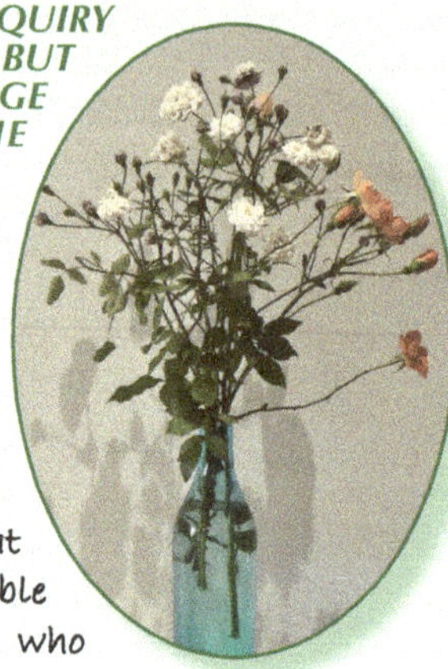

I hope there really will be an inquiry into the government's response to the pandemic, and they don't wriggle out of the real responsibility they have, particularly to families who have lost parents, grandparents, children, and other relatives and friends.

We fetch Bruce to work with us for a day, but at lunchtime, a friend calls to say he has had a possible coronavirus contact, so Bruce is collected by Sarah, who takes him home to quarantine. The danger is still not over yet.

I pick some of the remaining little roses from the new garden.

16th - A TEMPORARY CUT IN VAT COMES INTO FORCE TO HELP FOOD AND HOSPITALITY INDUSTRIES. ONLINE RETAILER ASOS SAYS IT WILL REPAY FURLOUGH CASH IT RECEIVED FROM THE GOVERNMENT AFTER SALES INCREASED BY 10% TO £1 BILLION IN THE FOUR MONTHS UP TO 30 JUNE.

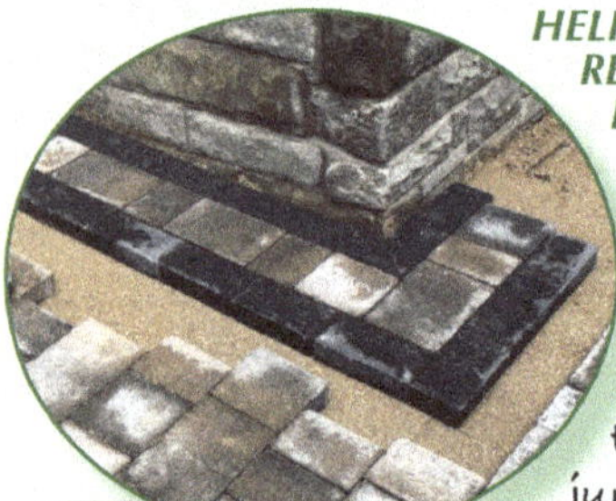

A new drive at the front...

Nando's, KFC & McDonald's restaurants announce price reductions, a relief for the many people who have missed their regular 'fix' of takeaways and junk food.

The build on the Children's House seems to have turned a corner, and gained some momentum. The front drive is finished and work moves to the back garden paving.

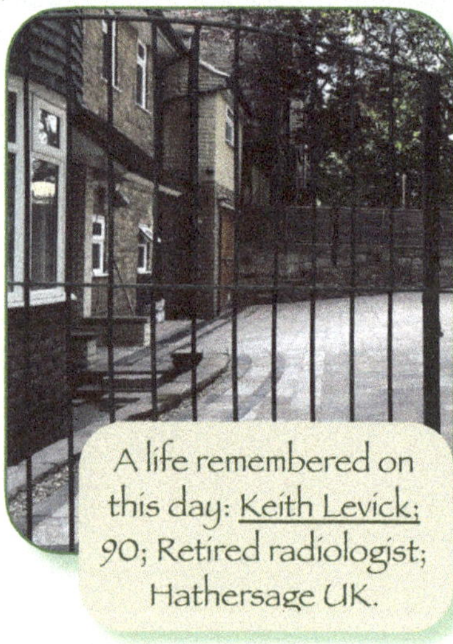

Phill had a haircut today - as my hair grows longer than it has ever been!

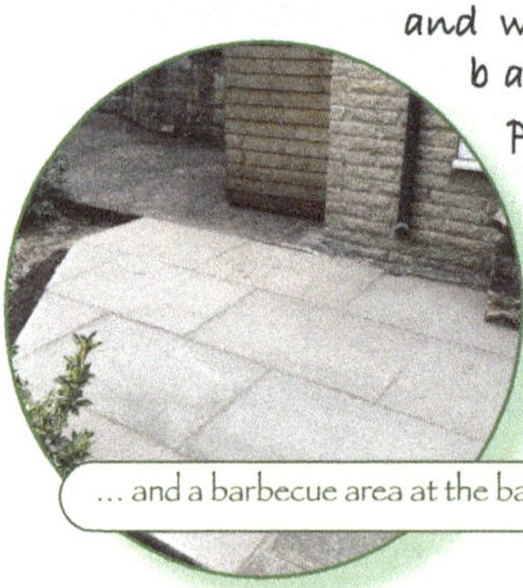

... and a barbecue area at the back

A life remembered on this day: Keith Levick; 90; Retired radiologist; Hathersage UK.

Pandemic Day: 126/127 Lockdown 1: day 112/113

From old stone wall to new pillar and flower bed in the new front garden.

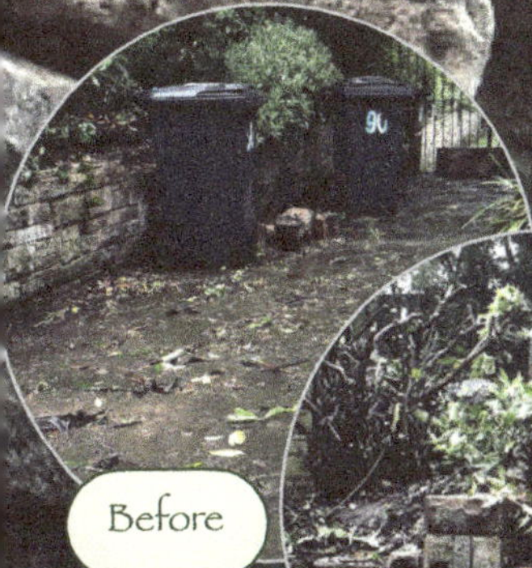

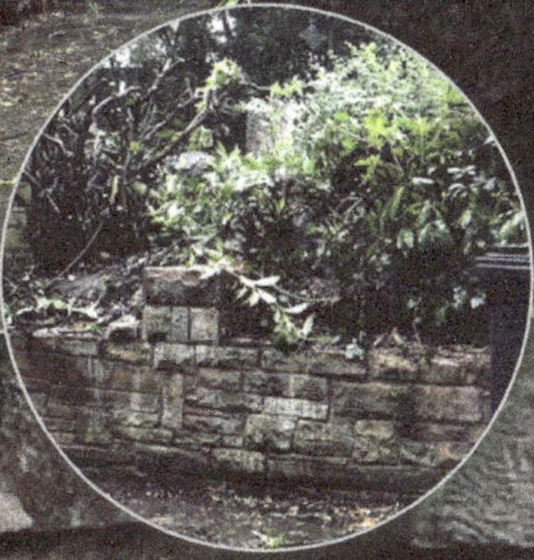

Before

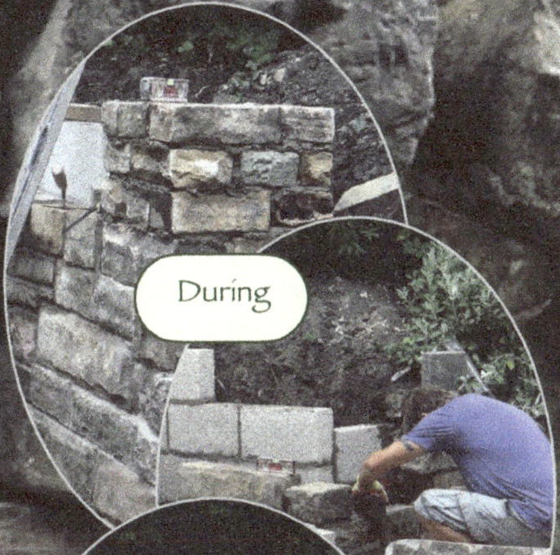

During

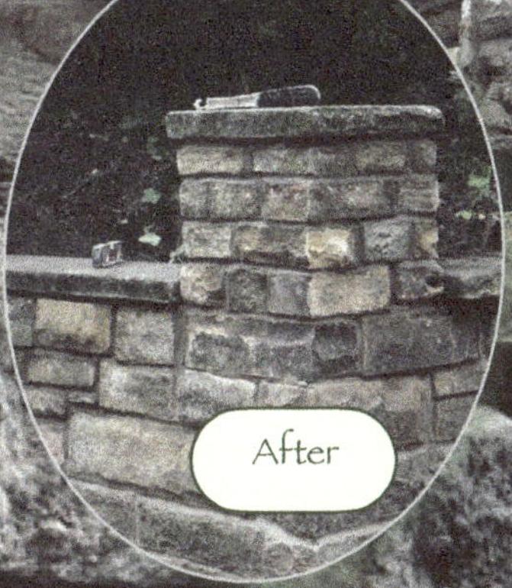

After

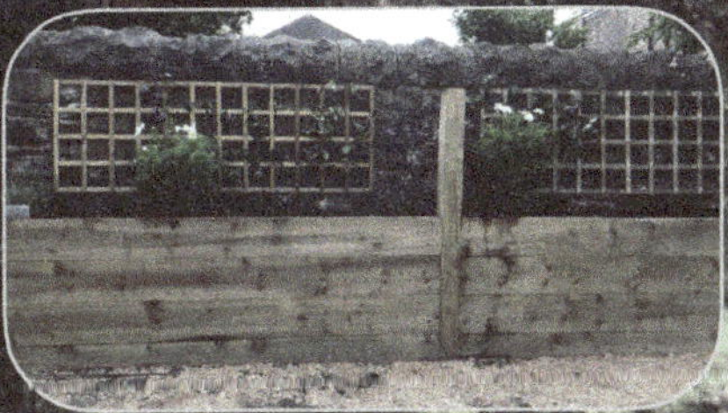

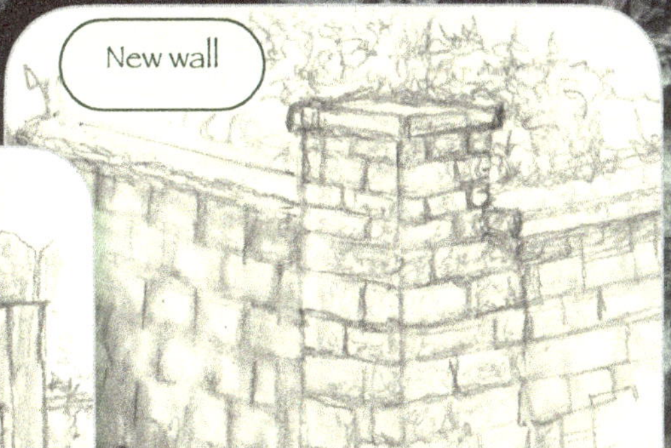

New wall

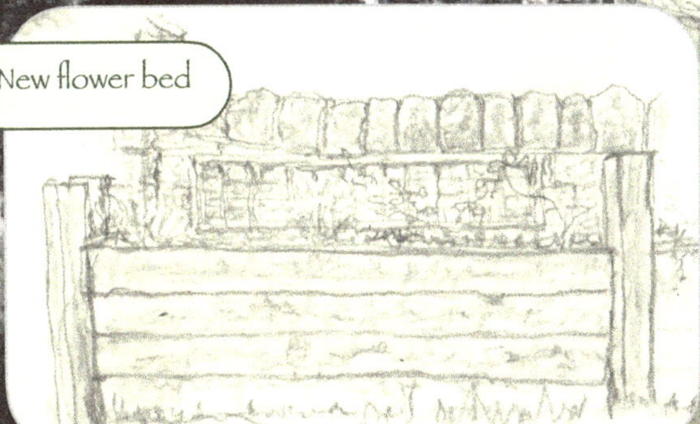

New flower bed

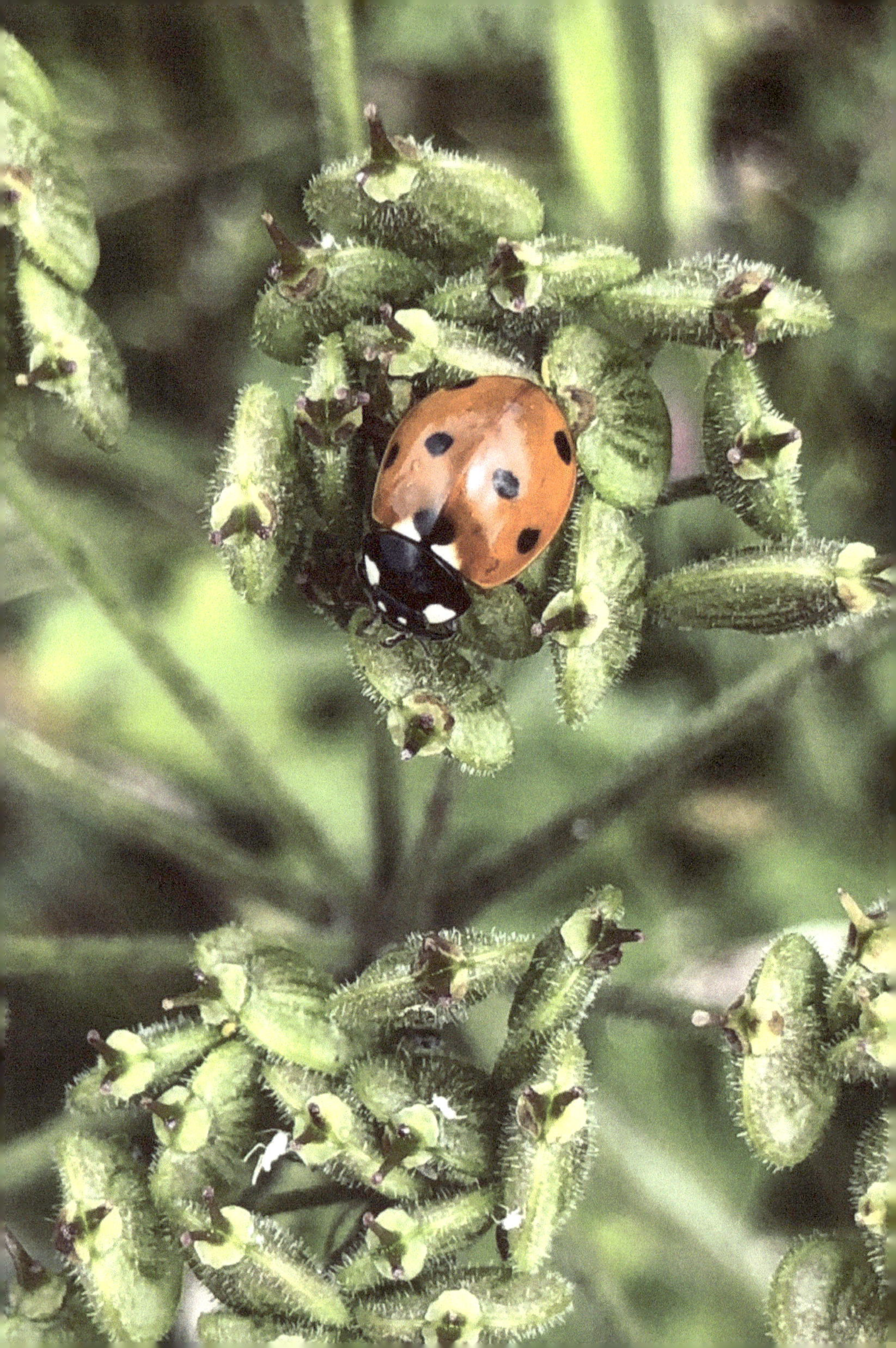

17th July 2020 Confirmed Cases: 252,300 Total deaths: 41,176

A life remembered on this day: <u>Habib Zaidi</u>; 76; Doctor; Southend; UK.

<u>UNLOCKING NEWS</u>: THE PRIME MINISTER ANNOUNCES A FURTHER EASING OF LOCKDOWN RESTRICTIONS FOR ENGLAND, WITH PLANS FOR A 'SIGNIFICANT RETURN TO NORMALITY' FROM AS EARLY AS NOVEMBER. THE NEW RULES ALLOW PEOPLE TO USE PUBLIC TRANSPORT FOR NON-ESSENTIAL JOURNEYS WITH IMMEDIATE EFFECT, WHILE EMPLOYERS WILL HAVE MORE DISCRETION OVER THEIR WORK PLACES FROM 1st AUGUST.

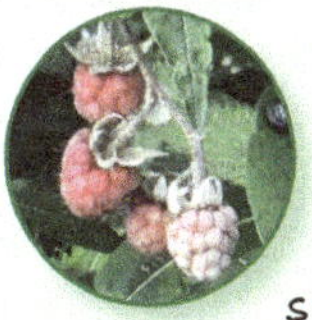

Today we spend another day in the wildflower meadows at Hartington. We walk to the meadows along the leafy, even more overgrown path, with still flowering blackberry and raspberry, and clouds of pale lilac scabious flowers. Butterflies flutter about, but are soon blown off-course by the breeze.

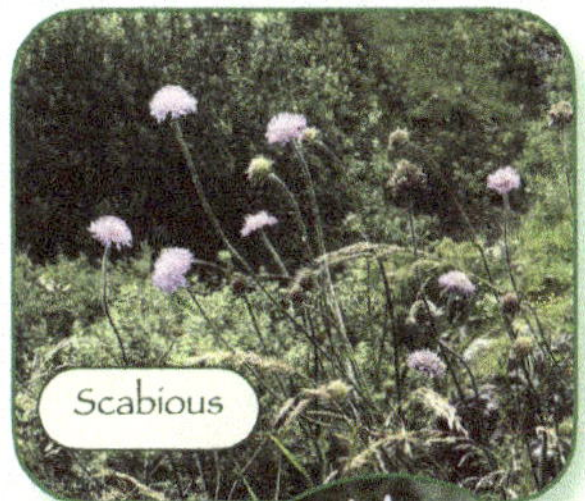

Scabious

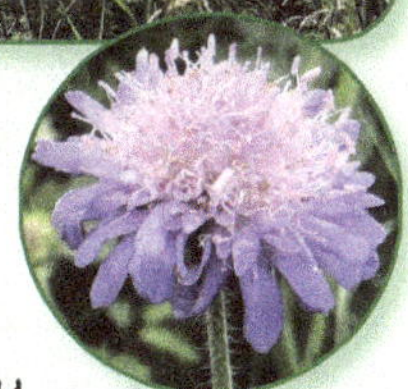

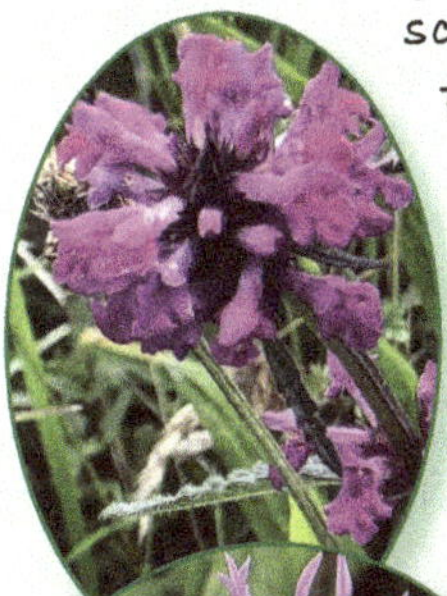

The yellows of catsear and dandelion have been overtaken by pinks of campion and the blues and pale mauves of scabious, blue geranium and harebells. The fields are liberally punctuated by big clumps of knapweed bursting out into starry magenta flowers atop their 'basketwork' buds, as a pink and blue mist gathers across the fields and beside the limestone walls.

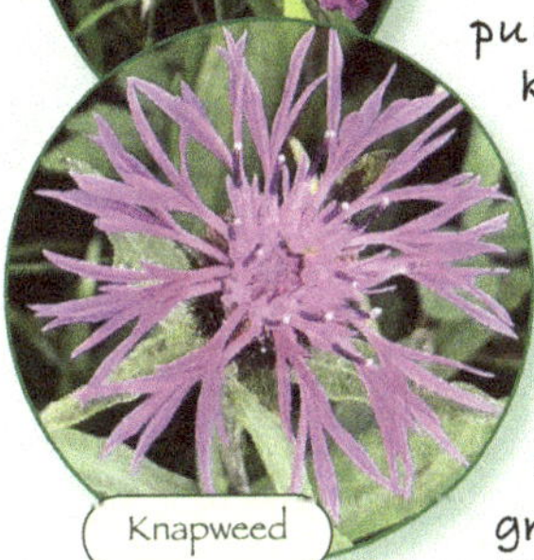

Knapweed

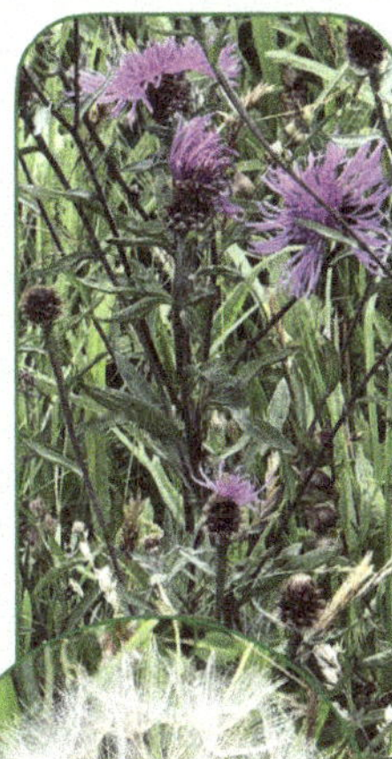

In the middle of the pale-ing grasses, ox-eye daisies, hogweed and the last of the orchids all hang on, and the seed heads of Jack-go-to-bed-at-noon, like fairy globes, nestle among the grass heads.

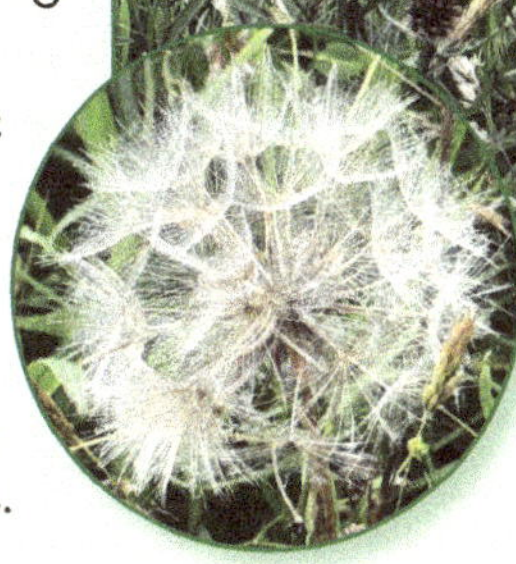

Swathes of lady's bedstraw gleam yellow in the watery sunlight as we climb the hill through the two big, grassy meadows, both full of flowers. Ladybirds, soldier beetles, ants and all sorts of flying insects hover and flit among the flowers as if they know the season is coming to a close. As we walk through the field, seeds of all sorts are beginning to pop, fly and fall.

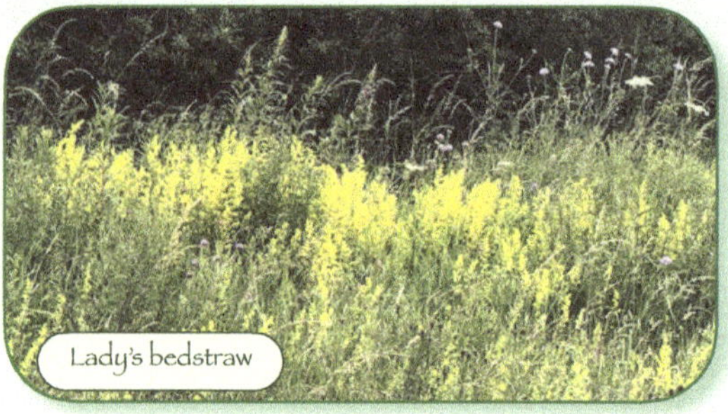
Lady's bedstraw

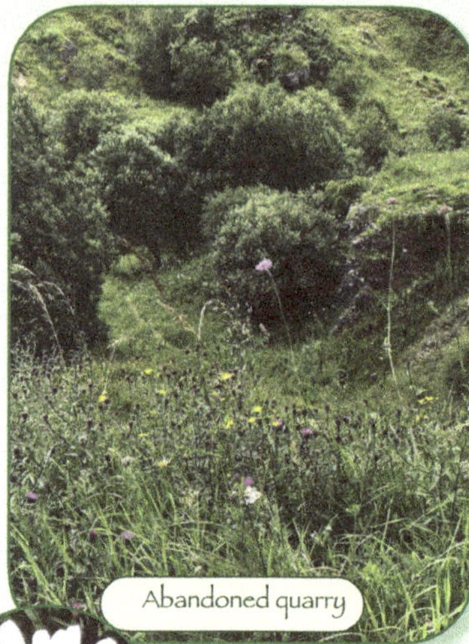
Abandoned quarry

Having climbed to the top of the meadows, we strike off to circle a disused stone quarry, long abandoned to nettles, brambles and hawthorn bushes. We resist the temptation to attempt its steep, wet sides, but may return another day!

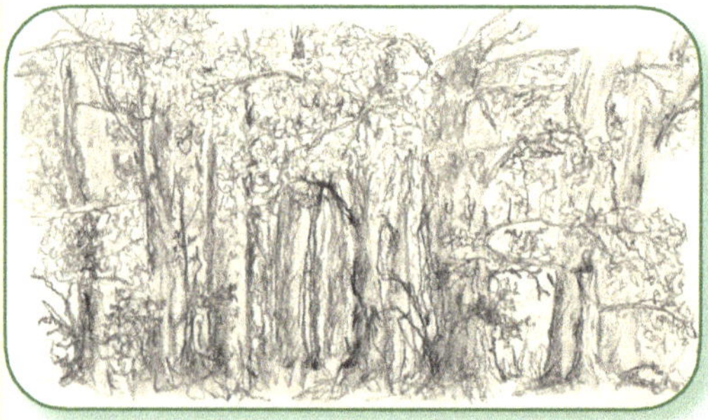

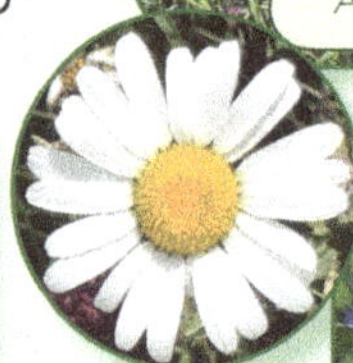

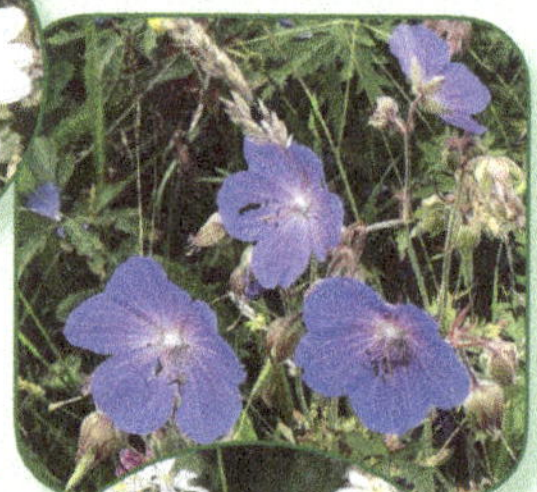

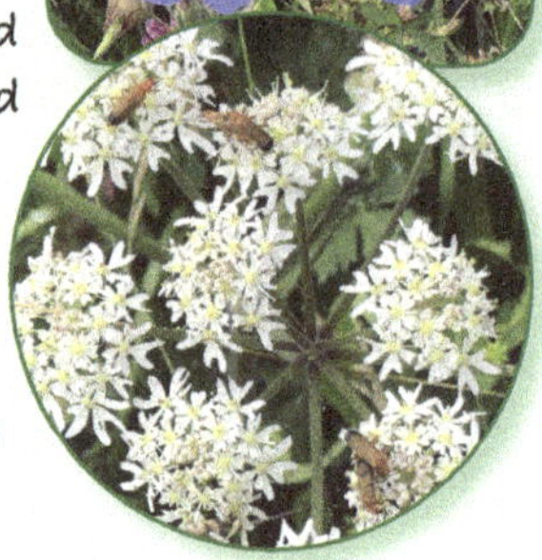

Avoiding hawthorn bushes and thistles, and carefully skirting the muddiest bits of the path, pockmarked by deep hoof prints of cows in the recent rain, we find a slightly clearer way that leads us through a landscape of hawthorn groves and spoil heaps, one of which we use as a picnic outlook.

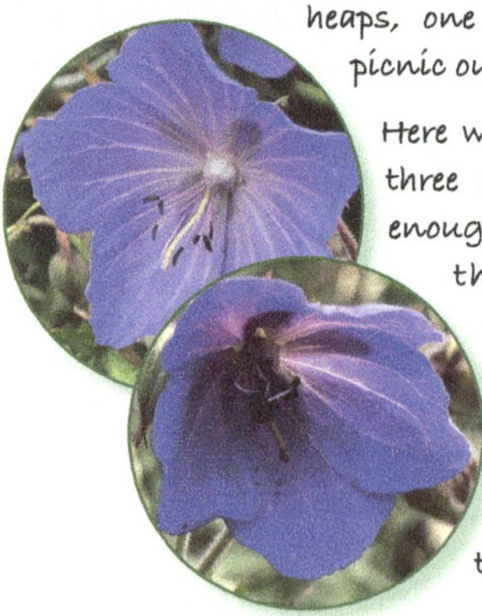

Here we lie and listen to insects, and three ravens croaking as they flap and soar, near enough to watch, but not close, their distant croaks continuing as we snack and doze in the sun among daisies, tormentil and scented dwarf thymes.

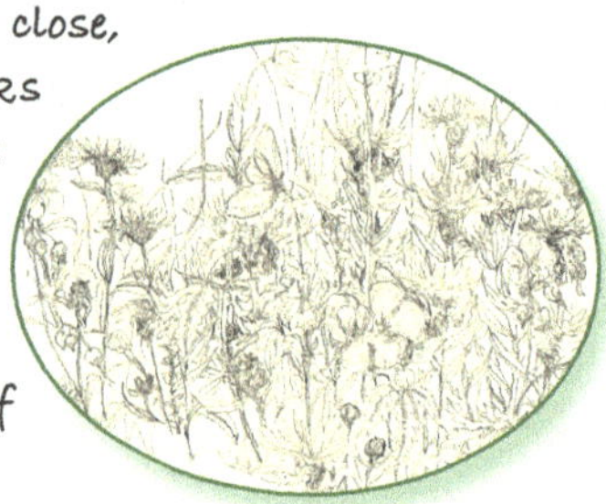

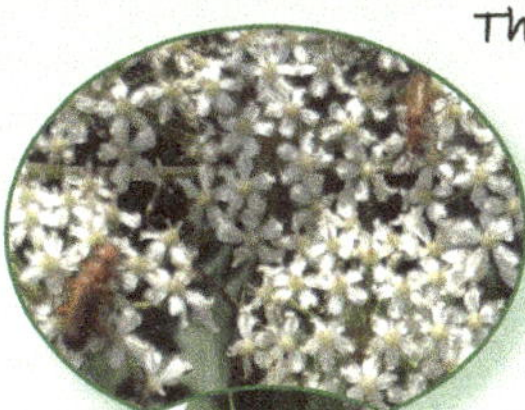

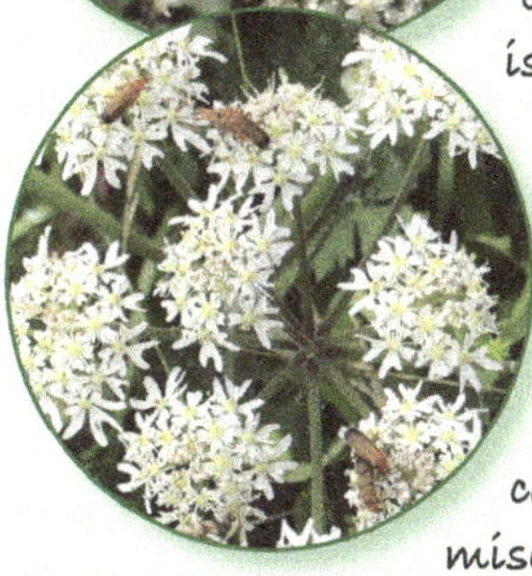

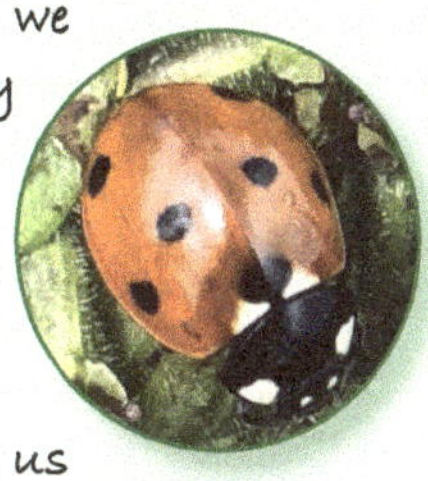

The view from the bottom of these meadows is very different from the top end, where we have rested before, a strange, lumpy landscape of old industrial workings, rubbing shoulders with these amazing wildflower meadows is like a half-remembered dream.

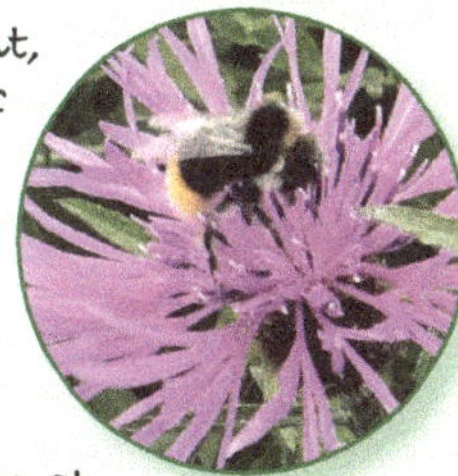

Before long, a chilly breeze sends us on our way from our viewpoint, circling back to the bottom of the meadows, watching the bravest of the butterflies, and collecting a damp pocketful of miscellaneous seeds as we walk.

We wander back along the path between the mossy walls at the bottom of the valley, watching red soldier beetles and ladybirds on the hogweed flowers, and bees on the magenta flowers of knapweed.

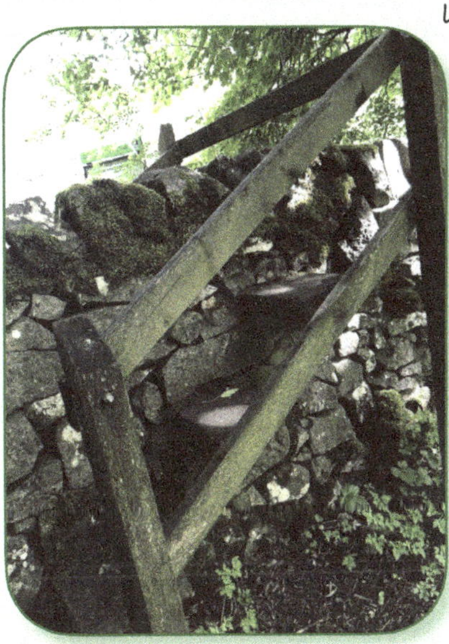

Walking lazily up and through the mossy wall onto the Tissington Trail, we reach the car park, to drive home after masked shopping for local pies and fat, red, greenhouse-scented, home grown tomatoes.

and as we rest: *The Prime Minister announces an extra £3bn for the NHS in England to help prepare for a possible second wave of COVID-19 over the coming winter. The Health Secretary calls for a review of the way deaths are recorded in England after Public Health England confirms it records deaths as COVID related even if the death occurs several months after someone has tested positive for the virus.*

A life remembered on this day: Leilani Dayrit; 47, Nurse; Rugby; UK.

Pandemic Day: 128 Lockdown 1: day 114

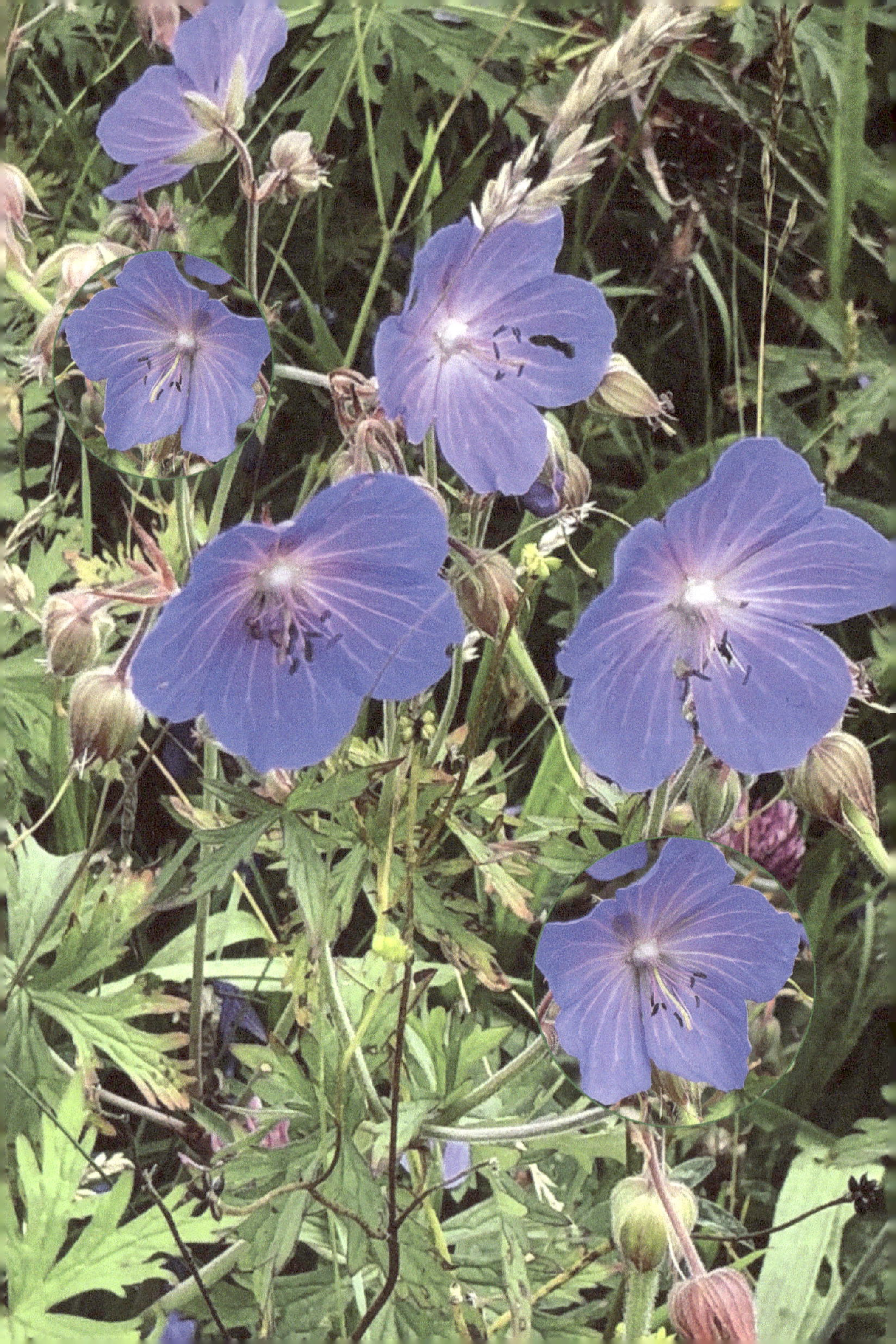

18th/20th - THE PM ANNOUNCES FURTHER EASING OF RESTRICTIONS WITH PLANS FOR 'A SIGNIFICANT RETURN TO NORMALITY' BY CHRISTMAS.

The Oxford Group have announced development of a successful vaccine, and the government swoops in, Trump-like, to buy up millions of doses. Anti-virus groups are increasingly vocal.

The left-behind garden swing is dismantled, and as we spend three more days of packing. We begin to realise that the major pressure on the renovation project is the constant decision-making as we really face working without a project manager, following our builder's diversion to his much bigger project.

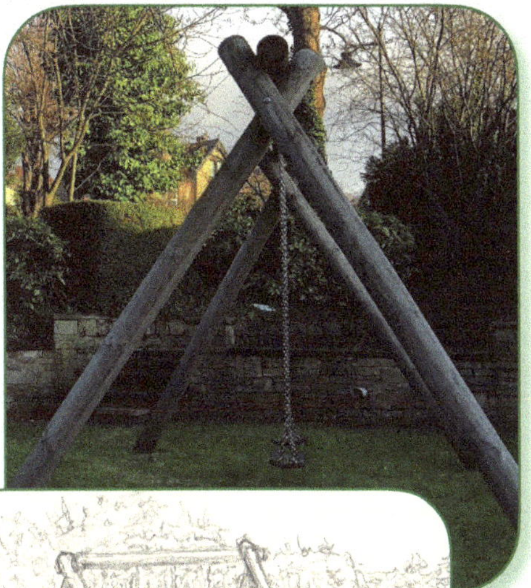

21st - THE PM SAYS HE IS CONFIDENT BUT NOT '100% CONFIDENT' THAT A VACCINE WILL BE AVAILABLE IN 2020.

Last night we watched a Panorama programme about the government response to this virus - a depressing list of suspect PPE orders, missed opportunities and botched or delayed decisions.

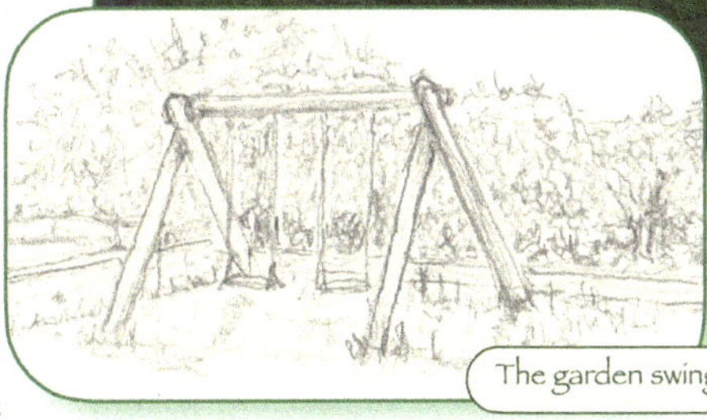

The garden swing

22nd - Joe Wicks presents his last on-line 'PE with Joe'. We pack up more belongings stored in the garage since we moved from the Pennines 2 years ago.

23rd - THE PUBLIC ACCOUNTS COMMITTEE CRITICISES THE UK GOVERNMENT FOR ITS 'ASTONISHING' FAILURE TO PLAN FOR THE ECONOMIC IMPACT OF THE COVID-19 PANDEMIC

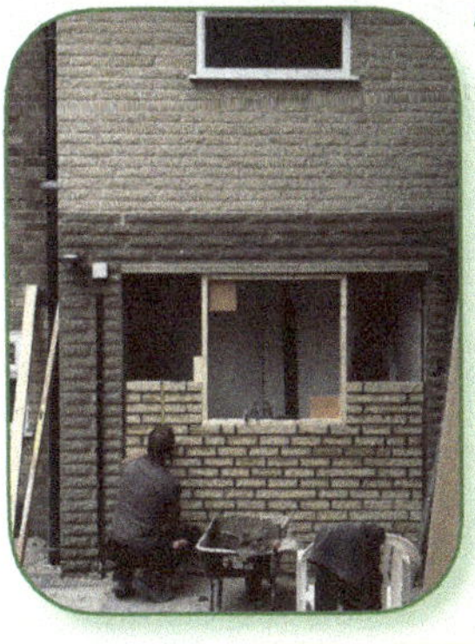

The walling up of the old garage is nearly done, and the window frames is in. It's a very good match with the rest of the house. When the builder is here and the workers are managed every day, the results are good, it's just the pace of progress that is so frustrating.

A life remembered: Donald Suelto; 51; Chemotherapy nurse; died alone in his flat in Bethnal Green, London.

Pandemic Day: 129/134 Lockdown 1: day 115/120

24th July 2020 Confirmed Cases: 257,138 Total deaths: 41,286

FACE COVERINGS BECOME COMPULSORY IN SHOPS AND MOST OTHER ENCLOSED PUBLIC PLACES IN ENGLAND, WITH £100 FINES FOR PEOPLE WHO DON'T OBEY THE RULES.

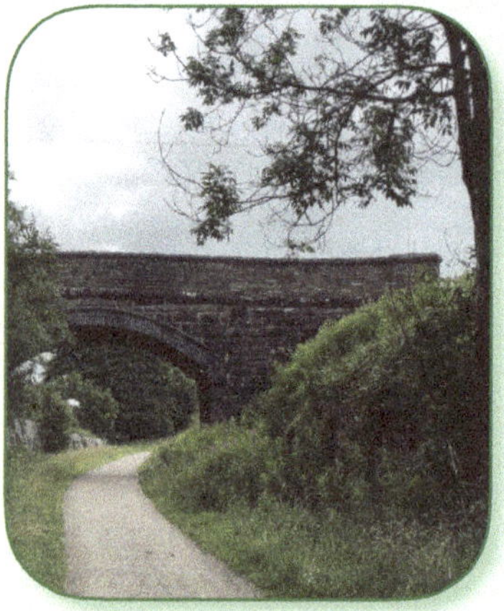

We have become so immersed in the building work that we have almost forgotten 'the green and the blue' of the countryside, so we leave for yet another walk along the Tissington Trail.

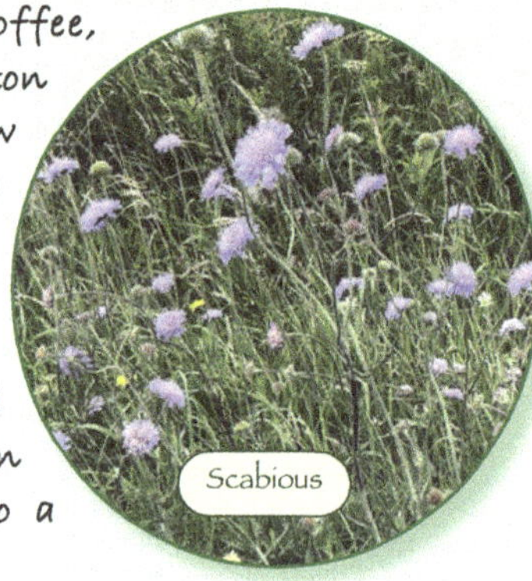

Scabious

Snacks and coffee, then to Hartington Station to follow the trail along the old railway track. We decide to resist the meadows, and walk along the path, to try to get some speed up in our walking which has recently developed into a stroll while we look at the views and take photos.

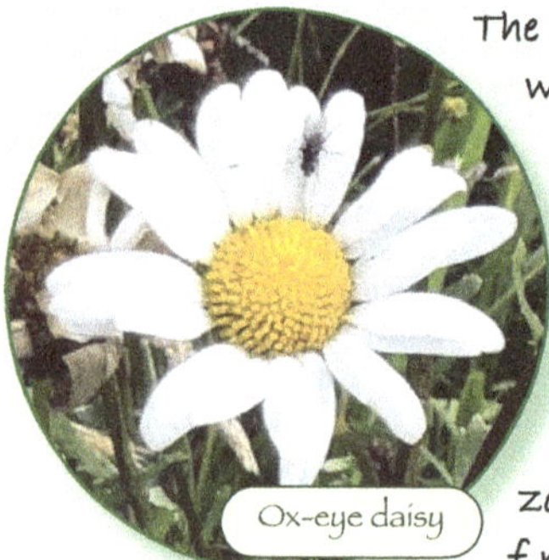

Ox-eye daisy

The trail is very busy today, and the first part of the walk is punctuated by passing cyclists, family groups of various sizes, ages and abilities from anxious novices to thrusting sportspeople. All seem to be convinced that they have right of way and that walkers will scuttle into the verges as they zoom past. Some are friendly and considerate, some are definitely not, with ear buds firmly in their ears, they are totally unaware of others. We need to listen all the time for the sound of tyres on gravel, particularly as many cyclists seem to come from behind us. This means that although we can keep up our promised faster pace, it is almost impossible to appreciate the natural world and the panoramic views at the same time.

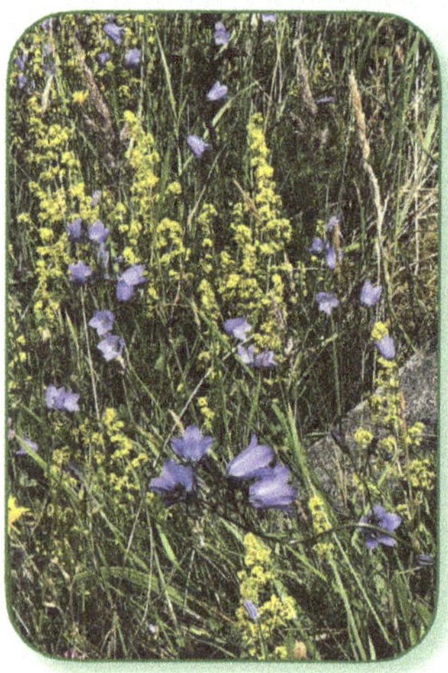

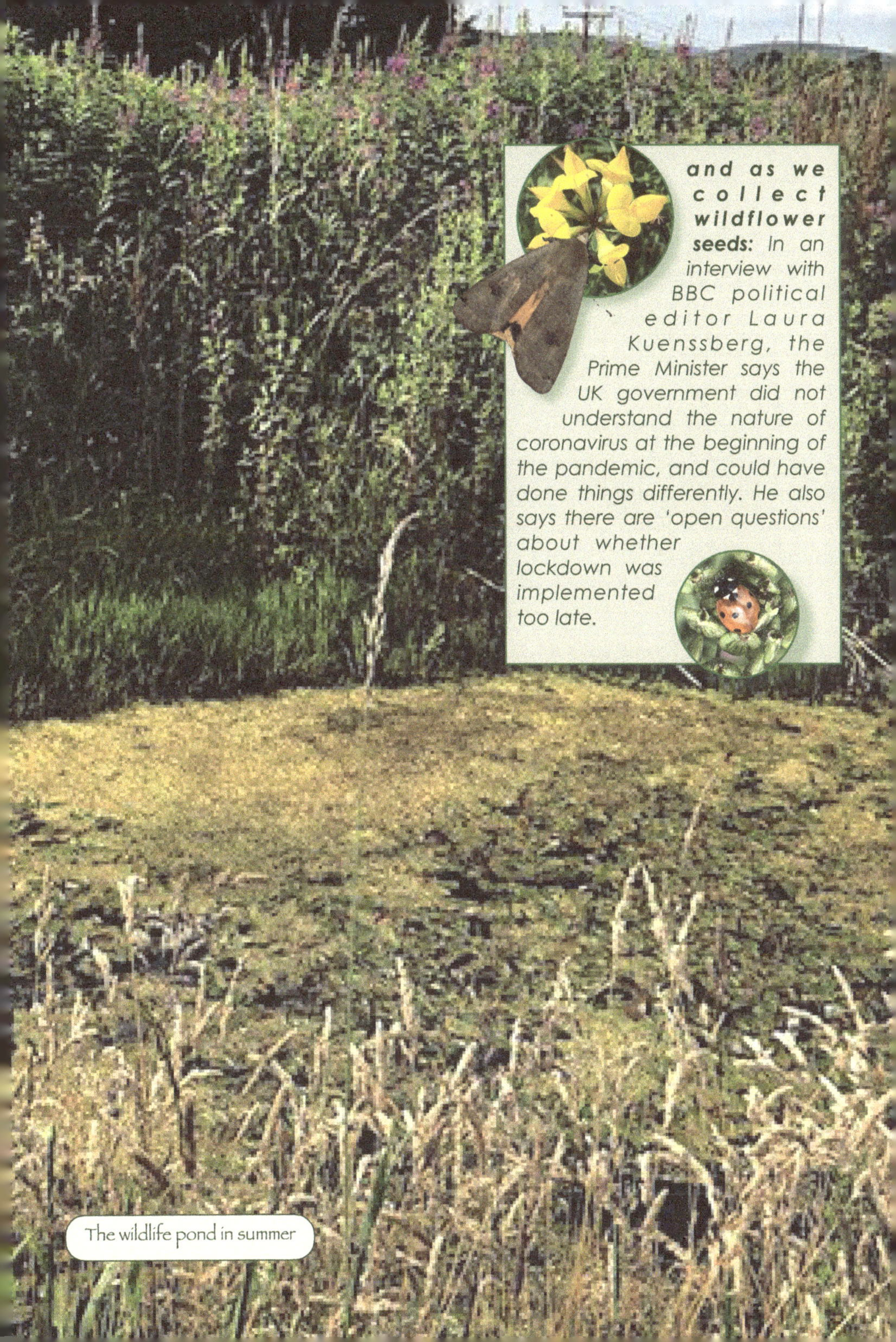

and as we collect wildflower seeds: In an interview with BBC political editor Laura Kuenssberg, the Prime Minister says the UK government did not understand the nature of coronavirus at the beginning of the pandemic, and could have done things differently. He also says there are 'open questions' about whether lockdown was implemented too late.

The wildlife pond in summer

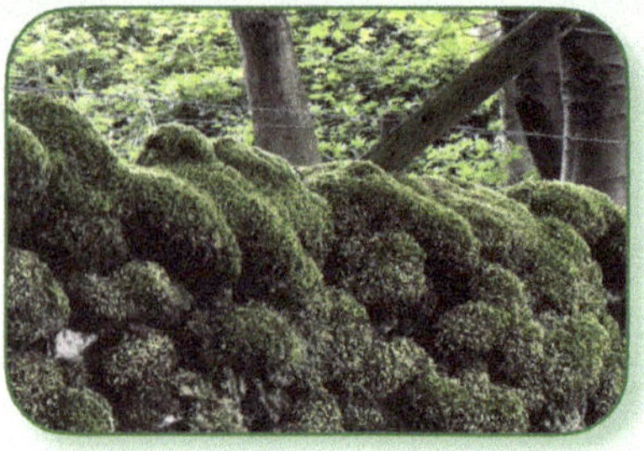

On the way back, we find, hidden among the trees beside one of the bridges, a little path along a limestone outcrop, climbing up beside a mossy wall between the railway line and the road, and worn smooth by the country boots of generations of feet, on a short cut from the railway line to the road. Perhaps there was a halt here, as the road over the bridge leads to the tiny hamlet of Heathcote.

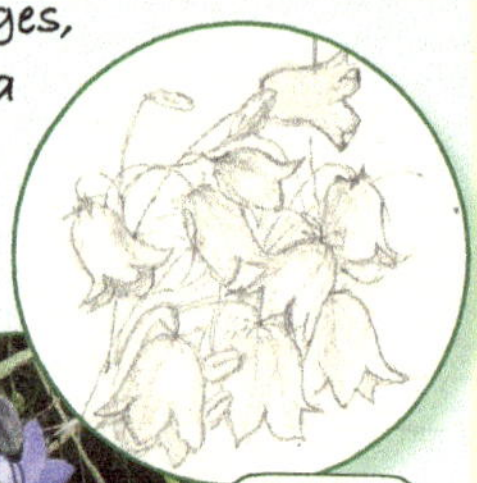

Harebell

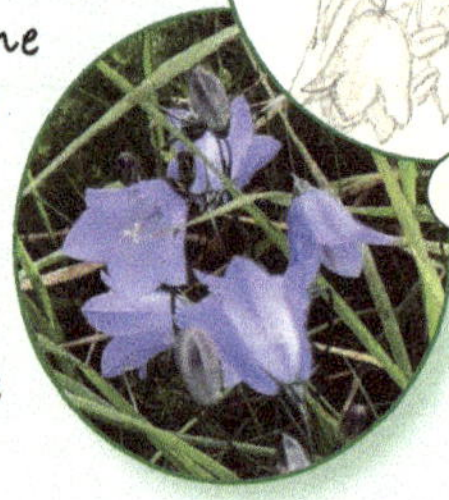

Turning right on the road, away from Heathcote, the remote road at the top is deserted, with shady trees and mossy walls. Surprisingly, the lane leads us to the top of the wildflower meadows we love so much. These have not yet been cut, so we are able to sit among the flowers again for a picnic, a rest, and a quick collection of more flower seeds from plantain, wild geranium, yellow rattle, daisy, knapweed and buttercup from the millions ripening all around us.

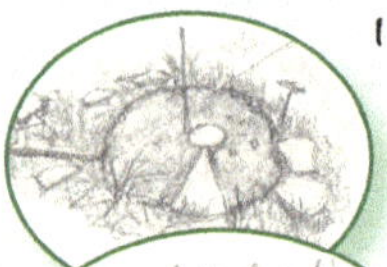

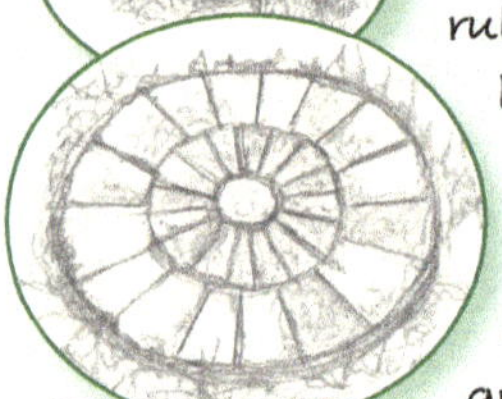

The stone circle

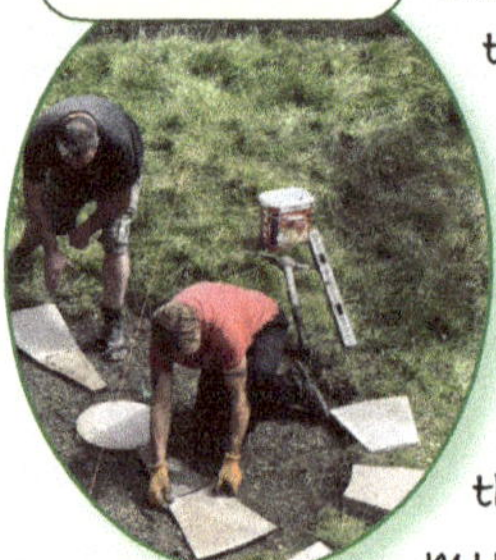

I'm sure we make only a tiny inroad into the number of seeds falling to the ground here, and wonder if we are breaking any rules by collecting them. When we get home I check, and am relieved to find that it is NOT illegal to collect wildflower seeds for your own use.

A life remembered on this day: Haji Tanveer Hussain; Taxi Driver; Rotherham; UK.

Sitting among the long summer grasses, gazing at the blue sky is one of the best ways to forget the worries and tensions of this extended lockdown, which no-one thought would last so long.

Later we walk down the hill, taking a detour to look at the wildlife pond, then through the lower meadows where a few orchids are still flowering. We tear ourselves away from the green and the blue, return to the car and drive home via the Children's House, where the stone circle in the lawn for my Japanese water lily bowl is finished!

Pandemic Day: 135 Lockdown 1: day 121

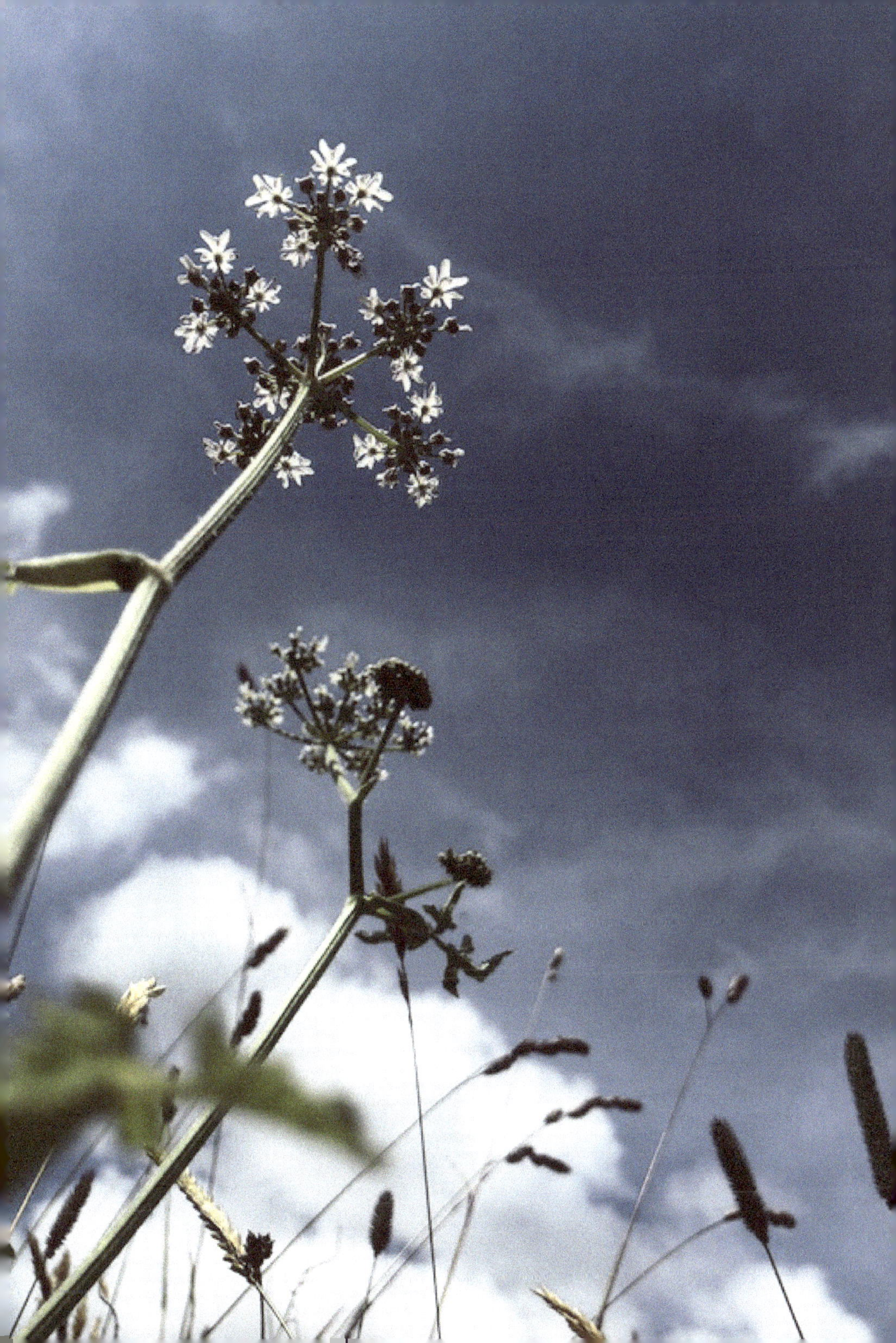

Remembered today: <u>Patrick Tighe</u>; 45; Carer Bridgnorth, Shropshire.

25th - A RISE IN COVID CASES IN SPAIN AND CONCERNS OF A SECOND WAVE, THE GOVERNMENT CONFIRMS TRAVELLERS RETURNING FROM SPAIN WILL NEED TO QUARANTINE FOR 14 DAYS FROM 26 JULY.

For just the second time in the many long days of writing this account, I make no diary entry.

Bournemouth Council declares a major incident after as many as half a million people travel to the Dorset coast.

26th - TRAVEL COMPANIES REPORT THAT BOOKINGS HAVE 'EXPLODED' SINCE THE GOVERNMENT EASED QUARANTINE RESTRICTIONS ON TRAVEL ABROAD.

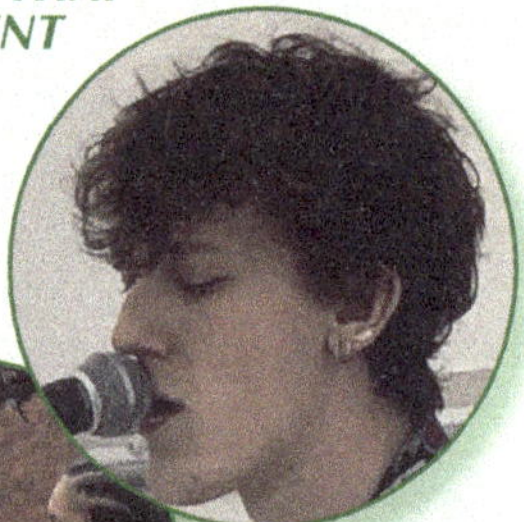

A local pub holds a music event in their car park, just off the main road, and after some discussion we decide to go. Other people are obviously feeling as anxious as I am, but we are pleased that our grandson Bruce's band can play again in public instead of endlessly practicing at home.

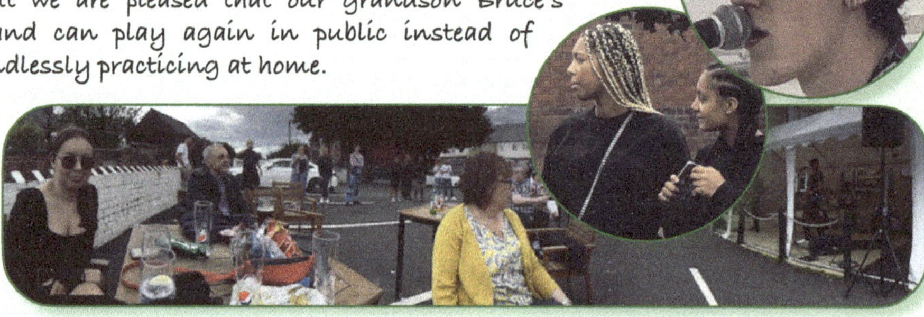

I don't like being in crowded places, or meeting people outside our immediate family. We don't stay long.

27th - BETWEEN MARCH 27TH AND JULY 20TH, 16,029 FINES WERE ISSUED BY POLICE IN ENGLAND FOR ALLEGED BREACHES OF COVID REGULATIONS.

Presumably some of these were fines for travelling too far for exercise, and we are very relieved that we never got caught!

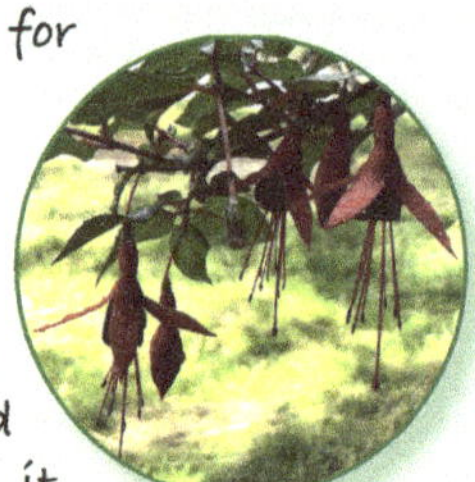

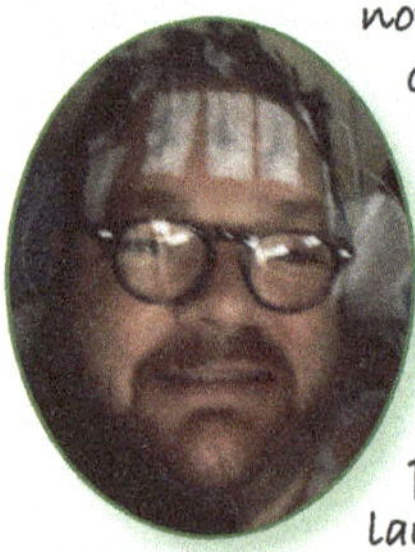

Our son John, in Arizona, is taken into hospital – not with Covid, but a collapse brought on by cycling in extreme heat. The Covid situation means that although we are worried and wish we could see him, Covid means no visitors, even his wife, so it would be pointless to travel even if we could.

I keep finding new plants in the garden. Today it's red and purple fuchsia flowers, hanging in the dark green shade of the laurel hedge.

Pandemic Day: 136/138 Lockdown 1: day 122/124

28th - THE NUMBER OF PEOPLE IN THE UK TESTING POSITIVE FOR COVID PASSES 300,000 WITH 45,759 DEATHS. THE PHANTOM OF THE OPERA ENDS ITS 33-YEAR RUN IN THE WEST END DUE TO THE PANDEMIC.

Thankfully John has recovered and is back home. The doctors are not sure what happened, but suggest he shouldn't do it again! Everyone, particularly his wife Kathy, is very relieved.

29th - EVERYONE IS WORRYING ABOUT SPAIN, AS A SECOND WAVE GAINS STRENGTH.

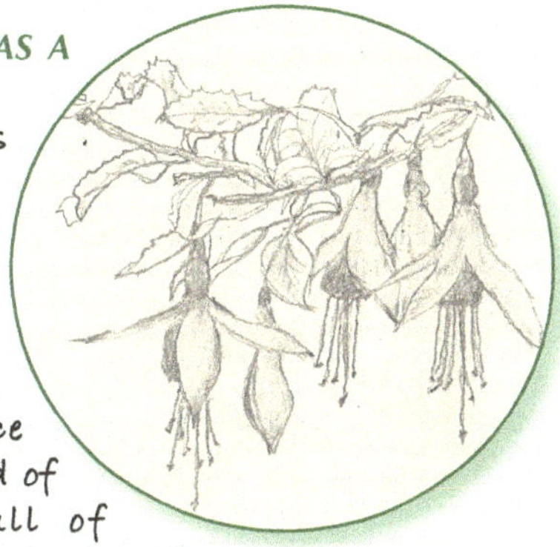

The National Trust plans 1,200 redundancies to save £100m; it has lost £200m in the pandemic. It will be a real loss to everyone if the work of the Trust is damaged, as they work hard to preserve the history of all of us, even if we don't all visit the properties.

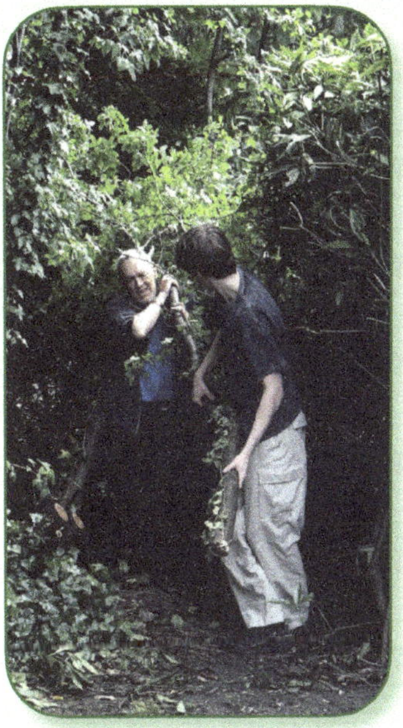

Phill and Bruce attack the far end of the garden, full of overgrown shrubs and self-seeded laburnum trees. They reduce the undergrowth until we can see that there must have been some sort of structure there, now overgrown with the self-seeded offspring of the hedges and trees left untended for many years. It is still strange to think that we now own this house. It always surprises men how big the branches from even a small tree are when cut down. Fortunately we still have a skip on the yard.

I draw the fuchsia flowers from the overgrown garden of the Children's House.

30th - AFTER AN 'INCREASED RATE OF TRANSMISSION', RESTRICTIONS ARE IMPOSED ON MANCHESTER, LANCASHIRE AND YORKSHIRE WHICH PROHIBIT HOUSEHOLDS FROM MEETING INDOORS.

People who test positive for coronavirus or display symptoms must now self-isolate for 10 days as Mr Hancock warns of a 'second wave starting to roll across Europe'.

The PM says the UK is 'not out of the woods' as he also warns of a resurgence of the virus.

A life remembered:
Khulisani Nkala;
46; Nurse; Leeds.

31st July 2020 Confirmed Cases: 261,348 Total deaths: 41,371

UNLOCKING NEWS: THE PRIME MINISTER POSTPONES SOME LOCKDOWN EASING MEASURES SCHEDULED TO BEGIN ON 1st AUGUST FOR TWO WEEKS AMID CONCERNS ABOUT RISING COVID-19 CASES. FROM 8th AUGUST THE WEARING OF FACE COVERINGS IN INDOOR SETTINGS SUCH AS CINEMAS AND PLACES OF WORSHIP WILL BECOME MANDATORY.

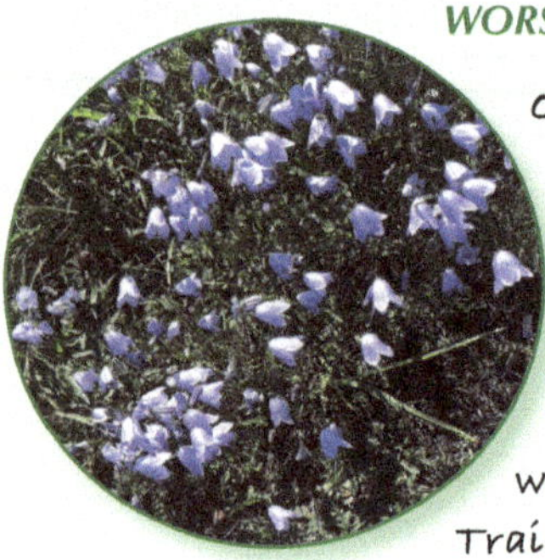

On what will prove to be our final visit to the flower meadows this summer, we set off once more across Derbyshire for Hartington.

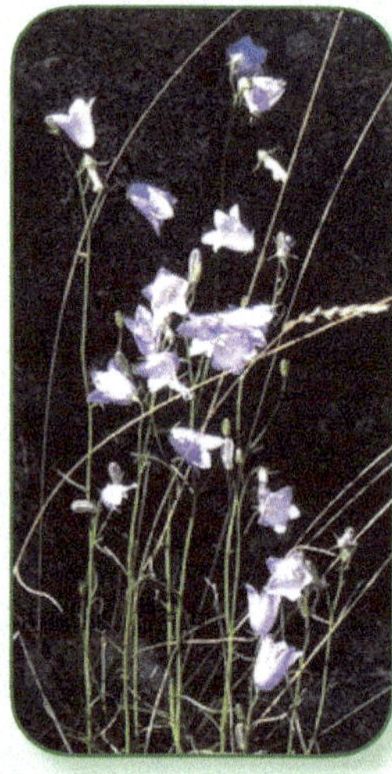

Carefully masked, we buy lunchtime supplies, park at the Station and decide to walk along the Tissington Trail towards the evocatively named tiny hamlet of Parsley Hey. This day would prove once again to be the hottest of the year (the third time the record has been broken), and there are few people on the glaring reflective white of the dry and sandy disused railway line.

This area has proved to be full of natural surprises for us during this dreadful time of Covid, and today is no exception. The banks and edges of the path, the bridges and rock faces are full of a sky blue flood of fragile harebells. These flowers are the epitome of 'the green and the blue' of summer, and we have never, ever seen so many flowering together as we do on this last day of July.

They bloom in clouds like shards of summer sky along the track, on every wall and in every crevice of the white limestone. Even the old bridges are festooned with the delicate blue bells, trembling on their thin, wiry stalks, and flowering in every nook, crack and ledge in the complex brickwork.

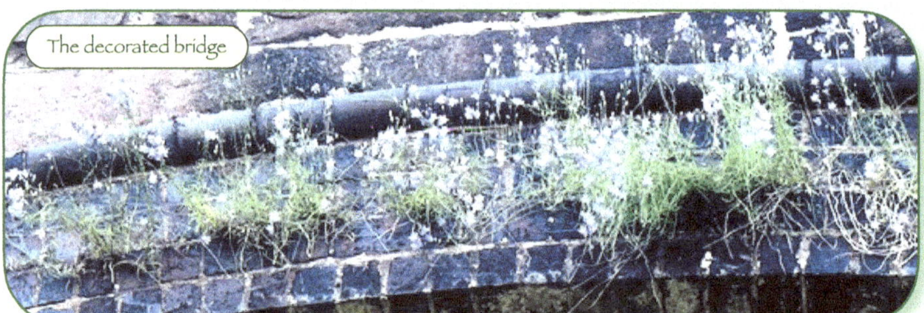

The decorated bridge

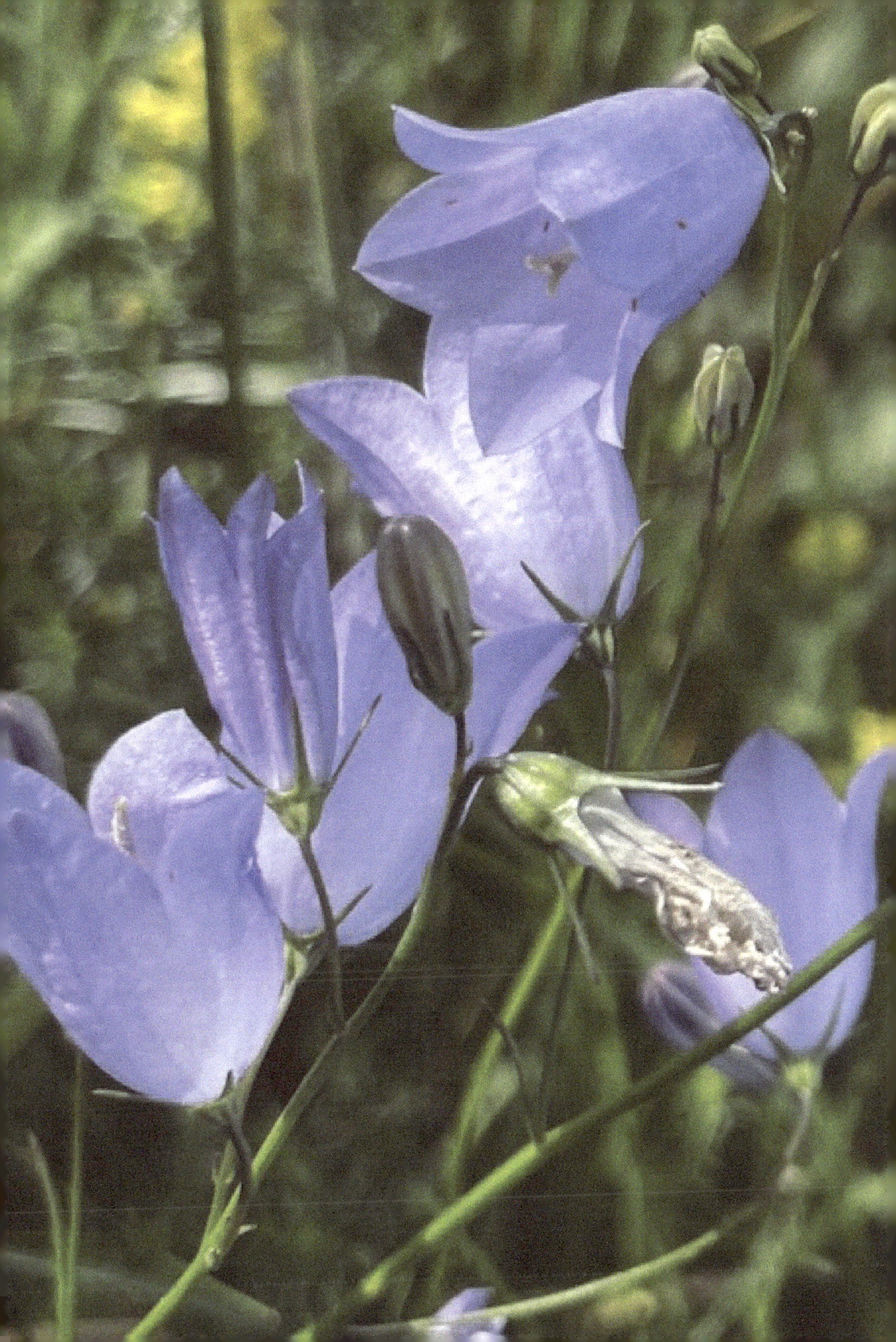

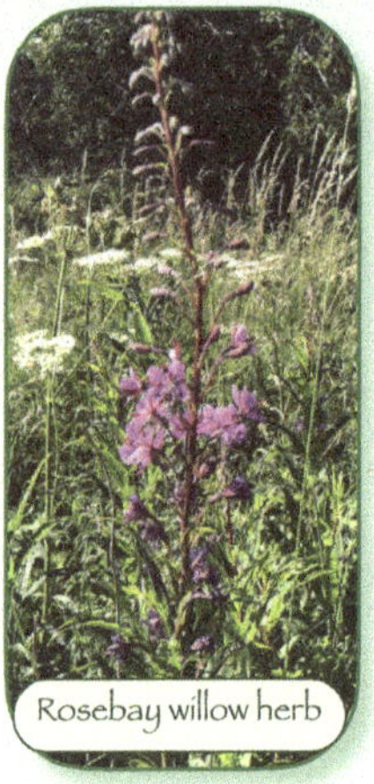
Rosebay willow herb

Banks of rosebay willow herb now flower in tall pink clouds, along with American willow herb, pink scabious and thousands of the delicate, pale yellow flowers of wall lettuce, balanced on thin, airy, maroon stems. Autumn hawkbit, and other dandelion flowers that I can't identify star the grasses, reminding us that August is on its way, and Autumn will be close behind. I can't believe that we have now been enduring this pandemic for five months.

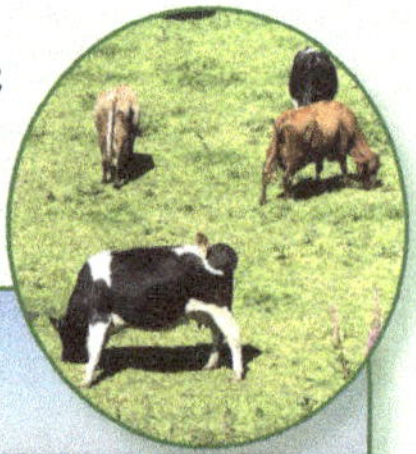

The path along the old line runs above the fields which lie in a panorama of greens, most cut now, but some still with the rusty hue of ripe natural meadow grass.

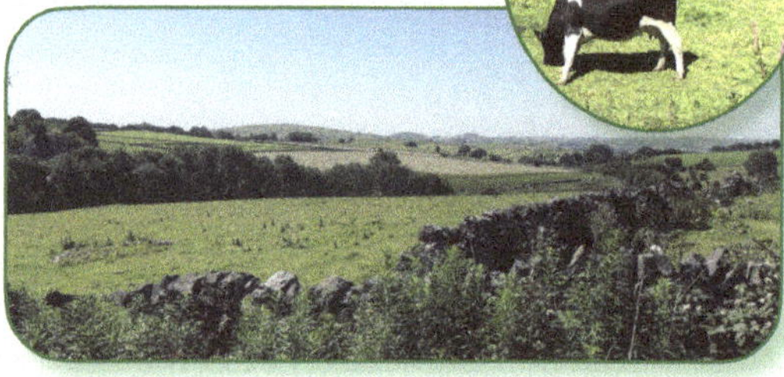

The elevated path also gives views over fields of cows with their young calves, and sheep with clinging teenage lambs, still not too old to butt their mothers for a last drink. Farmers are busy tedding and baling, using this hot day to bring in as much hay as they can before it rains again.

We turn back at Parsley Hey and walk back in the welcome breeze to Hartington meadows for our usual picnic, and a shady rest at the top edge of the fields. After drawing, thinking and resting, we walk down for a last look at the pond – even more overgrown than last time.

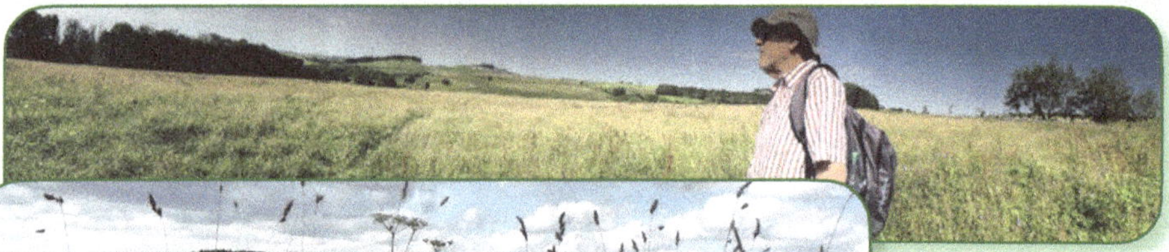

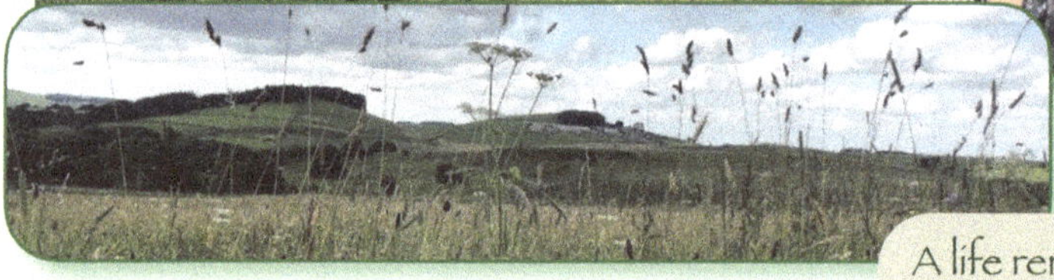

A life remembered today: Salina Shaw; 37; child-minder; Essex; UK; eight days after giving birth.

Martins are gathering on the wires in twittering flocks – a sign that the summer is ending as they urge their young to practise catching bugs on the wing.

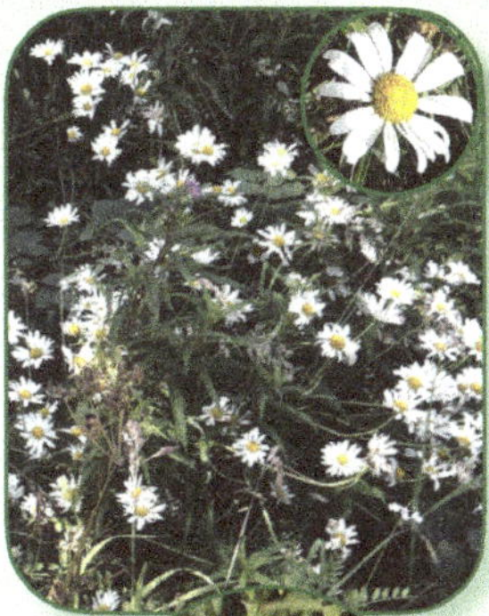

Apart from a few tufts of ox-eye daisies and the scabious still blooming everywhere, these meadows are sleeping now, leaving just a magenta memory. They have not been cut yet, as we think the Wildlife Trust and the farmer who manages it for them, may only really be interested in the flowers, which are all but gone. The odd pop of acid yellow ragwort, and the seed head skeletons floating above the grasses, are the only signs of the flowering here just a short month ago.

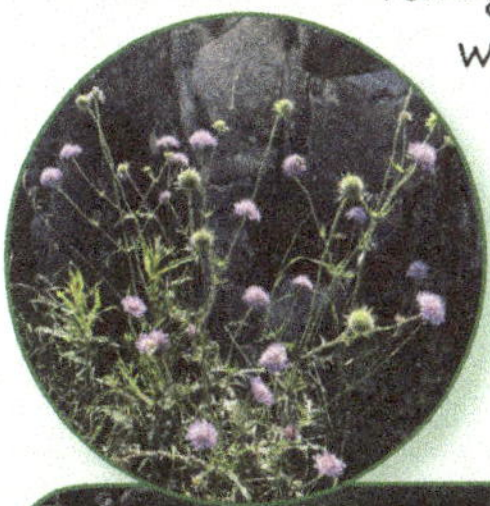

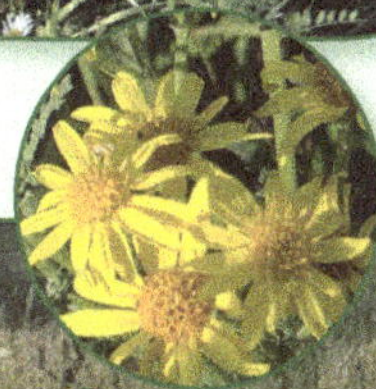

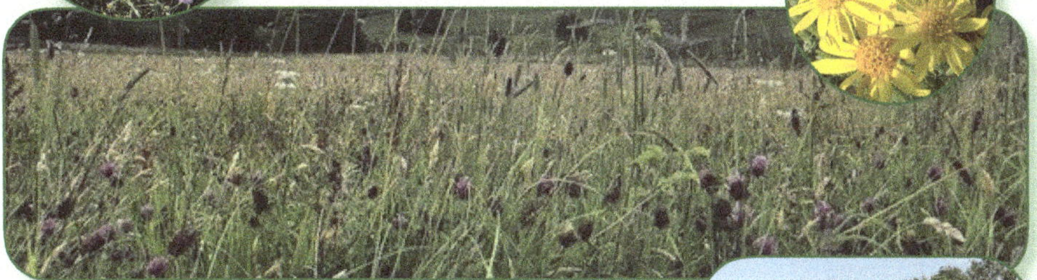

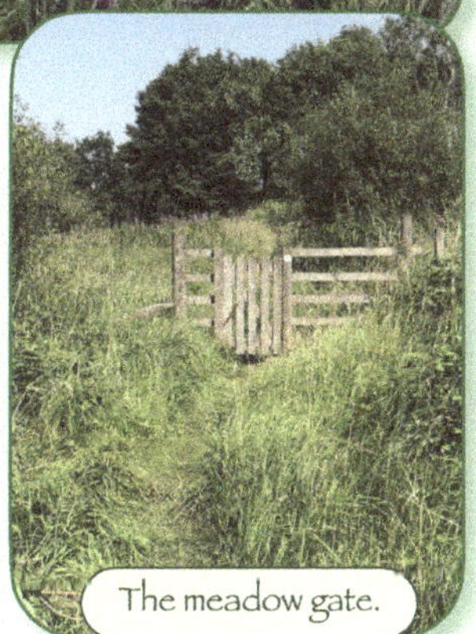

The meadow gate.

After a time gazing at the panorama of hills and fields through the pale stalks of the grasses, we leave these wonderful meadows, quietly close the gate, and drive home through a hazy afternoon, facing oncoming weekend traffic, and diverting to a new way along the limestone valleys where sheep make zigzag paths across the short grass, like tucks in a smocked green bedspread. These narrow roads are still edged with clover, scabious, and a last few ox-eye daisies.

and as we leave the meadows: The ONS household survey indicates COVID-19 cases in England are rising again, with an increase from 2,800 to 4,200 daily cases in the week of 20–26 July. Some measures due to be lifted on August 1st are delayed for at least two weeks.

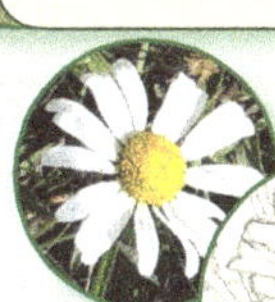

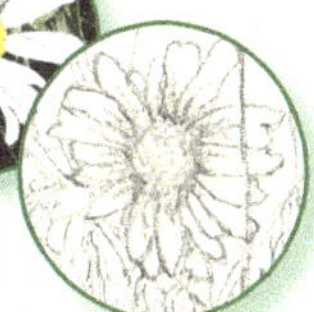

Autumn is surely approaching and a huge thunderstorm breaks as we reach home, with big drops making polka dots on the drive, but bringing little respite to a thirsty garden.

Pandemic Day: 142 Lockdown 1: day 128

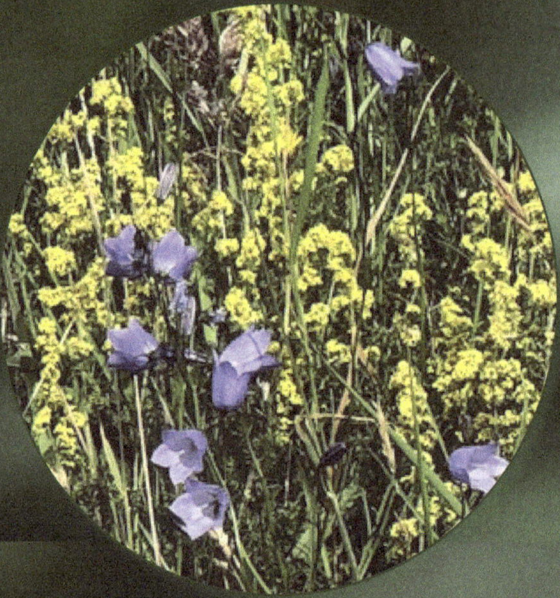

A little grasshopper lands on my pencil case as we sit in the summer flower fields, and rests for several seconds before leaving with a ping and disappearing into the harebells and lady's bedstraw.

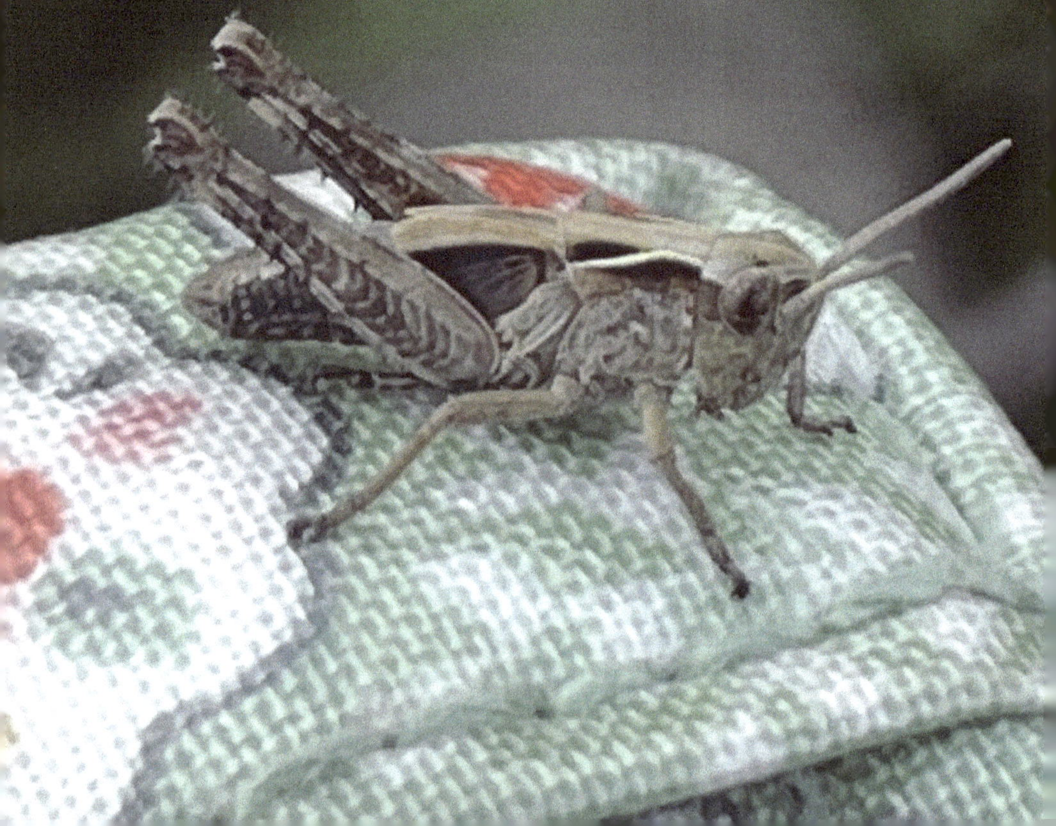

July 2020 ends

As the seemingly endless Covid procedures continue, with partial unlocking and constant changes, our respite has increasingly been in the July countryside. The isolated and mostly unvisited flower meadows near Hartington lift our spirits every time we visit them, and four long July days in these bee-filled flower fields have been a salvation for both of us. For me, the 'blue and the green' help to lift my mood on days when depression threatens, and I know that the space and uninterrupted thinking time in nature also give something immeasurable to Phill. Our 'free-range' country childhoods in the 1940's and 1950's must still run deep in both of us.

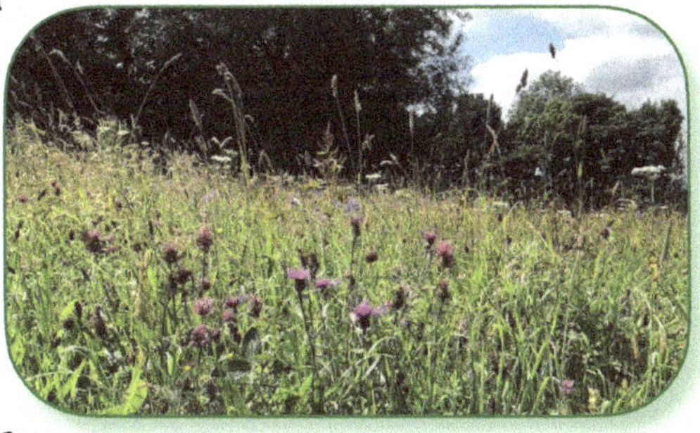

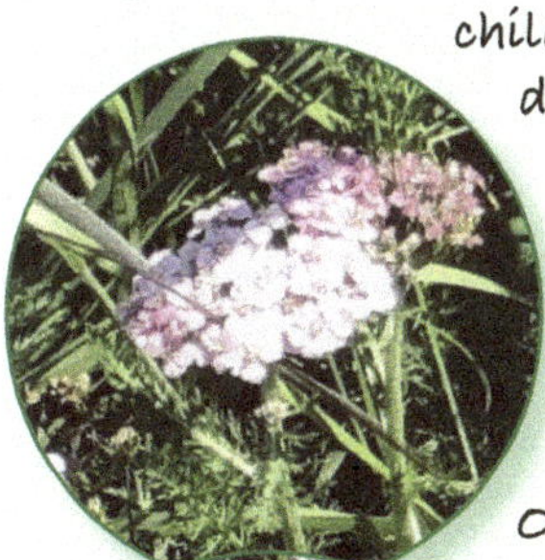

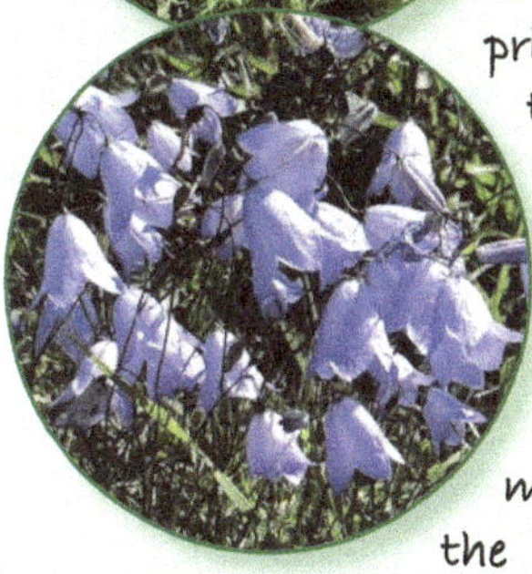

A final day in the meadows on the last day of July is not an official goodbye, although the flowers are almost gone, leaving only the last harebells, acid yellow ragworts, and pink-tinged yarrow among the seed heads and pale grasses. Only the millions of seeds remain, fallen to the soil, primed to begin the cycle again next year. We close the gate to the flower meadows, hoping that next year we can visit without the feeling of guilt that has accompanied us this year, but August must bring a change in priorities - less time escaping to the country, and much more time managing the renovation of our less than ordinary new house.

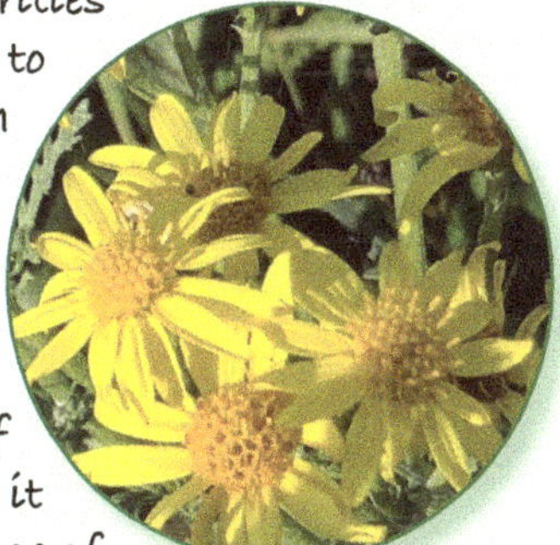

We thought that the renovation would provide a welcome change from the routines of lockdown life, but it is becoming obvious that it will be an increasing disclosure of our innocence of the intricacies and demands of the building trade.

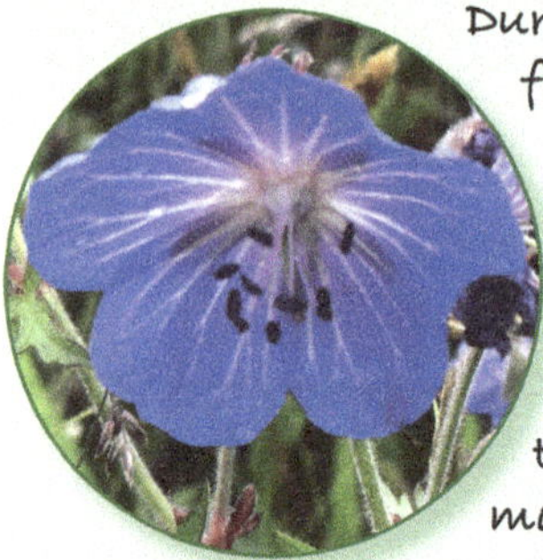

During July, our builder, who we thought was ideal for the project, loses concentration on the completion of our '12-week' job, distracted by a bigger and more lucrative project, and we reluctantly realise that if we are to make progress on this building, a major decision hangs over us. As July ends and August begins, it becomes clear that the original completion date of mid-August cannot possibly be met, and unless we become far more involved in day to day management, we may not even be moving by Christmas!

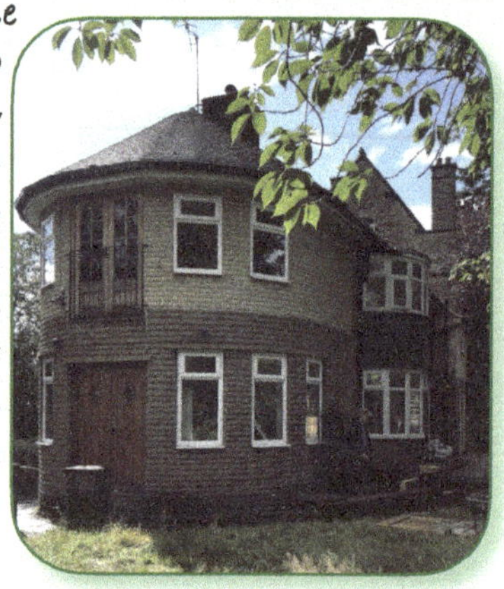

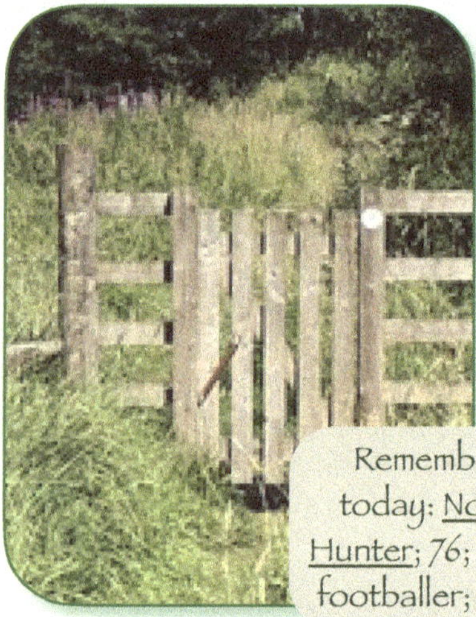

So the end of this month marks a significant change in our lives, and as the full 'unlocking' of England is delayed yet again, we will be forced to make personal decisions that will affect our daily lives, our freedom and even our personal wellbeing for the rest of 2020 and well into 2021.

Remembered today: Norman Hunter; 76; Retired footballer; Leeds.

Although the death rate appeared last month to be slowing, both the confirmed case numbers and the inevitable resulting deaths, sadly begin to rise again, so we are not out of the woods yet.

TOTAL UK CASES AND DEATHS: 31st July 2020

Total confirmed cases to date - 305,687 (up 20,928)

Total deaths to date - 41,361 (up 632)

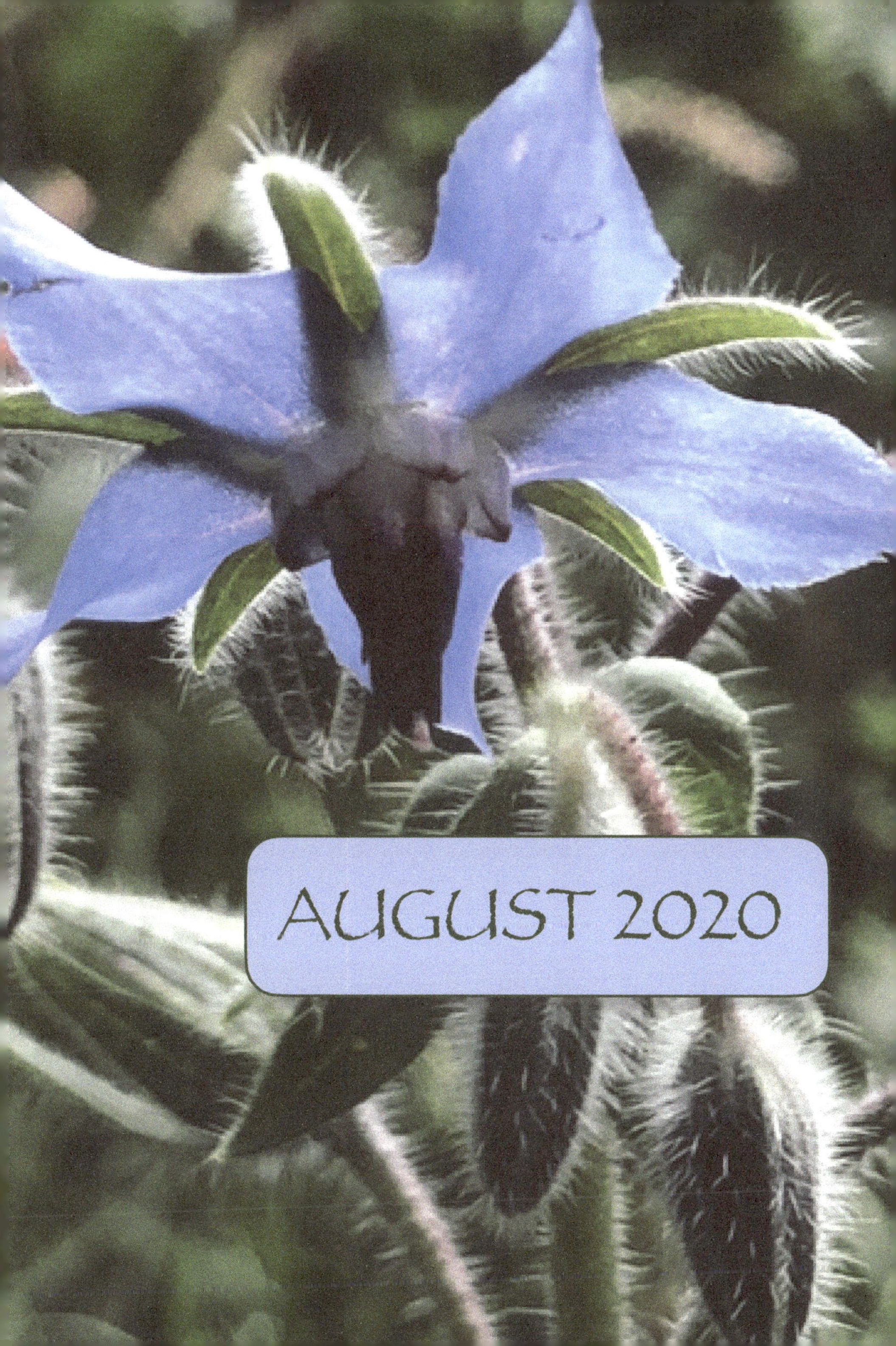
AUGUST 2020

August 2020 - The First Unlocking

31st July 2020 Confirmed Cases: 261,438 Total deaths: 41,371

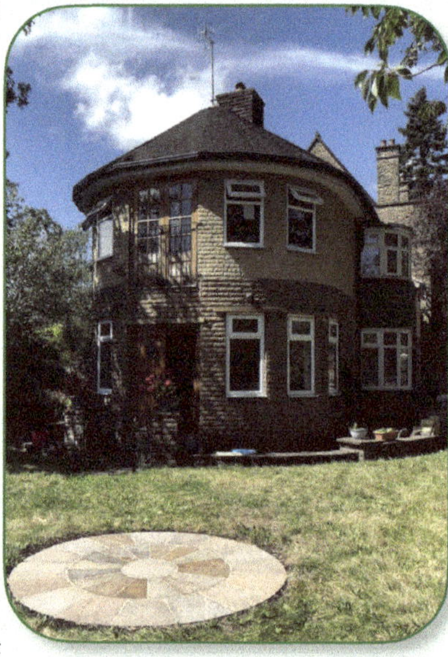

As August begins, and we complete nearly 150 days of lockdown chaos, we are still not safe. The ONS household survey indicates COVID-19 cases in England are slowly rising again. Restrictions due to be lifted on 1st August have been postponed until the 15th, although many people are surreptitiously pre-empting the lifting of the regulations and are meeting indoors and in their gardens. Trials of spectator sporting events are also paused. From 8th August the wearing of face coverings in additional indoor settings, such as cinemas and places of worship becomes mandatory.

We are all so very tired of this lockdown, of being in our storybook-like castles, but we are also anxious about the threat of a second wave of infections which seems to be inevitable, although none of us knows when it will come. So we are neither locked in, nor completely unlocked, and for the first 15 days of August things stay in very much the same limbo, except for those of us tempted by Rishi Sunak's 'Eat Out to Help Out' scheme. This government initiative, which cost around £500 million, is destined to bring a significant rise in infections in August and early September, accelerating the pandemic into its second wave. The economic benefits of the scheme are short-lived, and the enterprise is later dubbed by some as 'Eat Out to Spread it About'.

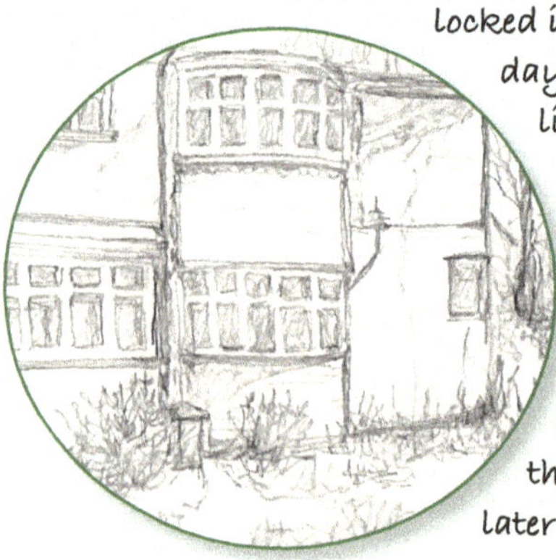

Pandemic Day: 143 Lockdown 1: day 129

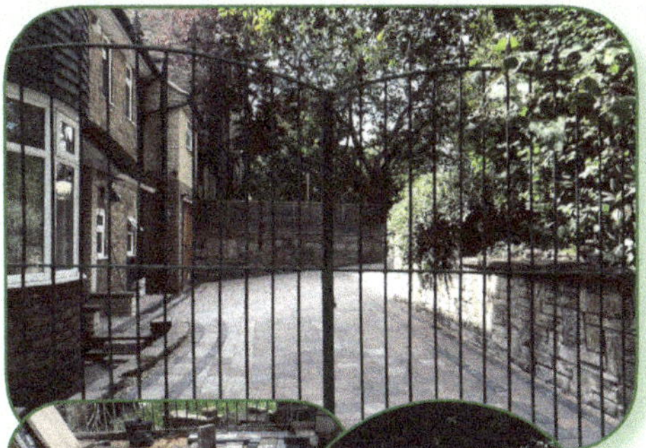

It is a great disappointment to us that the work on the house, which was started with such enthusiasm in June, when progress was noticeable every day, now begins to stall. From the beginning of August, Phill and I become increasingly involved in managing the renovation of the Children's House.

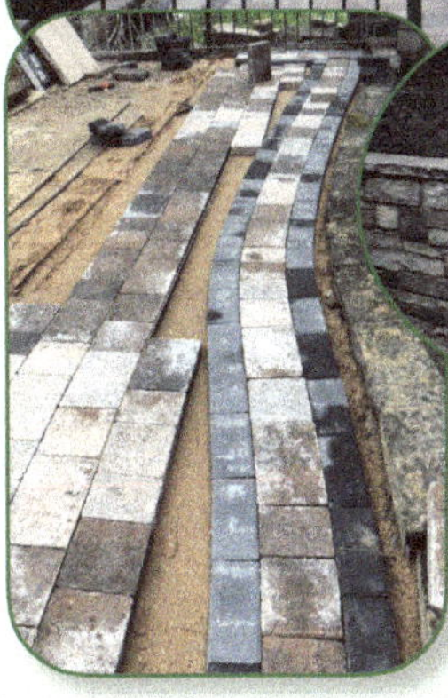

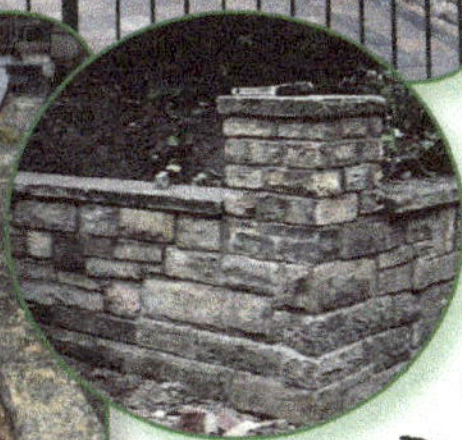

By the beginning of August, the house has been stripped of most of the layers of wallpaper, old paint, leaky radiators, kitchen and bathroom fittings, and miles of wire, piping and skirting boards. But at this point, we reach a wall of inaction and must make a decision about the management of the project. Expeditions into the country, and even worries about Covid must be put aside as we focus on the house.

However, we are not able to ignore for long that we are doing this renovation in the middle of a pandemic. Materials of all sorts, and the workers to use them, are in short supply, and we feel fortunate that the exterior work on the driveway and the garden has been completed, and the major structural work - relocation of walls, building of new doorways and windows, rewiring, and removal of kitchen fittings and plumbing from all the bedrooms have all been started although few of these jobs have been finished. Work elsewhere, on the driveway, removing shrubs, trees and their stumps, moving and rebuilding garden walls, and some of the works in the garden, have been brought forward to keep the two groundsmen busy. They have almost completed cutting the unruly laurel hedge when, without notice, they leave their scaffolding in the garden, and disappear.

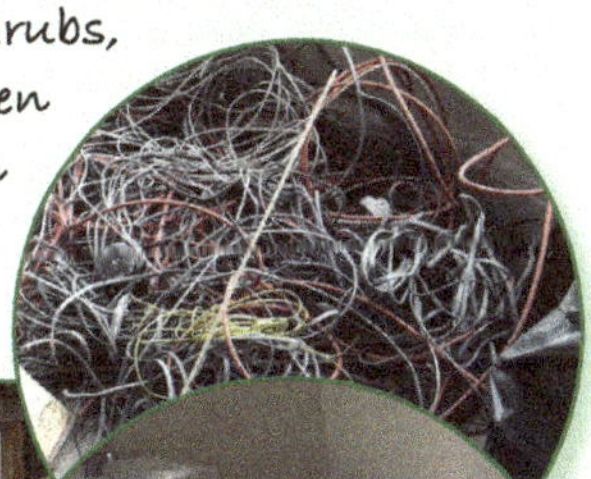

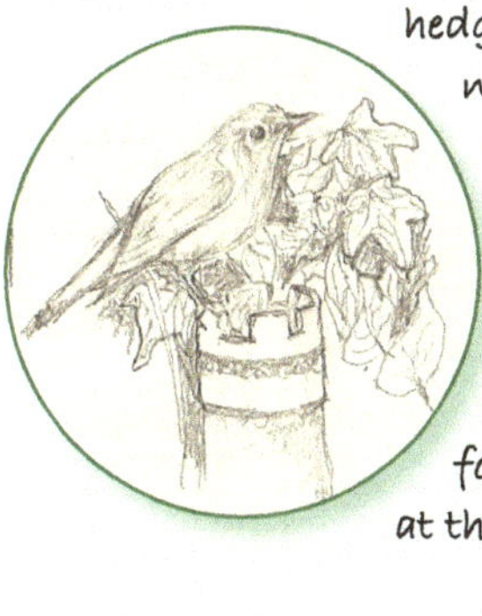

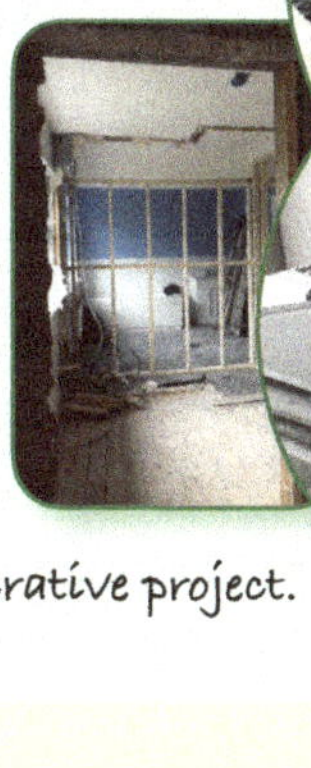

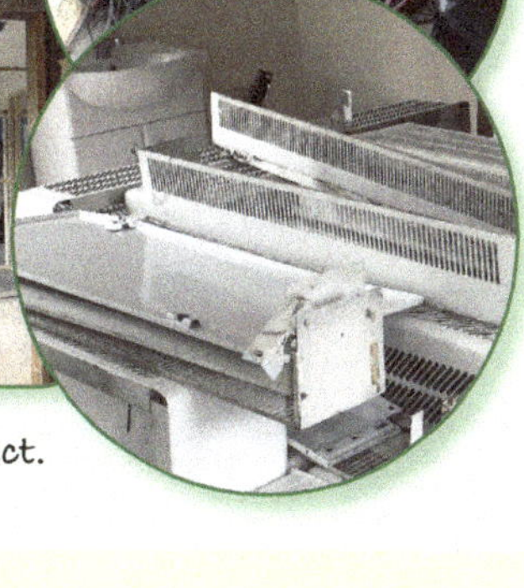

We guess they are now needed to for the groundwork at the new and more lucrative project.

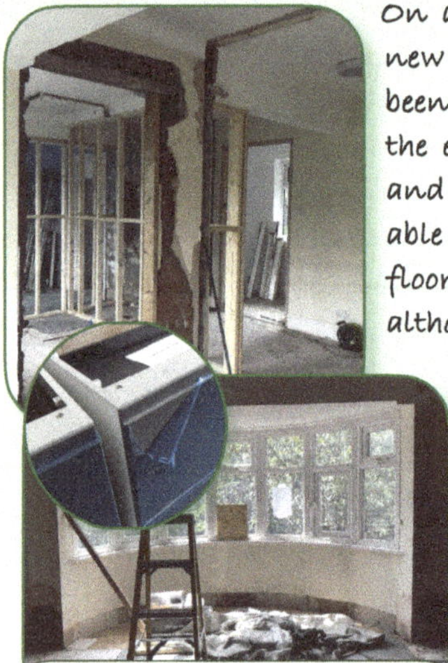

The new house begins to emerge

Remembered today:
Steven Pearson; 51;
Mental health nurse;
Northumberland.

On a more positive note, the new kitchen has already been designed and ordered, the electricians are efficient and punctual, and we are able to order most of the flooring, doors and bathroom fittings we choose, although our choice is sometimes limited.

June and then July pass, and the builder is rarely on site to maintain momentum, work slows to a halt, and workmen turn up with no instructions or materials, or fail to turn up at all. Late in July it becomes evident that he is not able to manage two jobs at once, or to delegate effectively to anyone else. Orders are not sent to suppliers, materials run out or are not delivered, meetings are missed, cancelled, full of empty promises, or a fruitless waste of energy. He now becomes unavailable on phone, text or email, and evasive excuses or impossible promises are all he can offer on the rare occasions when we do meet. We are really on our own now.

Cameron the carpenter valiantly struggles on, building a window seat in the dining room, moving and rebuilding storage, and working on the wooden flooring throughout the house, until the kitchen arrives and he can begin fitting. He is our lifeline, and he is left by the invisible builder to manage all the work as well as fielding our frustration and naivety. Without his commitment we would be in great difficulty, as we finally accept that the builder has abandoned us.

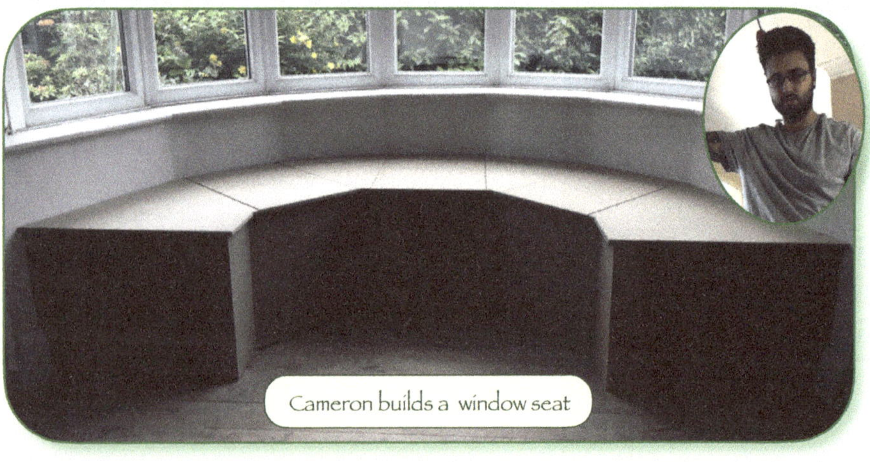

Cameron builds a window seat

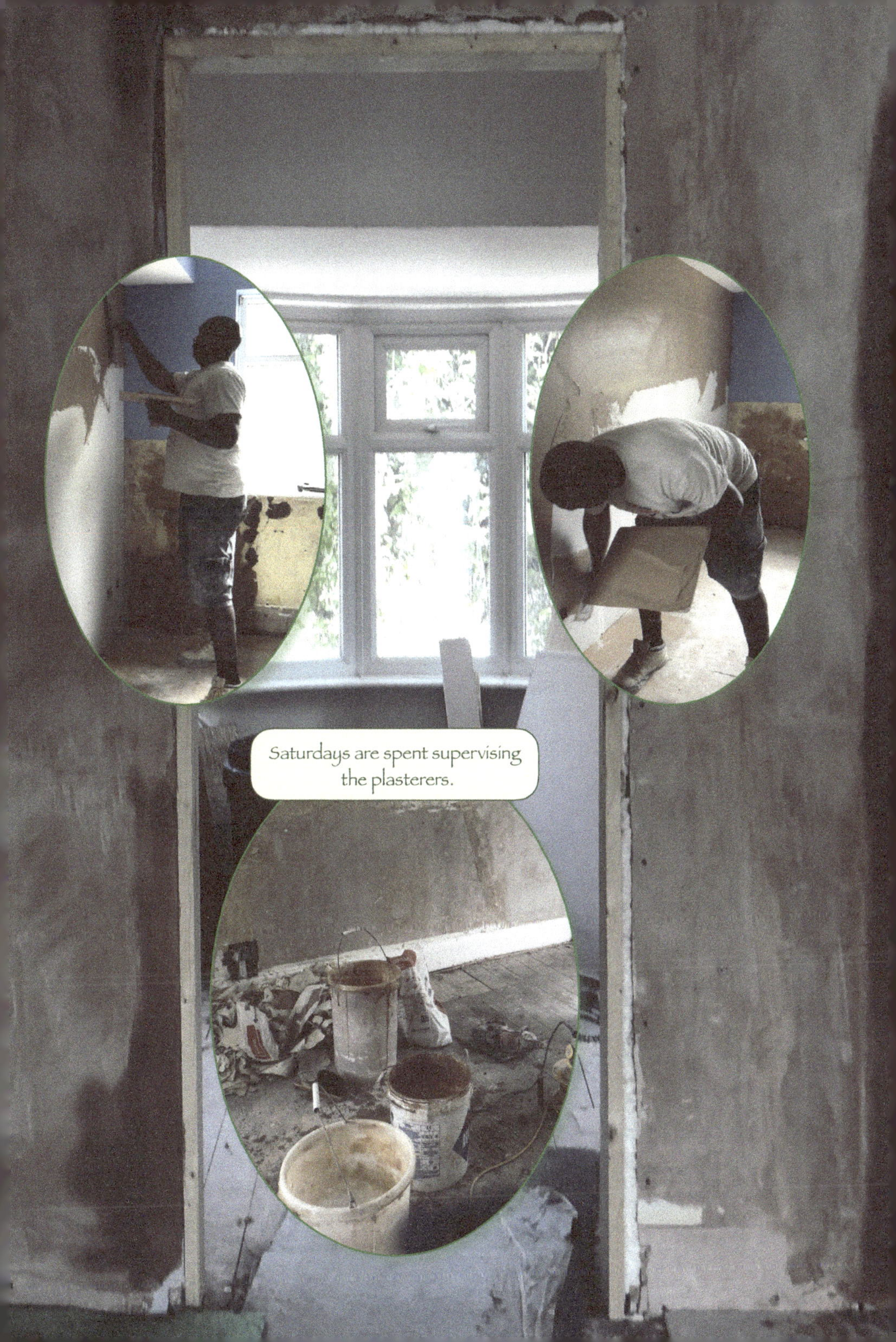

Saturdays are spent supervising the plasterers.

Long hot Spring and Summer months are now followed by more changeable weather as we take a deep breath and face the inevitable dive into project management. We are inexperienced project managers, so we make endless lists and schedules, to check what is happening (or might happen), and meanwhile, we do the 'grunt work' of making 'brews', and endless clearing up, alongside packing up the rental house in the hope that a moving date may eventually come. Taking over the scheduling of the job and being on site all day every day becomes challenging and exhausting, and the workforce swells and shrinks in response to Covid shielding, family demands, better managed projects, or the call of the builder as he continues to redeploy them for his other project. Builders' merchants' shelves get emptier by the day, and Phill spends some of each day, with instructions from workers, chasing obscure items from building suppliers. We embark on a different sort of lockdown and no respite of country walks.

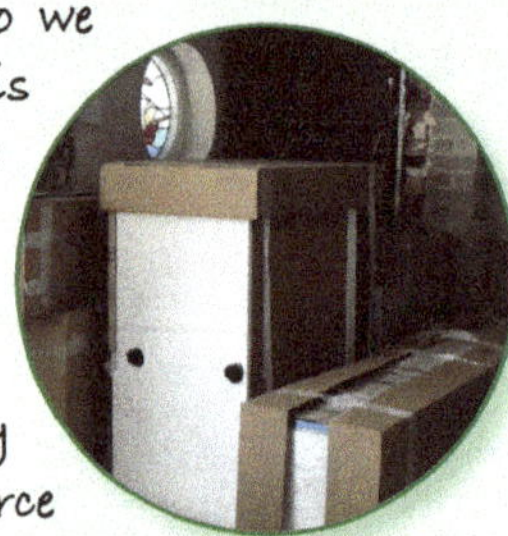

During August, we are able at last to celebrate family birthdays together, although we still stay in our gardens, alhough many people are now flouting this part of the guidance.

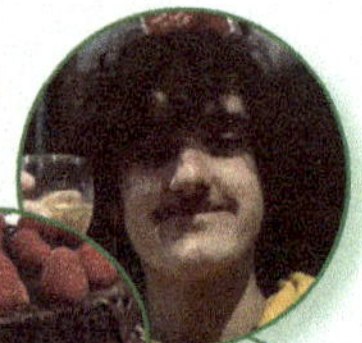

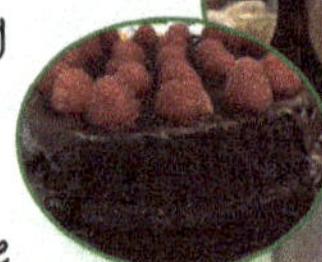

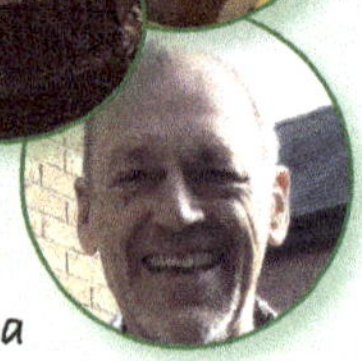

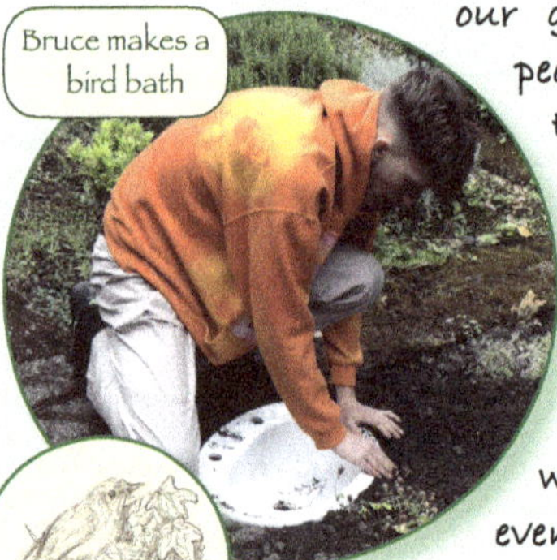

Bruce makes a bird bath

In the garden at the Children's House we make a start on trimming back the garden shrubs, as Bruce makes a bird bath in one of the little washbasins from the bedrooms. Small birds and even pigeons soon find it.

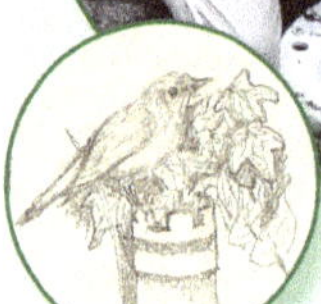

Autumn hawkbit flowers in the mossy lawn, buds emerge on the transplanted clematis, the wildflower seeds are germinating, blowsy white roses and cosmos bloom, and bees and butterflies visit the wet summer flowers in the garden – but we don't have time to do more than glance at them.

Remembered today:
Jenelyn Carter; 41; Health-care assistant; Swansea.

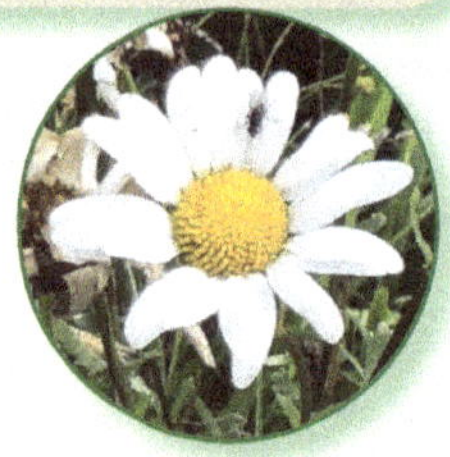

We even abandon our walks in the nearby Norfolk Park, the Botanical Gardens are just a leafy green memory, and the fields at Hartington lie sleeping until next year.

Endnote

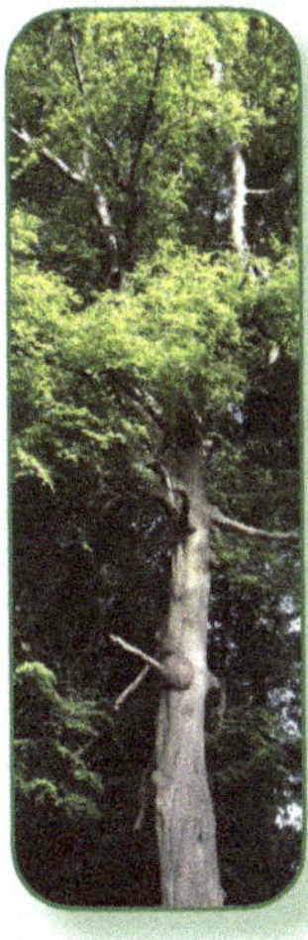

We have been so fortunate.

Unlike many others, a combination of voluntary isolation and carefully managed contacts has helped us to escape the virus ourselves, and our family have all stayed safe too. Up to this point, we have had none of the trauma of sickness, hospitalisation or death of family or friend, and our sympathy goes out to those who have suffered, and are still suffering, during this time.

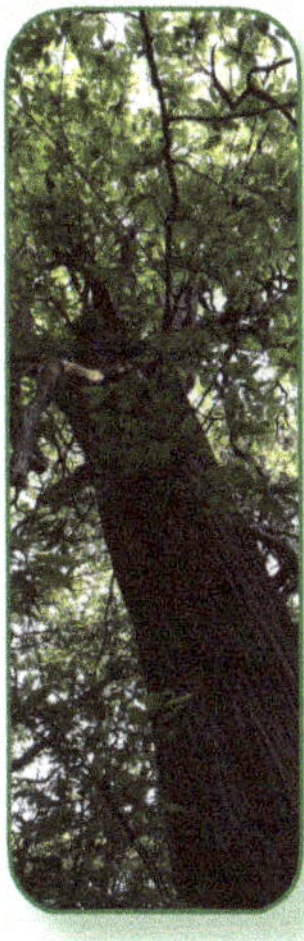

Without the support of Phill, my partner in life (and in our recent minor crimes), and contact with our two children, I know I would not have survived the uncertainty and isolation of these months of lockdown. This virus, with its dark grey ability to seep into body and mind, sapping energy and affecting both physical and mental health, reduces the days to a damp duvet of sameness. We forget which day, which month and even which year we are in, we stay locked in our solitary towers, watch too much television, submerge ourselves in social media, eat and sleep too much, as we wait for the daily news bulletin or government press conference with its inflated promises and endless statistics.

The first volume of these diaries, opened on 11th March 2020, contains the thoughts and activities of two ordinary people, coping as well as they can during a nightmare event, a challenge to every human on the planet. The first entry, made just one day before the announcement of the first lockdown, has been maintained until the beginning of August 2021, when we are promised that lockdown restrictions will soon be lifted.

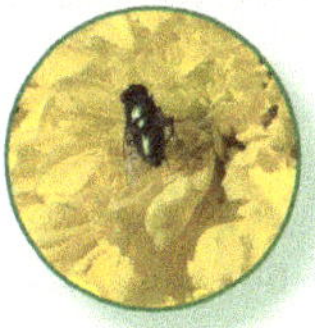

With an unfinished house conversion and little confidence that the virus has finished with us, we hang on, hoping that the summer will bring the promised respite, and the unlocking will continue until we get back to something like 'a new normal'.

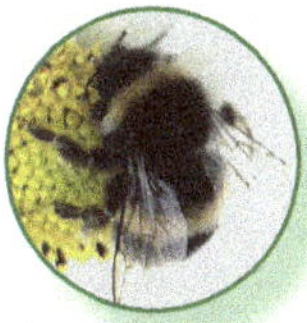

Little knowing what is to come, I wrongly assume that my account is at an end.

The second volume (Lockdown 2 & 3) continues from this point.

COVID Timeline December 2019 to August 2020

On the following pages I have attempted to present a timeline of the background events to this volume of the Lockdown Diaries. The choice of content is entirely my own, and I have not attempted to include everything that might be relevant or interesting. The information relates to the UK and, after the four countries developed independent guidance, to England. In constructing this timeline, I have referred to the following:

- **The BFPG Timeline**: The British Foreign Policy Group https://bfpg.co.uk
- **Wikipedia**: **Timeline of the COVID-19 pandemic in the United Kingdom** (January - August 2020): https://en.wikipedia.org/wiki/
- **UK government - Covid timeline** GOV.UKCoronavirus (COVID-19) in the UK https://coronavirus.data.gov.uk
- **The Institute for Government; Timeline of UK government coronavirus lockdowns and restrictions;** https://www.instituteforgovernment.org.uk/charts/uk-government-coronavirus-lockdowns
- **WIRED Magazine (May/June 2021) - COVID Timeline -** Rules Britannia: Laws of Lockdown https://wired.co.uk
- **Newspaper archives and TV and Radio reporting**

For the names of people who have died from Covid during 2020/21 -

- https://en.wikipedia.org/wiki - List of deaths due to covid.
- **BBC Coronavirus: Your tributes to those who have died** https://www.bbc.co.uk/news/uk-52676411

Dec 31 2019 - ***China contacts the WHO*** *and informs them of 'cases of pneumonia of unknown etiology' detected in Wuhan*

Jan 11 2020 - *Chinese state media report the* ***first known death*** *from an illness caused by the virus.*

Jan 20 2020 - *Chinese epidemiologists publish an article stating that the* ***first cluster of patients*** *with 'pneumonia of an unknown cause' were identified on 21st December 2019.*

Jan 22 - Public Health England moves the **risk level to the British public from 'very low' to 'low'**. *The PM misses 1st* ***COBRA*** *meeting.*

Jan 23 - ***Wuhan (population over 11 million) is cut off*** *by Chinese authorities.*

Jan 24 -*The PM misses 2nd* ***COBRA*** *meeting.*

Jan 29 - *The* ***UK's first two patients*** *test positive for Coronavirus in York.*

Jan 31 - *Government refuses offer to join* ***EU PPE scheme.***

Feb 5 - ***A cruise ship in Japan quarantines 3600*** *people after 218 people on board tested positive. The PM misses 3rd* ***COBRA*** *meeting.*

Feb 11 - ***The disease is named 'Covid-19'***, *an acronym that stands for Coronavirus Disease 2019. 1113 people in China have died.*

Feb 12 -*The PM misses 4th* ***COBRA*** *meeting.*

Feb 13 - *The PM fails to attend 1st & a further 7* ***conference calls with the EU.***

Feb 17 - *The PM misses 5th* ***COBRA*** *meeting.*

Feb 19 -***443 passengers leave the Diamond Princess cruise ship****. 621 people aboard the ship are infected.*

Feb 24 - *The PM is on retreat at Chevening.*

Feb 26 - *The Government says we need to achieve* ***'herd immunity'***.

Feb 28 - *The* ***first British victim dies*** *onboard the Diamond Princess.*

Feb 29 - ***NHS PPE shortage becomes critical.***

Mar 2 - *The government holds a* ***COBRA*** *meeting to discuss its preparations and response to the virus.* ***The PM fails to attend the meeting.***

Mar 10/13 - *The PM, against scientific advice, allows* ***Cheltenham Festival*** *to go ahead (250,000+ over a 4 day period) and the* ***Champions League tie between Liverpool and Madrid*** *(3,000 Atletico fans & 50,000 home support).*

Mar 11 - ***The WHO declares the virus a pandemic*** *and stock markets plunge. 3,000 Madrid fans fly to Liverpool.*

Mar 12 - ***The Government insists they are not closing schools.***

Mar 13 - ***Government turns down EU proposal to join ventilator scheme.***

Mar 14 -***5,000 pack Cardiff Arena for a Stereophonics gig****. UK retailers release a joint letter asking customers not to panic buy products after* ***supermarkets sell out of items such as pasta, and toilet paper***

Dec 31 2019 - China contacts the WHO and informs

Mar 15/16 - **Borders close across Europe**.

Mar 16 - **The PM begins daily press briefings**. He says 'now is the time for everyone to stop non-essential contact and travel'. The UK's **death toll rises to 55**. Six days after the UK stopped tracing, **WHO advises 'Test, test, test and contact trace'**.

Mar 17 - **The PM attends Six Nations match**.

Mar 18 - **Most schools across England, Wales, Scotland and Northern Ireland will be shut down from Friday 20th March until further notice**. Glastonbury cancelled.

Mar 19 - **The PM says UK can 'turn tide of Coronavirus in 12 weeks**. Education Secretary confirms **no exams will take place this year**. The government no longer deems Covid a 'high consequence infectious disease'. **Covid patients sent back to care homes from hospital –** with no protection for them or the care staff.

Mar 20 - The UK government orders **all pubs, restaurants, gyms and other social venues across the country to close**. Rishi Sunak announces government will pay 80% of wages for employees not working.

Mar 20 - **UK closes schools and pubs.**

Mar 21 - **Supermarkets around the UK struggle to keep up with demand.**

Mar 22 - The PM gives due **warning that lockdown will start immediately.**

Mar 23 - **Lockdown will be legally imposed** from 26th March, the public are instructed that they must stay at home, except for shopping; one form of outdoor exercise each day; for any medical need, or to provide care; to travel to and from work where this is 'necessary'. When the restrictions come into force on 26 March, law omitted any limit on the number of exercise sessions.

Mar 23 - **Home learning starts in earnest**, except for the children of key workers and those seen as 'vulnerable'.

Mar 25 - The **police will be given the power to use 'reasonable force' to enforce lockdown regulations**.

Mar 25 - The first two working **NHS doctors die** from Covid on the same day, a GP, & a surgeon.

Mar 26 - The **Government refuses another EU offer of PPE.** At 8pm, millions of people take part in the first **'Clap for Carers'** tribute.

Mar 27 - A government clarification confirms that we are not to drive out to walk and take exercise. **We must stay in 'The immediate locality'. Dominic Cummings, drives 250 miles to Durham** with his wife and child.

Mar 28 - The number of **fatalities passes 1,000.**

Mar 29 - The **first NHS nurse dies** from Covid.

Mar 30 - The government will spend £75 million on **flights** and airline tickets **to repatriate up to 300,000 Britons stranded abroad**.

Mar 31 - **A significant rise in anxiety and depression** among the UK population is reported following the lockdown. The number of people in hospital with Covid passes 10,000. Largest UK daily death toll reported.

Apr 1 - **Worldwide coronavirus cases passes one million**. **Shortages of PPE** cause friction between government and NHS, as hospitals and care homes are unable to get supplies.

Apr 3 - **UK deaths top deaths in China**.Figures published by the Cabinet Office indicate UK traffic levels have fallen by 73% since the lockdown measures were introduced

Apr 5 -The **PM is admitted to hospital** with Covid.

April 6 - **The Queen speaks to the nation. The PM** is admitted to an Intensive Care Unit. The **death toll exceeds 5,000**.

Apr 10 - **Jonathan Van-Tam**, England's deputy chief medical officer, at the daily briefing sys **the lockdown is 'beginning to pay off' but the UK is still in a 'dangerous situation'**.

Apr 11- **NHS workers still do not have the correct PPE.** Priti Patel tells a government briefing she is 'sorry if people feel there have been failings'.

Apr 12 - **Hospital death toll reaches 10,000**. No testing for arriving travellers.

Apr 14 - The **PM discharged from hospital**.

Apr 16 - **Lockdown extended for 'at least' three weeks. Tom Moore completes 100 laps of his garden**.

Apr 17 - **NHS bosses to ask Doctors and nurses to work without some PPE** as supplies begin to run out.

Apr 18 - Care England estimates a**s many as 7,500 care home residents may have died from Covid.**

Apr 18 - **The Communities Secretary says a further 400,000 gowns will be arriving from Turkey** but In the event, the shipment was delayed by several days, and was said on 7 May to be unusable.

Apr 21 - Dame Angela Maclean, scientific adviser, says number of confirmed cases is 'flattening'. **Death toll surges around Cheltenham.**

Apr 23 - **Deaths pass 20,000**.

Apr 25 - **The likely UK death toll will be 3rd highest in the world**.

Apr 25 - **The UK overtakes the Government 'worst case scenario'** - death toll exceeds 20,000.

Apr 27 - Government announces **families of NHS and care workers who die of Covid will be entitled to a payment of £60,000**

Apr 28 - ONS says **a third of Covid deaths in England and Wales are in care homes**.

Apr 30 - The **PM claims that the UK is 'past the peak'** of Covid.

May 1 - Matt Hancock claims the government's target of providing **100,000 tests a day by the end of April has been met**.

May 3 - Sir Patrick Vallance tells the House of Commons Select Committee that **earlier testing for Covid would have been 'beneficial' but would not have prevented the virus spread**.

May 5 - The number of recorded **deaths rises by 693 to 29,427**, giving the UK the highest number of Covid related deaths in Europe.

May 6 - At his first PMQ since returning to work the **PM says he 'bitterly regrets' the crisis in care homes and is 'working very hard' to tackle it.**

May 7 - An analysis from the ONS shows that **black men and women are nearly twice as likely to die from Covid** as white people.

May 11 - **A new alert system is announced**, ranging from green (level 1) to red (level 5). All cities and counties assigned to one of these.

May 12 - From today, new regulations mean **people can drive further, walk for longer**, and 'meet one person outside your house-hold in an outdoor, public place, staying 2m apart'.

May 13 - **Re-opening of** garden centres, sports courts and recycling centres. House moves and viewings are also permitted.

May 15 - A report on deaths in care homes from the ONS finds **9,039 additional deaths occurred from 2nd March to 1st May, and a further 3,444 deaths in hospital**.

May 17 - £84m is invested in a **Covid vaccine** being trialled by the University of Oxford and should be available by September.

May 19 - The office for national statistics reports that over **half the deaths from coronavirus have been in the community** (many in care homes) – and not in hospitals. As figures show there have been **11,600 deaths in care homes** as a result of Covid.

May 20 - Pressure from councils and teaching unions to reconsider Government plans to reopen primary schools from 1st June.

May 22 - **Travellers entering the UK will have to self-isolate for 14 days.** SAGE says the risk to pupils is 'very small, but not zero'.

May 24 - **UK schools will begin phased reopening beginning June 1st**.

May 25 - UK government announces **non-essential retailers may reopen from June 15th**. At a press conference in the Rose Garden at Downing Street, **Dominic Cummings** gives an unapologetic explanation of his actions, saying 'I don't regret what I did'.

May 26 - The WHO warns of '**second peak**' of Covid as countries begin to ease lockdowns. **Douglas Ross resigns** in protest at the PM's defence of Dominic Cummings.

May 27 - England to launch '**test & trace**' to replace lockdown restrictions.

May 29 - **Lockdown restrictions in England continue to ease**, groups of up to 6 people allowed to meet from June 1st.

May 30 - Government **scientific advisers warn of the risk associated with lifting lockdown restrictions in England too early**.

June 1 - UK records **lowest increase in Covid daily deaths and infections since the end of March**. Phased re-opening of schools; groups from more than one household limited to 6 outdoors, and prohibited indoors.

June 5 - The **number of recorded deaths in the UK passes 40,000.**

June 5 - **Covid-19 deaths in England pass 30,000 (34,095),** originally, the Government said 20,000 deaths would be 'a good result'.

June 7 - Professor John Edmunds says **he wishes the lockdown had been implemented earlier as the delay 'cost a lot of lives'.**

June 9 - **Lowest daily Covid death toll since March 22nd** (55 deaths). Non-essential retailers, zoos & safari parks reopen on 15 June, and pubs, restaurants & hairdressers on 4 July.

Jun 9 - The **government drops plans for primary school children to return before the end of the summer term**.

Jun 13 - Government introduces '**support bubbles**' between households.

Jun 15 - **Non-essential shops re-open in England.** The Government investigates summer schools & catch-up classes. **Face coverings become mandatory on public transport.**

Jun 16 - The majority of voters think lockdown was imposed too late. **Allowing Cheltenham races go ahead led to a huge spike.** ONS figures suggest 600,000+ people have lost their jobs between March and May.

Jun 17 - **Premier League football returns behind closed doors**.

Jun 19 - UK Minister accused of playing down the pandemic after **it was revealed the UK death count exceeded 1000 for 22 consecutive days, significantly higher than the figures given in daily briefings.**

Jun 23 - PM says 'national hibernation' coming to an end – announces relaxing of restrictions and 2m social distancing rule. **Pubs, restaurants & hotels to reopen on the 4th July.**

Jun 24 - Doctors discuss '**Long Covid**', and patients suffering this. **Scientists & health officials warn of risk of second wave.**

July 2 **-** The owner of **cafe Rouge and Bella Italia goes into administration**.

July 4 - The **Health Protection Regulations** come into force in England, replacing and relaxing the previous Lockdown Regulations.

July 5 - The UK stages a **national round of applause** to mark the 72nd anniversary of the founding of the National Health Service.

July 6 - **Scientific research has suggested the COVID-19 outbreak could result in several thousand extra cancer deaths** due to delayed diagnosis and treatment

July 7 - Downing Street rejects calls for the PM to issue an apology after comments the previous day that '**too many care homes didn't really follow procedures'**

July 9 - Two sets of data are released that show the number of **cases of COVID-19 are falling in England;**

July 15 - A **temporary cut in VAT** worth £4bn comes into force until 12 January 2021.

July 21 - The PM announces **a further easing of lockdown restrictions**, with plans for a 'significant return to normality' by Christmas.

July 19 - Prime Minister says **he does not believe it will be necessary to impose a second nationwide lockdown in the event of a spike in COVID-19 cases**, comparing the option to a 'nuclear deterrent'.

July 20 - **Clinical trials of the vaccine** being developed by the University of Oxford on 1,077 patients.

July 21 - The Chancellor announces that **900,000 public sector workers, including doctors and teachers, will get an above-inflation pay rise of 3.1%**

July 28 - The PM warns that there are signs of a **European second wave of the virus**

July 30 - The PM warns the UK is '**not out of the woods'**.

July 31 - The PM postpones some lockdown easing measures scheduled to begin in England on 1 August for two weeks amid concerns about rising COVID-19 cases.

Aug 3 - The month-long 'E**at Out to Help Out' scheme begins.**

Aug 5 - A report by the Home Affairs committee concludes that **the spread of COVID-19 could have been slowed by an earlier implementation of quarantine restrictions** on people arriving into the UK.

Aug 7 - **The R number for the UK rises** to between 0.8 and 1.0

Aug 9 - The daily figure of confirmed new **COVID-19 infections exceeds 1,000** for the first time since June.

Aug 17 - Following controversy over A Level grades, it is confirmed that both **A Level and GCSE results in England, Wales and Northern Ireland will be based on teachers' assessments**.

Sept 1 - The majority of **schools in England, Wales and Northern Ireland reopen for the autumn term.**

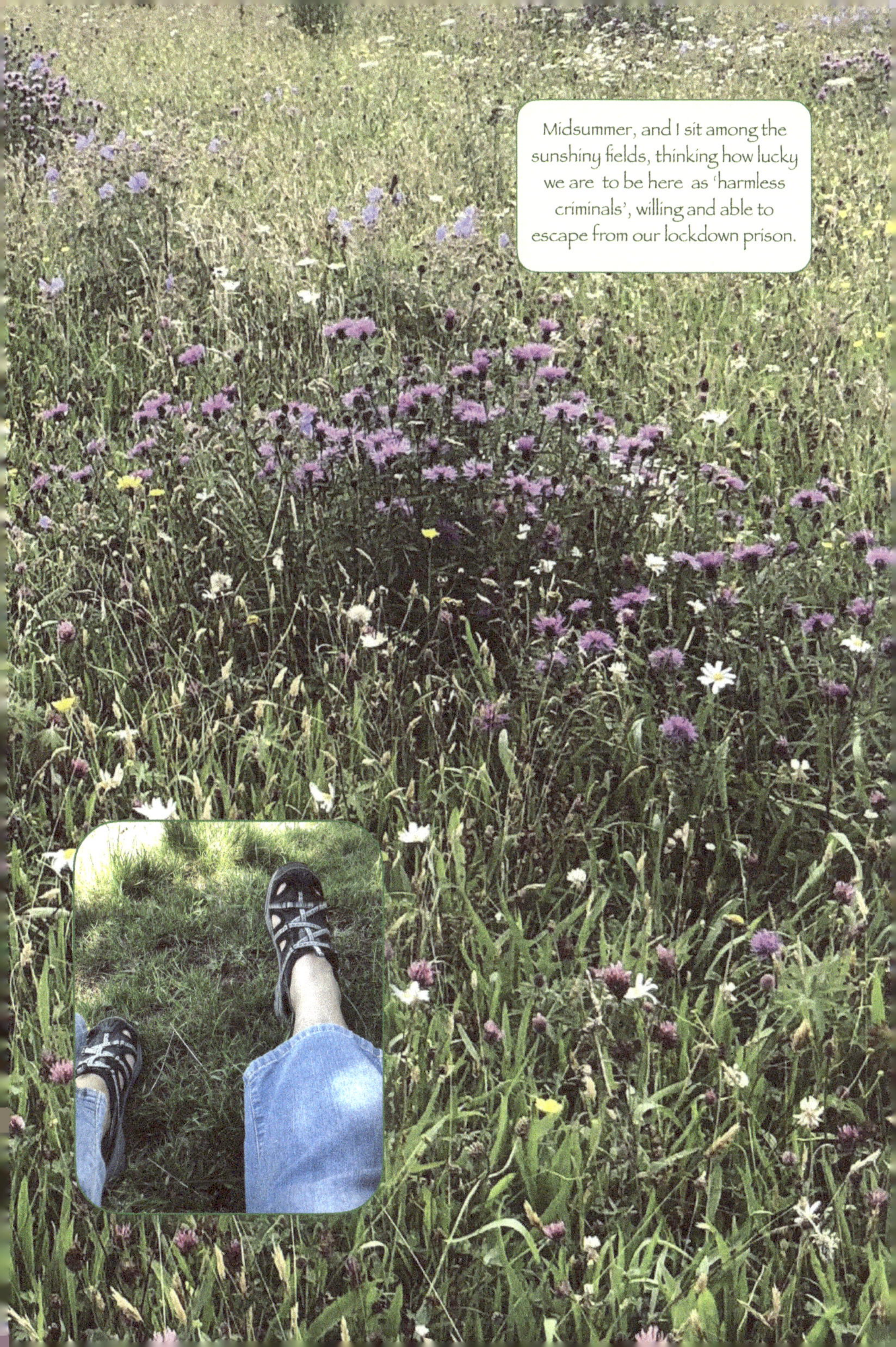

Midsummer, and I sit among the sunshiny fields, thinking how lucky we are to be here as 'harmless criminals', willing and able to escape from our lockdown prison.

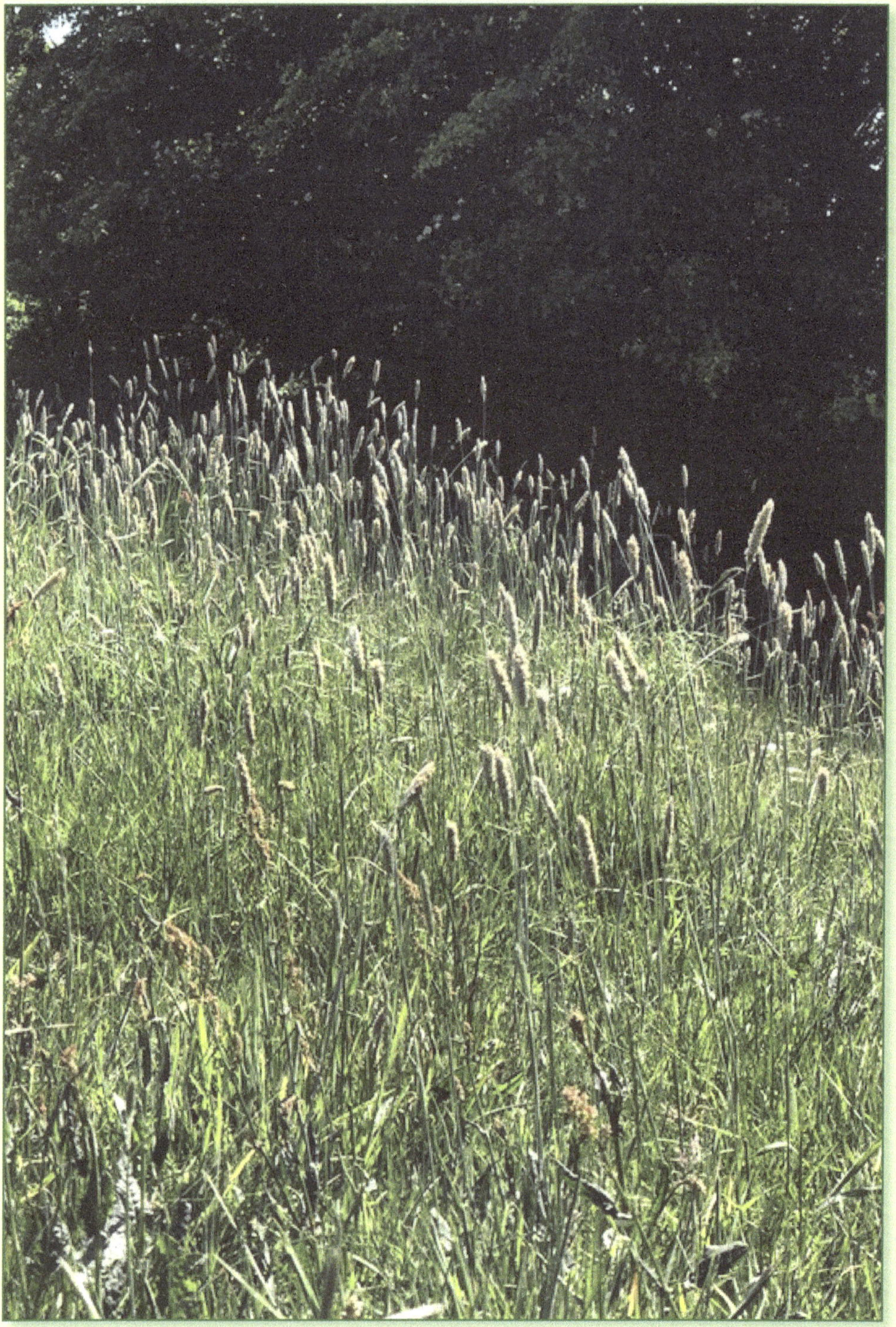

Lightning Source UK Ltd.
Milton Keynes UK
UKHW050217130422
401464UK00006B/221

9 781739 745509